Word 2016 For Professionals

for
dummies®
A Wiley Brand

by Dan Gookin

for
dummies®
A Wiley Brand

Word 2016 For Professionals For Dummies®

Published by: **John Wiley & Sons, Inc.**, 111 River Street, Hoboken, NJ 07030-5774, www.wiley.com

Table of Contents

Introduction

Welcome to *Word 2016 For Professionals For Dummies*, a book that uncovers the truth about parapsychology and the people in Asia who hand-place sesame seeds on the hamburger buns used by Burger King. I'm not serious, of course. I'm just checking to see whether you're actually reading this introduction.

This book goes way beyond the beginner's user level when it comes to word processing with Microsoft Word. This isn't a technical book, but rather a book geared toward the professional or anyone else who is serious about the words they write. Word is a powerful program, and few people venture into its more sophisticated levels. That's sad because many of Word's features can save you time and help you create a better document

About This Book

Are you still reading the introduction? That's really weird. Most people don't even bother. In fact, they simply take the copy of this book that they illegally downloaded, get the information they want, and then go on Facebook and lament how the economy is crumbling. I love that story.

Still, I'm proud of you for continuing to read the introduction. Truly, it's the best part of the book. That's because this is where I explain how this book covers a lot of material not found anywhere else. Google? Forget it. I've looked. Those people who put "help" up on Google don't know what they're talking about. If you really want to understand Word, and create outstanding documents, you have the best resource in your hands right now.

This book is a reference. It's designed to cover a topic quickly and let you get back to work. Each chapter covers a topic, and major sections within the chapter go into detail. Within each section are specific activities, complete with steps or further instructions that help you accomplish a task. Sample sections in this book include

>> Creating custom paragraph numbers

>> Splitting a table between two pages

- » Wrapping text around an object
- » Opening an Excel worksheet inside of Word

- » Creating the master document
- » Marketing your eBooks
- » Creating an AutoText building block
- » Recording a macro

The topics covered are vast, but you don't have anything to memorize. Information is cross-referenced. Technical tidbits are carefully shoved to the end of a section or enclosed in a box. Though it would be great to master all that Word offers, my sense is that you prefer to find out only what you need to know and then get back to your work.

How to Use This Book

This is an active book. When you explore a topic, you see steps you follow to accomplish a given task or create an example. These steps involve using Word and the computer — specifically, the keyboard and mouse. If you have a touchscreen, that works as well, but it's far more effective to use a mouse or another pointing device.

The mouse can point, click, double-click, and right-click. These are the basic mouse activities used through the text. The click always means a left-click. *Point* means to position the mouse at a certain location on the screen but not to click.

The mouse pointer is referred to as "the mouse pointer," and its common icon is shown in the margin. This pointer is often called the *cursor*.

In a document's text, the mouse pointer changes to the I-beam pointer, shown in the margin. When you click the mouse in the text, you move the insertion pointer, which shows where new characters appear as you type. I may also refer to the insertion pointer as the toothpick cursor.

Keyboard shortcuts are shown like this:

Ctrl+D

Press and hold the Ctrl (Control) key and then tap the D key.

Multiple key combinations are also presented:

Ctrl+Shift+S

Here you press Ctrl and Shift together and then tap the S key. Release all the keys.

Word presents its commands on a Ribbon. The commands are organized into tabs and then groups. Each command is a button, and the button's artwork appears in this book's margins.

 Some buttons feature menus. To view the menu, you either click the button itself or click a down-pointing triangle next to the button. The text directs you whether to click the button or its menu.

When a menu features a submenu, this text uses the following format to show how the submenu or command is chosen:

Page Number ⇨ Current Position ⇨ Plain Number

This direction tells you to click the Page Number button and, from its menu, choose the Current Position submenu and then the Plain Number item.

Other, more specific directions for some of the unusual things Word does are explained throughout the text.

Foolish Assumptions

This book assumes that you have a basic knowledge of Word. You know how the program works, and you've created crude and ugly documents. Perhaps you didn't believe them to be crude and ugly, but they are. And that's why you purchased this book, because you want to create more professional, respectable documents.

You are using Word 2016, which is the current version of Word as this book goes to press. Some of this book may apply to Word 2013 and possibly Word 2010, but the material isn't specific to those releases. You can have the stand-alone version of Word 2016, or you can use the Office 365 subscription version. Any differences between versions are noted in the text.

This book does not cover Word for the Macintosh. If you see an Apple logo on your computer, I can't promise that anything in this text applies to your software.

Parts of this book reference other Office applications — specifically, Excel and Outlook. Even so, you don't need to have these programs installed to get the most from the book.

If you need more basic information on Word, I can recommend *Microsoft Word 2016 For Dummies* (Wiley). That book covers material deemed too basic or common for this book, though it's still good material. For example, that book covers mail merge, which this book shuns like that steaming pan of gray goo at the back of an all-you-can-eat five-dollar buffet.

Icons Used in This Book

Festooning this book's pages are icons and micons. The icons consist of the traditional four *For Dummies* margin icons. They are:

TIP

This icon flags a useful suggestion or kindhearted tip. I'd like to think of all text in this book as a tip, but my editor dislikes it when I overuse the Tip icon. So only the very bestest tips are flagged.

REMEMBER

This icon appears by text that gives you a friendly reminder to do something, to not forget something, or to do something else, which I don't recall at the moment.

WARNING

This icon highlights things you're not supposed to do, like try to put sheet metal into a computer printer. That sounds cool, but if you really want a document to shine, I have better advice.

TECHNICAL STUFF

This icon alerts you to information you can happily avoid reading. I use it to flag parts of the text where I get technical, go off on a tangent, or mention material that's not really necessary to the topic, but my inner nerd just can't control himself. Feel free to avoid anything flagged with the Technical Stuff icon.

Along with the icons, you'll find margin art. These marginal masterpieces represent various items you see on the screen while using Word. They might be command buttons, doodads, controls, gizmos, or flecks of paint that look interesting. These micons (margin icons) help you navigate through steps in the text.

Beyond the Book

The publisher maintains a support page with updates or changes that occur since this book has gone to press. You'll also find bonus content in the form of an online cheat sheet, which isn't really cheating and definitely isn't a sheet.

To peruse the online content, visit `www.dummies.com`, but that's not the right page. You'll need to search for *Word 2016 For Professionals For Dummies*, and open the Download tab on this book's dedicated page. I'd offer more specific information, but I don't have any further details. Even I don't know where the online material is really hidden. When I asked, the publisher muttered something about "elves" and she then proceeded to consume dry coffee grounds.

Where to Go from Here

The first thing you need to do is stop reading the introduction. I'm serious: It's over. The book's vast pages await a bright reading light and your eager gaze.

Check out the table of contents and see what interests you. Peruse the index and look up a special topic. Or just flip to a page and become enlightened. Word does so much and offers so many tools to help you make better documents that you can truly start anywhere.

My email address is `dgookin@wambooli.com`. Yes, that's my real address. I reply to all email I receive, and you'll get a quick reply if you keep your question short and specific to this book or to Word itself. Although I enjoy saying Hi, I cannot answer technical support questions or help you troubleshoot your computer. Thanks for understanding.

You can also visit my web page for more information or as a diversion:

```
www.wambooli.com
```

This book's specific support page can be found at

```
www.wambooli.com/help/word
```

I provide frequent updates and posts on that page, offering bonus information on Word, supplements to this book, tips, tricks, trivia, and fun. And, there's only one little advertisement on the page and no pop-ups.

Enjoy this book. And enjoy Word as much as you can stand it.

1
Fancy Formatting and Froufrou

IN THIS PART . . .

Discover how to best use fonts.

Find out how to lay out a paragraph.

Learn how to organize text with tabs and lists.

Work with tables and information in a grid.

Customize columns of text in a document.

Get to know about page formatting.

Apply informative headers and footers to a document.

Use styles to quickly format text.

Get familiar with templates, and start creating documents quickly.

Chapter 1

Font Fun

When graphical computer operating systems appeared in the 1980s, users found themselves infectiously attracted to fonts. People played with text formatting, spicing up documents in frivolous and crude ways. It was fun, but odious: Documents looked like someone had hired a color-blind man to paint a house.

The adoration for fonts hasn't diminished over time, but people today have a bit more respect for a document's text. In a professional environment, you want to choose a font that's appropriate, tasteful, and consistent with a good layout and design. You can hire a graphic artist, but while you remain cheap, you can rely upon Word's various typeface tools to assist you.

A Knowledge of Fonts

I blame the Macintosh. A menu on the first MacPaint and MacWrite programs was called Font. It listed a variety of what are more properly termed *typefaces.* That's what the typesetters call them. A *font* is a combination of typeface, size, style, and other attributes. But never mind; the term *font* has stuck.

» A *typesetter* is someone who puts type on the page. The process once involved block letters, hot lead, and meticulous craftsmanship. Today, typesetters are considered layout artists. They follow the guidelines set by a graphic designer

» A *graphic designer* is someone who chooses elements that look good on a page. This list includes typefaces, margins, graphics, and other design elements. The designer and layout artist are often the same person.

» Though *typeface* is the preferred term, I use both *typeface* and *font* throughout this book. These days, both terms are interchangeable, though technically not the same.

Describing text

You might remember when you learned to write and your teacher handed out *ruled* paper. You copied letters and words and used the rules (lines) as a guide. Those rules weren't arbitrarily drawn on the page. They come from the history of printed text, where everything has a name and a purpose, as illustrated in Figure 1-1.

FIGURE 1-1:
Text essentials.

Here are descriptions of the text measurements shown in Figure 1-1:

Baseline: Text is written on the baseline.

Cap height: Capital letters extend from the baseline to the cap height.

X-height: Most lowercase letters rise to the x-height, which is named after the lowercase letter *x* and not anything mysterious.

Ascender: Taller lowercase letters extend to the ascender height, such as the *t* shown in Figure 1-1.

Descender: Lowercase letters that dip below the baseline drop to the descender.

The purpose of these lines is consistency. Though letters have different shapes and sizes, these rules help the reader absorb the text. When letters disobey the rules, the text becomes more difficult to read.

Text is also measured from side to side. The yardstick that's used is the width of the big *M*. That measurement is called an *em*. In digital typefaces, the *em square* is a box used for designing typefaces.

Half of an em is an *en*, which is also the width of the letter *N*. That measurement isn't as precise as the em, because, in many typefaces, the en isn't exactly half the width of an em.

Two ems make an M&M, which is delicious and often eaten in great numbers.

>> Grade-school lined paper features the baseline, x-height, and cap height lines. As you progress through school and even into the workplace, only the baseline remains as a guide, though the other lines still exist in the world of fonts.

>> In many fonts, the cap height and ascender are at the same position.

>> The x-height can be set high, as shown in Figure 1-1, but often it marks the midpoint between the baseline and cap height. Its location depends on the typeface design.

>> Font width varies depending on the font's design, whether the font is heavily weighted, and whether the font is proportionally spaced or monospaced. See the next section for details on these terms.

>> A dash equal in width to the M character is called an *em dash*. A space equal in width to the M character is an *em space*.

>> The *en dash* is equal in width to the letter *N*. An *en space* is a space of the same width.

>> A *hyphen* is a character, shorter than the en dash.

>> Use a hyphen to hyphenate words or as a minus sign.

>> The hyphen appears on the PC's keyboard, next to the 0 key on the top row and in the upper right corner of the numeric keypad.

>> Use an en dash to specify a range, such as pages 22–24.

>> The keyboard shortcut to generate an en dash in Word is Ctrl+Alt+(hyphen) where the hyphen key is next to the 0 on the PC's keyboard.

>> The em dash is used to create a parenthetical clause or as a replacement for the colon. Violent clashes erupt between copy editors over whether to add spaces on either side of the em dash. The current victors believe no spaces should cushion the ends of the em dash. These people are incorrect and will be punished eventually.

>> In Word, the keyboard shortcut Ctrl+Alt+Shift+(hyphen) produces an em-dash character, where the hyphen key is on the numeric keypad.

» In most modern typefaces, the en dash isn't exactly half the width of the em dash, but it remains equal to the width of the uppercase *N*.

» The typeface used in Figure 1-1 is Calibri, which is Word's default body text or Normal style font.

Understanding text attributes

A font has many attributes, which define the way the font looks and how it can be best put to use. Many of the font attributes are related to Word's text formatting commands. Here's the Big Picture:

Typeface: The font name is called the *typeface.* Yeah: Technically, a font is a typeface. Apple, you really screwed up everyone.

Serif / sans serif: The two styles of typeface are serif and sans serif. A *serif* is a decoration added to each character, a small line or embellishment. Serifs make text easier to read, so serif typefaces are preferred for body text. *Sans serif* typefaces lack the decorations and are preferred for document titles and headings. Figure 1-2 illustrates serif and sans serif typefaces.

Times New Roman
Serif typeface, proportional

Helvetica
Sans serif typeface, proportional

FIGURE 1-2:
Typefaces of differing styles.

Courier New
Serif typeface, monospaced

Proportional / monospaced: A proportionally spaced typeface uses different widths for each letter, so a little *I* and a big *M* are different widths. A monospaced typeface features letters all the same width, as you'd find on a typewriter. Figure 1-2 illustrates both proportional and monospace typefaces.

Size: Typeface size is measured in *points,* or units equal to $\frac{1}{72}$ of an inch. So, a typeface 72 points tall is 1 inch tall. The measurement is made from the typeface's descender to its cap height. On a computer, the size is measured by an *em square,* which is the width and height of the letter *M*.

Weight: The weight value is either part of the typeface itself or added as an effect, such as the bold text attribute. But for many fonts, the weight is selected with the typeface, as shown in Figure 1-3.

Myriad Pro Light

Myriad Pro Regular

Myriad Pro Semibold

Myriad Pro Bold

Myriad Pro Black

Myriad Pro Light Italic

Myriad Pro Italic

Myriad Pro Semibold Italic

Myriad Pro Bold Italic

Myriad Pro Black Italic

FIGURE 1-3:
Typefaces of
differing weights
and slants.

Typeface weights

Typeface weights & slants

Slant or slope: A typeface's slope refers to how the text is angled. The most common slope is italic. Oblique text is similar to italic, but subtler. The slant can also tilt to the right, which is more of a text effect than anything you'll commonly see associated with a typeface.

Width: Many typefaces feature condensed or narrow variations. These fonts include the same basic design, but the text looks thin or skinny.

Effects: Finally come the effects, which have little to do with the typeface. These affects are applied by Word to add emphasis or just look cool. See the later section "Text Effects Strange and Wonderful."

Text on a line can be manipulated to change the way it looks. For example, tracking can be adjusted to scrunch up characters on a line of text. Kerning can be applied to bring letters closer together. Later sections in this chapter describe the details.

TECHNICAL STUFF

>> Fonts are installed into Windows, not Word. You must access the Control Panel (even in Windows 10) and choose the Appearance and Personalization category. Click the Fonts heading to view installed fonts.

>> Fonts are installed on your PC in the Windows\Fonts folder.

>> Proportionally spaced typefaces are easier to read.

>> Computers traditionally use monospace fonts for programming and other historically text-only documents. The benefit is that the text's characters line up evenly into columns.

>> The old typewriters produced monospace text. The two styles, elite and pica, refer to text approximately 10 points and 12 points tall, respectively. The term *pica* is also a unit of measurement, equal to ⅙ of an inch — which is 12 points.

>> Beyond proportional and monospace and serif and sans serif, typ be scripted, foreign, decorative, ornamental, or a plethora of variations.

TIP

>> Select a heavy typeface over applying the bold text format. Word may select the heavy typeface automatically when you set the bold attribute. The result is that the heavy typeface looks better than when Word attempts to make text look bold.

>> Other typeface weights, not shown in Figure 1-3, include Book, Roman, and Heavy. Still other variations might be available, depending on how the font is designed and named.

>> Italic and oblique text are two different types of slant. *Italic* is often a specific design, whereas *oblique* is simply a subtle slant to the standard typeface.

>> Just as you should choose a heavy typeface instead of applying the bold text format, if an italic or oblique typeface is available, use it instead of applying the italic text format. See the next section.

Selecting the proper typeface

The general rule for text design is to use sans serif fonts for titles and headings and use serif fonts for document text. Like all rules, this one is broken frequently and deliberately. Even in Word, the default document theme uses sans serif Calibri as both the body text and headings typeface.

If you have trouble choosing fonts, take advantage of the Design tab's document themes in Word. Follow these steps:

1. **Click the Design tab.**

2. **In the Document Formatting group, select a theme.**

   Each theme combines typeface elements with colors and other tidbits to help your document maintain its overall appearance.

As you point the mouse at various themes, the document's text updates to reflect the theme's attributes.

WARNING

>> Avoid using decorative or ornamental typefaces in your document. They look nifty but make reading difficult.

>> A *scripted* typeface looks handwritten, and you might feel it adds a personal touch. For a short note, an invitation, or a thank-you card, that typeface works well. For a long document, however, a scripted typeface hinders readability.

>> Choosing a new document theme is optional. You can always create your own document styles to set heading and body typefaces.

TECHNICAL STUFF

>> Until Word 2007, the normal body text typeface was Times New Roman. The heading typeface was Helvetica or Arial.

Font Control

In Word, the term *font* is used over *typeface*, which is inaccurate but acceptable. Don't let the nomenclature get in the way. The purpose of the Font command is to select the type of text used in your documents.

Exploring the Font group

The first place you most likely go to control text in your document is the Font group on the Ribbon's Home tab. It hosts commands for basic typeface selection and manipulation, as illustrated in Figure 1-4.

TECHNICAL STUFF

FONT SPECIFICATIONS AND STANDARDS

Beyond typeface and other typographical nonsense, a few digital standards rule the world of computer fonts. You may have heard the names: TrueType and OpenType.

TrueType is a digital font standard created by Apple and Microsoft. It was designed to compete with Adobe's PostScript fonts, which rendered better on the computer screen back in the early 1990s. OpenType is the successor to TrueType, which was developed in the late 1990s.

To determine which font is which, open the Font dialog box. Choose a font, and its type is confirmed below the Preview window.

Other fonts are stirred into the mix and flagged as non-TrueType in Word. These fonts may not look as good as TrueType/OpenType fonts. You may also find that some of Word's advanced text-effect commands don't apply to non-TrueType/OpenType fonts.

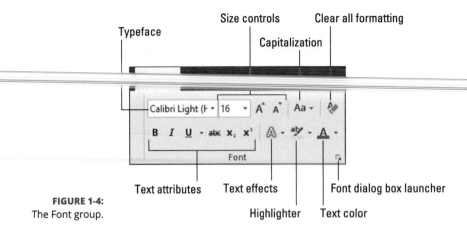

FIGURE 1-4:
The Font group.

The two key items in the Font group set the typeface and text size. Other common attribute commands are available, such as Bold and Italic, as well as commands for text effects, text color, capitalization, and highlighting.

>> Text formatting commands in the Font group are applied to any new text you type or to selected text.

>> Many of the commands shown in the Font group are echoed on the Mini Toolbar, which appears when you select or right-click text.

>> Capitalization and highlighting commands are not text formats or attributes. They manipulate the way text looks but don't affect the typeface.

>> The Clear All Formatting command resets all font attributes and modifications back to the underlying style. So, if the style is Calibri 11-point text, click the Clear All Formatting button to restore selected text to that style.

>> The keyboard shortcut for the Clear All Formatting command is Ctrl+spacebar.

Using the Font dialog box

For detailed control over the text format, use the Font dialog box. It offers far more controls than are found on the Ribbon. Follow these steps to summon the Font dialog box:

1. **Click the Home tab.**

2. **In the Font group, click the dialog box launcher.**

The Font dialog box is shown in Figure 1-5.

And now, the shortcut key: Press Ctrl+D to quickly summon the Font dialog box.

Font color

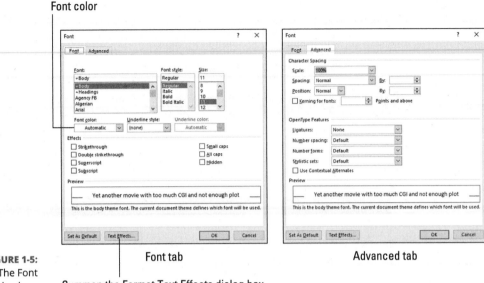

FIGURE 1-5:
The Font
dialog box.

Font tab

Advanced tab

Summon the Format Text Effects dialog box

The Font tab in the Font dialog box (on the left in Figure 1-5) is the traditional, go-to place for standard text-attribute application and formatting fun. More interesting and unusual text-manipulation commands are found on the Advanced tab (on the right in Figure 1-5). Even more text effects are available when you click on the Text Effects button, illustrated in the figure. These options are discussed in the later section "Text Effects Strange and Wonderful."

>> Settings made in the Font dialog box are applied to any new text that's typed or to any selected text.

>> The Automatic font color (refer to Figure 1-5) is the color set by the current style or the document theme. For the Normal style, the color is black.

>> Refer to the next section for information on the +Body and +Headings fonts, shown in the Font dialog box.

Choosing fonts with a theme

To spare you the expense of hiring a graphics designer, Word comes with multiple sets of document themes. These are organized by elements such as heading and body fonts, colors, and effects. The purpose isn't to replace styles, but rather to offer preset combinations that work well together. In fact, you don't need to mess with document themes, if you don't want to.

To view available documents, click the Design tab. Themes are available from the Themes button, which includes all theme elements: fonts, colors, and effects. The Style Set gallery is used to select specific fonts. Individual theme attributes can

The Fonts button in the Document Formatting group shows a list of fonts you can choose from to replace the current document theme. These fonts become the +Body and +Heading fonts, shown in the Fonts dialog box. (Refer to Figure 1-5.)

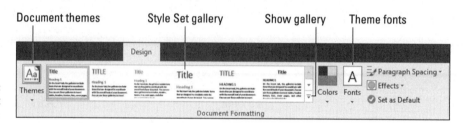

FIGURE 1-6:
Document
themes.

Selecting a new font, or any document theme element, immediately affects all aspects of the document — if you're using Word's standard styles from the Normal template. If you've set your own styles, theme changes may not have any effect.

Changing the default font

The default font is set in the Normal template, which Word uses for any new document without a specific template assigned. The Normal style in the Normal template is preset to match the document theme, but you can change that setting. Follow these steps:

1. **Press Ctrl+D.**

   The Font dialog box appears.

2. **Choose the typeface you want to use for all new documents opened in Word.**

   Say you want to use Times New Roman. If so, choose that typeface in the Font dialog box.

3. **Set the text size.**

4. **Set any additional text attributes.**

   You probably don't want to set any additional attributes, but if so, do it now.

5. **Click the button Set As Default.**

Word prompts you to indicate whether you want to make the change only for the current document or for all new documents based on the Normal template.

6. **Choose the option All Documents Based On the Normal.dotm Template.**

7. **Click OK.**

From this point onward, all new documents that you create use the typeface and size and any other attributes you selected.

>> To start a new document in Word, press Ctrl+N.

>> This change doesn't affect documents that use a template other than Normal.

Typography Control

Word offers some typeface options that go beyond standard text formatting. These controls let you manipulate the typeface in degrees beyond standard attributes. The modifications let you reset text size, spacing, and position. They also let you hide text, which is a curious attribute, yet it remains a valid option in Word.

Changing text scale

The Scale command changes the text size in a horizontal direction, so it's different from *point size*, which sets the typeface's overall size. Use the Scale command to fatten or thin your text, making it wider or narrower.

To adjust the width of a chunk of text, obey these directions:

1. **Select the chunk of text to modify.**

2. **Press Ctrl+D.**

3. **Click the Advanced tab in the Font dialog box.**

4. **Choose a percentage value from the Scale menu, or type a specific scale.**

The larger the percentage, the wider each character becomes.

TIP

Use the Preview box in the Font dialog box to get an idea of how the command affects the selected text (from Step 1).

5. **Click OK.**

The new width is applied to your text.

Figure 1-7 illustrates the effect of changing the text scale. For each scale percentage, note that the text *height* (size in points) remains the same. Only the text's width changes.

I suppose I'll start the diet tomorrow

Scale 66%

I suppose I'll start the diet tomorrow

Scale 100%

FIGURE 1-7:
Examples of
text scale.

I suppose I'll start the diet tomorrow

Scale 150%

REMEMBER

>> I don't recommend setting the text scale for your document's body text. This type of command is best suited for headings or other document elements where unusually sized text draws attention.

>> Setting a very narrow text width is one way to generate a font size that's otherwise too small to produce.

>> If the typeface offers a Narrow or Wide variation, use that rather than the Scale command.

>> Some typefaces don't scale well at the larger end of the spectrum. You must decide whether a scaled typeface is worth any ugliness generated by the effect.

Setting character spacing

You probably don't think about the spacing between characters, which is exactly what a typeface designer wants. Despite all that talent and effort, Word lets you override the decisions of a typeface designer and reset the amount of space between characters in a line of text.

To condense or expand spaces between each letter, obey these steps:

1. **Select the text you want to expand or condense.**

2. **Press Ctrl+D to bring up the Font dialog box.**

3. **Click the Advanced tab.**

4. **From the Spacing menu, choose Expand or Condensed to increase or reduce the space between letters in the selected text.**

5. **Manipulate the By gizmo to set how wide or narrow to set the spaces between letters.**

   Use the Preview box to see how the settings affect the selected text. Figure 1-8 illustrates some of the settings.

6. **Click OK to set the character spacing.**

As with changing the text scale (refer to the preceding section), I recommend manipulating character spacing only for document titles and headings.

Expanded by 1.5 pts   Great Places to Hide the Body

Expanded by 1.0 pts   Great Places to Hide the Body

Normal spacing   Great Places to Hide the Body

Condensed by 1.0 pts   Great Places to Hide the Body

FIGURE 1-8:
Character spacing
settings.   Condensed by 1.5 pts   Great Places to Hide the Body

Adding kerning and ligatures

To adjust the spaces between specific letters in a typeface, you can apply kerning to the text or use special character combinations known as ligatures.

Kerning is a character-spacing command that involves only specific letters. It scrunches together those characters, such as the *A* and *V*, to make the text more readable. To kern text in your document, heed these directions:

1. **Press Ctrl+D.**

   The Font dialog box appears.

2. **Click the Advanced tab.**

3. **Place a check mark by the setting Kerning for Fonts.**

4. **Set a text size value in the Points and Above box.**

5. **Click OK.**

Unlike other items in the Font dialog box, kerning is applied to all text throughout the document, as long as the text's point size is larger than what's set in Step 4.

letters is to apply ligatures. A *ligature* connects two or more letters, such as the F and I in the word *file*. Converting text in this manner is a feature of the OpenType font, so it's not available to all typefaces. If you want to try it, follow these steps:

1. **Select the chunk of text to which you want to apply a ligature.**

2. **Press Ctrl+D.**

3. **In the File dialog box, click the Advanced tab.**

4. **From the Ligatures menu, choose Standard Only.**

   If this choice has no effect on the text, choose All.

5. **Click OK.**

The All setting (refer to Step 4) adds just about every ligature possible, which may produce some funky results in the text. If so, consider scaling back your choice to Standard and Contextual.

TECHNICAL STUFF

REMEMBER

>> Without kerning, some words appear to have extra space in them. Kerning addresses that issue.

>> Technically, kerning intrudes upon the integrity of the virtual em square around each character in a digital font. Because kerning is applied only to specific letters, the effect improves readability.

>> If you desire to kern all letters on a line of text, adjust the character spacing. Refer to the preceding section.

>> Not every font (typeface) sports ligatures.

>> You can also insert ligatures directly. On the Insert tab, choose Symbol and select More Symbols. In the Symbol dialog box, the *fi* and *fl* ligatures are found in the Symbol dialog box, under the subset Alphabetic Presentation Forms.

Adjusting text position

The two basic text-positioning commands are Superscript and Subscript, found in the Home tab's Font group. These commands allow you to reduce the text size and shift the baseline up or down to create subscripts such as H_2O and superscripts such as $E=mc^2$. You can apply a similar effect to your text by shifting the baseline up or down, as illustrated in Figure 1-9.

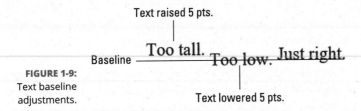

FIGURE 1-9:
Text baseline adjustments.

To adjust text position above or below the baseline, heed these directions:

1. Select the text you want raised or lowered.

Ensure that it's a small chunk of text. Raising an entire line of text would be impractical.

2. Press Ctrl+D to bring forth the Font dialog box.

3. Click the Advanced tab.

4. From the Position menu, choose Raised or Lowered.

5. Select a point value from the By gizmo.

For example, to raise a word 3 points from the baseline, choose Raised and then 3 pt from the box.

6. Click OK to apply the new text position.

To remove raised or lowered text, repeat these steps and choose Normal in Step 4, and then click OK.

>> Raising or lowering text can affect line spacing within a paragraph as well as spacing between paragraphs. If you have paragraph line spacing at the Exactly setting, the text may bump the line above or below. See Chapter 2 for more information on paragraph line spacing.

>> The Subscript command button is shown in the margin. Its keyboard equivalent is Ctrl+=. Use this command to subscript a single character of text.

>> The Superscript command button is shown in the margin. Its keyboard equivalent is Ctrl+Shift+=. This command is preferred when you want to superscript a single character.

Text Effects Strange and Wonderful

If you really want to have fun with fonts, you can apply some of Word's text effects. These aren't typeface attributes, but rather special effects applied to a font. And like all strange and wonderful things in the world of fonts, these effects are best suited for headings and titles, not for body text.

TIP

ment. For most fancy text times, choosing this command saves you a lot of time and frustration. See Chapter 13 for information on WordArt.

Accessing the Format Text Effects pane

To apply text effects, you summon the Format Text Effects pane, illustrated in Figure 1-10.

To display this pane, follow these steps:

1. **Press Ctrl+D to bring forth the Font dialog box.**

2. **Click the Text Effects button.**

The button is found near the lower left corner of the dialog box. If it's disabled, the current typeface cannot be manipulated.

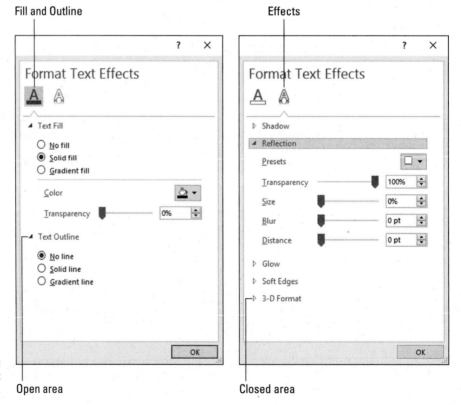

FIGURE 1-10:
The Format Text
Effects pane.

The Format Text Effects pane features two tabs, illustrated in Figure 1-10. The left tab handles text fill and outline options. The right tab lists a host of effects.

Each item in the Format Text Effects pane is collapsible. Click the triangle to expand the item; click again to collapse, as illustrated in Figure 1-10.

To make adjustments, select the text you want to format. Work the pane to apply the effects, which, sadly, cannot be previewed. After making adjustments, click the OK button to apply, and then click OK again to close the Font dialog box.

Changing text fill

The Font dialog box, as well as the Font group on the Home tab, features the Font Color button. To apply color to the font's outline as well as use more than just a solid color, you access the Text Fill area of the Format Text Effects pane; refer to Figure 1-10.

The Solid Fill option works just like the Font Color command: Choose Solid Fill and select a color. Use the Transparency slider to add a transparent, or ghost, effect to the text.

When you choose Gradient Fill, the pane changes to show many more controls. A gradient features different colors or shades that fade into each other, similar to the text shown in Figure 1-11, which features a gradient fill effect.

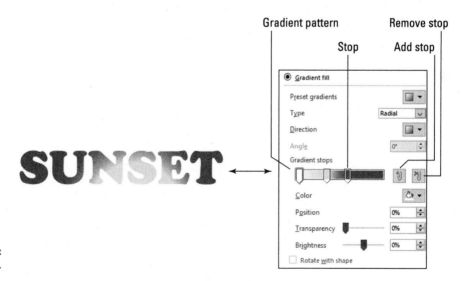

FIGURE 1-11:
Gradient fill.

The options available for Gradient Fill are numerous, as illustrated on the right in Figure 1-11. The key is the Gradient Stops bar, which features different color settings at different positions. The settings blend along the bar to build the gradient pattern.

Here are the general steps taken to create a gradient fill pattern:

1. **Select the text.**

   Gradient fill works best on titles and perhaps on a caption or another graphical element. It would look horrid if applied to a heading or body text.

2. **Press Ctrl+D.**

3. **Click the Text Effects button in the Font dialog box.**

4. **Click the Fill and Outline tab on the Format Text Effects pane.**

   Refer to Figure 1-10 for the tab's location.

5. **Expand the Text Fill area.**

6. **Choose Gradient Fill.**

7. **Select a fill from the Preset Gradients button or create your own fill.**

8. **Click OK to apply the fill, and then click OK again to close the Font dialog box.**

If you opt to create your own fill (refer to Step 7), you set two or more stops on the Gradient Stops bar, selecting a color for each stop: Click on the bar to set a stop, and then choose a color from the Color button menu.

To remove a stop, use the mouse to drag it from the Gradient Stops bar. You can also use the Remove Stop and Add Stop buttons, illustrated in Figure 1-11.

Four types of gradients are available, as chosen from the Type menu. In Figure 1-11 you see a Radial gradient, which fans out from a center point. The Position box is what sets the center point. Use the Direction button to see how the gradient is applied to the text.

TIP

Unfortunately, the Gradient settings changes aren't previewed live in your document. The best way to see the effect is to click OK. Use the Preview portion of the Font dialog box to check your work.

Setting a text outline

A font has both a fill color and an outline color. The Font Color command affects only the fill, not the outline. To add an outline or a border to text, you apply the Text Outline effect.

Obey these steps to add a text outline:

1. **Select the text.**

   The text doesn't need to have a fill color; the Automatic color (usually, black) works fine. You can, however, set No Fill as the text color, in which case only the outline shows up.

2. **Press Ctrl+D and click the Text Effects button in the Font dialog box.**

3. **Ensure that the Fill and Outline tab is chosen in the Format Text Effects pane.**

4. **Expand the Text Outline area.**

5. **Choose Solid Line or Gradient Line to set the type of outline.**

   For Gradient Line, you can configure the gradient color stops and other options, as discussed in the preceding section.

6. **Use the Width gizmo to set the outline width.**

   Width is measured in points. Larger values show a heavier outline.

7. **Set other options to customize how the line looks.**

8. **Click OK, and then click OK again to view your effects.**

   The text modifications may not show up in the Font dialog box's Preview window, so you must return to the document to view your efforts.

In Step 7 you can further manipulate the line's look, depending on which line attribute you choose:

Compound Type: Use the Compound Type menu to choose line styles, such as a double line, thick and thin lines, and more.

Dash Type: The Dash Type menu sets whether the line is solid or composed of dashes or dots in various patterns and lengths.

Cap Type: Items on the Cap Type menu set how the border goes around a curve. The options are Square, Round, and Flat. This effect doesn't really show up unless the text is quite large or the outline is thick.

Join Type: The Join Type menu determines what happens when lines meet. As with the cap type, this effect requires large text or thick lines to show up.

As with other settings in the Format Text Effects pane, you must set your options and then click OK to view the results in the Font dialog box.

Adding a text shadow

The Shadow effects can help a title or graphical element stand out, almost as if it's

gallery of preset options, or you can toil on your own with various settings in the Format Text Effects pane.

Preset shadow effects

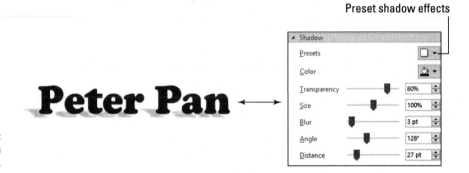

FIGURE 1-12:
Text with a
shadow attached.

The Shadow effect is found in the Format Text Effects pane. Obey these directions to apply the effect to selected text in your document:

1. **Select the text.**

The Shadow effect works best on titles and perhaps decorative text elements.

2. **Press Ctrl+D to bring up the Font dialog box.**

3. **Click the Text Effects button.**

4. **Click the Effects tab in the Format Text Effects pane.**

Refer to Figure 1-10 for the tab's appearance and location.

5. **Expand the Shadow area.**

6. **Choose an item from the Presets menu button.**

TIP

The best way to apply a text shadow is to choose an item from the Presets menu, shown on the right in Figure 1-12.

7. **Use the remaining items in the Shadow portion of the Format Text Effects pane to make fine adjustments to the preset options.**

8. **Click OK, and then click OK again to view the shadow effect.**

You may have to repeat these steps a few times to get the effect just right, but choosing a preset shadow (refer to Step 6) really helps to expedite the process.

Configuring text reflection and glow

The Reflection and Glow text effects work similarly to the Shadow effect, covered in the preceding section. These effects and their settings are illustrated in Figure 1-13.

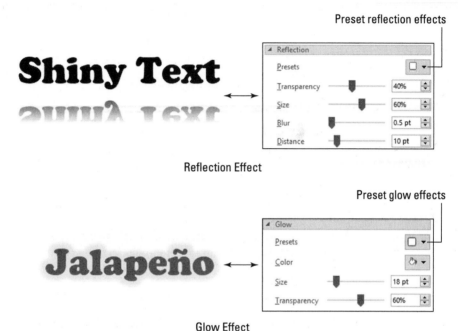

Reflection Effect

Glow Effect

FIGURE 1-13:
Reflection and glow text effects.

To best apply text reflection and glow effects, first select text and then choose a preset from the Presets button. (Refer to Figure 1-13.) You can make further adjustments to the effects, which requires that you click OK (twice) to view the text and then return to the Format Text Effects pane to jiggle the various controls.

>> The Reflection effect does increase the text's line height. Again, this type of effect works best on a chapter title or other graphical element, not on body text.

>> The Soft Edges effect doesn't apply to most text (if any). It's an echo of the Soft Edges effect applied to other graphics in a document. See Chapter 12.

Creating hidden text

Perhaps the strangest font attribute is hidden text. You won't find this setting in the Format Text Effects dialog box, because it's more of a deception than an effect: What's the point of writing something that doesn't show up on the screen or in a printed document? I honestly can't think of any proper situation, but the command is available.

To hide text, follow these steps:

1. **Select the text you want to disappear.**

   The text isn't deleted; it's merely hidden.

2. **Press Ctrl+D to summon the Font dialog box.**

3. **Place a check mark by the Hidden item.**

   The Hidden item is found on the Font tab in the Effects area.

4. **Click OK.**

   The text is hidden.

Now that the text is hidden, the big question is, "How do I get it back?" In fact, how do you even find the text?

¶ The easy way to view hidden text is to use the Show/Hide command, located on the Home tab in the Paragraph group. Its icon is shown in the margin. Click the button, and hidden text appears in the document with a dotted underline, as shown in Figure 1-14.

Hidden text   Dotted underline

I think Dan is a doody head but others think that he is a nice guy.

You can also direct Word to show hidden text all the time. Heed these steps:

1. **Click the File tab.**

2. **Choose Options.**

   The Word Options dialog box appears.

3. **Choose Display from the list of categories on the left side of the dialog box.**

4. **In the Always Show area, place a check mark by the option Hidden Text.**

5. **Click OK.**

Though you can make hidden text visible, it doesn't print unless you direct Word to also print the hidden text. To do so, repeat Steps 1 through 3 in the preceding list, but also place a check mark by the item Print Hidden Text.

Then again, if you're going to show and print hidden text, why hide it in the first place?

» Hidden text affects document proofing. That's because the proofing tools (spelling and grammar) ignore the hidden text.

» I suppose one reason to hide text is that you might want to resurrect it later. I wouldn't use this option as an editing tool, but rather as a way to customize a single document for multiple purposes. For example, you might hide more technical information so that you can provide a shorter document as an executive summary.

» Hidden text is used on web pages to obscure various elements. For example, a web page template may list an item that's unused on a page, in which case it can be hidden to avoid confusion. See Chapter 30 for information on Word and web page publishing.

» The Hidden text attribute isn't the same as the Clear All Formatting command. That command resets any added text attributes to their settings as defined in the underlying style. So, if the style is Normal, the Clear All formatting command removes any applied text formats that aren't part of the Normal style.

» To unhide text, you must remove the Hidden format: Repeat the first step list in this section, but in Step 3 remove the check mark (or ensure that the box is blank). You can also use the Clear All Formatting command (Ctrl+spacebar), but that removes all text attributes, which may not be what you want.

Find and Replace Text Formatting

One item that relates to fonts but has nothing to do with aesthetics is Word's capability to find and replace fonts and text formatting. Using this variation of the standard Find and Replace command is tricky, so pay attention!

To replace formatting, you must add and then *subtract* the text attributes. Before diving in, I have some bits of advice:

» If you use styles, it's easier to modify a style than to globally search-and-replace a text format. That's the best way to change an underlying typeface or text size.

>> When you find and replace a text format, you must search for the first text format and then replace with the second format while removing the first. This sounds odd, which is why if you try this type of operation on your own, it

REMEMBER

>> Always remove the formatting attributes from the Find and Replace dialog box when you're done. If you don't, Word continues to search for text attributes, which may limit future searches.

Obey these steps to find and replace a text attribute, such as underline with italics:

1. **Press Ctrl+Home to position the insertion pointer at the tippy-top of the document.**

2. **Press Ctrl+H to bring up the Find and Replace dialog box, with the Replace tab forward.**

3. **Click the More button to expand the Find and Replace dialog box.**

4. **Click the Find What text box, but leave it blank.**

5. **Click the Format button and choose Font from the menu.**

   The Font dialog box appears.

6. **Select the format you want to find.**

   For example, click the Underline Style button and choose the single underline.

7. **Click OK to close the Font dialog box and return to the Find and Replace dialog box.**

8. **Click the Replace text box and leave it blank.**

9. **Click the Format button and choose Font.**

   The Font dialog box appears again.

10. **From the Font Style list, choose Italics.**

11. **From the Underline Style menu, choose None.**

    These two steps (10 and 11) carry out the important task of not only selecting the replacement text format but also removing the original text format. In this example, you're choosing underline and replacing it with no underline and italics.

12. **Click OK to close the Font dialog box.**

13. **The Search and Replace dialog box should look similar to Figure 1-15.**

Replace with (and remove)

Format to find

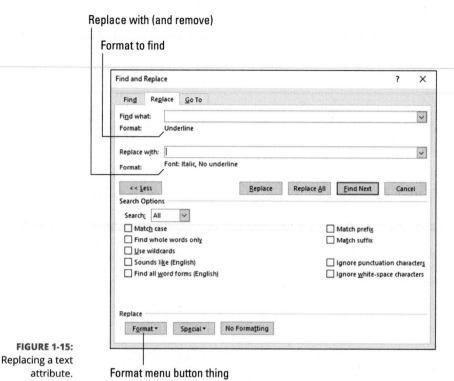

Format menu button thing

14. **Click the Replace All button to search and replace the text attribute throughout the document.**

A summary box appears, listing the number of replacements made.

15. **Click OK to dismiss the summary.**

Now come the important steps of removing the formatting attributes.

16. **Click the Find What text box and click the No Formatting button.**

17. **Click the Replace With text box and click the No Formatting button.**

These steps (16 and 17) remove formatting options from the next find-and-replace operation. That way, these options won't mess up the next search or search-and-replace operation.

18. **Click the Close button to dismiss the Find and Replace dialog box.**

If you were to replace italics with underline, you'd need to search for the Italic text style and replace it with the regular text style as well as the single-underline format. If you forget to remove the original text format, you end up with double

You cannot use the steps in this section to peel away text effects. The Text Effects button isn't available in the Font dialog box you summon in Steps 5 and 9.

BRING BACK THE OLD FIND DIALOG BOX

Starting with Word 2010, Microsoft set the standard Find command in the Navigation pane; gone is the old Find dialog box, which is now called the Advanced Find dialog box. You can bring back that dialog box by mapping it to the Ctrl+F keyboard shortcut.

Generally speaking, I don't recommend that you re-assign Word's default keyboard shortcuts. For the old Find dialog box, I'm willing to make an exception to that rule. If you're okay with changing a default keyboard shortcut, follow these steps:

1. Choose Options to conjure forth the Word Options dialog box.

2. Choose the category Customize the Ribbon.

3. Click the Customize button next to Keyboard Shortcuts to bring up the Customize Keyboard dialog box.

4. From the Categories list, choose Home Tab.

5. From the Commands list, choose EditFind.

6. Click the mouse in the Press New Shortcut Key box.

7. Press Ctrl+F.

8. Click the Assign button.

9. Click the Close button to close the Customize Keyboard dialog box.

10. Click the Close button to close the Word Options dialog box.

The Ctrl+F keyboard shortcut now summons the Advanced Find dialog box, which I believe is better suited to a high-end Word user than the Search Document text box on the Navigation pane.

Chapter 2

Paragraph Layout

Word's formatting commands parallel the structure of all documents. The most basic tidbit you can format is the character. Characters form words, sentences, and then paragraphs. Word's next level of formatting is the paragraph. In fact, the paragraph is the basic building block of all documents. Select the proper paragraph format to make your document presentable and readable.

A Typical Paragraph

In Word, a *paragraph* is defined as a chunk of text that ends when you press the Enter key. That chunk can be empty, or it can contain a single letter, word, line of text, or sentence or a collection of sentences. As long as you press the Enter key, and gener–ate a paragraph character in Word, the paragraph formatting commands apply.

>> A *sentence* is a linguistic unit designed to express something. It must have meaning, but also the typical parts of speech: noun, verb, and other junk you forgot about in French class. (That's because grammar is only a remote

concept in English, like the national debt or how paper can possibly defeat rock.)

>> A *paragraph* is grammatically defined as a writing unit that expresses an idea. It can be composed of a single word or sentence, sentences.

>> A new paragraph begins a new concept or idea. Even experienced writers find it difficult to determine where a paragraph can be split or when a new paragraph starts. No exact rules exist, though reading over your text can help clue you in to when a new idea begins and a new paragraph is necessary.

>> See Chapter 31 for information on displaying the paragraph, or Enter, key character.

>> The paragraph character, ¶, is officially called the *pilcrow*. This symbol is normally hidden in Word.

>> To quickly select a paragraph of text in word, click the mouse three times.

>> If you move the mouse into the page's left margin, the pointer changes to a northeasterly arrow, shown in the margin. Double-click the mouse in this position to select a paragraph of text.

Understanding paragraph formatting

To best format a paragraph of text, you need to understand the terms Word uses to describe a paragraph's elements. You also need to know what the elements are and how Word lets you adjust them.

In the Big Picture, paragraphs feature alignment. The four values are shown in Figure 2-1: Align Left, Align Right, Center, and Justify. These formats are covered in the later section "Using justification."

Align Left

In Word, a *paragraph* is defined as a chunk of text that ends when you press the Enter key. That chunk can be empty, or it can contain a single letter, word, line of text, or sentence or a collection of sentences. As long as you press the Enter key, and generate a paragraph character in Word, the paragraph formatting commands apply.

Align Right

In Word, a *paragraph* is defined as a chunk of text that ends when you press the Enter key. That chunk can be empty, or it can contain a single letter, word, line of text, or sentence or a collection of sentences. As long as you press the Enter key, and generate a paragraph character in Word, the paragraph formatting commands apply.

Center

In Word, a *paragraph* is defined as a chunk of text that ends when you press the Enter key. That chunk can be empty, or it can contain a single letter, word, line of text, or sentence or a collection of sentences. As long as you press the Enter key, and generate a paragraph character in Word, the paragraph formatting commands apply.

Justify

In Word, a *paragraph* is defined as a chunk of text that ends when you press the Enter key. That chunk can be empty, or it can contain a single letter, word, line of text, or sentence or a collection of sentences. As long as you press the Enter key, and generate a paragraph character in Word, the paragraph formatting commands apply.

FIGURE 2-1: Paragraph justification or alignment.

Of the four available paragraph alignment formats, you'll probably use Align Left most often. If you use Justify, review the later section "Hyphenation." Word's Hyphenation feature works with justification to make text more readable.

The next formatting item involves spacing. A paragraph features multiple spacing formats, illustrated in Figure 2-2.

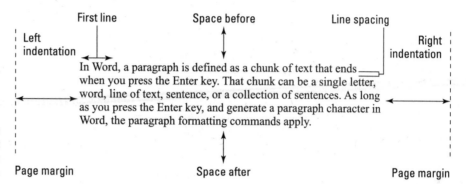

FIGURE 2-2: Things to format in and around a paragraph.

The spacing to the right and left of a paragraph is called *indentation*. It's measured from the page margin, which is itself measured from the edge of the page. In Figure 2-2, the left indentation and right indentation are exaggerated. Typically, the indentation is zero.

A special indentation can be applied to the first line of each paragraph. This indentation is either the first-line indent or a hanging indent. These formats are covered in the later sections "Setting a first-line indent" and "Creating a hanging indent."

Above and below the paragraph you find the space-before and space-after areas. These areas provide a buffer between paragraphs, such as between a heading and body text or after a title.

Finally, a paragraph can feature *line spacing.* This space pads the lines of text in a paragraph. Setting the line spacing is covered in the later section "Adjusting line spacing."

>> Center alignment works best for single-line titles and chapter breaks.

>> When a paragraph features a first-line indent, the paragraph spacing is usually set to zero.

>> When a paragraph features no first-line indent, paragraph spacing after is set to equal approximately one blank line in size.

>> Whether you use a first-line indent or a space after the paragraph, the end result is the same: to make the text readable.

>> See Chapter 6 for information on setting page margins.

Finding paragraph control in Word

Rather than let you retain your sanity, Word offers not two, but *three*, locations where you can format a paragraph of text. That's probably because a paragraph plays multiple roles in your text and it depends on how you look at a paragraph when it comes to formatting the thing.

The first location for paragraph control is found on the Home tab, in the Paragraph group, shown on the left in Figure 2-3. On the Layout tab, a second Paragraph group is found, located on the right in Figure 2-3.

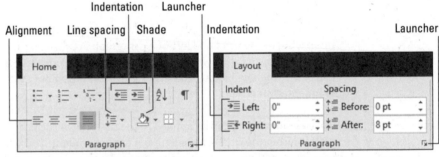

Alignment   Line spacing   Indentation   Shade   Launcher   Indentation   Launcher

Paragraph group on the Home tab   Paragraph group on the Layout tab

FIGURE 2-3:
The two
Paragraph groups
on the Ribbon.

Each Paragraph group features different controls, and each set of controls is related to the tab upon which the group squats: The Home tab features more basic paragraph-formatting items, and the Layout tab features items that relate to page formatting.

For both groups, click the Launcher icon to display the Paragraph dialog box, illustrated in Figure 2-4.

All the basic paragraph-formatting commands and settings are shown in the Paragraph dialog box. Further, the dialog box shows the current paragraph format, such as 8 points of space after the paragraph, as illustrated in Figure 2-4.

>> The Paragraph group on the Layout tab features Indent command buttons similar to the Indent buttons found on the Home tab's Paragraph group. The

difference is that the Home tab's command set the indent at ½-inch increments only. On the Layout tab, you can set specific indent values.

» As with the Font dialog box (refer to Chapter 1), the Paragraph dialog box
features a Set As Default button. Use the button to recajigger Word's paragraph format for all new documents. Most people don't mess with this setting
as much as they change the default font.

Current paragraph's Space After setting

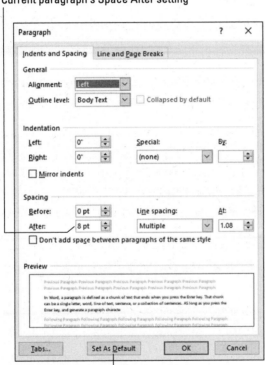

FIGURE 2-4:
The Paragraph
dialog box.

Save settings for all new documents

Working with the Ruler

Gizmos on the Ruler directly manipulate various paragraph formats. Specifically,
they control the left and right indentation, first-line indentation, and tabs. The
topic of tabs is covered in Chapter 3. Indentation is referenced in Figure 2-1. The
Ruler is illustrated in Figure 2-5.

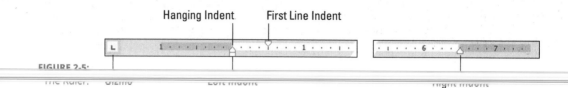

Hanging Indent   First Line Indent

FIGURE 2-5:

The Ruler doesn't normally appear in the document window. You must specifically summon it. Obey these directions:

1. **Click the View tab.**

2. **In the Show group, place a check mark by the Ruler item.**

The Ruler appears.

Settings made on the Ruler affect the current paragraph or any group of selected paragraphs. The gizmos show current settings.

TIP

›› The big advantage of the Ruler is that you can use the mouse to manipulate the controls and get instant visual feedback.

›› For more precise adjustment of paragraph indents, use the Paragraph dialog box instead of the Ruler. See the preceding section.

›› Click the gizmo on the left end of the Ruler to cycle through the various tab stops and paragraph indents. Whichever item appears in the gizmo is set when you click on the Ruler. In Figure 2-5, the left tab stop is shown in the gizmo.

›› The Left Indent marker moves both the Hanging Indent and First Line Indent gizmos.

›› The First Line Indent marker affects only the first line of the paragraph.

›› The Hanging Indent marker affects all lines *but* the first line of the paragraph.

›› The Ruler shows up in Print Layout, Web Layout, and Draft views. You can also configure a Vertical Ruler, as described in Chapter 31. The Vertical Ruler is simply a reference; it's not used to set any formatting options.

Pure Paragraph Formatting

All the command buttons residing in the Home tab's Paragraph group affect paragraph formatting. Only a handful, however, directly address how the paragraph sits on the page. The rest of the commands apply other attributes to the paragraph, such as page numbering and borders. This section focuses on what I refer to as *pure* paragraph formatting.

>> The Sort button, shown in the margin, is really a table command. It's covered in Chapter 4, but it does affect a group of selected paragraphs. Typically, you'd use the command on single-line (or single-word) paragraphs to sort a list alphabetically. More details on using this command are found in Chapter 4.

¶

>> The Show/Hide command, also found in the Home tab's Paragraph group, honestly has nothing to do with paragraphs. It displays hidden characters and text.

>> For information on the border paragraph format, refer to the book *Word 2016 For Dummies* (Wiley).

Using justification

Justification, or paragraph alignment, determines how the outer edges of a paragraph line up. It's perhaps the most basic of all paragraph formatting options, and you have only four choices, each of which appears as a button in the Home tab's Paragraph group:

Align Left: Line up the left side of the paragraph's text, which graphic artists wearing oversized sweaters have determined is the best way for human eyeballs to read text. The right side of the paragraph is not lined up. Keyboard shortcut: Ctrl+L.

Align Right: Line up the right side of a paragraph's text, which leaves the left side uneven. This alignment isn't good for reading, but it looks cool in some situations. Keyboard shortcut: Ctrl+R.

Center: Each line in the paragraph is centered, left to right. This alignment works best for titles and headings, but not for text longer than a single line. Keyboard shortcut: Ctrl+E.

Justify: Both sides of the paragraph are lined up, which is a format usually found in newspapers and magazines. Especially for multiple columns of text, the Justify paragraph format works well. Keyboard shortcut: Ctrl+J.

When justification is even, the paragraph's edges line up with the left or right indents (or both). When justification isn't even, words that cross the left or right indent boundary are placed on the following line. The official term for moving words to the next line is *word wrap*.

>> The Align Left justification is also known as *rag right* by graphic designers. This term refers to the right edge of the paragraph, which doesn't line up, so it's "ragged."

>> The Align Right justification is known as *rag left*.

>> The Justify alignment is often called *full justification*.

tab stop to position a chunk of text in the center of a line without formatting the entire paragraph with center alignment.

>> See Chapter 5 for information on marching text into columns.

Working with paragraph indents

The largest document element you can format is the page. It's the base upon which all other document formatting rests.

Figure 2-6 illustrates how Word sees a page as a formatting element. The key item is the *margin*, or indent from the edge of the page.

Formatting page margins is covered in Chapter 6. They're relevant to paragraph formatting in that the paragraph's Left Indentation and Right Indentation settings are relative to the page margins.

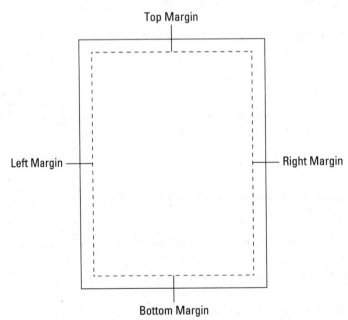

Top Margin

Left Margin ————   ———— Right Margin

FIGURE 2-6:
Page margins.

Bottom Margin

To set paragraph indents, you have a host of choices. Rather than list them all, follow these steps to quickly set the indents:

1. **Select the paragraph(s) you want to format.**

   If nothing is selected, only the current paragraph is affected. (The current paragraph is where the insertion pointer is located.)

2. **Click the Layout tab.**

3. **In the Paragraph group, use the gizmos by the Left and Right Indent boxes to set the paragraph(s) indentation.**

   As you adjust the gizmos, the paragraph(s) in your document reflect any changes. You also see the gizmos on the Ruler shuffle around, if the Ruler is visible.

TIP

If you know the exact indentation values, type them into the Left and Right boxes. (Refer to Step 3.)

>> Page margins aren't fixed. They can be adjusted, which is a topic covered in Chapter 6. They do, however, affect paragraph indentation, which is always relative to the page margin — not to the edge of the page.

>> The Normal style sets Word's default paragraph with zero indentation and zero first-line indentation.

>> It's possible to set negative values for left and right indentation. When you do so, the paragraph's edges slip into the page margin.

Setting a first-line indent

The first-line indent is special. You can adjust it in a number of ways to create some interesting paragraph formatting. Two such formats are illustrated in Figure 2-7.

FIGURE 2-7:
A first-line indent and a hanging indent.

The first line indent is special. You can adjust it in a number of ways to create some interesting paragraph formatting. Two such formats are illustrated in Figure 2-7.

First Line Indent

The first line indent is special. You can adjust it in a number of ways to create some interesting paragraph formatting. Two such formats are illustrated in Figure 2-7.

Hanging Indent

The first-line indent is pretty common (on the left in Figure 2-7). In fact, Word may automatically format all paragraphs that way if you press the Tab key when you start typing. Or you can follow these steps to apply a first-line indent:

1. **Select the paragraph(s).**

   You can select one or more paragraphs or simply click the mouse in a paragraph to affect only its format.

2. **Click the Home tab.**

3. **Click the Launcher in the Paragraph group.**

   The Paragraph dialog box appears.

5. **In the Indentation area, click the Special menu and choose First Line.**

6. **In the By box, type** 0.5 **for a ½-inch indent.**

   The half-inch indent is pretty standard.

7. **Click OK.**

TIP

If you prefer this type of text format, create or modify the current style so that it includes a first-line indent.

To adjust both the first-line indent and left indent together, use the mouse to drag the Left Indent marker on the Ruler. Refer to Figure 2-5 to identify the Left Indent marker.

Creating a hanging indent

The hanging indent is more unusual than the first-line indent, as shown in Figure 2-7. It often appears in lists or in a series of descriptive paragraphs. To set this indent, heed these directions:

1. **Select the paragraph(s) to modify.**

2. **Click the Home tab, and in the Paragraph group, click the Launcher.**

   The Paragraph dialog box appears.

3. **On the Indents and Spacing tab, in the Indentation area, click the Special menu and choose Hanging.**

4. **In the By box, type** 0.5 **for a ½-inch hanging indent.**

   The first line doesn't change, but the rest of the paragraph is indented by the value you set in the By box.

5. **Click OK.**

You can adjust the first-line indent if you like, but it's best to use the Ruler for this operation: Adjust the First Line and Hanging Indent markers on the Ruler to set the paragraph's format. That way, you can get immediate visual feedback on the effect.

TIP

The keyboard shortcut to create a ½-inch hanging indent is Ctrl+T.

Increasing space before or after a paragraph

When most Word users desire space between two paragraphs, they commit the deplorable sin of pressing the Enter key twice. This trick works, but it's not proper formatting; an empty paragraph is a sad thing. The proper solution is to add space after the paragraph.

To add space between your document's paragraphs, follow these steps:

1. Select all paragraphs you want to format.

Or you can format the first paragraph and then all the subsequent paragraphs inherit the format.

2. Click the Home tab.

3. In the Font group, note the text size.

For example, it may read 12 points.

4. Click the Layout tab.

5. In the Paragraph group, click the After box and type the same size value you remember from Step 3.

For example, type **12 pt** for a 12-point font.

For document titles and headings, you probably want to add more space, which helps distance that element from the text around it. In fact, adding space *before* a heading helps keep that line separate from the text that comes before it.

To add space before a paragraph, repeat the steps in this section, but in Step 5 click the Before box.

> ❯❯ You can set spacing both before and after a paragraph. Because text lines up at the top of the page, most body-text paragraph formats specify space after, not before.

> ❯❯ If you use a first-line indent, do not add extra space after a paragraph. The indent is added for readability, to mark the start of a paragraph. Space is added after a paragraph when the first line isn't indented, which also helps with readability. You don't need to mix the two.

Adjusting line spacing

Within a paragraph, the area between lines of text is called the *line spacing.* This value when you don't increase line spacing too much. Also, editors and collaborators might want more line spacing on a printed document so that they can write nasty notes.

The visual way to adjust line spacing is to select one or more paragraphs and follow these steps:

1. **Click the Home tab.**

2. **In the Paragraph group, click the Line and Paragraph Spacing button.**

3. **Point the mouse at the menu items to see how each one affects the paragraph.**

   As you move the mouse, the paragraph's spacing changes to reflect the new values. If this trick doesn't work, the paragraph's spacing is preset to an exact value.

4. **Click to choose a spacing value.**

   The line spacing is applied to the current paragraph or a group of selected paragraphs.

For more precise line spacing control, you must summon the Paragraph dialog box. Obey these steps:

1. **Select the paragraph(s) you want to format.**

2. **Click the Home tab.**

3. **In the Paragraph group, click the Launcher icon.**

   The Paragraph dialog box appears.

4. **In the Spacing area, click the Line Spacing menu.**

   You see six items. Here's what they mean:

   Single: Lines are spaced close together, using the typeface's em square to determine the line spacing.

   1.5 Lines: Lines are spaced 1½ times as far apart as they are with single spacing.

   Double: Lines are spaced twice as far apart as single spacing.

   At Least: Lines are spaced at a minimum point value. Word can increase the spacing within a paragraph for exceptions such as an in-line graphic, a larger text size, or special-effects text.

Exactly: Lines are spaced at a set value. The value cannot be increased for larger text elements, which can overwrite the line above or below.

Multiple: Lines are spaced to a specific line value, similar to the Single, 1.5 Lines, and Double settings. For example, if you want triple line spacing, you choose this option and specify **3** in the At box.

Most of the time you'll probably choose Single or Double from the Line Spacing menu.

5. **Use the At box gizmo to set the line spacing amount.**

   You don't need to use the At gizmo for Single, 1.5 Line, and Double options. If you do, the Multiple option is chosen automatically.

6. **Click the OK button to apply the line spacing format.**

REMEMBER

The point of line spacing is to make text readable. Single line spacing is okay, but 1.5 line spacing is more readable, as is double line spacing. The only drawback to larger spacing values is that the text occupies more room on the page.

>> Line spacing values for the At Least and Exactly options are set in points.

>> Line spacing for the Multiple item is set at the number of lines.

TECHNICAL STUFF

>> Word's default line spacing value is Multiple at 1.09. I have no idea why this setting was chosen. In fact, when Microsoft made the change in Word 2007, I received a lot of puzzling emails about why the default line spacing was set to such an odd value.

TECHNICAL STUFF

WHAT'S THE DIFFERENCE BETWEEN LINE SPACING AND LEADING?

The typographical term for *line spacing* is *leading*. It's the distance between the baselines of two lines of text. In the days of manual typesetting, a strip of lead was placed between blocks of moveable type to create the space. That's why the term is *leading*.

The amount of leading added to a line is traditionally equal to 120 percent of the line height. So, if a 10-point typeface is used, the leading is set to 12 points. That's the distance between baselines for two lines of text. The 120 percent, or 12/10, ratio is determined to be the best for reading. Single line spacing is approximately 120 percent of the line height, though Word doesn't strictly adhere to this rule.

Adding some shade

One paragraph format that has little to do with distance is the Shading command.

the command isn't available in the Paragraph dialog box.

The Shading command sets the background color for text. It doesn't need to apply to an entire paragraph. In fact, the command is more of a text background attribute than a full paragraph format, which is probably why the command isn't available in the Paragraph dialog box.

To shade a chunk of text, follow these shady steps:

1. **Select text in a paragraph.**

2. **Click the Home tab.**

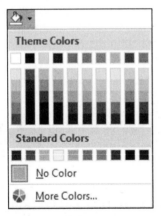

3. **In the Paragraph group, click the Shading button.**

The button hosts a menu, shown in Figure 2-8. You can choose from a preset color or create your own color. And the menu really is in color, though it appears in grayscale in this book.

FIGURE 2-8:
Picking a
paragraph
background
color.

4. **Choose a color from the Shading palette.**

The color is applied to the text's background.

As an example of how this effect is applied, you can set the paragraph shading to black and then use the Font Color command to set the text color to white. The result is white-on-black text.

If you choose to apply the Shading command to an entire paragraph, prepare to be disappointed: The shading attribute affects only the paragraph within the confines of its left and right indentation settings. Further, any space before or after the paragraph is not shaded.

When applied to multiple paragraphs, the Shading command does affect the space between the paragraphs, but again, not the space before the first paragraph or after the last.

TIP

>> To remove any shading, repeat the steps in this section but choose No Color in Step 4.

>> The colors shown on the Shading menu (refer to Figure 2-8) relate to the document theme. Click the Design tab to review the current document theme and its associated colors.

>> When the document theme is changed, the shading color may change as well.

>> If you plan to create white-on-black text, consider building a style. That way, you can apply the effect to multiple expanses of text in your document and change them all at once. See Chapter 8 for information on styles.

>> If you're creating a list of items and you desire to shade every other line, consider placing the list into a table. See Chapter 4.

>> A better option than applying background shading might be to create a text box. See Chapter 11.

Hyphenation

Thanks to proportional typefaces, and Word's capability to adjust spacing between words, rarely do you think about hyphenation. You can still hyphenate a long word, splitting it between two lines, and readers will understand and accept. Often it's better to hyphenate a word than to keep the word intact and destroy any uniformity with a paragraph's right indentation.

>> Hyphenation is used most often when paragraphs are formatted at full justification. This feature allows for better word and letter spacing within the paragraph.

>> Hyphenation is an optional thing. I recommend using it only when the hyphenated word improves a paragraph's visual presentation.

Adding a manual hyphen

Word's Hyphenation feature can check a document and automatically apply
hyphen character (−), also called the *minus sign.* That character splits words at the
end of a line, such as the one illustrated in Figure 2-9. See the ugly gap?

Paragraph before hyphenation

> The pale blue house was unremarkable, looking like every other home in the village. The street was quiet. A cat played in the yard. Nearby, an old woman watered her plants. Yet no one in the German town of Fuerstenfeldbruck was aware that little Johann was about to activate what would become his most infamous invention.

Click here to place the hyphen   Ugly gap

Paragraph after hyphenation

> The pale blue house was unremarkable, looking like every other home in the village. The street was quiet. A cat played in the yard. Nearby, an old woman watered her plants. Yet no one in the German town of Fuersten-feldbruck was aware that little Johann was about to activate what would become his most infamous invention.

FIGURE 2-9:
Hyphenating a
long word.

Hyphenated word

To hyphenate the word, follow these steps:

TIP

1. **Click the mouse to place the insertion pointer at the appropriate spot.**

   You hyphenate a word between two syllables or double letters. If you don't know the exact position, refer to a dictionary.

2. **Press the − (hyphen) key.**

   The word is split between two lines, as illustrated in Figure 2-9.

For better results, in Step 2 press Ctrl+(hyphen), the optional hyphen character. Unlike the standard hyphen character, the optional hyphen character vanishes from view when the word doesn't need to be hyphenated. It's still in the text, but appears only when needed.

>> To view optional, hidden hyphens, use the Show/Hide command. The optional hyphen character appears as the ¬ symbol. This character is known as a *logical negation* symbol, which is pronounced "not."

Automatically hyphenating text

You don't need to fuss with hyphenation, providing that you activate Word's Hyphenation feature. When activated, Word automatically inserts the optional hyphen characters in your text as needed.

To activate automatic hyphenation, obey these directions:

1. **Click the Layout tab.**

2. **In the Page Setup group, click the Hyphenation button.**

3. **From the menu, choose Automatic.**

Once active, Word hyphenates all text in the document, as well as new text you type. You may see hyphens added and removed quickly as you work on the text.

TIP

If you prefer to review Word's hyphenation choices, choose Manual in Step 3. You see the Manual Hyphenation dialog box, shown in Figure 2-10. Click to place the hyphen and then click Yes to hyphenate the word. Click No to leave the word unhyphenated.

FIGURE 2-10:
The Manual
Hyphenation
dialog box.

Manual Hyphenation: English (United States)	?	X

Hyphenate <u>a</u>t: | pref|er-en-tial |

[<u>Y</u>es] [<u>N</u>o] [Cancel]

Continue to work the Manual Hyphenation dialog box to hyphenate (or not) the entire document. When hyphenation is complete, click OK.

Manual hyphenation isn't interactive; it's done all at once. So, after you choose Manual, the None option is chosen from the Hyphenation menu and automatic hyphenation is disabled.

Inserting an unbreakable hyphen

An unbreakable hyphen prevents Word from splitting text you don't want split,

To insert the unbreakable hyphen character, press Ctrl+Shift+(hyphen). It looks like a regular hyphen, but Word won't split the text between two lines.

TIP

Just as you can insert an unbreakable hyphen, you can also insert a nonbreaking space when you don't want words split between two lines. The nonbreaking space character keyboard shortcut is Ctrl+Shift+spacebar.

Of Widows and Orphans

If you can judge a culture by how it treats widows and orphans, you can also judge a document. That's because many graphic designers detest having one or two lines from a paragraph split between two pages.

>> A single line lingering atop the page is called a *widow*.

>> A single line lagging at the bottom of the page is called an *orphan*.

In both cases, the single line is part of a paragraph that couldn't all fit on the previous or next page. Word features various remedies to cure these typographical troublemakers.

Word is preset to automatically adjust paragraphs so that you don't unintentionally create widows and orphans in your document. To confirm that this setting is active, follow these steps:

1. **Click the Home tab.**

2. **In the Paragraph group, click the Launcher.**

   The Paragraph dialog box appears.

3. **Click the Line and Page Breaks tab.**

4. **Ensure that a check mark is set by the Widow/Orphan Control option.**

5. **Click OK.**

Three other options in the Paragraph dialog box, on the Line and Page Breaks tab, also control paragraphs and how they flow on a page. Choose one of these options in Step 4 to create the desired effect:

Keep with Next: This setting keeps a group of paragraphs on the same page, no matter how the document is formatted.

Keep Lines Together: This option prevents a single paragraph from splitting between two pages.

Page Break Before: This setting starts a paragraph at the top of a page, regardless of how text lays out on the preceding page.

The mnemonic for widows and orphans is, "An orphan has no past; a widow has no future." An orphan is "born" at the bottom of a page. A widow is "left behind" at the top of a page.

WARNING

Never try to fix the widow/orphan problem by inserting empty paragraphs into your document! Sure, press the Enter key a few times, and the paragraph pops up on the next page. The problem is that as you edit and reformat your document, those empty paragraphs cause undue formatting woe.

Chapter 3

Tabs and Lists

Tabs and lists are directly related, though they are separate features in Word. The goal of these features is to automate some routine formatting chores. The end result is that you have a list of items or an arrangement of text that doesn't look like crap. In fact, one of the earmarks of amateur Word users is when they use a series of spaces to line up text instead of using a tab stop. That's understandable because the process of using tabs, as well as applying list formatting, isn't the easiest thing to understand in Word.

TECHNICAL STUFF

» The words *tab* and *table* have the same root — the Latin word *tabula,* for table or list.

» The Tab key on a keyboard is designed to line up text in columns, which help to create a list. The key was called Tabulator on early typewriters.

The Whole Tab Thing

Word's system for setting tab stops and using tabs is damn confusing. That's because the notion of tabs involves two separate items: the tab character and the tab stop. The tab character is generated when you mash the Tab key. The character's width is variable, determined by the next tab stop on the line.

>> Any time you plan on typing more than one space, you need a tab stop: Never use spaces to line up or indent text.

>> The reason you don't use spaces is that, for most typefaces, the space character is of a variable size. Word shrinks or expands the space character to help fill text on a line. The effect of using spaces is uneven text because the width of the space characters is inconsistent.

TECHNICAL STUFF

>> You don't need to type two spaces after the period in a sentence. This rule was developed for typewriters because their monospaced typeface was more readable when two equal-width spaces were appended to a sentence. In fact, if you use a monospace font in Word, you can still use two spaces at the end of a sentence. For all other (proportionally spaced) fonts, one space is good.

Understanding tab stops

A *tab stop* is a gizmo that sits at a specific horizontal position in a paragraph. It sets the width of a tab character typed at a position before the tab stop. The tab character becomes a wide space that moves text over the tab stop.

The reason the tab stop concept is difficult to understand is that almost every character you type in a document has a given width. Most people assume that the tab works just like those other characters — for instance, that the tab character is $\frac{1}{2}$-inch wide. Instead, the tab character is as wide as the distance between the insertion pointer's position and the location of the next tab stop.

Figure 3-1 illustrates the basic tab-stop / tab-character concept. In the figure, after the word *Tab*, the Tab key is pressed. A variable-size character is inserted, extending to the next tab stop.

To further confuse you, Word comes with several tab stop types. The difference between them is how text lines up when the Tab key is pressed. Here are the various tab stop types:

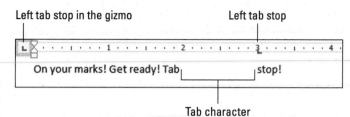

FIGURE 3-1:
Tab stops and
tab characters.

Default: These tab stops are preset by Word at half-inch intervals across the page. They work like Left tab stops and format your text when no other tab stops are set on the line.

Left: The standard tab stop. Text typed after the stop is left-aligned.

Right: Text typed after the Right tab stop is right-aligned.

Center: Text typed after this tab stop is centered on the line.

Decimal: This tab stop keeps a column of numbers lined up at the decimal place. Text typed after the tab is right-aligned, and then the decimal (period) is aligned with the tab stop, and then the rest of the text flows normally after the decimal.

Leader: The Leader attribute can be applied to any tab stop. It fills the tab character's space with a series of characters — dot, underscore, or hyphen — to create what the graphic designers call a *leader*.

Bar: This tab stop doesn't affect the tab character at all. Instead, a vertical line is inserted at the Bar tab stop's position. The Bar tab stop is more of a decorative element than a tab stop.

Examples of each of these tab stops and how they're best used appear in the "Tab Cookbook" section, later in this chapter.

Each of these tab stops is set specifically in Word. The next section describes the methods for setting a tab stop.

>> The Right and Center tab stops work best in headers and footers, for single lines of text, in lists, and so on.

>> If you desire to have an entire line centered or right-aligned, use the paragraph alignment formats instead. See Chapter 2.

>> Tab stops are paragraph-formatting attributes because they affect all lines within the paragraph. Even so, most paragraphs that exploit the more exotic tab stops contain only a single line of text.

>> The default tab stops continue on a line after you've set your own tab stops.

>> If you set a tab stop to the far right of the page (on the right page margin), all default tab stops are ignored.

>> See the later section "Using the Tabs dialog box" for information on messing with the default tab stops.

Setting tab stops on the Ruler

The most convenient way to set tab stops is to use the Ruler. The tab stop type is chosen from the gizmo, and then you click on the Ruler at the position where you want to set the tab stop. The tab stop affects the current paragraph or any other paragraphs selected before you set the tab stop.

To adjust the tab stop, use the mouse to drag it left or right on the Ruler. As you drag, a line extends through the document, graphically showing how the tab stop affects text. Figure 3-2 illustrates how this technique works.

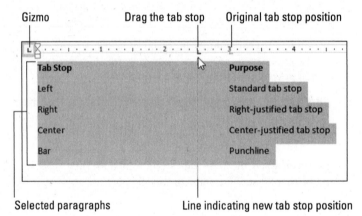

FIGURE 3-2:
Adjusting a tab stop on the Ruler.

Generally speaking, setting a tab stop on the Ruler works like this:

1. Select one or more paragraphs.

If you don't select any paragraphs, the tab stop is set only for the current paragraph (where the insertion pointer blinks).

2. Click the gizmo on the Ruler to select the proper tab stop type.

The tab stop types are illustrated in Table 3-1.

TABLE 3-1

Tab Stop Symbols on the Ruler

Symbol	Tab Stop
L	Left tab stop
⅃	Right tab stop
⊥	Center tab stop
⊥.	Decimal tab stop
▌	Bar tab stop

3. **Click in the Ruler to set the tab stop.**

The tab stop affects any existing tabs in the text, adjusting the paragraph(s) accordingly.

You may need to drag the mouse right or left to fine-tune the tab. Also see the next section, on using the Tabs dialog box.

>> You can type text before or after you set tab stops. Just boldly press the Tab key where you want the tab to go, and then set and line up the tab stops later. That way, you can visually see how text lines up.

>> Dragging a tab stop on the Ruler can be tricky! You must click the mouse directly on the Tab Stop symbol. If you miss, you create a second, unwanted tab stop.

>> To remove a tab stop, drag it from the Ruler: Point the mouse at the tab stop and drag downward. If this trick doesn't work, use the Tabs dialog box instead; see the next section.

>> Occasionally, you may see ghost tab stops on the Ruler. They show up when multiple paragraphs are selected. The ghost tab stop means that not all selected paragraphs use that tab stop. You can click to set the stop in all paragraphs or drag it from the Ruler to remove it.

Using the Tabs dialog box

The most precise way to set tab stops is to use the Tabs dialog box. The only issue ~~the dialog box: it's not directly available in Word. Instead,~~ follow these steps to get to the Tabs dialog box:

1. **Click the Home tab.**

2. **In the Paragraph group, click the Launcher icon in the lower right corner.**

   The Paragraph dialog box appears.

3. **Click the Tabs button.**

   The Paragraph dialog box bows out, and the Tabs dialog box, illustrated in Figure 3-3, finally shows up.

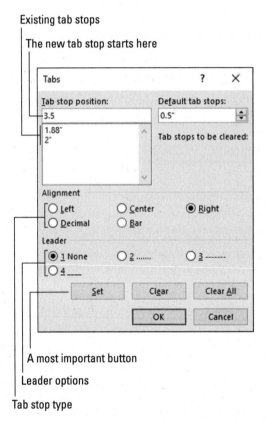

Existing tab stops

The new tab stop starts here

A most important button

FIGURE 3-3: The Tabs dialog box.

Leader options

Tab stop type

In the Tabs dialog box, you choose the tab stop's position, the type of tab stop, and whether it features a leader. The most important part is to click the Set button to create the tab stop. Too many people forget to click Set, and they simply click OK. Then they have to repeat the process and remember to click Set and then OK.

As an example, here is how you'd use the dialog box to set a Left tab stop at the 2-inch position in the current paragraph:

1. **Click the mouse in the current paragraph.**

   Or you could select a buncha paragraphs.

2. **Click the Home tab.**

3. **In the Paragraph group, click the Launcher.**

4. **Click the Tabs button in the Paragraph dialog box.**

5. **In the Tab Stop Position box, type** 2.

   You don't need to type the " (inches) symbol.

6. **In the Alignment area, choose Left.**

7. **In the Leader area, keep None selected.**

8. **Click the Set button.**

   This is the step everyone forgets. After you click the Set button, you see the tab stop appear in the list of existing tab stops. That's good.

REMEMBER

9. **Click the OK button.**

   The tab stop is set.

To use the tab stop, start typing and press the Tab key. The insertion pointer zooms to the tab stop position.

>> Tab stops positions are measured from the page's left margin. This location isn't the same thing as the paragraph indent. Refer to Chapter 2.

>> You can set negative tab stops, in which case the position is measured to the left of the page's left margin. I see no reason to set such a tab stop.

>> To remove a tab stop in the Tabs dialog box, click to select the tab stop in the list. (Refer to Figure 3-3.) Click the Clear button. You can repeat this action or click the Clear All button to remove them all. Click OK to confirm deleting the tab stop(s).

>> Tab stops slated for removal appear in the Tab Stops to Be Cleared area of the Tabs dialog box.

>> The Tabs dialog box is the only way to set (or remove) a tab stop set on a paragraph's right indent. That's because if you click on the indent, the mouse moves the indent and doesn't set a tab stop.

>> The Tabs dialog box also plays host to the Default Tab Stops setting, shown in Figure 3-3. These are the tab stops Word uses in any line of text that doesn't have a tab stop set. You can use the Default Tab Stops gizmo in the Tabs

value to zero. Click OK in the Tabs dialog box to change the Default Tab Stops interval, which affects all paragraphs in the current document.

Viewing tab characters

Like the space character, the tab character doesn't appear in a document. You see the tab character's effect, but not the character itself. If you want to see the tab character, use the Show/Hide command. Follow these steps:

1. **Click the Home tab.**

¶

2. **In the Paragraph group, click the Show/Hide button.**

The document changes to show all sorts of hidden and nonprintable characters.

→

The tab character appears as a right-pointing arrow, similar to what's shown in the margin. This character sits squat in the middle of the tab character's space. If you have multiple tabs in a row, you'll see multiple tab characters. Sometimes they get squished together.

>> Seeing the tab character in your document can help you unravel some formatting mysteries. For example, a tab in the middle of a paragraph may jiggle and jostle text in an unanticipated manner. By revealing the tab character, you can quickly determine what the problem is.

>> See Chapter 31 for information on making the tab character visible all the time.

>> By the way, if you need two tabs in a row, you've incorrectly set the line's tab stops. As with spaces, a document doesn't need two or more tabs together on a line of text. If you're creating a table or list with a missing item, that's okay. Otherwise, reset the line's tab stops so that you don't need to press the Tab key more than once.

Tab Cookbook

I don't know of any universities that offer a degree in Word's tab science. I'm sure an online course or two is available. They probably ship you a handsome certificate, suitable for framing, when you complete the course. That's awesome. What's even better is when the author simply coughs up good examples of the different ways you can use Word's crazy tab stops. Like a food cookbook, look at a picture, follow the recipe, and be done with it.

>> If you're in the habit of pressing the Tab key at the start of a paragraph, you probably want to use the first-line indent instead. In fact, Word can automatically convert that indent into a paragraph format, which is what you want. See Chapter 2.

>> The hanging indent is also a tab-like format you can apply to a paragraph. The next section covers a variation on that format that uses tabs. Otherwise, see Chapter 2 for details.

Building a hanging-indent list

On its own, the hanging-indent paragraph format looks kind of odd. Yet when you use that format with a tab, it creates an interesting sort of item-paragraph list, as illustrated in Figure 3-4.

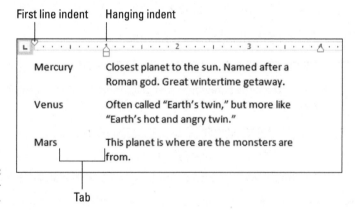

FIGURE 3-4:
A hanging-indent list.

Rather than type text up to the hanging indent, you type a word and then press the Tab key. The result is similar to what's shown in Figure 3-4, where the hanging indent is set at the 1-inch mark.

>> You don't use the Tab dialog box to create a hanging-indent list. You just take advantage of the tab to indent text to where the hanging indent is set.

>> Refer to Chapter 2 for information on setting a hanging indent, though the easiest technique is to drag the hanging-indent marker on the Ruler, as illustrated in Figure 3-4.

Building a double-tab hanging-indent list

The hanging indent can pull overtime with a tab stop to create a two–item/

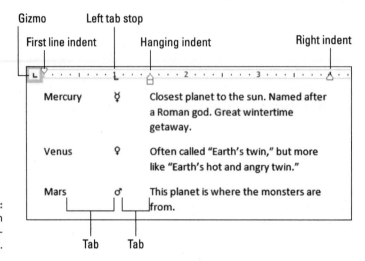

FIGURE 3-5:
A two-item
hanging-
indent list.

To create such a thing, obey these directions:

1. **Click the mouse in the current paragraph, or select a group of paragraphs.**

   I prefer to type the paragraphs first, but formatting first may help you better create the list.

2. **Adjust the hanging-indent control on the Ruler.**

   Slide it to the right to create the paragraph indent, as illustrated in Figure 3-5.

3. **Click the gizmo on the Ruler until the Left tab stop appears.**

4. **Click the mouse at a position between the first-line indent and hanging indent to set the tab stop.**

   Refer to Figure 3-5 for a potential location, which shows the tab stop at the 1-inch mark.

5. **Type the paragraphs, if you haven't typed them already.**

   Each paragraph starts with a word, and then a tab, and then another word (though a single character is shown in Figure 3-5), and then another tab and the paragraph text. The paragraph text wraps between the right indent and the hanging indent.

6. **Adjust the Left tab stop and hanging indent, if necessary.**

   Ensure that you select all the paragraphs before you adjust the layout.

You could even add a third item to the list: Set another Left tab stop between the first-line indent and hanging indent. You'll need to adjust the hanging indent to the right, which makes the paragraph rather squat and ugly, but that's the limit of what can be done with this particular technique.

Creating a tabbed list

The simplest way to use the Left tab stop is to create a tabbed list. The list can have two or more columns. The first column could even be at the start of the line, in which case you need only a single tab stop. In Figure 3-6, two Left tab stops create a 3-column list.

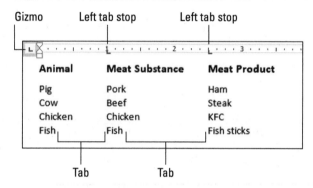

FIGURE 3-6:
A tabbed list.

To build this type of list, heed these steps:

1. **Ensure that the Left tab stop is selected from the gizmo on the Ruler.**

Refer to Figure 3-6 for the gizmo's location.

2. **Click the mouse to set a Left tab stop at the 1-inch position.**

3. **Click the mouse to set a Left tab stop at the 2.5-inch position.**

4. **If you haven't yet written the text, write it now.**

5. **If necessary, use the mouse to adjust the tab stops so that the text aligns evenly.**

You can set the tab stops before or after you type the list. If you type first, press the Tab key to separate the items, but don't fret over how the line looks. You fix the alignment when you set the tab stops later.

A more convenient way to create a multicolumn list is to use Word's Table function. See Chapter 4.

Setting a Center tab stop

The Center tab stop works best on a single line of text where it's mixed with other

in Figure 3-7. Otherwise, for a title or heading, use the center paragraph alignment, covered in Chapter 2.

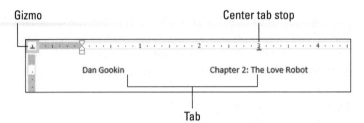

Gizmo   Center tab stop

Dan Gookin   Chapter 2: The Love Robot

Tab

FIGURE 3-7:
A center tab title.

Follow these steps to use the Center tab stop:

1. **Click the gizmo on the Ruler until the Center tab stop appears.**

2. **Click at the 3-inch position on the Ruler to set the Center tab stop.**

   Or you can observe the right paragraph indentation marker, mentally or visually split that width in half, and set the Center tab stop at that spot.

3. **To center the text, press the Tab key and then type.**

   As you type, Word jiggles the text to position it on the center of the line. In Figure 3-7 you see that the tab character extends to the tab stop, not to the first word in the centered chunk of text.

And now, the rest of the story: Word automatically sets tab stops as shown in Figure 3-7 for a document's header and footer. You can use Center tab stops anywhere else in your document, but it works best for a single line of text, as illustrated in the figure.

Typically, there will be only one Center tab stop on a line. You could have two for two columns of centered text items, but that's getting a little whacky.

Building a left-justified, right-justified list

The Right tab stop right-aligns text after you press the Tab key. That may seem kind of weird, and using such a tab stop is funky: As you write the text, it shuffles off to the left. Yet it's the Right tab stop that creates the common type of list shown in Figure 3-8.

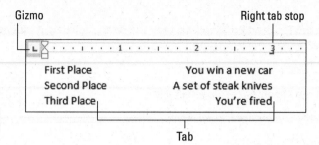

FIGURE 3-8:
The left-justified,
right-justified list.

To build a left–justified, right–justified list, follow these steps:

1. **Click the gizmo until the Right tab stop appears.**

2. **Click on the Ruler to set the Right tab stop.**

You can adjust its position later.

3. **Type the first column text, which is left-justified.**

4. **Press the Tab key.**

The insertion pointer hops to the Right tab stop.

5. **Type the second-column text.**

The text pushes off to the left, maintaining the Right tab stop's position as its rightmost edge.

6. **Press the Enter key to end the line.**

7. **Repeat Steps 3 through 6 as necessary to build the list.**

8. **Select the paragraphs and adjust the Right tab stop, if need be.**

Use the mouse to drag the Right tab stop left or right on the Ruler until the text looks great.

If you need to set the Right tab stop exactly at the right paragraph indentation, you must use the Tabs dialog box, not the Ruler. If you try to use the Ruler, you end up messing with the right indentation marker instead of setting a tab stop. Heed these directions:

1. **Make a note of the paragraph's right indent on the Ruler.**

Say that it's set at 6.5 inches.

2. **Click the Home tab.**

3. **In the Paragraph group, click the Launcher icon.**

4. **Click the Tabs button.**

The Tabs dialog box appears.

5. **In the Tab Stop Position box, type the paragraph's right indent position, which you noted in Step 1.**

   For example, type **6.5** for 6½ inches.

6. **In the Alignment area, select Right.**

7. **In the Leader area, keep None.**

8. **Click the Set button.**

   You must set the tab stop before you click OK.

9. **Click OK.**

   The Right tab stop is set precisely at the right margin indent.

Also see the later section "Creating a leader tab list." Often, this type of left-justified, right-justified list uses a leader tab, especially when the distance between the columns is wide.

Building a back-to-back list

I don't know how best to describe this type of list, so refer to Figure 3-9. You see such a format used often for credits, or in a program. It's built by properly setting a Right tab stop and then a Left tab stop, as illustrated in the figure.

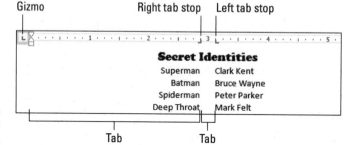

FIGURE 3-9:
A back-to-back
list.

To create a right-justified, left-justified list, follow these steps:

1. **Type the list before you set the tab stops.**

   Unless you're familiar with this technique, I recommend that you type each line: Press Tab, and type the first column item. Press Tab again, and type the second column item. Type the entire list.

2. **Select all lines in the list.**

3. **Choose a Right tab stop from the gizmo.**

4. **Click on the Ruler just to the left of the center page mark.**

   For example, at the 2⅞-inch mark.

5. **Choose a Left tab stop.**

6. **Click on the Ruler just to the right of the center page mark.**

   For example, at the 3⅛-inch mark.

After you set the tab stops, the text lines up as shown in Figure 3-9. You can make further adjustments: With the text selected, use the mouse to move the tab stops left or right to clean up the list's presentation.

>> This type of back-to-back list is best created as described in this section. If you attempt to build such a list by whacking the spacebar to line things up, the results will suck.

>> The first tab character shown in Figure 3-9 extends to the Right tab stop. Text typed at that point (or before the tab stop was created) extends to the left of the tab stop.

Lining up values with a decimal tab

The decimal tab is designed to line up numbers in a list. The key is the period character: When you press the Tab key, text is right-aligned until you type a period. After that, text continues from the Decimal tab stop across the page. Figure 3-10 illustrates such a list.

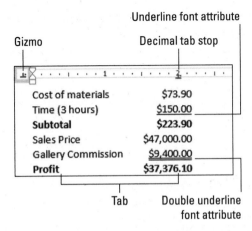

FIGURE 3-10:
The decimal tab aligns numbers.

Obey these steps to build a numeric list, lined up at the decimal place:

1. **Click the gizmo on the Ruler until you see the Decimal tab stop.**

   Refer to Figure 3-10.

2. **Click on the Ruler to set the tab stop.**

   Don't worry if the position isn't perfect; you can change it later.

3. **Type the items in the first column (if any), and then press the Tab key.**

   The insertion pointer hops over to the Decimal tab stop.

4. **Type the value.**

   As you type, text is right-justified. When you type the period, the text begins to flow normally across the line. That's how the Decimal tab stop lines up a column of numbers.

A better solution for the type of list shown in Figure 3-10 is to use a table. In fact, you can set a decimal tab inside a column of cells in a table. Tables also support formulas that can perform basic calculations, as described in Chapter 4. These feats aren't possible in a simple tabbed list.

Creating a leader tab list

The leader tab isn't really a tab stop, but rather a tab character decoration. It applies a dot, a dash, or an underline to the tab character so that instead of it showing up blank, you see dots, dashes, or a solid underline. The leader attribute is often used for 2-column lists, especially when the columns are set wide apart, as illustrated in Figure 3-11.

With a leader tab, you're best off using the Tabs dialog box to create the tab stops and apply the leader attribute. Follow these steps:

1. **Type the list.**

   Type the first column's text, and then a tab, and then the second column. Don't worry about things not lining up.

2. **Select the list.**

   For a leader tab list, I recommend that you add a little air between paragraphs:

TIP

3. **Click the Home tab.**

4. **In the Paragraph group, click the Launcher icon.**

   The Paragraph dialog box appears.

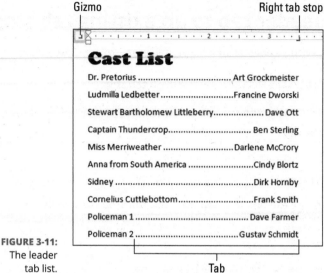

FIGURE 3-11:
The leader
tab list.

5. **From the Line Spacing menu, choose 1.5 lines.**

Or you can set any value. In Figure 3-11, 1.5 line spacing is used.

6. **Click the Tabs button.**

The Paragraph dialog box goes away, and the Tabs dialog box appears.

7. **Type a value into the Tab Stop Position text box.**

For example, type **5** to set the tab stop at the 5-inch mark on the Ruler. You can adjust this stop later.

8. **In the Alignment area, choose a Right tab stop.**

9. **In the Leader area, choose a leader.**

In Figure 3-11, the dotted underline leader (option 2 in the dialog box) is chosen.

10. **Click the Set button.**

11. **Click OK.**

12. **Use the mouse to adjust the tab stop on the Ruler.**

Drag the tab stop left or right until the list looks just so.

Many of Word's list functions, such as Index and Table of Contents, use this very same type of leader tab. See Chapter 21 for specifics on these document references.

Adding a leader tab to an existing tab stop

If you need to apply the leader to an existing tab stop, follow these steps:

1. **Select the paragraphs that already feature a tab stop.**

   The tab stop can be any variety, but it helps if it's the only tab stop on the line.

2. **Click the Home tab.**

3. **In the Paragraph group, click the Launcher icon.**

4. **Click the Tabs button.**

5. **Click to select the existing tab stop from the Tab Stop Position list.**

   You're not creating a new tab stop; you're applying the leader attribute to an existing tab stop.

6. **Choose the proper leader from the Leader area.**

7. **Click the Set button.**

   This step updates the existing tab stop, applying the leader attribute.

8. **Click OK.**

If you want to remove the leader, repeat these steps. In Step 6, choose the None leader, option 1.

Building fill-in-the-blanks underlines

The worst way to build a fill-in-the-blanks item in your document is to endlessly whack the underline key. Yes, that works, but the result can look sloppy, depending on the width of the character.

The next worst way is to apply the underline text attribute to a series of spaces. But — oops! — you're not really supposed to type more than one space in a row. Can you underline tab characters? Yes, but that's not the trick.

The trick, and the best way to build a fill-in-the-blanks item, is to create a Left tab stop and use the underline leader attribute. Follow these steps:

1. **Type the text you want as a prompt before the blank line.**

   For example, the classic *Your name* prompt, shown in Figure 3-12.

2. **Press the Tab key.**

   The insertion pointer unimpressively hops over to the next default tab stop.

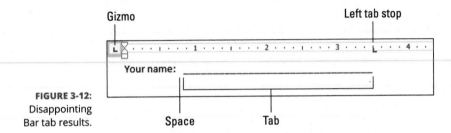

FIGURE 3-12:
Disappointing
Bar tab results.

3. Click the gizmo on the Ruler until the Left Tab Stop icon appears.

4. Click on the Ruler to set the Left tab stop.

Its position can be adjusted later. For now, you need to add the leader attribute to the tab stop.

5. Click the Home tab.

6. In the Paragraph group, click the Launcher icon.

7. Click the Tabs button.

The Tabs dialog box appears.

8. Select the tab stop from the Tab Stop Position list.

9. In the Leader area, choose the underline leader, option 4.

10. Click the Set button.

11. Click OK.

The fill-in-the-blanks underline appears next to the prompt, similar to what you see in Figure 3-12.

12. Adjust the tab stop, if necessary.

You could also add a space after the prompt, which looks cleaner.

Each prompt can have its own Underline leader tab stop, or you can format all paragraphs identically. The only time this solution gets tricky is when setting a fill-in-the-blanks item in the middle of a paragraph. In that case, it actually works better to whack the underline character a few times to create the blank space. That's because, if you use a tab stop and then edit the paragraph, its location and size change.

>> This section describes an underline that works great on the printed page. If you want an underline where someone types in a document, my advice is to use a content control instead. See Chapter 27.

>> If the underline leader doesn't look smooth, choose another font for the paragraph. For example, in Figure 3-12, the Calibri font renders what looks like a dashed line. Switching to the Times New Roman font fixes the line's

Finding an excuse to use the Bar tab

The Bar tab is a purely decorative element; its position doesn't even affect the tab character. You use a bar tab to scribble a vertical line in your text at a specific position. You can mix this tab decoration with other tabs to create an interesting list, as shown in Figure 3-13.

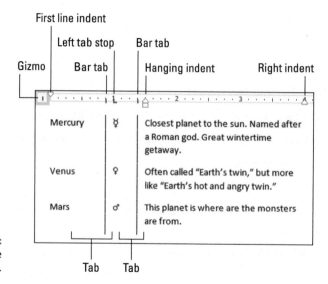

FIGURE 3-13: The decorative bar tab.

Figure 3-13 is an update to Figure 3-5. All I did was select the Bar tab from the gizmo and use the Ruler to apply the Bar tab to the existing paragraphs. You can see how it decorates the text, extending through the lines, but doesn't affect existing tab characters.

>> An advantage of using Bar tabs as opposed to drawing lines in your text is that the Bar tab is a paragraph format; it sticks with the paragraph no matter where you move the paragraph in the document.

>> I hope you're delighted that I wrote this entire section without making at least one Bar tab pun.

Numbered Lists

You can use Word's tab stops to manually construct a numbered list. The decimal tab is ideal for a numbered list, but you also want to use the hanging-indent format. That's a little complex, so a shortcut is available: the Numbering command.

> » If you want an indented list of numbers, like an outline, use the Multilevel List command instead. See the later section "The Multilevel List."
>
> » Also see Chapter 17 for information on numbering lines on a page.

Numbering paragraphs

Word's Numbering command supplies automatic numbers to sequential paragraphs. It updates the numbers for you, keeping them in order if you edit or add paragraphs. In fact, the format might be applied automatically via the AutoFormat As You Type feature, though you can apply it manually to any clutch of paragraphs.

To number paragraphs, follow these steps:

1. **Type the paragraphs.**

   Don't type the numbers. If you do, you'll engage Word's AutoFormat As You Type feature, which you might find annoying. Therefore, just type out the list one line (or paragraph) at a time.

2. **Select the paragraphs.**

3. **Click the Home tab.**

4. **In the Paragraph group, click the Numbering button.**

   If you click the button itself, the paragraphs are formatted with sequential numbers, 1 through n. Otherwise, you can click the menu button and choose a number format from the list, as shown in Figure 3-14.

If you apply numbering to text as you type, press the Enter key twice to stop numbering. Or you can click the Numbering button again or choose the None format (refer to Figure 3-14) to remove the number from a paragraph.

> » To change the numbering style for a group of numbered paragraphs, select the lot of them and choose a new format from the Numbering button menu.
>
> » Don't edit the paragraph numbers! If you need to renumber the paragraphs, see the later section "Skipping paragraph numbers."

>> Numbered paragraphs are formatted with a hanging indent. A tab character is added after the number. You can change the character, as shown in the next section.

Menu

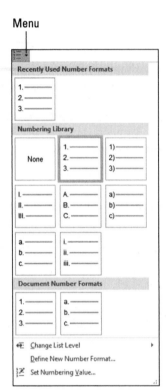

FIGURE 3-14:
The Numbering menu.

Adjusting numbering indents

You can use the Ruler to adjust the numbering positions for the Numbering command, but the process may frustrate you. Instead, use the Adjust List Indents dialog box. Heed these directions:

1. **Select all numbered paragraphs.**

2. **Right-click the selection.**

3. **Choose the command Adjust List Indents.**

   The Adjust List Indents dialog box appears, illustrated in Figure 3-15.

4. **Use the gizmos in the box to set the number and text-indent positions.**

   These two items actually control the first-line and hanging indents, as illustrated in Figure 3-15.

First line indent

Hanging indent

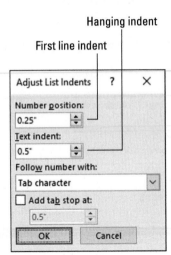

FIGURE 3-15:
The Adjust
List Indents
dialog box.

5. **Select the character to follow the number.**

   Options are a tab, a space, or nothing.

6. **Click OK.**

If you choose a tab to follow the number (refer to Step 5), the Text Indent item and Tab Stop settings (on the Ruler) are affected. If the text indent is too close to the number position, text slides over to the next tab stop position. That might not be what you want; click OK to confirm. Otherwise, use the Adjust List Indents dialog box to set a new tab stop to line up text.

Skipping paragraph numbers

Not every list is consistent. You may find the desire to insert extra paragraphs after a specific numbered item. When you do so, you want the list to continue numbering again later. Word actually does that trick for you automatically, but you may find its behavior to be inconsistent.

A good approach is to number all paragraphs in a list. Then go back and remove numbering for certain paragraphs. Obey these steps:

1. **Apply numbering to the original set of paragraphs.**

   For example, in Figure 3-16, all paragraphs were originally numbered, 1 through 6. The numbering on paragraph 3 was removed and the remaining paragraphs automatically renumbered.

2. **Click on the paragraph where you want numbering to stop.**

3. **Click the Home tab.**

Left Indent gizmo

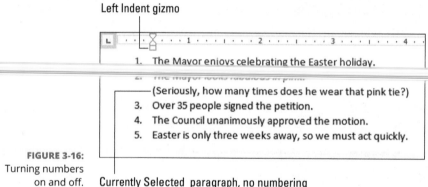

1. The Mayor enjoys celebrating the Easter holiday.
2. The Mayor looks fabulous in pink.
   (Seriously, how many times does he wear that pink tie?)
3. Over 35 people signed the petition.
4. The Council unanimously approved the motion.
5. Easter is only three weeks away, so we must act quickly.

FIGURE 3-16:
Turning numbers
on and off.

Currently Selected paragraph, no numbering

4. **In the Paragraph group, click the Numbering icon.**

   The number is removed from the single paragraph, but the paragraph loses its indentation formatting.

5. **Adjust the Left Indent gizmo on the Ruler to line up the paragraph's text with the rest of the numbered paragraphs.**

   Refer to Figure 3-16: The Left Indent gizmo (the square box) is adjusted to line up the unnumbered paragraph with the rest of the paragraphs.

If you need to remove numbering from more than one paragraph, select all the paragraphs in Step 2. You'll need to reapply formatting to the group, as described in Step 5.

Restarting numbered paragraphs

Suppose that you need to start a new set of numbered paragraphs, yet Word stubbornly insists on continuing the previous series. So it keeps slapping *6.* on your paragraph when you really need to start over at *1.* To address that issue, follow these steps:

1. **Right-click the mouse on the paragraph where you want Word to start renumbering at 1.**

2. **Choose the command Restart at 1.**

   The paragraphs start numbering all over again at 1.

Conversely, if you want Word to continue the previous set of numbers but it won't, choose the Continue Numbering command from the right-click shortcut menu. This command works no matter how distant the current paragraph is from the last set of numbered paragraphs.

Numbering paragraphs starting at a specific value

Word doesn't always need to number paragraphs starting with 1. For example, when you're starting a new document and need to continue numbering from another document, you can reset the initial paragraph numbering value. Obey these steps:

1. **Apply the numbering format to the paragraphs.**

   Use the Numbering command button as described elsewhere in this section.

2. **Right-click the paragraph where you want the new numbering series to begin.**

3. **Choose the command Set Numbering Value.**

   The Set Numbering Value dialog box appears.

4. **Ensure that the option Start New List is selected.**

5. **Use the Set Value To gizmo to specify the starting number value.**

6. **Click OK.**

Creating custom paragraph numbers

The Define New Number Format dialog box is used to specify numbering schemes not available on the Numbering menu. (Refer to Figure 3-14.) You can even craft your own numbering style, such as the colon format, shown in Figure 3-17. To mess with the number formats, follow these directions:

1. **Click the Home tab.**

2. **Click the Numbering button's menu.**

3. **Choose the command Define New Number Format.**

   The Define New Number Format dialog box appears.

4. **Choose a style from the Number Style menu.**

   Only a given list of styles is presented; you cannot create a new number style.

   Not all styles shown on the Number Style menu are available on the Numbering button's menu, such as the cardinal and ordinal options.

5. **Edit the number format.**

   You don't want to change the number, but you can add text after the number, such as the colon shown in Figure 3-17.

Colon

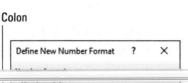

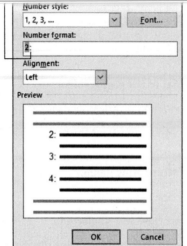

6. **Select a new alignment for the number and its format.**

   Use the Preview window to examine how the settings will appear.

7. **Click OK to confirm the custom number settings.**

The advantage of Word's Numbering command is that it applies the numbers automatically. If the numbering schemes or methods don't meet with your approval, you can manually number and format the paragraphs. The only drawback is that the numbers aren't automatically updated as you edit or add to your text.

Bulleted Lists

When it comes to page layout, the term *bullet* refers to a symbol next to a paragraph of text. In fact, the · character is called the *bullet*. You don't need to do any fancy footwork to apply that character, or any special symbol, to the front of a paragraph. You don't even need to hone your paragraph formatting skills. That's because Word's Bullet command does all the work for you.

To apply bullets to a series of paragraphs, follow these steps:

1. **Select the paragraphs you want to bullet.**

2. **Click the Home tab.**

3. **In the Paragraph group, click the Bullets command button.**

   The standard bullet is applied to each paragraph, which is reformatted with a hanging indent.

If you want a custom bullet, click the menu button next to the Bullets command button. Choose a preset bullet from the list. Or, to dream up your own bullet symbol, choose the Define New Bullet command and then use the Define New Bullet dialog box to choose something fun or inspirational.

>> To remove bullets from a paragraph, repeat the steps in this section.

>> When bullets are removed from a paragraph, its standard formatting returns. If you want the paragraph to be consistent with other items in the bulleted list, you must adjust the paragraph's indents.

>> Word's AutoFormat As You Type command converts any paragraph starting with an asterisk (*) and space into a bulleted list. See Chapter 23 for more details, as well as for information on how to disable this feature.

>> A bulleted paragraph is often called a *bullet point*. That term refers to both the paragraph and the symbol.

The Multilevel List

A multilevel list is an interesting concoction, combining elements of both numbered lists and bulleted lists, but also borrowing a tad from Word's Outlining capabilities. Figure 3-18 illustrates a typical multilevel list.

The problem with a multilevel list is how to edit it and maintain it. To best correct that problem, remember two basic multilevel-list editing rules:

>> Press Alt+Shift+→ to demote a topic (move it right).

>> Press Alt+Shift+← to promote a topic (move it left).

These two keyboard commands are also used in Word to adjust topic levels, but within the multilevel list format, they move paragraphs within the list.

1) No one is allowed to chew gum in School.
   a) "School" refers to the entire school grounds. This area includes:
      i) The parking lot
      ii) The playground
   b) "Gum" refers to any chewing gum or similar candy that is put into the mouth with the potential of being spat out at some point
   c) "No one" means everyone
      i) Teachers may not chew gum
      ii) Staff may not chew gum
      iii) Students may not chew gum
      iv) Parents may not chew gum
         (1) Includes all adult relatives
         (2) Includes all children
      v) Friends and anyone else may not chew gum
   d) "Chewing" means having gum in your possession

FIGURE 3-18:
A multilevel list.

Obey these directions to create a multilevel list in Word:

1. Start on a blank line.

2. Click the Home tab.

3.  In the Paragraph group, click the Multilevel List button.

The first paragraph indents to form a *1)* or whichever other format was previously selected from the Multilevel List menu.

4. Continue typing the multilevel list.

If you need to demote a topic (move it right), press Atl+Shift+→.

To promote a topic (move it left), press Alt+Shift+←.

5. When you're done typing the list, press Enter to start a new line, and then click the Multilevel List button again.

Or, you can press the Enter key twice, which also deactivates the multilevel list format.

To end the list, press the Enter key one last time. Click the Multilevel list button on the Ribbon, and the format is removed from that paragraph.

And now: the tricky part. If you need to edit the list, you must be careful! You can use the keyboard shortcuts shown in Step 4 to shuffle around paragraphs. That works well. Other edits to the text may not have the desired effect:

>> To add a new line to the multilevel list, place the insertion pointer at the end of a line and press Enter. The new line is inserted at the same list level. You can also press the Enter key at the start of a line.

>> To split a line, click the mouse to set the insertion pointer somewhere in the text. Press the Enter key. The line is split, but both new lines remain at the same level.

>> To remove a line, select the entire paragraph and press the Delete key. Word closes the rest of the list, renumbering it if necessary.

>> To set a specific level for a line, click the Multilevel List button, and from the menu, choose the Change List Level command. Select a specific level from the list to reset the current line in the list.

>> As with an outline, you can press Alt+Shift+↑ and Alt+Shift+↓ to move a line up or down in the list. (These keyboard shortcuts are paragraph-moving commands, not truly outlining commands.)

TIP

>> Right-click on an item in the list to renumber, continue numbering, or set a new numbering value. The commands covered in the earlier sections "Skipping paragraph numbers," "Restarting numbered paragraphs," and "Numbering paragraphs starting at a specific value" all apply to a multilevel list.

>> A multilevel list isn't an outline! It looks like an outline, but it's really just a formatted series of indented paragraphs. If you really need to move things around and brainstorm, you need to use Outline view and all Word's outlining tools.

Chapter 4

Custom Tables

orget tabs: If you want to organize information in a grid, shove a table into your document. Word's cup overflows with table creation options, formatting choices, and superpowers you probably weren't aware of or just didn't care about — until now.

>> Word's table commands are not a substitute for using a spreadsheet like Excel. Truly, if you need information organized into a grid, use Excel and not Word.

>> See Chapter 13 for information on the frightening prospect of inserting an Excel worksheet into a Word document.

Let's Build a Table

The programmers at Microsoft went insane when it came to tables. They just couldn't figure out a single, best way to cobble together a table in a document.

I'm assuming that a committee met to resolve the problem. The committee had at least five members because that's the total number of ways — insane and rational — that you can add a table to your document.

The following sections are presented historically, based on how the Table command has evolved over the years in various versions of Word.

Creating a table the original way

Word's first table command is still available, nearly 30 years after it was introduced. It's mechanical, but it works and it's very right-brain-oriented. Follow these steps:

1. **Position the insertion pointer wherever you want the table to appear.**

A table is a paragraph-level element. It sits in its own paragraph, which you can align, like any paragraph. No other text should appear on the line.

2. **Click the Insert tab.**

3. **In the Tables group, click the Tables button.**

It's a menu button-thing.

4. **Choose Insert Table.**

The Insert Table dialog box appears. It's shown in Figure 4-1, on the left. On the right you see the same dialog box as it appeared in Word for Windows 2.0 running under Windows version 3.1.

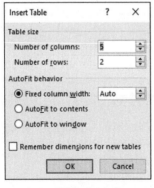
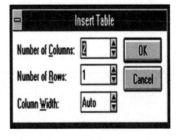

FIGURE 4-1:
The Insert Table dialog box.

Insert Table dialog box
Word 2016

Insert Table dialog box
Word for Windows 2.0

5. Set the number of columns and rows.

Use the Number of Columns and Number of Rows gizmos to set the approximate size of your table, or just type in the row and column values. Don't worry if you mess up; the table can be adjusted later.

The rest of the items in the dialog box are okay as is. You can reformat and adjust the table as you create it or afterward. This chapter covers all the details.

6. Click the OK button.

The table is set into the document, as shown in Figure 4-2.

Table handle   Cell margin   Table resize

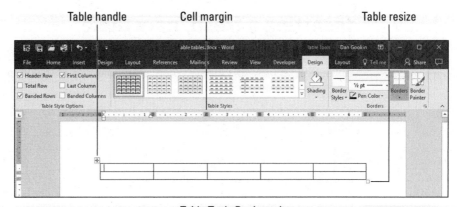

Table Tools Design tab

FIGURE 4-2:
A table, ready
for stuff.

Table Tools Layout tab

The table contains as many rows and columns as you set in Step 5. Every cell is sized evenly, which is what the Auto setting decrees.

Also visible are two new tabs on the Ribbon: Table Tools Design and Table Tools Layout, illustrated in Figure 4-2. These tabs show up anytime a table is selected or when the insertion pointer dwells inside the table.

In Figure 4-2, you also see that each cell in the table sports its own margins on the Ruler. Effectively, each cell in the table features its own paragraph formatting.

At this point you can further format the table, apply table styles, or fill in the cells. Details on what you can do with the table are littered throughout this chapter.

>> See Chapter 31 for more information on the Ruler.

TECHNICAL
STUFF

>> The Insert Table dialog box, shown on the right in Figure 4-1, was a screen capture I took for the book *Word For Windows For Dummies*, published in 1993 by IDG Books. The image size is a bit off; monitors back in those days had a resolution of 800-by-600 pixels, so if you compared the actual size of the two dialog boxes, the original would be one-fifth the size shown in the figure.

Inserting a fresh, new table

A quick way to create a table is to use the grid on the Table button menu, shown in Figure 4-3. I use this method more often than any of the other four ways to set a table in my documents.

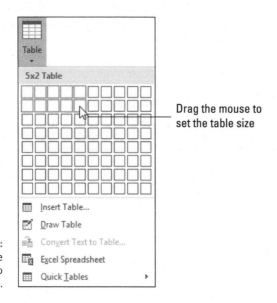

Drag the mouse to
set the table size

FIGURE 4-3:
Using the
Table menu to
build a table.

Follow these directions:

1. Position the insertion pointer at the spot where you desire the new table to appear.

Tables work best on a line by themselves.

2. Click the Insert tab.

3. **In the Tables group, click the Table button.**

The Table menu appears, as illustrated in Figure 4-3.

4. **Drag through the grid to set a specific size for the table.**

In Figure 4-3, a table of 5 columns and 2 rows is selected.

5. **Lift the mouse button (end the drag operation) to create the table.**

Don't fret when you get the size wrong; you can adjust the table after it's created, as discussed elsewhere in this chapter.

TIP

You don't have to drag the mouse through the grid in Step 4; you can simply point at the table grid, then click the mouse (Step 5) to create the table.

Converting tabs to a table

Tabs and tables are related, as words and as a document feature. As words, *tab* and *table* share the same root: the Latin word *tabula.* In fact, primitive word processors used tabs and not tables to present tabular information.

If you already have a set of tabbed paragraphs in your document, follow these steps to convert those paragraphs to a table:

1. **Select the paragraphs.**

2. **Click the Insert tab.**

3. **In the Tables group, click the Table button and choose the command Convert Text to Table.**

The Convert Text to Table dialog box appears. It makes a good guess of the number of rows and columns needed — as long as the text uses tabs and paragraphs to represent those rows and columns.

4. **If the Convert Text to Table dialog box guesses wrong, adjust the column and row values.**

You can adjust other items in the dialog box, such as the separator character, if it isn't a tab.

5. **Click OK.**

Word attempts to translate the text into a table. Figure 4-4 illustrates one such conversion.

The table may not be perfect. If not, you can adjust column widths, add cells, split cells, and perform other table magic, as described in this chapter.

FIGURE 4-4:
Converting
tabbed
paragraphs
into a table.

Beast	Habitat	Favorite Food
Lion	Jungle	Zebras
Bear	National Park	Jelly Sandwiches
Elephant	Savanna	Peanuts

Tabbed text in four paragraphs → Table with 3 columns and 4 rows

TECHNICAL STUFF

>> If the text doesn't use tabs as separators, use the Convert Text to Table dialog box to choose another character, such as the space or comma or another character you specify.

>> If you copy and paste a comma-delimited file, also known as a *CSV* file, you can convert it to a table in Word, but you must specify the comma as the cell separator.

>> *CSV* stands for *Comma Separated Values*. It's a text document that contains a table of information. Each line in the CSV file is a row, the items separated by columns represent cells in the row, which stack up as columns in a table.

>> You can convert a single line of text to a table. As long as the line features tabs (or another separator character), you can convert it into a single row table.

>> I cheated a bit in Figure 4-4: The Convert Text to Table command set the table's third column too wide, all the way to the page's right margin. I adjusted the table size so that the columns were more proportionate to the text. This topic is covered in the later section "Setting the table size."

>> Conversion between text and table goes the other way as well. See the later section "Converting a table to text."

>> Refer to Chapter 3 for information on tabs and tab stops.

Drawing a table

The most unique, and possibly least popular, way to create a table in your document is to draw it. This completely left-brain approach works, but I believe the other table creation methods are more effective.

If you want to dabble in table-drawing, obey these directions:

1. **Click the Insert tab.**

Unlike the other table creation techniques, this one doesn't require that you preset the insertion pointer.

2. **In the Tables group, click the Table button.**

3. **Choose Draw Table.**

The mouse pointer changes to the Pencil icon, shown in the margin. Your task is to doodle in the document to create the table.

4. **Drag a rectangle in the document.**

Start at the upper left corner. Drag down and to the right. When you release the mouse button, you see a 1-cell table approximately the same size and position where you dragged the mouse.

The mouse pointer retains its pencil powers. On the Table Tools Layout tab, in the Draw group, you see the Draw Table button highlighted. That's your clue that Word remains in table drawing mode.

5. **Draw lines within the table to create rows and columns.**

Drag the mouse downward to create columns. Drag right or left to create rows. The lines don't need to be even, and you can split cells so that row 1 has four cells but row 2 may have five.

6. **When you're done drawing the table, click the Draw Table button.**

The button is shown in the margin. It's found on the Table Tools Layout tab, in the Draw group.

You can now begin filling in the table or formatting the table, as described throughout this chapter.

» If you goof up while drawing, hold the Shift key. The mouse pointer changes to the eraser. Click the mouse on a line in the table to remove that line.

» You can also select the Eraser tool from the Table Tools Layout tab, in the Draw group.

» To cancel the eraser or even the Draw Table tool, press the Esc key.

Adding a quick table

The most recent addition to Word's table creation tools is perhaps the easiest and most rewarding. You pick a predesigned table from a gallery and — boom! — it's in your document.

Do tables go "Boom"?

Follow these steps to slide a quick table into your document:

1. Place the insertion pointer at the spot where the new table will bloom.

2. Click the Insert tab.

3. Click the Table button and, from the menu, choose Quick Tables.

   You see a host of different tables, including calendars (which are tables, after a fashion).

4. Choose a table from the list.

   Instantly, the table is inserted into your document, including all its placeholder text.

Your next step is to replace the placeholder text with your own text, if you like. You can also further modify the table. I would recommend reading the later section "Applying instant table formats," which describes a quick way to format a table.

Table Editing

Creating the table is only the first step. After the grid is set in your document, you fill the grid with interesting, gridlike information. Anything that can be set into a paragraph of text fits into a cell in a table, including graphics. And when you need more cells, rows, or columns, you can add those as well.

Filling the table

Type text into a table's cells just as you would type any text in Word. A cell can contain a character, word, or paragraph or multiple paragraphs. You don't want to get wacky in a table with too much text, though, because it destroys the table's uniformity.

>> You can jam as much text into a cell as possible. Word automatically adjusts cell size to accommodate the text — unless you've set specific cell widths. See the later section "Adjusting row and column size."

>> To move from one cell to the next, tap the Tab key.

>> To move backward through the cells, press Shift+Tab.

>> If you press the Tab key in the far right column's cell, the insertion pointer moves to the first cell in the next row.

>> If you press the Tab key in the bottom right cell in the table, Word adds a new row to the table.

>> On the off-chance that you need to type a tab character in a cell, press Ctrl+Tab. Keep in mind, however, that tabs in tables are ugly.

>> You can click the mouse in any cell to begin typing in that cell.

>> Pressing the Enter key in a cell starts a new paragraph inside the cell.

>> All text and formatting commands apply to a cell. If you need to center a cell's contents, apply the center-justification attribute to the paragraph: Press Ctrl+E.

>> Tabs and indents are adjustable for every cell in the table. If you refer to Figure 4-2, you see that each cell in the table sports its own, tiny portion of the Ruler. Use the controls on the Ruler to adjust cell margins or add tab stops. See Chapters 2 and 3 for details on paragraph and tab formatting.

Selecting stuff in a table

Tables add an extra layer of frustration to the selection process. You can select text within the table, or you can select parts of the table itself. To best describe how these techniques work, I've placed them into . . . a table! Refer to Table 4-1 for the details.

TABLE 4-1

Table Selection

Object	Mouse Pointer	What You Do
Cell		Point the mouse at the lower left corner of the cell. Click to select.
Row		Point the mouse at the left side of the row. This technique is used in Word to select paragraphs.
Column		Point the mouse at the top of the column, above the table.
Table		Click the mouse on the table's handle, located in the upper left corner of the table. If you don't see the handle, click the mouse in the table.

If you find any of the techniques listed in Table 4-1 to be awkward, follow these steps to select items in the table:

1. Click the mouse inside the table.

   If you need to select a cell, column, or row, click inside that object.

   After the table is active, the Table Tools tabs appear.

2. **Click the Table Tools Layout tab.**

3. **In the Table group, use the Select menu to select a specific part of the table.**

To deselect any part of the table, tap any of the cursor keys (such as the left-arrow key) or click elsewhere in the text.

Inserting rows or columns

No table is born perfect. Adding rows or columns is something you may frequently do, especially when Bill in Finance discovers a new month between October and November.

To add a new row or column to a table, follow these steps:

1. **Click the mouse in a cell above or below or to the left or right of the new row or column you want to add.**

   For example, if you need a new column between existing Columns 2 and 3, click the mouse in a cell somewhere in Column 2.

   You don't need to select an entire row or column to insert a new row or column.

2. **Click the Table Tools Layout tab.**

3. **In the Rows & Columns group, click the proper command button.**

   Your choices:

   Insert Above

   Insert Below

   Insert Left

   Insert Right

4. **Repeat the command to add more rows or columns.**

All new rows and columns are inserted empty. Existing columns may be resized to accommodate the addition.

TIP

>> To add a new row to the bottom of a table, click the mouse in the far right cell in the last row and press the Tab key.

>> If you find accessing Ribbon commands tedious, point the mouse to the left of the table, between the rows you want to add. When the Add Row gizmo appears, as shown in the margin, click the Plus Sign icon to insert a new row at that spot.

>> Likewise, when you want to add a new column, point the mouse above the column gridline where you want the new column to appear. Click the Plus in the gizmo (shown in the margin) to insert a new column at that spot.

>> Also see the later section "Deleting rows or columns."

Merging and splitting cells

A table grid need not harbor the same number of cells in each row or column. Word lets you split and merge cells. It's not something you do for every table, but it does address some unique situations.

To combine two cells, follow these steps:

1. **Select the cells.**

They can be left-right or top-bottom to each other. You can select two or more cells, but they must all be in the same row or column.

2. **Click the Table Tools Layout tab.**

3. **In the Merge group, click the Merge Cells button.**

The two cells are combined.

The text from the right or lower cell is placed in a new paragraph in the combined cell.

To split a cell, follow these steps:

1. **Click the mouse in the cell you want riven.**

2. **Click the Table Tools Layout tab.**

3. **In the Merge group, click the Split Cells button.**

The Split Cells dialog box appears. It gives you control over how the cells are

direction(s).

4. **Set the number of rows or columns for the split.**

5. **Click the OK button.**

The single cell is split into multiple cells.

Figure 4-5 illustrates how a single tall cell is split into three cells in a column.

In Figure 4-5, the three cells were originally merged to form a single cell. The split command reversed the merge. The content remained in the top cell, so if you needed to move some lines to the new cells, you'd have to select, cut, and paste the text one line at a time.

Original table, cell selected

Split set to 1 column, 3 rows

Result

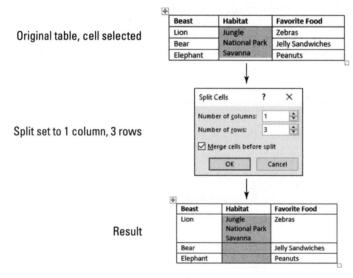

FIGURE 4-5:
Splitting a cell.

>> A simple way to split a cell is to use the Draw Table command: On the Table Tools Layout tab, in the Draw group, click the Draw Table button. Use the mouse pointer drawing tool (shown in the margin) to draw a line in a cell, effectively splitting the cell.

>> Just as you can draw lines to split a cell, you can use the Eraser command to remove lines. Click the Eraser button on the Table Tools Layout tab. The mouse pointer changes to the Eraser icon. Click a line between two cells to remove that line.

>> Refer to the earlier section "Drawing a table" for details on using the mouse to create a table.

>> You can split a single cell in a table, dividing it into two or more cells horizontally or vertically. This technique doesn't change the table size, but it does add more cells to a single row or column.

Setting the table size

For a quick adjustment to the table's width in your document, follow these steps:

1. **Click the mouse inside the table.**

2. **Click the Table Tools Layout tab.**

3. **In the Cell Size group, click the AutoFit button.**

4. **Choose AutoFit Window.**

   The table instantly expands to fill the paragraph's indentations.

If you want to tighten up the table, choose the AutoFit Contents command in Step 4.

You can also adjust the table size by dragging the box located in the table's lower right corner. This method isn't as precise as using the AutoFit commands.

Adjusting row and column size

Word accommodates both your left- and right-brain abilities to mess with a table's inner arrangement.

For the left brain, you can use the mouse to adjust rows and columns. In fact, Word features a quick shortcut to adjust the column width to match the widest line of text in the column. Heed these steps:

1. **Point the mouse at a column separator.**

   When you get to the sweet spot, the mouse changes to the left-right pointer, illustrated in the margin.

2. **Double-click the mouse.**

   Instantly, the column is resized to reflect the widest cell to the left of the separator line.

Rather than double-click, you can drag the mouse to resize the cells. Point the mouse at the line between cells and the pointer changes as shown in the margin. Drag up or down to resize.

The mouse-pointing method can be imprecise, so Word offers a solution for your right brain: First, click the Table Tools Layout tab. In the Cell Size group, four gizmos are available to precisely set cell height and column width, as illustrated in Figure 4-6.

Table Row Height

Distribute Rows

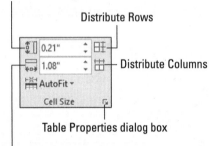

Distribute Columns

AutoFit ▾

Cell Size

Table Properties dialog box

FIGURE 4-6:
The Table Tools
Layout tab's Cell
Size group.

Table Column Width

Use the Table Row Height and Table Column Width gizmos to set the specific height or width for the selected row(s) or column(s).

The Distribute Rows and Distribute Columns buttons split the table evenly, allocating dimensions to rows or columns without regard to the contents.

WARNING

>> I recommend that you select multiple rows and columns if you want to effectively use the gizmos in the Cell Size group. (Refer to Figure 4-6.) Otherwise, you may screw up the table's presentation.

>> Column size can also be adjusted if you drag the Cell Margin control, found on the Ruler. Refer to Figure 4-2.

>> Click the Launcher icon in the Cell Size group to behold the Table Properties dialog box. Use the Row and Column tabs in that dialog box to make more specific adjustments across the table.

>> On the Table Tools Layout tab, in the Alignment group, you'll find the Cell Margins button. Click that button to view the Table Options dialog box, which contains controls to set interior cell margins.

>> Adjusting row width and column height does affect the table's size. This effect can't be avoided, so you may end up adjusting the overall table size after resetting the row or column size. Refer to the preceding section.

Make the Table Less Obnoxious

Word really crammed a whole truckload of table commands onto the Ribbon. Your goal isn't to use all of them when you craft a table for your document. Instead, you just want to make the table look presentable. It must convey information in an organized manner without detracting from its own content or other items on the page.

Adding a table heading

Tables often contain a header row. Most of the time, the header row is the top row, though some tables feature the header on the left side. Some tables feature both top row and left column as headers.

No secret exists to create a table heading. What I do is select the entire row and press Ctrl+B to make it bold. You could apply a style to the header, or you could use a preset style, as covered in the later section "Applying instant table formats."

One question to ask is whether you plan to manipulate the table's contents — for example, to sort the rows. If so, you must tell Word that the table contains a header row. Obey these directions:

1. **Click the mouse in the table.**

2. **Click the Table Tools Design tab.**

3. **In the Table Style Options group, place a check mark by the item Header Row.**

   The item might already be selected: Word is smart, and it may set this item whenever it sees bold text applied to the table's top row.

See Chapter 12 for information on adding a caption to the table. That chapter's topic is pictures and illustrations, but the same caption techniques also apply to tables.

Aligning text

Paragraph formatting commands can align text within a table's cell. These commands cannot, however, set the text's vertical alignment. To do so, follow these steps:

1. **Select the cells you want to align.**

   Drag to select individual cells or rows or columns or the entire table.

2. **Click the Table Tools Layout tab.**

3. **In the Alignment group, click the appropriate Align button.**

position according to the icon's graphic.

The top three buttons align text the same as the paragraph formatting commands: Left, Center, and Right. The rows set the text's vertical alignment.

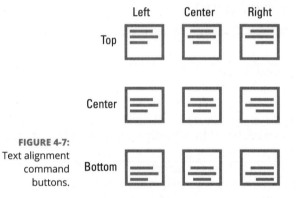

FIGURE 4-7:
Text alignment command buttons.

Setting text direction

Text in a table need not flow from left to right. When you prefer another direction, or you simply enjoy watching your readers turn their heads, reset the text direction. Heed these instructions:

1. **Click the cell containing the text you want to reorient.**

   Or select a group of cells.

2. **Click the Table Tools Layout tab.**

3. **In the Alignment group, click the Text Direction button.**

   Every time you click the button, the text changes direction by 90 degrees.

4. **Keep clicking the button until the text is properly oriented.**

Flinging around the text direction adjusts the cell size to accommodate your text. You may have to resize rows and columns afterward to make the table more presentable. Refer to the earlier section "Adjusting row and column size."

Setting gridlines

When you add a table to your document, it's set with a border style applied to the table grid. That style applies color and thickness to the table's grid. You can remove the grid's border style or selectively apply it. Follow these steps:

1. **Select the entire table.**

   Click the table's handle in the upper left corner.

2. **Click the Table Tools Design tab.**

3. **In the Borders group, click the Borders button.**

   The Borders menu appears.

4. **To remove the grid, choose No Border.**

   The table border vanishes, but you probably would appreciate still viewing gridlines while you work on the table, so:

5. **Click the Borders button again and choose the View Gridlines command.**

   A faint, dashed line appears to delineate the table's presence in your document. This gridline does not print.

The Borders group on the Table Tools Design tab features a host of controls to set border styles, line types, thicknesses, and colors.

If you want more control over border formatting, click the Borders button and choose the Borders and Shading command. The Borders and Shading dialog box sets how lines are applied to various elements within the table.

Also on the Table Tools Design tab, you can use the Shading button in the Table Styles group to apply background color to selected portions of a table.

Applying instant table formats

If you want to get really wacky with a table's design, skip over all the details and use one of Word's table styles. Follow these steps to best apply a table style:

1. **Create the table.**

   Fill in the cells' contents, adjust the table's presentation, and get everything *just so.* Using a table style works best when you have some semblance of a table to work with.

2. **Click the Table Tools Design tab.**

3. **In the Table Styles group, point the mouse at one of the styles.**

The style is previewed on the selected table.

~~select a style to apply its attributes — colors, shading, line styles, and so on — to your table.~~

to your table.

To view more styles, Click the More button in the lower right corner of the Gallery. This list is quite extensive.

To remove the attributes applied with a table style, follow Steps 1 and 2, and then click the More button to display all the styles. Choose the Clear option.

TIP

Word's Table Styles gallery contains options to allow for every-other-row shading. It's much easier to select a preset style to apply that format than to apply shading manually. Ditto for other presentations, such as header rows and columns, which can be applied from the same Table Styles gallery menu.

Some Table Tricks

The only table trick I knew as a kid is the old Up Table game. I could never figure out whether Uncle Ed kept rulers up his sleeves to make the thing work. Word's table tricks aren't as sneaky, but they aren't that obvious, either.

Sorting a table

Word isn't Excel, but with its table commands, it tries to be. One example of borrowing heavily from Word's spreadsheet sibling is the capability to sort contents in a table. This command is also used to sort paragraphs, though it adds more horsepower when used in a table.

TIP

The best way to sort a table is to ensure that it has a header row. Refer to the earlier section "Adding a table heading."

When you're certain that the table features a header, obey these directions to start sorting:

1. **Click to select the table.**

2. **Click the Table Tools Layout tab.**

3. **Click the Sort button.**

   The Sort dialog box appears. When a header row is defined in the column, the header column text appears, similar to the word *Beast,* shown in Figure 4-8. (The sorted table is shown in Figure 4-4.)

Header column text

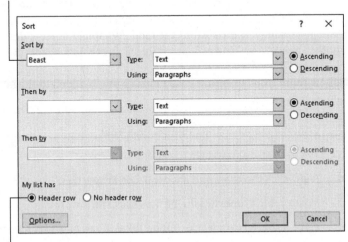

FIGURE 4-8:
The Sort
dialog box. Header row setting

4. **Choose a column heading from the Sort By list.**

5. **Choose how to sort from the Type list.**

   Choose Text for an alphabetic sort, Number for a numeric sort, or Date for a time sort.

6. **Set Ascending or Descending to determine the sort order.**

   For example, A-to-Z is an ascending text sort.

7. **If you want to sort by a second column, choose a column heading from the Then By menu.**

   For example, you could sort first by the Date column and then by the Amount column. These values, Date and Amount, would be the column heading in the table.

8. **Confirm that the Header Row option is set, as illustrated in Figure 4-8.**

   This setting confirms to Word that the table features a header row, which is not included in the sort.

9. **Click the OK button.**

   The table is sorted.

The Sort command button is also found on the Home tab, in the Paragraph group. It's used to sort lines of text, which don't necessarily need to be organized into a table.

Splitting a table between two pages

If possible, try to keep tables on their own page. Some tables get rather long, so Word dutifully splits the table between two pages. The problem is that the header row appears only at the start of the table. Whatever you do, don't manually insert another header row! Instead, properly set the table's header row property.

Follow these steps to ensure that a header row is added to the table, should it split between two pages:

1. **Click the mouse in the table's header row.**

   The header row must hold the insertion pointer.

2. **Right-click the table and choose Table Properties.**

3. **In the Table Properties dialog box, click the Row tab.**

4. **Place a check mark by the option Allow Rows to Break Across Pages.**

5. **Place a check mark by the option Repeat As Header Row at the Top of Each Page.**

6. **Click OK.**

The table is now configured so that, should it split across a page break, the first row — the *header* row — is echoed on that second page.

WARNING

>> Some of Word's preset tables automatically split across two pages.

>> Don't manually insert header rows. When you do, you run the risk that the table split may move as you edit and update your document.

>> I recommend setting a larger table in its own section. That way, you can keep the table on its own page. See Chapter 6 for details on sections in a document.

>> Instead of starting a table's section at the start of the page, you could reset the page orientation to horizontal for the table. This trick works only when you split your document into sections.

>> On the Table Tools Layout tab, in the Merge group, you'll find the Split Table button. Use that button to break a table into two separate tables. The split is made above the current row, and it doesn't reproduce the header in the second table.

Applying table math

One area where Word's tables horn into Excel's spreadsheet turf is table math. It's possible in Word to add formulas to a table. These formulas provide for simple calculations and other operations within a table's cells.

In Figure 4-9, you see a table filled with boring numbers. A formula, inserted into the bottom row, adds the total of the items above it. The Formula dialog box is shown, which is how the formula is inserted into the table.

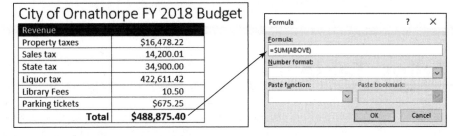

FIGURE 4-9:
Formulas
in a table.

To stick a formula into a table, heed these directions:

1. Click the mouse in the cell.

For example, click in the cell at the bottom of a column into which you want to place the total (sum) of the values in the cells above it.

2. Click the Table Tools Layout tab.

3. In the Data group, click the Formula button.

The Formula dialog box shows up. Word is clever at this point: The formula you most likely need is presented in the dialog box. If not, delete the formula and choose a new one from the Paste Function menu.

4. Click OK.

The formula is inserted into the cell, reflecting the proper result.

The formula is actually a field. If you modify the table, you need to refresh the field: Right-click on the cell and choose the Update Field command. See Chapter 24 for more information on fields.

>> Word features a variety of functions that you can paste into the Formula field in the Formula dialog box. The list is shown on the Paste Function menu.

>> The four major table references are ABOVE, BELOW, LEFT, and RIGHT, which refer to cells above or below or to the left or right of the current cell.

>> You can combine two references, such as =SUM(ABOVE,LEFT), to get the sum of a row and column's values.

Rn, or RnCn. C is the column containing the formula's cell; R is the row. The value n represents a specific cell in the column or row where 1 is the first cell.

TIP

>> Don't bother getting fancy with the formulas in a table. I've never used anything beyond the =SUM() formula. That's because, whenever I need more power, I use Excel. Then I can squeeze an Excel worksheet into my Word document so that I don't have to compromise on anything. See Chapter 13 for details.

Adios, Table

Word offers several methods to banish some or all of a table. You can zap a single cell, row, or column; delete all text in the table but leave its grid skeleton; or simply vaporize the entire table.

Removing a cell

It's quite possible to snip a single cell from a table. Your only concern is what to do with the surrounding cells: Move them left or up?

To remove a cell, heed these directions:

1. **Click the mouse in the cell you want to zap.**

2. **Click the Table Tools Layout tab.**

3. **In the Rows & Columns group, click the Delete button.**

4. **Choose Delete Cells.**

   The Delete Cells dialog box shows up. The command you choose determines how Word deals with the remaining cells in the table.

5. **Choose either Shift Cells Left or Shift Cells Up.**

6. **Click OK.**

   The table is adjusted to account for the missing cell.

Yes, the table can look uneven. That's the effect of removing a cell.

If you want a better way to remove a cell, refer to the earlier section "Merging and splitting cells." Merging two cells might be a better solution for you.

Deleting rows or columns

Word is efficient when it comes to removing table rows and columns. Follow these steps:

1. **Click the mouse in the row or column you want to remove.**

You can also select a row or column as covered in the earlier section "Selecting stuff in a table." Select multiple rows or columns to purge more than one at a time.

2. **Click the Table Tools Layout tab.**

3. **In the Rows & Columns group, click the Delete button.**

4. **Choose Delete Rows or Delete Columns.**

The row or column is gone.

If you delete all rows or columns in a table, the table disappears.

Converting a table to text

Before you decide to remove the table from your document, consider the option to convert the table's contents to text. This process removes the table structure but keeps all that typing. It even converts table cells into tab stops, so the result isn't too horrific.

To convert a table's content into text, heed these steps:

1. **Click the mouse in the table.**

2. **Click the Table Tools Layout tab.**

3. **In the Data group, click the button Convert to Text.**

The Convert Table to Text dialog box appears. Your job is to determine how text cells are separated. The best choice is usually tabs, which is the preset option.

4. **Ensure that the Tabs setting is chosen.**

5. **Click OK.**

The table goes away. In its place you see the table's text, separated by tabs with each row on its own line.

The text will *not* look pretty. You need to adjust each line, fixing tab stops and adding other paragraph formatting. Yet the text remains and the table is gone, which is what you wanted.

TIP

Sometimes it's better to choose the Paragraph Marks setting instead of Tabs in Step 4. With that option chosen, the table is split into multiple lines, which you might find easier to reformat into something more presentable.

Deleting a table's text

To remove text from a table and leave only empty rows and columns, follow these steps:

1. **Click the table handle.**

The table's handle is located in the upper left corner of the table. It's visible only when the table is selected or when the insertion pointer lurks somewhere in the table's midst.

2. **Tap the Delete key on the keyboard.**

The table's text is gone.

The funny thing about deleting a table's text is that it's the command you most often use when you want instead to delete the table. See the next section.

Deleting a table

To nuke a table, obey these directions:

1. **Click the mouse inside the table.**

The table must be active so that the Table Tools tabs are visible on the Ribbon.

2. **Click the Table Tools Layout tab.**

3. **In the Rows & Columns group, click the Delete button.**

4. **Choose the Delete Table command.**

The table disappears.

The shortcut is to right-click in the table and then choose Delete ➪ Delete Table from the Mini Toolbar.

Chapter 5

Custom Columns

Here's a surprise: Word documents always use a column setting. You just don't think about it. That's because your document traditionally has only one column of text — *the* column of text. It goes from page margin to page margin and flows down from one page to the next. It's only when you decide to make your document more interesting and add more columns that you can get into trouble.

The Columns Philosophy

The physical column, or pillar, predates the text column by a few thousand years. Even so, columns in Egyptian temples featured hieroglyphics, which is probably the first example of the modern opinionated editorial.

Understanding columns

A column of text is nothing more than a stack of paragraphs. The stack is recognized as a column only when more than one stack appears on a page, such as in a magazine or newspaper:

The reason why newspapers use
multiple column layout is
readability; it's easier on the eye to
read short lines of text than to read
long lines.

Reading speed greatly diminishes when your eyeballs have to track a tediously long line of text across a page. Shorter lines are better.

Then
again,
when the
width is
too
narrow,
reading
slows
again and
long words
require
hyphen-
ation.

Typography lacks specific rules for setting a column's minimum or maximum width. As the width gets narrow, text size can shrink to retain readability — but not by much. It's the page size that determines what looks best.

A standard sheet of paper in portrait orientation easily handles about two columns of text. In landscape orientation, three columns become feasible, as illustrated in Figure 5-1.

Any more columns of text in either the portrait or landscape page orientation becomes problematic because the individual column width becomes too narrow.

Setting columns in Word

All text in a Word document flows into columns. This page attribute has been available since Word was introduced, in the 1950s. It's just that most people leave the number of columns at 1 and never explore further possibilities.

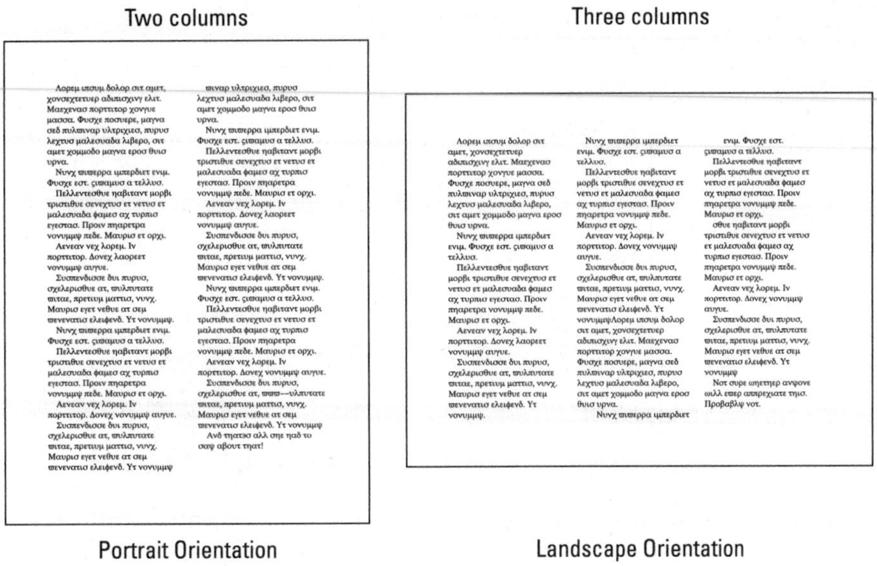

Two columns

Three columns

Portrait Orientation

Landscape Orientation

FIGURE 5-1:
Columns of text
on a page.

To reset the number of columns on a page, use the Columns command or the Columns dialog box. Obey these steps:

1. **Write something.**

   It helps to have text already written on the page, which provides visual feedback to the process.

2. **Save your document.**

   That, too.

3. **Click the Layout tab.**

4. **In the Page Setup group, click the Columns button.**

   The Columns menu shows five quick column formats, including the current format, which is most likely One.

5. **Choose More Columns.**

   The Columns dialog box appears, illustrated in Figure 5-2.

6. **Make settings in the Columns dialog box.**

   Information about using the dialog box is littered throughout this chapter.

7. **Click the OK button when you're done.**

   The effects chosen in the dialog box are applied to the document's text.

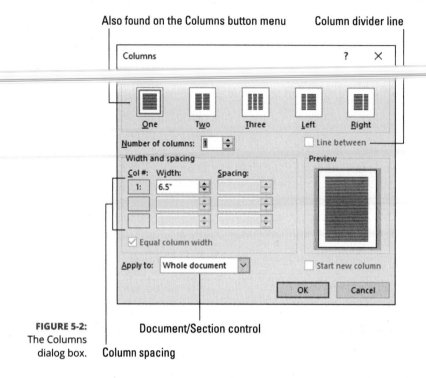

Also found on the Columns button menu   Column divider line

FIGURE 5-2:
The Columns
dialog box.

Document/Section control

Column spacing

As a page-level format, columns are affected by section breaks. If your document contains one section, the columns apply to all the text; otherwise, multiple columns apply only to the current section.

>> Text in a column flows to the bottom of the page and then to the top of the next column, whether that column is on the same page or the next page. The only thing that interrupts the flow is the column break. See the later section "Using a column break."

>> Columns do not show up in Draft view. Don't even bother using Draft view when you plan on structuring columns within your document.

>> See Chapter 6 for information on document sections and how they affect page formatting.

>> Each column supports its own region or chunk of the Ruler. If you use the Ruler to set paragraph indents or place tab stops, you must apply these settings to each column's chunk on the Ruler. See Chapters 2 and 3 for information on paragraph indentation and tab stops, respectively.

More than One Column

In architecture, a single column would be an oddity. In a document, it's the norm. When your desires expand more toward the architectural side of text, consider creating a 2-column document. Word makes it easy to apply that format, but the results aren't without some minor complications.

Creating 2-column text

To cleave your document's text in twain, heed these directions:

1. Click the Layout tab.

You don't need to set the insertion pointer when you reset column text in Word. That is, unless you've divided a document into sections. See the later section "Applying columns to part of a document."

2. In the Page Setup group, click the Columns button and choose Two.

The document's text is divided into two columns.

If your document features a section break, resetting the number of columns affects only the current section; otherwise, the entire document changes.

>> The Two command (refer to Step 2) splits the text into two, even columns separated by a half-inch of air. If you desire a wider or narrower split, see the section "Adjusting the column gutter."

>> Two other options on the Columns menu split the text into uneven columns: The Left option creates a narrow column (just under 2 inches wide) next to a wider column. The Right option creates a wider column followed by a narrower column.

>> My advice is to use the mouse to move the insertion pointer through multicolumn text. You can use the cursor keys, but sometimes the results can be frustrating.

TIP

Applying full justification

You might find that multiple columns on a page look better when full paragraph justification is applied. The column boundaries seem more defined with full justification than with the default left justification.

To apply full justification to an entire document, follow these steps:

1. Press Ctrl+A.

All text in the document is selected.

2. **Press Ctrl+J.**

Full justification is applied to all the text.

If you need to apply justification to only a portion of the document, select only the relevant paragraphs and then press Ctrl+J.

A problem with fully justified text is the appearance of gaps between words. The gaps help even out the paragraph's left and right indentations. If this visual burp bugs you, apply hyphenation to the text. Refer to Chapter 2.

Adjusting the column gutter

Visually, I think the space between columns, or *column gutter,* should be related to the page margins. If page margins are wide, the gutter could be wide, to make the page more visually appealing. Word's programmers don't agree. They set the column gutter to half an inch, no matter how many columns line up on a page or how wide the page's margins are set.

You can adjust the column gutter to set it however wide you want, or even set multiple columns with different spacing between them. Follow these steps:

1. **Place the insertion pointer where the columns are set in the document or where you want to create columns.**

2. **Click the Layout tab.**

3. **In the Page Setup group, click the Columns button and choose More Columns.**

The Columns dialog box appears.

4. **If you haven't yet set multiple columns, choose a preset from the list or use the Number of Columns gizmo to set the number of columns.**

Each column appears in the Columns dialog box, numbered 1 through *n.* By each column's number are width and spacing settings. (Refer to Figure 5-2.)

5. **Set the Spacing value.**

Wide values are good for fewer columns or when the page margins are set wide. If you venture above three columns per page, setting a narrow value, such as a quarter-inch (0.25"), might present text in a better way.

6. **Click OK.**

While the Columns dialog box shows a tiny preview, you can't really see the results of your changes until you click OK and look at the text. If you need to make further adjustments, repeat these steps.

- The default value for column spacing is 0.5", or half an inch.

- All column width and spacing values are applied equally. To set individual values, remove the check mark by the Equal Column Width check box.

Using a column break

Like a page break, the column break interrupts the flow of text. Its effect is to stop text in a column at the break's position. Text after the break appears at the start of the next column, whether that column is on the same page or the next page. Figure 5-3 illustrates examples of a column break.

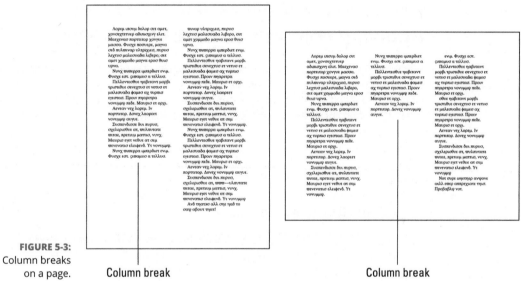

FIGURE 5-3:
Column breaks on a page.

Column break   Column break

To insert a column break into your text, follow these steps:

1. **Click to set the insertion pointer where you want the new column to start.**

   Set the blinking toothpick cursor at the start of a paragraph. That paragraph ends up starting the top of a new column of text.

2. **Click the Layout tab.**

3. **In the Page Setup group, click the Breaks button.**

4. **Choose Column.**

   The column break is inserted, and text after the break jumps to the top of the next column.

The column break remains in the text even if you add or remove columns. If you return to single-column layout, the column break works like a page break. (That effect makes sense when you think about it.)

¶

>> Column breaks are a booger to remove. Use the Show/Hide command to best see them: Click the Home tab and, in the Paragraph group, click the Show/Hide button. The column break appears in the text as a dotted line with the words *Column Break* in the center. Place the insertion pointer at the top of the next column, and press the Backspace key to remove the column break.

>> If a column break coincides with a page break or the column sits on the far left end of the page, the column break is effectively a page break. This configuration changes as you edit and modify the document.

Applying columns to part of a document

When your document needs multiple columns in one part and not another, the best solution is to divide the document into sections. Because the column is a page-level format, you can apply a single column to one section, and two columns to another, and then return to single column in a third.

Chapter 6 offers details on document sections. The following steps illustrate how to break a document into one single-column section and a second, 2-column section:

1. **Write the document's text.**

   It's best to write stuff first and then apply section breaks later. Even if you're just a wee bit into the next section, text on that page is beneficial to the formatting process.

2. **Save the document.**

3. **Position the insertion pointer where you want multiple columns to start.**

   If that location is at the start of the document, good. If it's in the middle of page 9, good.

4. **Click the Layout tab.**

5. **In the Page Setup group, click Breaks and choose Next Page.**

   A Next Page section break appears in the document. It looks like a typical page break, but the break starts a new document section, one that can contain different page formatting.

6. **Click the insertion pointer in the document section where you want columns to appear.**

7. **In the Page Setup group, click the Columns button and choose the number of columns for that section.**

   The column format is applied only to the current section. The other section remains single-column.

You can also create a new section from within the Columns dialog box: After setting the number of columns, click the Apply To menu (at the bottom of the dialog box) and choose the option This Point Forward. When you click OK, Word inserts a next-page section break and starts multiple columns in the next section.

» Choose a continuous section break in Step 5 when you want the columns to start in the middle of a page. Text above the continuous section break is formatted with a single column; text below, with multiple columns. This column trick is one of the few ways you can use a continuous section break.

» See Chapter 6 for further details on section breaks and page formatting.

Triple Columns — and More!

If you want to build a classic Greek temple, you'd follow the column number formula: $2n+1$. As an example, the Parthenon features 8 columns on the short side and 17 columns on the long side: $2(8)+1 = 17$. This math has absolutely nothing to do with placing multiple columns on a page in Word.

Building a triple-column page

A single sheet of paper can play host to three columns — barely. In portrait orientation, the three columns are pretty thin: just under two inches wide. That's okay, but not the best. In the landscape orientation, three columns are a bit wider, about $2\frac{2}{3}$ inches wide.

If you keep in mind that the goal of columns is to keep text readable, and if you want to please your reader (and you do), you set more than two columns on a page oriented horizontally. Follow these steps:

1. **Click the Layout tab.**

2. **In the Page Setup group, click the Orientation button and choose Landscape.**

   The page goes wide on the screen.

3. **Click the Columns button and choose Three.**

You can perform these steps before or after you compose the text. The result is that the document works like a trifold brochure.

- » You can further design the page — for example, by setting half-inch margins instead of 1-inch margins. That allows for wider columns and more text per column.

- » Use the Columns dialog box to adjust the column spacing and width. Generally speaking, if you plan to fold the paper three ways, everything lines up when you use Word's default column and spacing widths.

Setting four or more columns

It's time to get crazy with columns! How many can you march across a page?

The physical limit for columns is based on paper width. If you want to set Word to use a page size of 11-by-17 inches in landscape orientation, you can easily fit seven columns across the page. That's awesome, but would it be effective?

Consider these points when you decide to go with a large number of columns in any document:

- » If you have the proper paper and the printer can accept it, use a larger paper size to accommodate more columns. If the printer can't accept anything larger than letter or legal size, use the landscape page orientation, as covered in the preceding section.

- » Adjust page margins to allow more room for the columns. A 1-inch margin is standard in Word. A half-inch margin gives you more room for columns to dance across the page.

- » Reset the column spacing (gutters) to allow for more text in the columns. Refer to the earlier section "Adjusting the column gutter."

- » Finally, consider reducing the text size to ten points or smaller. Some fonts look better in smaller sizes, so changing the typeface might help you squeeze more information into multiple columns.

Chapter 6

Page Control

The pinnacle of Word's formatting pyramid is the page. Pages hold formats in Word that affect an entire document. These are big picture items that include the paper size, margins, and page orientation. They impact other document elements as well. All that makes sense until you throw in the concept of a section break. Then you can toss up your hands and surrender your common sense.

All about Page Formatting

When you start a new document in Word, you see a page. It's the foundation upon which your document rests. And it can be changed.

Finding the page formatting commands

Word boldly sets the page formatting commands on the Layout tab, in the P~~...~~

~~...~~ commands relevant to this section are Margins, Orientation, and Size, illustrated in Figure 6-1.

Page formatting commands

FIGURE 6-1:
Page formatting
commands on
the Ribbon.

Launcher

Commands in the Page Setup group also affect page formatting: Columns are covered in Chapter 5; line numbers are referenced in Chapter 17; hyphenation is covered in Chapter 2. Breaks are covered elsewhere in this chapter.

Nestled in the lower right corner of the Page Setup group you find the Launcher icon. Click it to behold the Page Setup dialog box, illustrated in Figure 6-2. This dialog box is home to the same commands found on the Ribbon, but with more settings and options and stuff like that.

One important item in the Page setup dialog box is the Apply To menu, found near the lower right corner on every tab. This command tells Word how to apply the page formats — specifically, whether the formats affect the entire document, from the insertion point forward, or only within the current document section.

>> Page formatting extends from the first page to the last; it affects the entire document. Even when the document is split into sections, if you choose the Whole Document command from the Apply To menu (refer to Figure 6-2), the formatting affects the entire document.

>> Sections are containers designed to hold separate page formats in a single document. See the later section "The Big Deal with Sections."

>> When you choose the option This Point Forward from the Apply To menu, you insert a next-page section break at the insertion pointer's position. This choice creates a new section *and* applies page formatting to that section of the document.

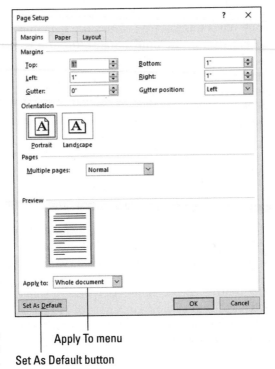

FIGURE 6-2:
The Page Setup
dialog box.

Apply To menu

Set As Default button

>> The Page Setup dialog box can be accessed from the Print screen. This option allows you to modify page formatting that you may not have considered when you first created the document.

>> The Set As Default button (refer to Figure 6-2) allows you to change the page formatting options for each new document you open in Word. So, if you want tighter margins or a different page size, choose those options in the Page Setup dialog box and click the Set As Default button.

**TECHNICAL
STUFF**

>> The Set As Default button modifies Word's Normal template. Word uses that template for each new, blank document you open in Word.

Choosing the paper size

You would think that paper size selection would happen when you print, but the printing operation comes way too late. Word must know the paper size so that it can set page margins and paragraph indentation.

Because most people don't think of paper size when they first create a document, Word sports a default size. In the United States, the size is a standard sheet of paper, 8½ inches wide by...

To reset the paper size, or to confirm the current size, follow these steps:

1. **Click the Layout tab.**

2. **In the Page Setup group, click the Size button.**

3. **Choose a new size from the menu.**

For example, choose Legal.

Word instantly updates the page size for the document. In Print Layout view, you can see the size reflected on the screen when the document window is wide enough or tall enough or when you've set the zoom properly to view the entire page.

For more paper size control, choose More Paper Sizes in Step 3. You see the Paper tab in the Page Setup dialog box, shown in Figure 6-3. Use this dialog box to set a custom-size sheet of paper or even to choose separate paper sources from the printer, as illustrated in the figure.

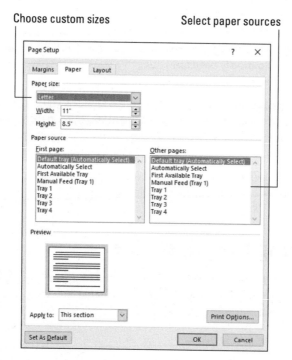

FIGURE 6-3: Setting paper size in the Page Setup dialog box.

>> The paper size in Word must match the size of the paper stocked in the printer.

>> One of the preset paper sizes is Envelope #10. This size represents the standard U.S. envelope, and it's selected when you use Word to print envelopes. See the next section.

>> To set a custom paper size, such as the 11-by-17 tabloid format, choose Custom Size from the Paper Size menu. (Refer to Figure 6-3.) Use the Width and Height gizmos to set the page's dimensions.

>> If you want to reset an 8½-by-11 sheet of paper to be 11-by-8½ inches, just change its orientation. See the later section "Changing orientation."

REMEMBER

>> The Paper Source area is useful when you have a printer that sports two paper trays and they're stocked with different paper. For example, Tray 1 may hold corporate letterhead, and Tray 2 may hold plain stock. If you're printing a document with a cover sheet, select the proper tray in the Page Setup dialog box for the first page, as illustrated in Figure 6-3.

>> Though you can fabricate any paper size you like in the Page Setup dialog box, the printer has the final say-so on which paper size you can truly use.

>> See Chapter 14 for more information on cover sheets, or how to set aside the first page from the rest of a document.

Creating envelopes

An envelope is really a document you print on a sheet of paper of a specific size. You can go to the trouble of formatting a page to look like an envelope, use text boxes to house the sender and return addresses, and even print a stamp. Or you can use Word's Envelope command.

Follow these steps to print an envelope:

1. If the recipient's address is written in your document, select it.

Word copies the address and places it into the Envelopes and Labels dialog box.

2. Click the Mailings tab.

3. In the Create group, click the Envelopes button.

The Envelopes and Labels dialog box appears, with the Envelopes tab forward. Any address you selected (refer to Step 1) appears in the box, as shown in Figure 6-4.

4. If the return address isn't filled in automatically, type the return address.

Word remembers the return address. If you don't want it included, click the Omit box and it won't print.

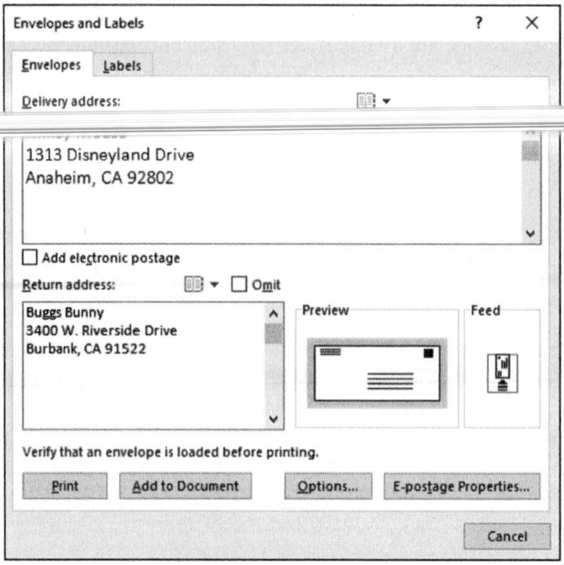

Envelopes and Labels
Envelopes
Labels
Delivery address:
1313 Disneyland Drive
Anaheim, CA 92802
Add electronic postage
Return address:
Omit
Buggs Bunny
3400 W. Riverside Drive
Burbank, CA 91522
Preview
Feed
Verify that an envelope is loaded before printing.
Print
Add to Document
Options...
E-postage Properties...
Cancel

FIGURE 6-4: The Envelopes and Labels dialog box.

5. **To instantly print the envelope, stick an envelope in the printer's manual feed maw and then click the Print button.**

   Printing may happen at once, or you might have to press a button on the printer so that it accepts manual input.

In Step 5, you can also elect to set the envelope as part of your document. To do so, click the Add to Document button. The envelope "page" is inserted at the top of the document, in its own section. Figure 6-5 illustrates how the results look in the document window, with the zoom setting at 30 percent.

When you print such a document, the printer may demand that you first insert an envelope into the manual feed. The rest of the document processes from the standard paper tray. Not all printers may be so smart.

If you want to create an envelope document, I recommend that you build a new envelope template. Set the envelope paper size, and create text boxes to hold the recipient and return addresses. See Chapter 9 for details.

Adding more than one page per sheet

Word calls the document's foundation a *page*, but when you print, you set that page on a sheet — specifically, a sheet of paper. You won't notice the difference, because Word sets the Multiple Pages option to Normal, which sets one page per sheet. Other options are available.

Section breaks   Envelope   Rest of the document

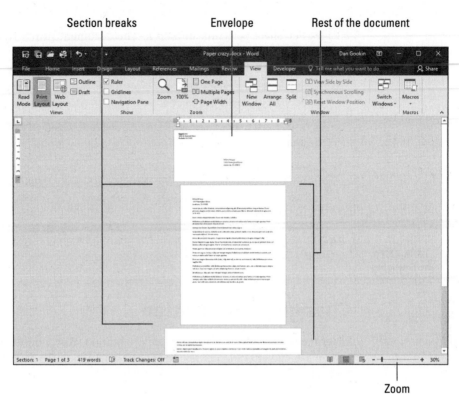

FIGURE 6-5:
An envelope
in a document.

Zoom

To print two pages per sheet, obey these instructions:

1. **Click the Layout tab.**

2. **In the Page Setup group, click the Launcher icon.**

   The Page Setup dialog box appears.

3. **Ensure that the Margins tab is forward.**

4. **In the Orientation area, choose Landscape.**

   Two-pages-per-sheet looks better in landscape orientation.

5. **From the Multiple Pages menu, choose 2 Pages Per Sheet.**

   The Preview window shows the pages side-by-side on a sheet of paper.

6. **From the Apply To menu, choose Whole Document.**

7. **Click OK.**

The document presents itself in Print Layout view as half-width. That's because Word's page, which was set at a standard sheet of paper, was cut in half by the

2 Pages Per Sheet selection in Step 4. The document prints two of those Word pages on a single sheet of paper, side by side.

>> The other options on the Multiple Pages menu may not affect your document. Especially if you use Portrait orientation, you may see no printed effect at all.

>> To reset Word to print a single page on a sheet of paper, choose Normal from the Multiple Pages menu.

>> It makes sense to think of a page in Word and a sheet of paper as different things. After all, printing is just a form of publishing a document. You can also publish a document electronically, as a web page or PDF. In that case the "sheet" remains ethereal.

>> Also see Chapter 15, which covers printing more than one page on a sheet of paper.

Changing orientation

Paper feeds into a printer in only one orientation. Word, on the other hand, sets text on a document in landscape or portrait orientation. To make the change, obey these steps:

1. **Click the Layout tab.**

2. **In the Page Setup group, click the Orientation button.**

3. **Choose Landscape.**

   The document's text adjusts to fill the left-right page margins, which are now wider on the screen.

To restore the document to a vertical presentation, choose Portrait in Step 3.

It's entirely possible to mix portrait and landscape orientations in a document. For example, you can present a wide table in the middle of your text on a landscape sheet of paper. The secret is to divide the document into sections and apply the page orientation format to a specific section. Details are covered elsewhere in this chapter.

Setting the page margins

Word sets a typical page with 1-inch margins — top, bottom, left, and right. These values can be changed, which allows for more or less text on the page.

To quickly reset page margins, heed these directions:

1. **Click the Layout tab.**

2. **In the Page Setup group, click the Margins button.**

3. **Choose a preset margin configuration from the list.**

   For example, choose the Narrow option to set half-inch margins around the page.

If the assortment of preset margins on the Margins button menu displeases you, choose the Custom Margins command in Step 3. In the Page Setup dialog box, on the Margins tab in the Margins area, you can set specific margins for the top, bottom, left, and right sides of the page. Work the gizmos in the dialog box, and then click the OK button to assert your document's new margins.

>> Paragraph indentation formatting is relative to page margins. For example, if you've formatted paragraphs to be exactly three inches wide, resetting page margins requires you to adjust the paragraph indents. See Chapter 2.

WARNING

>> Avoid setting a margin of zero. Not every printer can set ink that close to the edge of the page. Also, printing text right up to the page edge is visually annoying.

>> Like other page formatting commands, margins are affected by sections. See "The Big Deal with Sections," later in this chapter.

>> Also see Chapter 14 for information on the gutter settings in the Page Setup dialog box.

Behold! A New Page!

One of the most grievous word processing sins is to repeatedly whack the Enter key to force a new page. This sin is such an abomination that I would probably faint if I ever encountered such a poorly formatted document. The true solution is to use Word's Page Break and new Blank Page commands.

TECHNICAL STUFF

The problem with a stack of empty paragraphs (caused by multiple Enter key presses) is that its span remains the same height no matter how you edit the document. So, after a while, the multiple Enter key presses may not generate a new page at all, but rather appear as just an ugly empty space in your document.

Adding a hard page break

To ensure that the current paragraph starts at the top of the next page, you use a

To insert a hard page break, follow these easy steps:

1. **Place the insertion pointer at the start of a paragraph.**

It's the paragraph that you want to ensure will always be at the top of a page.

2. **Click the Insert tab.**

3. **In the Pages group, click Page Break.**

The paragraph now sits at the top of a new page.

The hard page break tracks with your text. No matter where the previous paragraph ends on a page, the next paragraph (chosen in Step 1) will be at the top of the next page.

» The keyboard shortcut to set a hard page break is Ctrl+Enter.

» If you set the hard page break at a location other than the start of a paragraph, you may experience weird formatting between the paragraphs before and after the break. See the nearby sidebar, "The formatting hangover."

WARNING

» On the Layout tab, in the Page Setup group, you can click the Breaks button and choose Page to set a hard page break.

» A *soft page break* occurs when text crosses the boundary between one page and the next. It happens naturally.

» To see hard page breaks, use the Show/Hide command, found on the Home tab in the Paragraph group. The breaks show up as a short string of dashes with the text *Page Break* in the center.

» To remove a hard page break, use the Show/Hide command to expose the break in your document. Use the Delete key or Backspace key to remove the break. This method is far more successful than trying to use Delete or Backspace when you can't see the break.

Inserting a blank page

Blank pages are added at the end of your document, inserted there as you write. You'll never run out! Whenever you need a new, blank page in the middle of a document, however, you can use Word's Blank Page command.

THE FORMATTING HANGOVER

Word's hard page breaks feature an undesirable side effect that I call the formatting hangover. Lamentably, no drinking is necessary to experience this type of stupor.

The formatting hangover affects the last paragraph on the page before the hard page break. You may discover that the paragraph features weird indentation or attempts to ghost the style of the first paragraph at the top of the next page. That effect seems to be a Word quirk, and there's nothing you can do about it.

If you try to remove the formatting hangover effect, you may end up deleting the hard page break or reformatting the first paragraph on that page. My advice: Ignore this oddity.

Suppose that you want to add a graphic to your document and place it on a page by itself. If so, follow these steps to create that extra page:

1. **Position the insertion pointer at the start of a paragraph.**

The paragraph above the insertion pointer will be the last paragraph before the new, blank page. The paragraph where the insertion pointer blinks will be on the page after the blank page.

2. **Click the Insert tab.**

3. **In the Pages group, click the Blank Page button.**

4. **Snap your fingers.**

Presto! There's the new, blank page!

The blank page is a unit. It's surrounded by two hard page breaks — one after the previous paragraph (refer to Step 1) and one before the next paragraph (also in Step 1).

>> Don't add a blank page just because you need to add text in the middle of your document. If you simply need to write more text, click to set the insertion pointer, and write. Word keeps moving the rest of the document around to accommodate new text.

>> Also see Chapter 14 for information on cover pages, which work similarly to a blank page but are inserted at the start of a document.

>> Snapping your fingers (refer to Step 4) is optional.

The Big Deal with Sections

Page formatting is the base upon which all other formatting commands are built. It's a document-long format, but it can be broken up. So, if you desire to switch the paper size or page orientation or to reset margins in the middle of a document — and have that change affect only a page or more of text — you can do so. The secret is to divide your document into multiple sections.

>> A *section* is a container for page formatting.

>> All documents have a single section: Section 1.

>> A document can contain as many sections as needed. Each section is the size of a page, though the continuous section break might split a page as opposed to starting a new page.

>> An example of changing the paper size is found in the earlier section "Creating envelopes." After you add an envelope to a document, you create a section that sports envelope-size paper, and then another section with standard page-size formatting.

>> Sections play a role in other page-level formatting as well. Commands affected by sections include columns, headers/footers, line numbers, and automatic page numbering.

Understanding sections

All documents have at least one section. This section encompasses the entire document, setting the document's page formatting: margins, orientation, and paper size.

To add another section, you insert a section break. Word offers four different types of section break:

Next Page: This break works the same as a hard page break, but the next page starts a new section in the document.

Continuous: A continuous break allows a section to start anywhere on a page. This comes in handy for setting columns in the middle of the page or resetting margins, but if you change page orientation or paper size, the continuous section break works like a next-page section break.

Even Page: The section break starts at the top of the next even-numbered page. If the current page number is even, a blank, odd-numbered page is inserted before the next even-numbered page.

Odd Page: The section break starts at the top of the next odd-numbered page. If the current page number is odd, a blank, even-numbered page is inserted before the next odd-numbered page.

 The section commands are found on the Layout tab, in the Page Setup group. Click the Breaks button to choose a section break. The break is placed at the insertion pointer's position. Ideally, the insertion pointer should be positioned at the start of a new paragraph.

TIP

>> To confirm which section you're viewing, ensure that the Section item is visible on the status bar. See Chapter 18 for details on activating that item.

>> The next-page section break is the most common.

>> The even-page and odd-page section breaks are ideal for bound material where, for example, you want a page to start on the righthand side. That would be an odd-numbered page.

>> If necessary, Word adds a full, blank page to satisfy the requirements for the even-page and odd-page section breaks.

>> Word's Master Document command places next-page section breaks between chapters. You don't need to end every subdocument with a section break. See Chapter 20 for details on master documents.

Creating a section break

To create a new section in your document, follow these steps:

1. **Place the insertion pointer at the start of a paragraph.**

The paragraph appears in the next section. All text above the insertion pointer will lie in the preceding section.

2. **Click the Layout tab.**

 3. **In the Page Setup group, click the Breaks button.**

4. **Choose Next Page.**

Or you can choose another type of section break, though Next Page is the most common.

Visually, the section break looks like a hard page break. If the Section item on the status bar is visible, move the insertion pointer between pages to confirm that both are in separate sections.

REMEMBER

» After the sections are created, you can apply different page formatting to each one. When you do, remember to use the Apply To menu in the Page Setup dialog box and choose the This Section option.

» You may find that the This Section option is already selected from the Apply To menu. That's Word's default choice when your document has sections.

» You could change page formats *and* create a section break at the same time. Rather than set a next-page section break, summon the Page Setup dialog box, as described elsewhere in this chapter. Change the page formatting from the Apply To menu, and then choose This Point Forward. A new section is created at the insertion pointer's location, and the new page format is applied to that section.

» When you set a section break, any command you choose from the Margins, Orientation, Size, Columns, or Line Numbers menus affects only the current section.

» If you need to apply landscape orientation to a single page in your document, you must set two next-page section breaks: one before the landscape page and a second one after it. The second section break allows you to return to portrait orientation for the remainder of the document.

» The steps in this section also apply to setting the continuous, even-page, and odd-page section breaks.

Removing a section break

When you no longer want a section break, delete it. Follow these enjoyable steps:

1. Click the Home tab.

¶ **2. In the Paragraph group, click the Show/Hide command button.**

The button is shown in the margin. With the document's details visible, you see the section break appear. It looks like a row of double-dots with the section break name in the middle, such as *Section Break (Next Page)*.

3. Place the insertion pointer just before the section break.

Click the mouse just after the pilcrow (¶) character marking the end of a paragraph.

4. Press the Delete key.

The section break is gone.

5. Click the Show/Hide command button again.

With the section break eliminated, page formatting from the second section takes over the first part of the document. You may need to reformat that section to put things back in order.

Chapter 7

Headers and Footers

I t's probably the last thing you think of when you craft a document: Not the cover sheet, not the artwork, not any fancy photos or doodles — but what most people do last is to stick a number on the page. When you do so, you're creating a header or footer in Word.

Headers and footers can be simple or complex. They add consistent information to each page in the document. For example, in this book you see different odd or even page headers with the page number, part name, and chapter name. Look up there! Yep, that's how headers (and footers) can help you build a presentable, informative document.

Headers, Headings, Footers, Footings

Once again, you can't dive into a new technology topic without facing the onslaught of similar and confusing terms. Headers and footers are no different. Here are some terms to ponder:

Header: A header is the top part of a page. It starts a half-inch below the top page edge, which usually places it within the top page margin but above the first paragraph on a page.

Footer: A footer is the bottom part of page. It rests a half-inch above the bottom page edge and below the final paragraph on the page.

Heading: A heading is a section title in your document. It's also the name Word uses for styles that match headings at various levels, such as Heading 1, Heading 2, and so on.

Footing: A footing is used in construction to stabilize a load, such as the foundation part of a structure that holds up the walls.

Footnotes: In Word, a footnote is the text that appears at the bottom of a page, referenced inside the text. See Chapter 21.

Headers and footers are similar with regard to their contents. In fact, no hard-and-fast rules exist for what goes in a header versus what goes in a footer. Word's Header & Footer Tools Design tab offers the same commands and settings whether you're editing a header or a footer.

» Headers and footers show up as dimmed text when your document is presented in Page Layout view. They don't appear in the Word window when you work in Draft view.

» Large headers and footers can extend into the text area of the page. Therefore, they can affect where the first paragraph starts and the last paragraph ends. To address this issue, increase the page's top and bottom margins. See Chapter 6.

» Both the header and footer are preset to a half-inch from the top and bottom page edges, respectively. This setting can be changed. See the later section "Resetting the header position."

» You do not need a header or footer for documents you plan to publish as a web page. See Chapter 30.

» In construction, *header* is the term applied to a support structure over a window or door or another opening in a wall.

TECHNICAL STUFF

Quick-Slap a Header or Footer

When you're in a hurry and you don't mind that your document looks like everyone else's document, you can quick-slap into your document a preset header or footer. This process saves you time in creating a header or footer and in not having to endure reading the remainder of this chapter.

To quickly add a header or footer to your document, obey these fast steps:

1. **Click the Insert tab.**

2. **In the Header & Footer group, click the Header button.**

A gallery of preset headers appears on a scrolling menu.

3. **Choose the quick-and-easy header from the list.**

Use the mouse to click the header. It instantly appears in your document.

4. **Use the Header & Footer Tools Design tab to further customize the header.**

Most of the options are set, though you may have to add text or fill in some blanks.

5. **Click the Close Header and Footer button when you're done making changes.**

You're returned to the document's text. In Print Layout view, the header remains visible at the top of every page, though it's dimmed.

To set a footer, repeat the steps in this section, but click the Footer button in Step 2.

WARNING

If you quick-slap a preset header or footer into your document, it replaces any items you've already set in the header or footer. These items include any page numbers or text or other items you've set.

Your Very Own Headers and Footers

Many Word commands affect a document's header or footer. For example, the Page Numbering command can insert its field into a header or footer. The best way to set a header or footer, however, is to create your own. It's not that difficult to do — plus, it has the distinction of making your document look unique. I consider that an advantage over using a preset header (lamentably covered in the preceding section).

One important note!

The following sections list commands that affect both headers and footers. For
header or footer, it's noted in the text.

Creating a header

The header is nothing more than an extension of your document. The big difference is that its text is echoed over every page. Therefore, the information you set
in a header can be whatever is required for consistency, such as your name, the
document title, the date, page numbers, your blood type, and so on.

To build your own header, or to edit the current header, follow these steps:

1. **Click the Insert tab.**

2. **In the Header & Footer group, click the Header button.**

3. **Choose Edit Header.**

The document's text goes dim, and the insertion pointer blinks inside the
Header area, illustrated in Figure 7-1. Visible is the Header & Footer Tools
Design tab, also shown in Figure 7-1.

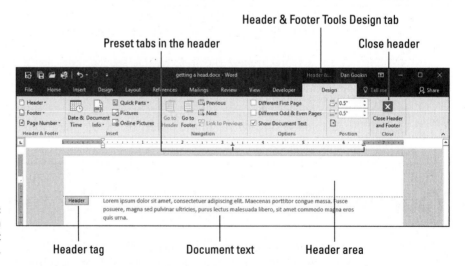

FIGURE 7-1:
Creating a
document
header.

The sections that follow detail what you can do in the header. Beyond text, the
tools you need in order to place specific items in the header or footer are found
on the Header & Footer Tools Design tab on the Ribbon.

When you finish editing the header, click the Close Header and Footer button, illustrated in Figure 7-1.

TIP

To quickly access the document header, double-click the mouse at the top of the page. Similarly, to exit the header, double-click the mouse in the document's text.

Switching between the header and footer

You don't need to exit the Header & Footer Tools Design tab every time you switch between the document's header and footer. Instead, in the Navigation group, use the Go To buttons:

To switch from the header to the footer, click the Go to Footer button.

To switch from the footer to the header, click the Go to Header button.

The commands on the Ribbon don't change whether you're working on the header or footer. Also, the paragraph format is the same in both header and footer, with a center tab stop and right tab stop, as illustrated in Figure 7-1. The tag says *Header* or *Footer*, depending on which one you're editing; in Figure 7-1, the Header tag is shown.

Typing text in a header

Anything you can type or place into a document can go into a header. Any formatting that's set in a document can also be set in a header. This formatting includes text attributes, tab stops, styles, and so on.

To add text to a header, heed these steps:

1. **Edit the header.**

If the header exists, double-click its text. Otherwise, follow the steps from the preceding section to access the document's header.

2. **Type the text.**

Be brief. Headers are not wordy.

3. **Close the header when you're done adding the text.**

Examples of great header text include your name, the document's title, the chapter number, the course name, your evil corporation's name, and so on.

TIP

The header is preformatted with two tab stops: a center tab stop in the middle of the page and a right tab stop at the right paragraph indent. (Refer to Figure 7-1.) Use these tab stops!

In Figure 7-2, you see my name, the document title, and the page number set in the header. Tabs separate each element, which align at the tab stops, as shown in the figure.

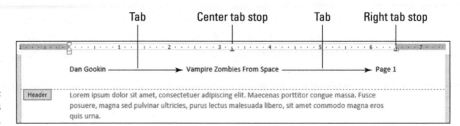

FIGURE 7-2:
Using tab stops
in a header.

You don't have to use all the tab stops. In fact, you can remove the preset tab stops or replace them with other tab stops.

As an example, if you simply want to set the page number on the far right end of the header, press the Tab key twice and insert the page number, per the directions in the following section.

WARNING

>> Avoid the temptation to burden the header with obnoxious quantities of information. A single line of text in the header is ideal.

>> If you need a second line — for example, to accommodate a long document title — do so. Line spacing within the header is set *tight* to accommodate multiple lines — when such things are deemed necessary.

>> The footer is not the place for explanatory text. If you need text at the bottom of the page, use a footnote. See Chapter 21.

>> Typically, a header's text is formatted like a heading but with a smaller point size. That's not a hard-and-fast rule, but keep in mind that header text is designed as a reference and the reader will seek it out.

>> Word features built-in Header and Footer styles. That's how the tab stops are preset, but neither style modifies the document's text format.

Adding page numbers

The most popular thing to stick into a header (or footer) is the page number. It's not just any old page number, either: What you insert into the header is a page number field. That way, each page's header shows the current page number, which is exactly what you'd expect.

To place the current page number in a header, obey these steps:

1. Edit the header.

Refer to the section "Creating a header," earlier in this chapter.

2. Place the insertion pointer at the position where you desire the page number to roost.

For example, simply keep the insertion pointer at the left margin, or press Tab once to center it, or press Tab again to right-align the page number, similar to what's shown in Figure 7-2.

3. Click the Header & Footer Tools Design tab.

They could have come up with a shorter name, don't you think?

4. In the Header & Footer group, click the Page Number button.

5. From the menu, choose Current Position ⇨ Plain Number.

A field representing the current page number appears in the header.

You can decorate the page number with whatever text you like, such as the word *Page*, shown in Figure 7-2, or the dash–number–dash thing I see in college papers.

TIP

If you also desire to insert the total number of pages into the header, use the NumPages field. On the Header & Footer Tools Design tab, in the Insert group, click the Quick Parts button and choose Field. Select the Document Information category, and then choose the NumPages field. Click OK to insert the field.

The total number of pages is often used in a header to display page numbers, as in

Page 1/32

where 1 is the current page and 32 is the total number of pages reported by the NumPage field.

See Chapter 24 for additional information on fields.

>> Other document properties you can include in the header are the current date, the date and time, the document filename, your name, the document title, chapter numbers, and so on. Some of these items are fields, which are covered in Chapter 25. The document filename field is demonstrated in Chapter 14.

>> If you've configured the document to sport different headers for odd- and even-numbered pages, you might want to set the page number on the left for an even page and on the right for an odd page. See the later section "Creating

>> There is no need to duplicate information in a header or footer. For example, if your name or the page number is in the header, don't put identical information in the footer.

Placing objects in the header

Anything that can go into a document's text can land in a header. This list includes graphics, such as pictures, or (more likely) shapes and text boxes.

My only advice for sticking objects into the header is to keep them small enough so as not to crowd the document's text. Large objects can be placed with the Behind Text layout, which might alleviate overcrowding.

>> Use the preset header and footer examples to get an idea of what kind of graphics can be set in a header or footer. Refer to the earlier section "Quick-Slap a Header or Footer."

>> See Chapter 10 for layout options, such as Behind Text.

>> Shapes are covered in Chapter 11.

Resetting the header position

Word positions the header half an inch from the top of the page. For most margin settings, that location is well within the page margin and above where the text starts. If you've set custom margins, or you desire a different page look, you can adjust the header position relative to the top of the page. Heed these directions:

1. **Click the Insert tab.**

2. **In the Header & Footer group, click the Header button and choose Edit Header.**

   The Header & Footer Tools Design tab appears.

3. **In the Position group, use the gizmo to adjust the Header from Top value.**

   The distance that's measured is the location of the top of the header from the top of the page.

You don't want to get the header too close to the top of the page, because it may not print on some printers.

The further you move the header from the top of the page, the more it encroaches on the document's text.

REMEMBER

These same steps apply to the footer. Just substitute *footer* for *header* and *bottom* for *top* and *below* for *above*.

Removing a header

The complicated way to remove a header is to simply edit away all its text. A better, swifter way is to follow these steps:

1. **Click the Insert tab.**
2. **In the Header & Footer group, click the Header button.**
3. **Choose Remove Header.**

   And it's gone.

If the document is split into sections, these steps affect only the current section. See the later section "Working with headers in sections."

If you're using different odd/even headers, these steps remove both odd and even headers.

When Headers and Footers Change

A header and footer need not be the same throughout your document. For example, you can have different headers for different sections. That way, you can suppress the header and footer for the document's cover page, or you can add a special header and footer for the introduction.

The two common ways to change headers and footers are to split the document into sections or set different headers and footers for odd- and even-numbered pages. You can even mix the two.

As with other parts of this chapter, this section refers only to headers. The same information also applies to footers.

Working with headers in sections

A document header is a page-level format. As such, it's affected by section breaks within a document. As long as you don't mess with the header, it extends or links between all sections in a document. When you break the link, you can set different headers for different sections.

In Figure 7-3, you see headers from a document with two sections. Each section is referenced in the header tag: Section 1 and then Section 2.

The headers in Section 1 and Section 2 are identical in Figure 7-3. That's because they're *linked:* If you change one header, both are updated.

To separate the headers, you must break the link. Follow these steps:

1. **Edit the header.**

   Double-click the mouse at the top of the page, in the header's text.

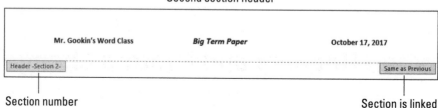

First section header

Mr. Gookin's Word Class   *Big Term Paper*   October 17, 2017

Header -Section 1-

Second section header

Mr. Gookin's Word Class   *Big Term Paper*   October 17, 2017

Header -Section 2-   Same as Previous

FIGURE 7-3: Headers, linked across two sections.

Section number   Section is linked

2. **On the Header & Footer Tools Design tab, in the Navigation group, click the Next button.**

   You need to be in the second header, or any section header that follows another section's header.

3. **In the Navigation group, click the Link to Previous button.**

   The Same As Previous tag disappears from the header. (Refer to Figure 7-3.) The header's text isn't removed, but you're free to change it and have the new header in use for the current section.

If you change your mind and you desire to keep the links between section headers, click the Link to Previous button in Step 3 to assert that setting. Click Yes in the confirmation dialog box, and the previous section's header is restored. The Same As Previous tag reappears, as shown in Figure 7-3.

>> If your document has additional sections, you can link or unlink each one. Use the Next button to page through the sections, hopping from header to header.

>> The Previous button, also found in the Navigation group, is used to hop to the previous section's header. Use the Next and Previous buttons to review headers in the document's different sections.

>> It's possible to have one header in Section 1, and then no header in Section 2, and then the same header from Section 1 in Section 3. To do so, unlink all sections as described in this book. Next, copy the header from Section 1 and paste it into Section 3.

>> One of the ways section links can bother you is when you try to edit a second section's header and the changes don't stick. The reason is that the headers are linked. Unlink them as described in this section.

>> If you're creating a master document, all sections are linked. To manage them — for example, to set an original header for each chapter — you must unlink each section. See Chapter 20 for details on Word's Master Document feature.

TIP

Creating odd and even headers

Another way your document can sport different headers is to set one for the odd pages and another for the even. This book uses that configuration, with the even page headers showing the part title and the odd page headers showing the chapter title.

To set different headers on odd and even pages, obey these steps:

1. **Edit or create the header.**

Double-click the mouse at the top of the page, in the header's text.

2. **On the Header & Footer Tools Design tab, in the Options group, place a check mark by the option Different Odd & Even Pages.**

Word splits the header in twain, creating separate odd and even page headers, as illustrated in Figure 7-4.

Odd page header

The Mysterious Bump on Grandma's Leg   Page 1

Even page header

Page 2   Dan Gookin

FIGURE 7-4:
Odd and even
page headers.

Even Page Header

3. **Edit the odd page header.**

Click the Previous button to ensure that you see the odd page header, identified by its tag in the lower left corner. (Refer to Figure 7-4.)

4. **Edit the even page header.**

Click the Next button to hop over to the even page header.

When you break up your document into sections, they also hold the odd/even format, with each section having its own set of odd/even headers. The links between sections are as a unit, with both odd and even headers linked between sections.

REMEMBER

>> The odd page header comes first because Page 1 is the first page of your document.

>> When the document contains multiple sections, the section name and number follow the odd or even header tag, as in "Odd Page Header –Section 2–."

>> Odd and even headers are affected when you choose to reset page numbering. The header that's used always reflects the odd or even page number, regardless of how many physical pages the document uses until that point.

>> The Next and Previous buttons hop between odd and even headers and then to the next or previous section's odd or even header.

TECHNICAL
STUFF

>> In a bound book, odd pages are always on the right, even pages on the left. That's because the first page is presented on the right side of the binding.

Page Numbering Galore

I see page numbering as a header-and-footer thing. That's where page numbers normally go, but your choices in Word aren't limited to sticking a number atop a page or at the bottom of it. And though you can keep the numbers in sequence, Word lets you restart page numbering and set new numbering styles. You cannot, however, number pages backward, which I would find hilarious, but apparently the programmers at Microsoft don't agree.

>> Page numbers are affected by a document's sections. You can restart page numbering or start new page numbering values or styles within any section in a document.

>> Also see Chapter 24, which covers document fields. It includes detailed information on creating various page number references in a document.

Adding an instant page number

I find that experienced Word users prefer to set their own page numbers within a header or footer, and they use their own styles and format. When you don't have time, or you don't know better, you can use Word's instant page-number feature.

To add an instant page number to your document, follow these steps:

1. **Click the Insert tab.**

2. **In the Header & Footer group, click the Page Number button.**

   A menu appears, listing popular locations for page numbers.

3. **Select a location from the menu.**

   For example, Top of Page.

4. **Choose a page number style from the submenu.**

   The page number is inserted into the document.

If you choose Top of Page or Bottom of Page, the insertion pointer lands in the document's header or footer, respectively. Double-click in the document's text to exit the header or footer — or continue building the header or footer.

WARNING

>> If your document already has a header or footer, choosing an item from the Top of Page or Bottom of Page submenus replaces the current header or footer, leaving only the chosen page number.

>> The Page Number button and its menu are echoed on the Header & Footer Tools Design tab, in the Header & Footer group. (The entire group is duplicated.)

>> When you choose an item from the Page Margins submenu, you insert a text box on the page. The In Front of Text layout option is set for the text box, and it's anchored to the header's text. The text box contains a page number field.

>> See Chapter 11 for more information about text boxes.

>> Items chosen from the Current Position submenu place a page number field in the document at the insertion pointer's position. The page number field can be accompanied by other text and formatting froufrou, as illustrated in the submenu.

>> The steps in this section place a page number field into the document. The field shows the current page number, no matter where you place it in the document. See Chapter 24 for additional information on document fields.

Restarting page numbering

Not every page needs to be Page 1. For example, if you're not numbering the document's cover page, the document's second page should begin as *Page 1*. Or, perhaps you want to use Roman numerals for the introduction and then start over with *Page 1* for the main part of the manuscript. Either way, you must change the page numbering scheme.

To restart page numbering at a value other than the current, physical page number, obey these steps:

1. **Right-click a page number in your document.**

The page number you right-click is where you want to start new page numbering in your document.

2. **Choose the Format Page Numbers command.**

The Page Number Format dialog box appears, shown in Figure 7-5.

FIGURE 7-5:
The Page Number Format dialog box.

3. **Click the Start At button.**

   The Continue from Previous Section option keeps the page numbering continuous through all the document's sections.

4. **Use the gizmo to choose a new page number.**

5. **Click OK.**

   Page numbering is reset to the value you chose in Step 4.

The change in page numbering affects all page numbers in the current section. If the document is one section long, all page numbers are affected.

Any additional document sections retain the new page numbering sequence as well. To change that sequence for those sections, in Step 1 choose a page number from the new section.

>> Refer to the preceding section for information on how to insert a page number into a document.

>> The Format Page Numbers command is also found on the Page Number button's menu.

>> If the document's cover page is *not* in another section, choose 0 in Step 4. That way, the cover page is numbered 0, and the first page is numbered 1.

>> A master document holds different sections for each subdocument or chapter. The default is to continue numbering through each chapter. Use the steps in this section to modify page numbering in a subdocument. See Chapter 20 for information on master documents.

>> See Chapter 14 for more information on cover pages.

>> See Chapter 24 for information on page number fields.

Choosing another page number style

Word's automatic page-numbering feature doesn't limit your numbering choices to the standard ordinal numbers. You can number pages with letters. You can use Roman numerals. You can also include chapter numbers, if your document is formatted in a manner Word appreciates.

For example, consider a document with two sections, as shown in Figure 7-6.

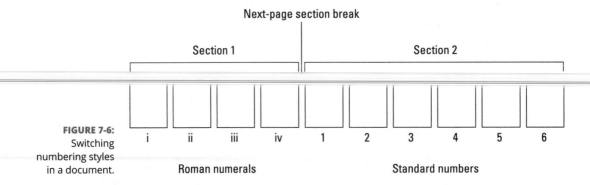

FIGURE 7-6:
Switching
numbering styles
in a document.

The first section, illustrated in Figure 7-6, is the introduction — with Roman numerals used to number the pages. The second section contains the document's text and standard numbers, starting with Page 1. This feat is entirely possible, when you obey these directions:

1. **Write the document's text.**

   Or at least write the introduction. You want to place a section break between the introduction and the rest of the manuscript. That task works best when you have some text to work with in the document.

2. **Position the insertion pointer where you want the section break; at the start of the first paragraph for the document's main text.**

   If the main part of the document features a title, set the section break at the start of that paragraph.

3. **Click the Layout tab.**

4. **In the Page Setup group, click Breaks and choose Next Page.**

   The next-page section break is inserted. It separates the document's introduction from the rest of the manuscript.

5. **Press Ctrl+Home to zoom to the tippy-top of the document.**

   The insertion pointer is in the document's first section. This is where you set the Roman numeral page-numbering style.

6. **Click the Insert tab.**

7. **In the Header & Footer group, click the Page Number button and choose the Format Page Numbers command.**

   The Page Number Format dialog box pops up on the screen.

8. **Click the Number Format menu and choose the Roman numeral type.**

   It's labeled "i, ii, iii, . . ."

148 PART 1 Fancy Formatting and Froufrou

9. Click OK.

10. Insert the page number in the document.

Refer elsewhere in this chapter for various techniques on how to set a page number in the header or footer or elsewhere.

11. Navigate to the start of the second section.

Or, you can set the insertion pointer to any location within the second section. Use the Section indicator on the status bar to guide you.

12. Confirm that the page number style in the second section is different from the first section.

The page number in the second section is set at the same location as for the first section. (Refer to Step 10.) But because the page number is in a new section, the numbering format returns to the default, such as *Page 5* instead of *Page v.*"

13. To adjust page numbering in the new section, click the Insert tab and, in the Header & Footer group, click the Page Number button and choose the Format Page Numbers command.

The Page Number Format dialog box pops up again.

14. Choose the new section's format.

If the item chosen from the Number Format menu is okay, you're good.

15. Select the Start At option and choose to start page numbering at 1.

The new section not only has a different page number format but also starts at Page 1, as illustrated in Figure 7-6.

16. Click OK.

You can use these steps to split page numbering in any two sections of a document and apply any change in format.

» To suspend page numbering in a section, unlink the section's header or footer. Then, in the new section, simply remove the page number field. Refer to the earlier section "Working with headers in sections."

» Also see Chapter 14 for information on cover pages, which is also a situation where you may want different page numbers (or no page numbers) in each document section.

Chapter 8

Style Methods and Madness

I confess that I avoided styles when I first used Word. My priority was writing. Formatting text? Styles were something I didn't think about. As my documents grew more complex, however, eventually I realized the value — and power — of creating and applying styles to the document's text.

Styles make the formatting job easy. They save time so that you can concentrate on writing. Once I understood that reality, I never avoided styles again. I hope you share the same view.

The World of Styles

You don't need to mess with styles to write a novel, report, or term paper. You can simply use plain text to create the manuscript and be as boring as boring can be. Or you can take a few moments to apply some styles. Word supplies sample styles for your pleasure, and you can select a new document theme if you don't like the particular sample styles presented.

the possibilities of styles, it helps to know a few basics.

Understanding style types

A *style* is a container for various formatting commands. Word uses five style types to represent the various formatting commands and how they're applied within a typical document.

The five types of styles are

Character: The style affects only text. It contains character formatting commands such as font, size, bold, text color, and all other text attributes.

Paragraph: It's the most common style, applied to full paragraphs of text. The formatting commands include alignment, tabs, spacing, and indents. Paragraph styles also include font formatting, though unlike a character style, a paragraph style is applied to the entire paragraph, not to individual words or a selection of characters.

Linked: This combination of character and paragraph styles can be applied to either individual text or entire paragraphs. The difference depends on what text is selected when the style is applied.

List: The list style is specific to lists of items, formatting indents, and the way the list is presented. Though that sounds interesting, the list style itself is difficult to implement. It's better to use the paragraph style for lists.

Table: As with the list style, the table style is difficult to properly implement. You can apply character, paragraph, and linked styles inside a table. To format the table, use the Table Styles gallery, covered in Chapter 4.

You choose a style type when you create a new style. The icons for the style types appear next to the style name in the Styles pane, covered in the next section.

Finding Word's style commands

Word doesn't hide its style commands; it overwhelms you with them. Again, I blame a committee. Rather than come up with a single, solid method of working with styles, Word's programming team tosses all sorts of options your way.

To start at the obvious, on the Home tab in the Styles group, you see the Styles gallery, illustrated in Figure 8-1. Click the More button to view the full Styles gallery, as shown in the figure.

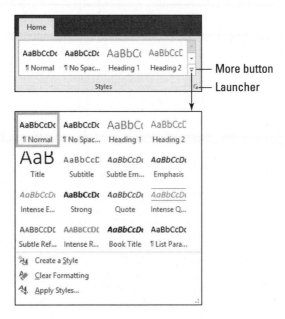

FIGURE 8-1:
The Styles gallery.

But wait! There's more . . . .

At the bottom of the Styles gallery you see the Apply Styles command. (Refer to Figure 8-1.) Choose that command to show the Apply Styles pane, shown in Figure 8-2. You can choose a style from the menu or type the style name.

The Apply Styles pane is rather limited. Instead, click the Launcher in the Styles group (refer to Figure 8-1) to see the Styles pane, also shown in Figure 8-2. You can also click the Styles button in the Apply Styles pane to summon the Styles pane, illustrated in Figure 8-2.

>> The keyboard shortcut to summon the Apply Styles pane is Ctrl+Shift+S.

>> The keyboard shortcut to summon the Styles pane is Alt+Ctrl+Shift+S.

>> I'm sure that if the keyboard had a fourth modifier key, it too would be used to summon some form of the Styles command.

>> I find the Styles pane so useful that I keep it open in all my document windows. See the next section.

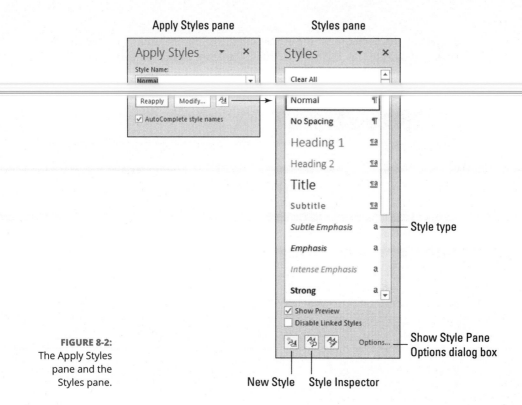

Apply Styles pane

Styles pane

Style type

Show Style Pane Options dialog box

New Style Style Inspector

FIGURE 8-2:
The Apply Styles pane and the Styles pane.

>> Click the Show Preview button in the Styles pane to enable the style names to appear in context, as shown in Figure 8-2. Deselect that check box to see a brief, though not-as-fancy list of style names.

>> To dock the Styles pane to the left side of the document window, point the mouse at the top of the pane. The mouse pointer changes, as shown in the margin. Drag the mouse to the document window's right edge. The Styles pane snaps into place.

REMEMBER

>> Word's styles are affected by the document theme. On the Design tab, the current theme reflects fonts, colors, and other elements that Word's standard set of styles use as a base. If you change the theme, or a specific aspect of a theme (such as fonts or colors), you affect a document's styles.

>> The document themes affect Word's own styles, such as those used in the Normal template. The themes can affect your custom styles or styles saved in any of your own templates, but only when those styles inherit theme attributes (typeface, color) from the Normal template.

Applying a style

Text in a new Word document is preset with the Normal paragraph style. To change that choice, you apply a new style. Follow these steps:

1. **Click the Home tab.**

2. **Choose a new style from the Styles gallery.**

If necessary, click the More button (refer to Figure 8-1) to display the full gallery.

The new style affects the current paragraph or any selected text. It affects any new text you type as well; subsequent paragraphs inherit the style of the current paragraph.

The Styles gallery is rather limited in how many styles it shows. For a better configuration, I dock the Styles pane to the right side of the document window, as described in the preceding section. To apply a style, click to select the style from the pane.

TIP

To help keep the Styles pane usable, I recommend that you limit the number of styles displayed. To do so, summon the Style Pane Options dialog box. Follow these handy steps:

1. **Click the Home tab.**

2. **In the Styles group, click the Launcher icon to display the Styles pane.**

3. **At the bottom of the Styles pane, click Options.**

The Style Pane Options dialog box appears.

4. **From the Select Styles to Show menu, choose In Current Document.**

This item directs Word to show only the styles held in the current document template in the Styles pane.

5. **Place a check mark by the option Paragraph Level Formatting.**

This setting directs Word to list only paragraph level styles. It keeps the list short.

6. **Click OK.**

The Styles pane shows a more useful list with a limited amount of options.

In my documents, I choose the option In Use in Step 4, which limits the styles shown to only those currently used in the document.

>> Most styles are of the paragraph type. If you try to use a paragraph style on a smaller chunk of text, the entire paragraph is affected. Confirm the style type in the Styles pane. The type appears to the right of the style name, as shown

>> New paragraphs inherit the preceding paragraph's style unless the style is programmed to generate a second, follow-on style. See the later section "Setting the next style."

>> To determine which style is in use, look at the Home tab's Styles group. The current style is highlighted in the gallery. If not, display the Styles pane, and the current style is highlighted there. If it isn't, click the Style Inspector button at the bottom of the Styles pane and (finally) it reveals the text's style.

>> It's possible to reapply the same style to text. This process may seem redundant, but it's useful when the text has been altered. For example, if somehow the font size changes in a paragraph of text, just choose the same style from the Styles gallery or Styles pane. The text is refreshed to match the original style.

>> The Clear Formatting command also refreshes text to match the underlying style. Click the Home tab and, in the Font group, you'll find the Clear Formatting button. The keyboard shortcut is Ctrl+spacebar.

Unapplying a style

You don't really remove a style as much as you reset the current style to Word's default, the Normal style. To do so, apply the Normal style as you would any other style.

WARNING

AVOID THE FORMAT PAINTER

A quick way to duplicate a specific text format from one chunk of text to another is to use the Format Painter tool. Because this tool represents a form of copy-and-paste, it's located on the Home tab in the Clipboard group.

Copying and pasting text format is handy and quick. I've used it many times. It's not a substitute, however, for using styles in Word. If you want two paragraphs to share the same formatting, you create a style and apply it to both paragraphs.

The benefit of using styles is that style updates and changes apply to all paragraphs that host the style. So, if you change the font, the change is reflected throughout the document. If you instead use the Format Painter tool, you're giving yourself a lot more work when you don't need to.

The Style Inspector pane is used to reset any style to Normal. Click the Style Inspector button (shown in the margin) at the bottom of the Style pane. Click the Reset button to the right of a style to reset it to Normal. Close the Style Inspector pane when you're done.

A New Style

Styles are created, or they evolve. In my experience, I've seen both practices. It's often better to experiment first with text formatting and then base a style on the results. I suppose, however, if you really know Word's formatting commands, you could create a style from scratch. At least Word gives you the option.

>> When you clear text formatting, you reassert the Normal style to the text. That's because all text must have a style, and the Normal style is the base.

>> Creating a style is easy, but knowing all of Word's formatting commands is not. The more practice you have formatting text and paragraphs, the easier it is to know what you want in a style.

>> Styles become part of a document and are saved with that document.

>> If you want to use your custom styles in other documents, you create a document template that houses those styles. See Chapter 9.

Formatting text and then creating a style

When I need a new style, I experiment with text to get the format just right. Then I build a style based upon my formatting efforts. This process is most likely what you do in your document already. If so, follow these steps to create a new style based on your efforts.

1. **Select the text you've already formatted and made just-so.**

    Don't worry if it's not exactly perfect. Any style can be modified.

2. **Click the Home tab.**

3. **In the Styles group, click the More button to display the full Styles gallery.**

    Refer to Figure 8-1.

4. **Choose the command Create a Style.**

    The Create New Style from Formatting dialog box appears, shown on the left in Figure 8-3.

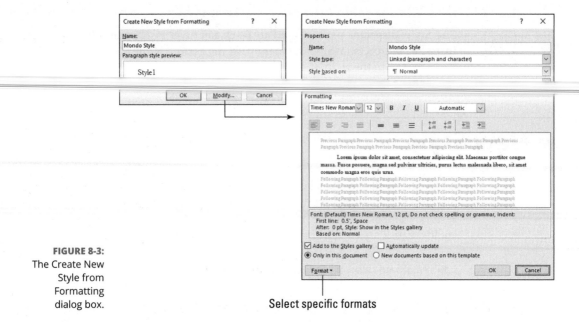

FIGURE 8-3:
The Create New
Style from
Formatting
dialog box.

Select specific formats

5. Type a name for the style.

Be short and descriptive. You can use letters, numbers, spaces, and upper- and lowercase. You cannot, however, use an existing style name. If you attempt to do so, Word pops up a warning; try again.

6. Click OK.

The Style is created and added to the current document. A tile representing the style appears on the Home tab's Styles gallery.

To view the more advanced version of the Create New Style from Formatting dialog box, click the Modify button. (Refer to Figure 8-3.) The advanced version of the dialog box, shown on the right in the figure, features more controls and options and a preview window.

You can also use the New Style button on the Styles pane to create a new style: Click the New Style button at the bottom of the pane, shown in the margin and illustrated in Figure 8-2. You're taken directly to the Create New Style from Formatting dialog box, shown in the right in Figure 8-3.

Making a style from scratch

Word lacks a command to build a style from nothing. That's because all styles are based on other styles, like inherited theft. At the root of all styles is the Normal style, Word's default. At minimum, making a new style from scratch is simply modifying the Normal style.

To build a new style from scratch, obey these steps:

1. **Summon the Styles pane.**

If the Styles pane isn't visible, click the Home tab and, in the Styles group, click the Launcher icon.

2. **Click the New Style button.**

The Create New Style from Formatting dialog box appears, as shown on the right in Figure 8-3.

3. **Type a name for the style.**

4. **Choose the style type.**

If you're in doubt, select Linked.

5. **If the style closely matches an existing style, choose it from the Style Based On menu.**

For example, if you're creating a B-Head style based on the A-Head style, choose A-Head from that list.

See the later section "Setting the next style" for information on using the Style for Following Paragraph menu.

6. **Use the controls in the Formatting area of the box to set the style's basic attributes.**

You can choose font, size, paragraph alignment, and so on. The preview window shows how the font will look. Below that window you see the specific formatting attributes.

7. **To set an additional formatting item, click the Format button at the bottom of the dialog box.**

A menu pops up, listing many format categories, including Font, Paragraph, and Tabs. Each category is linked to a dialog box that contains additional formatting options.

8. **Choose a formatting item from the Format button menu to summon a specific formatting dialog box.**

For example, choose Font to view the Font dialog box.

9. **Make additional formatting choices, just as you would if you were formatting text directly.**

10. Repeat Steps 8 and 9 for each individual item that requires additional formatting choices.

11. Click OK.

The new style is created and applied to text in your document.

Also see the next section, should you wish to change the style after you click OK.

>> If you know that you're creating a text-only style, such as the Redaction style demonstrated in Chapter 17, select Character from the menu.

>> Paragraph styles can be applied only to paragraphs, not to smaller chunks of text.

>> When you choose a predefined style from the Style Based On menu (refer to Step 5), any changes to the base style might be inherited with the current style. This effect is a bonus. For example, if all your heading styles are based on the top-level heading, changing that style's font changes the font for all the heading styles.

Modifying a style

Follow these fast steps to quickly modify a style:

1. Locate text in your document where the style is applied.

For example, the style is applied to a paragraph, but you're not happy with the paragraph's line spacing.

2. Modify the text to reflect whichever updates you want to apply to the style.

3. In the Styles pane, point the mouse to the right side of the style.

You see a menu button appear, as illustrated in Figure 8-4.

4. Click the menu button.

5. Choose the command Update Mondo Style to Match Selection.

The style is updated in the document. All instances of the style (all the text and paragraphs) are updated as well.

If the modifications require more work, choose the Modify command in Step 5. Use the Modify Style dialog box to make any adjustments. The Modify Style dialog box looks identical to the Create New Style from Formatting dialog box, shown on the right in Figure 8-3.

Hidden menu button

Style in the Styles pane

FIGURE 8-4:
Modifying or
updating a style.

>> As an alternative to hunting for the menu button (refer to Step 3), you can right-click a style name in the Styles pane.

>> If you want to assign a style a shortcut key, you must summon the Modify Style dialog box: Click the Format button and choose Shortcut Key. Press a new shortcut key combination and ensure that it's not already assigned to an existing command. If it isn't, click the Assign button and then click OK.

>> Shortcut keys are kept with the style in the current document.

>> I recommend using Ctrl+Alt key combinations, because few of them are used for other Word commands.

>> See Chapter 31 for more information on assigning shortcut keys in Word.

>> If the style isn't already in the Styles gallery (on the Home tab), choose the command Add to Style Gallery from the menu. If the style is already in the gallery (refer to Figure 8-4), choose the command Remove from Style Gallery to remove it.

TIP

>> I don't mess with adding or removing styles from the Styles gallery. That's because I find the Styles pane to be far more useful.

Setting the next style

Styles can sport a follow-on attribute. This feature allows you to preset one style to follow another.

As an example of a follow-on style, your Chapter Head style might be followed by the First Paragraph style, and that's followed by the Body Text style. The result is that when you type the first paragraph (Chapter Head) and press Enter, the First Paragraph style is automatically applied to the next paragraph. Press Enter again, and the following paragraph takes on the Body Text style.

To set the next style, follow these steps:

1. **Modify the first style.**

   Refer to the preceding section.

2. **In the Modify Style dialog box, click the Style for Following Paragraph menu.**

   A list of available styles appears.

3. **Choose the follow-on style from the list.**

   For example, choose Body Text style if the current style is First Paragraph, as discussed at the start of this section.

4. **Click OK.**

   The style is updated.

When you finish typing a paragraph with the first style applied, the second style (chosen in Step 3) formats the next paragraph.

TIP

These steps assume that the follow-on style has already been created. If not, create it! Then repeat the steps in this section.

Creating a heading style

Word comes with preset heading styles. These represent heading levels within a document, and the styles parallel such a format: Heading 1 for the top-level heading, Heading 2 for the next level, and so on.

REMEMBER

You may desire to create your own heading styles. When you do, don't forget to set the outline-level paragraph attribute. This attribute tells Word how to treat the style and the outline level used by various features, such as the Table of Contents command, to help automate document production.

To set the outline-level paragraph attribute when creating a new style, follow these steps:

1. **Build the heading style in your document.**

   It's best to format the paragraph first. In fact, create the top-level heading style for your document. This text isn't the title, but rather a section heading. For example, the title of this section, "Creating a heading style," is formatted at outline level 2.

2. **On the Styles pane, click the New Style button.**

If the Styles pane isn't visible, click the Home tab and then click the Launcher icon in the lower right corner of the Styles group.

3. **In the Create New Style from Formatting dialog box, click the Format button.**

4. **Choose Paragraph.**

The Paragraph dialog box appears.

5. **Ensure that the Indents and Spacing tab is selected.**

6. **Click the Outline Level menu.**

7. **Choose Level 1.**

Level 1 is the top level for the document's primary heading style.

8. **Click OK.**

9. **Make whatever changes are necessary in the Create New Style from Formatting dialog box.**

For example, you may want to choose a style for the next paragraph from the Style for Following Paragraph menu. I choose the Body Text style to follow my document's headings.

10. **Continue creating the style.**

Add whatever other formatting the style needs.

11. **Type the style's name.**

12. **Click OK.**

The heading style is created with the proper outline-level attribute set.

When you create the next level heading in your document, base it on the top-level heading format: Use the Style Based On menu in the Create New Style from Formatting dialog box. Also, repeat Steps 3 through 7 to set the outline level, but set it at the next level down, such as Level 2.

>> Ensure that all headings in your document support an outline-level attribute. That way, other Word tools recognize and use the headings as described elsewhere in this book.

>> The top-level heading style generally uses the largest point size. The heading styles decrease in size with each level.

>> Graphic designers prefer sans serif fonts in boldface type for document headings. Refer to Chapter 1.

>> For plain text, you choose the Body Text outline level. This option is the default for new styles based on the Normal style.

>> I use the style name *A Head* for my document's top-level heading. The next level is *B Head*, and then *C Head*, and so on. This is the nomenclature used in the publishing industry to refer to document heading levels.

>> Word's default heading styles are used when creating an outline. See Chapter 19.

>> See Chapter 21 for more information on creating an automatic table of contents in a document.

Style Management

The best way to control styles is to view them all together. You can use the Home tab's Styles gallery, but the Styles pane is what you need to see to best control all styles in a document.

To view the Styles pane, follow these steps:

1. **Click the Home tab.**

2. **In the Styles group, click the Launcher icon.**

   The Styles pane appears.

Managing the styles involves clicking the style's menu button. That button appears whenever you point the mouse at a style, as illustrated in Figure 8-4. You may see more or fewer commands on the menu, depending on how the style is used in the document.

Selecting instances of a style

A style's menu indicates how many times that style is applied in your document. In Figure 8-5, the style is used once. If you choose the command Select All 1 Instance(s), the style's application to text is highlighted in the document. At that point, you can apply a new style, delete the text, or do whatever.

I use the Select All Instances command to locate altered styles in a document. For example, when I see a modified style in the Styles pane, such as the one illustrated in Figure 8-5, I need to fix it. So I select the instance of that style and then reapply the original style.

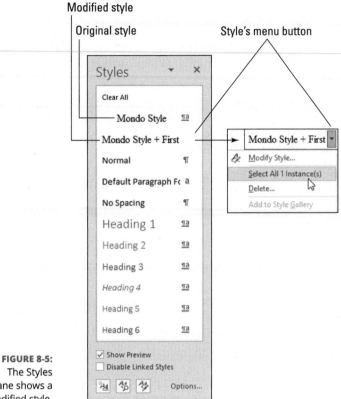

FIGURE 8-5:
The Styles pane shows a modified style.

Here are the steps I follow to fix modified styles:

1. **Click the modified style's menu.**

Refer to Figure 8-5.

2. **Choose Select All 1 Instance(s).**

If the style is applied multiple times, this menu item changes.

3. **Choose the original style from the Styles pane.**

In Figure 8-5, the original style is named Mondo Style.

When the style is updated, the altered style reference is removed from the Styles pane.

To confirm that the Styles pane displays changed styles, click Options. (Refer to Figure 8-5.) In the Style Pane Options dialog box, ensure that a check mark is by the option Paragraph Level Formatting. Click OK.

>> If a style isn't used, the Select All menu item says No Data.

>> I prefer to configure the Styles pane to show only styles in use. Refer to the earlier section "Applying a style" for information on setting that option for the Styles pane.

TIP

>> Your clue that a style has been modified in a document is the plus sign (+) in the Styles pane, shown in Figure 8-5. The plus sign indicates that the base style has the addition of another element. In Figure 8-5, that element is the First Line Indent, which doesn't appear in the figure but shows up if you point the mouse at the style.

Deleting a style

I don't recall ever needing to delete a style. In fact, when a style goes unused, it also goes unnoticed. Deleting a style isn't something you're compelled to do.

If you need to remove a style, heed these directions:

1. **Click the style's menu button in the Styles pane.**

Refer to Figure 8-5 for the menu button's location.

2. **Choose the Delete command.**

3. **Click the Yes button to confirm.**

The style is gone.

If the style is applied to the document's text, that text reverts to the Normal style.

>> See the earlier section "Finding Word's style commands" for information on displaying the Styles pane.

>> Removing a style from a document doesn't remove it from the document's template. You must edit the template directly to remove the style. Chapter 9 covers templates.

Stealing a style from another document

Don't bother trying to re-create your favorite styles in each document you edit. Though you can use a template to host those styles, you can also purloin styles from other templates and documents. You have two methods to accomplish this theft.

The first and easiest method is to copy text from one document and paste it in another. Along with the copied text rides the style. That pasted style is added to the Styles gallery and appears in the Styles pane. Ta–da!

The second way is to use the Organizer dialog box, shown in Figure 8-6. This tool lets you copy styles between any two Word documents.

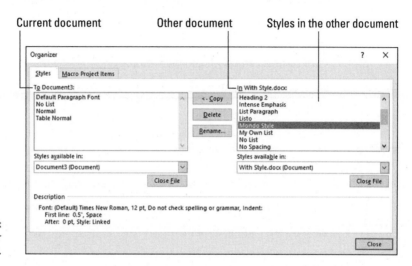

FIGURE 8-6:
The Organizer
dialog box.

To access the Organizer dialog box and steal styles, follow these perfectly legal steps:

1. **In the Styles pane, click the Manage Styles button.**

   The Manage Styles dialog box appears.

2. **Click the Import/Export button, located at the bottom left of the Manage Styles dialog box.**

   The Manage Style dialog box vanishes, and the Organizer dialog box takes its place, as shown in Figure 8-6. The open document appears on the left, and the Normal template is shown on the right (though not in Figure 8-6).

3. **Click the Close File button on the right side of the dialog box.**

4. **Click the Open File button.**

   It replaces the Close File button from Step 3.

   You see an Open dialog box. Your job is to find the file that contains the style you want to copy. Word automatically chooses the current location for any document templates.

5. **Work the controls in the Open dialog box to locate the document that contains the style you want to copy.**

If the document isn't a template, change the file type from All Word Templates to All Word Documents. Navigate to the folder that contains the document you need.

6. **Select the Word document, and then click the Open button.**

The document isn't opened. Instead, you see a list of its styles shown in the Organizer dialog box, as illustrated in Figure 8-6.

7. **Click to select the style you want to copy.**

For example, select Mondo Style, shown in Figure 8-6.

8. **Click the Copy button.**

The style is copied to the current document.

9. **Repeat Steps 7 and 8 to copy more styles.**

Or you can Ctrl+click to select multiple styles and copy them all at once.

10. **Click the Close button when you're done copying the files.**

11. **Save the current document.**

Using the Organizer dialog box is a bit more involved than the copy-and-paste method, but it does allow you to select styles without having to open another document.

Styles copied or imported from another document remain in the current document, even when that style isn't applied in the text.

Chapter 9

The Tao of Templates

emplates are document starter kits. They store styles, graphics, macros, and preset or common text. All these document elements help you begin the writing task with renewed vigor, like pushing a kid in a swing. Even if you don't choose a template, Word picks one for you. It's an unavoidable topic, especially in this chapter.

Template 101

A template is powerful yet friendly. All its elements are designed to help you start a new document. In fact, you've been using templates all along in Word. That's kinda sneaky, but it's still a positive thing.

Understanding templates

A template is the foundation upon which all Word documents are built. You can't have a document without a template attached. Even the blank document you see when you press Ctrl+N is associated with a template. It's called the Normal template.

The *Normal* template is host to all of Word's built-in styles. These include the Normal style, the Heading styles, and other styles.

a new document, which is covered in the next section. No matter what, any document you create or edit in Word has a template attached.

>> The template may come with preset text and graphics, or it may not.

>> All templates play host to various styles. Refer to Chapter 8 for information on styles in Word.

>> In addition to custom styles, templates inherit styles from the Normal template.

>> The New Document command's keyboard shortcut is Ctrl+N. This command displays a new Word window with a blank document based on the Normal template.

>> On the File tab's New screen, the Normal template appears as the Blank Document thumbnail.

>> Templates stay with your document for eternity. You can replace templates, covered in the later section "Reassigning templates." You cannot remove a template from a document, unless you replace it with the Normal template.

>> The Normal template's full filename is Normal.dotm. The dotm extension means that Normal is a macro-enabled template. See Chapter 25 for details on macros.

TECHNICAL STUFF

>> The standard filename extension for a template is dotx. The macro-enabled template filename extension is dotm. These extensions are different from the document filename extension, which is docx, and the macro-enabled document filename extension, which is docm.

>> And here's another nerdy secret: The docx file format is really a zip file archive. Don't tell anyone!

Starting a new document

When you start a new document in Word, you're infusing the new document with a copy of a template. You choose the template from the New screen and a new document is created based on the template's settings. You're not editing the template; instead, you're working on a new document based on the template.

To conjure forth a new document, you choose the template from the New screen, illustrated in Figure 9-1.

Template categories   Search   Pin icon

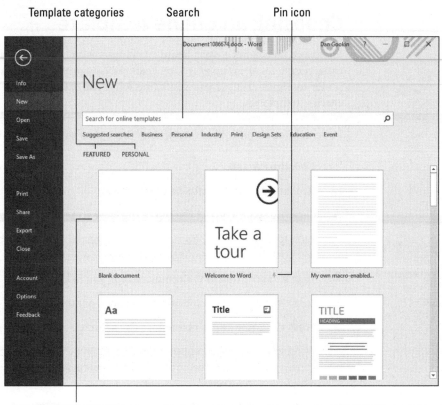

FIGURE 9-1:
The New screen.   Normal template

Templates on the New screen are divided in two categories: Featured and Personal.

Featured: The Featured category includes templates obtained from Office Online as well as templates you use frequently. It also includes any templates you've pinned to the New screen, as shown in Figure 9-1.

Personal: The Personal category lists only those templates you've created yourself or obtained from other sources and copied to your PC's local storage.

Click a category heading to view templates specific to that category.

After you choose a template, a new document window appears. The template's formatting is available in that document. Any preset text or graphics also appear. Macros and custom tabs on the Ribbon show up, if they are included with the template.

REMEMBER

Opening a new document based on a template doesn't change the template. The new document simply inherits all the template's attributes and settings.

Choosing an online template

Microsoft maintains a vast hoard of templates you can access online. Many of

(Refer to Figure 9-1.) If you don't find what you want, you can search for more-specific templates.

To search for an online template, obey these directions:

1. Click the File tab.

2. Choose New on the left side of the screen.

3. Click the Search box at the top of the New screen.

Refer to Figure 9-1. You also see a list of suggested searches below the Search text box. These suggestions aren't clickable.

4. Type a description of the template type you're looking for.

For example: résumé, invitation, term paper, or ransom note.

5. Press the Enter key to commence the search.

Word scours its online repository, looking for matching templates. The results appear on the New screen. You see additional categories appear in a list on the right side of the screen.

6. Click a template to view a larger preview.

You see more details about the template. If it's not what you want, click the left or right arrows to page through additional templates, or click the X (Close) button to search again. Otherwise:

7. Click the Create button to start a new document based on that template.

The template is downloaded and a new document is created, ready for editing.

If the search proves fruitless after Step 5, click the Home button (shown in the margin) to return to the New screen.

>> The steps in this section don't work when the Internet is unavailable or the Microsoft Office website is down.

>> The template you download (refer to Step 7) is saved on the New screen under the Featured category.

>> To keep the template prominently listed on the New screen, click its Pin icon. When the pin is pointed left, as shown in the margin, the template is prioritized on the New screen.

>> Those fill-in-the-blanks items you see in many of the online templates are content controls. See Chapter 27 for information on using them in your own templates.

Using one of your own templates

Word must not like your own templates because you must take one extra step to access them; they're shown on the Personal tab, which doesn't initially appear when you first view the New screen.

To use one of your own templates to start a new document, follow these steps:

1. **Click the File tab.**

2. **Choose New.**

3. **Click the PERSONAL heading.**

4. **Choose one of your templates from the list.**

   A new document is created with all the template's goodness.

If you prefer to have your own templates on the main New screen, pin it: Click the Pin icon next to the template's name. Pinned templates appear under the FEATURED heading, as shown in Figure 9-1.

Make Your Own Template

When you create the same type of document over and over or you work on a project that involves many similar documents, you need to build your own document template.

>> Templates offer document consistency. They also provide standard elements, such as a letterhead or company logo.

>> The most common feature in a template is a collection of styles. That way, the template's documents all feature the same text formats. Refer to Chapter 8 for details on creating styles in Word.

>> If you're writing a novel, ensure that all chapters use the same template. See Chapter 20 for details.

>> Not every document needs a custom template. For a one-off document, it's perfectly okay to use the Normal template: Press Ctrl+N to start a new, blank document.

Building a custom template

As with creating styles, no one really sets out to build a template from scratch. It's

common elements. Hone how the document presents itself, and then build a template based on that prototype.

Generally speaking, here are the steps I take to create a custom template:

1. **Create the prototype document.**

Build styles, set graphics, design the layout, program macros, apply page formatting. Not all these tasks are necessary for every document, but the point is to have a foundation upon which to build a document.

2. **Remove the document's specific text.**

A template can contain text, but that text is effective only when it applies to *all* documents the template creates; for example, your name and address for a Letter template.

3. **Add content controls.**

If your template is used by others, content controls can help direct them where and how to type text. See Chapter 27.

4. **Save the template as a template.**

When using the Save As dialog box, choose Word Template as the file type. When you do, Word automatically chooses the Custom Office Templates folder as the file's location.

5. **Close the template document.**

You don't want to further edit the document, because it's now a template. Any changes that are made affect the template itself. To start a new document based on the template, obey the steps in the earlier section "Using one of your own templates."

As a more specific example, the following steps build an envelope template:

1. **Press Ctrl+N.**

Start off with a new document. As with all new documents, this one is based on the Normal template.

2. **Click the Layout tab.**

3. **In the Page Setup group, click the Size button and choose Envelope #10.**

The document's only page changes to reflect a common envelope, but the orientation is wrong.

4. Click the Orientation button and choose Landscape.

There's your envelope.

5. Click the Margins button and choose Narrow.

The page's margins are set to a half-inch around the envelope.

6. Type your return address, pressing Shift+Enter to end each line.

Type your name, and then press Shift+Enter. Type the address, and then press Shift+Enter. Type the city, state, and zip code.

The Shift+Enter keyboard shortcut inserts a soft return at the end of each line, keeping the return address intact.

The next few steps create a style for the return address.

7. Select the return address text.

8. Click the Home tab.

9. In the Font group, choose a font, size, and format for the return address.

For example, I choose Tahoma 11-point bold.

10. With the return address still selected, create a new style named Return Address.

The style helps you recover the text's formatting, should the return address be accidentally deleted or you need to replace that text.

Refer to Chapter 8 for details on how to create a style.

11. Click the Insert tab.

For the recipient's address, I recommend using a text box. That way, the address can be positioned properly on the page without the need to mess with paragraph formatting.

12. In the Text group, click the Text Box button and choose Simple Text Box.

Don't worry about the text box's current position.

13. Click the mouse on the text box's border.

You want to see the Layout Options button, shown in the margin.

14. Click the Layout Options button and choose In Front of Text as the layout.

Refer to Chapter 10 for more details on how objects appear on a page.

15. Drag the text box to the approximate location of the recipient's address on the envelope.

Point the mouse at the edge of the text box and drag.

16. On the Drawing Tools Format tab, in the Shape Styles group, click the Shape Outline button and choose No Outline.

17. Select the placeholder text inside the text box.

18. Choose the Return Address style for the text.

This style was created in Step 10.

19. Right-click the text in the text box and, on the Mini Toolbar, type 13 points as the text size.

20. Create a new style for the recipient's text; name the style Recipient Address.

In this instance, you want to base the style on the Return Address style, which shows up automatically in the Create New Style from Formatting dialog box. Refer to Chapter 8 for details on creating a style.

21. Delete the placeholder text in the text box.

22. Click the Developer tab and, in the Controls group, click the Rich Text content control.

Refer to Chapter 27 for additional details on content controls.

23. In the content control, type [Recipient's Address].

The document should appear similar to the one shown in Figure 9-2. The various added elements are illustrated in the figure.

With all elements added, it's now time to save the envelope template.

24. Press Ctrl+S.

The Save As screen appears, which for this advanced operation is kind of a waste of time.

25. Click the Browse button.

The Save As dialog box appears.

26. From the Save As Type menu, choose Word Template (*.dotx).

The Save As dialog box automatically shows the location of all Office templates.

27. Type a name for the template, such as Standard Envelope.

28. Click OK.

The template is saved.

29. Press Ctrl+W to close the document window.

You don't want the template to linger on the screen. That's because it's now a template and not a document you want to edit.

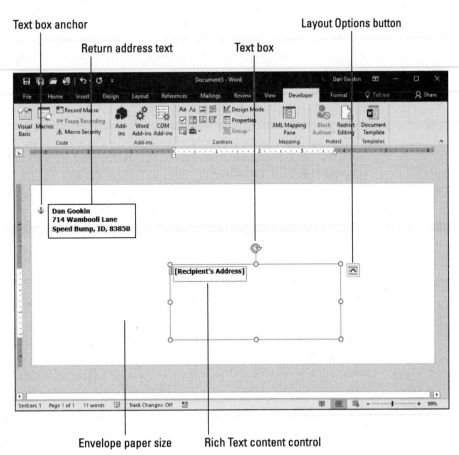

Text box anchor

Return address text

Text box

Layout Options button

Dan Gookin
714 Wambooli Lane
Speed Bump, ID, 83850

[Recipient's Address]

FIGURE 9-2:
An envelope
template in
the making.

Envelope paper size

Rich Text content control

To confirm that the template operation was successful, click the File tab and choose New. Click the PERSONAL heading and locate the Standard Envelope template, or whichever template you just created. You don't see a preview, as you do with Word's own templates, but the template is available. Choose it to create a new envelope document.

REMEMBER

>> Use these steps to create any template: Add the document elements you need, and then save the document as a template.

>> The only text you want to keep in a template is text that's needed for every document the template creates. If your template document contains any surplus text, remove it before you save the template.

>> For Office 2016, user templates are saved in the Custom Office Templates folder. This folder is located in your user account folder, in the Documents or My Documents subfolder. This location is standard in all Office applications. It's where Word looks for any personal template files.

>> If template files are stored in another location, move them to the Custom Office Templates folder so that they're easily accessible within Word.

Modifying a template

You can't just open a template file to make changes. When you do, you create a new document based on that template. To modify a template, you must be specific. Follow these steps:

1. **Press Ctrl+O to summon the Open screen.**

2. **Click the Browse button.**

   The Open dialog box is the best tool for locating template files.

3. **From the file type menu, choose All Word Templates (*.dotx, *.dotm, *.dot).**

4. **Navigate to the Documents\Custom Office Templates folder.**

   Figure 9-3 offers some visual assistance on how to locate this important folder.

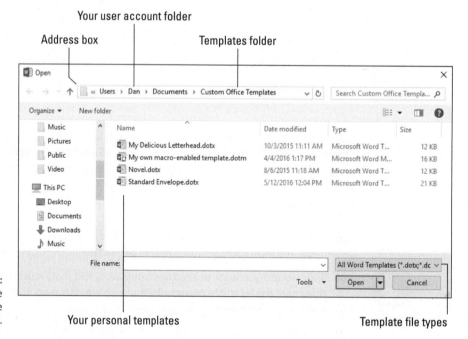

Your user account folder

Address box   Templates folder

Your personal templates   Template file types

FIGURE 9-3:
Finding where Word keeps the template files.

Start with your account folder, which has the same name as your sign-in ID. Click that item in the address bar, shown in Figure 9-3. Then open the Documents or My Documents folder. Finally, open the Custom Office Templates folder.

5. **Select the template file you want to edit.**

6. **Click the Open button.**

   You're editing a template — not a document. A good clue is that the template filename, not the generic "Document *n*," appears on the window's title bar.

7. **Edit the template.**

   Modify styles, add or remove text, create other elements, and do whatever is necessary to update the template.

8. **Save the template.**

   Because you're editing the template directly, the changes you save are made to the template, not to a new document.

9. **Press Ctrl+W to close the template.**

A logical question at this point is, "Are all my documents updated?" The answer is a vague, "They could be!" Whether or not existing documents change depends on the settings you make when you create a style. See the next section.

>> Generally speaking, changing a template affects only new documents created with the template as a base.

>> Styles in an updated template can be applied to all documents attached to the template. See the next section.

>> Anything beyond a style, such as text and graphics, appears only in new documents created by selecting the template.

Updating template documents

When you change a template, you affect only new documents. Any older documents associated with the template remain unchanged — unless you alter how template updates affect a document.

To keep a document's styles updated to reflect any changes to the template, follow these steps:

1. **Click the File tab.**

2. **Choose Options.**

   The Word Options dialog box appears.

3. **Choose Add-Ins from the left side of the Word Options dialog box.**

4. **At the bottom of the dialog box, click Manage and choose Templates.**

5. Click the Go button.

The Templates and Add-Ins dialog box appears, illustrated in Figure 9-4.

Refresh styles from template

Current template

Select new template

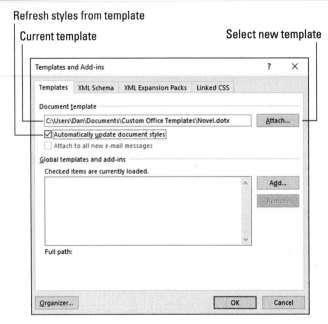

FIGURE 9-4:
The Templates
and Add-Ins
dialog box.

6. Click to place a check mark by the item Automatically Update Document Styles.

7. Click OK.

The document is now refreshed whenever the template is edited and changes are made to the styles.

If perchance your copy of Word shows the Developer tab, click the Document Template button on that tab. That way, you can skip Steps 1 through 5.

>> The document may not instantly reflect changes, so close it and then open it again.

>> Only changes to the template's styles are reflected in the document. Any other changes or additions, including text or graphics, are reflected only in new documents created.

>> See Chapter 25 for details on the Developer tab.

Template Management

Don't fret over managing templates. It isn't a regular, required maintenance chore. It's nothing you need to do, not like regularly changing the bit oil in your PC. Instead, template management addresses some of the more specific and advanced things you can do with a template in Word.

TECHNICAL STUFF

I'm kidding about the bit oil.

Finding the templates

Word 2016 stores your template files in a specific folder on the computer's mass storage system. The folder is shown earlier, in Figure 9-3. The specific location is written like this:

```
%USERPROFILE%\Documents\Custom Office Templates
```

If you type this line of text into any File Explorer window's address bar, you'll see the templates in the folder window.

Reassigning templates

All documents must be attached to a template. You can reattach a document to a template, or you can replace the template with the Normal template. To do so, follow these steps:

1. **Click the File tab and choose Options.**

2. **In the Word Options dialog box, choose Add-Ins.**

3. **Click the Manage button menu, located at the bottom of the dialog box.**

4. **Choose Templates and click the Go button.**

   The Templates and Add-Ins dialog box appears. (Refer to Figure 9-4.)

5. **Click the Attach button.**

   The Attach Template dialog box appears. It works like an Open dialog box, but it's used to hunt down templates. In Figure 9-5, you can see that the dialog box is focused on the location for Microsoft's templates.

Address for Microsoft's templates

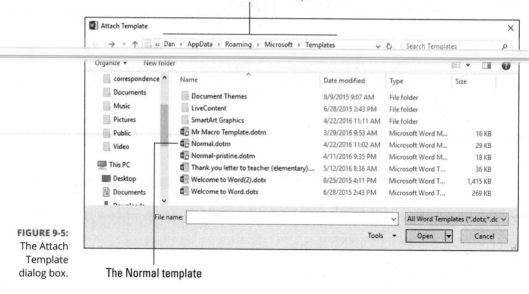

FIGURE 9-5:
The Attach
Template
dialog box.

The Normal template

6. **If you're attaching one of your own templates, click in the dialog box's address bar and type the location for your personal templates.**

   That location is

   ```
   %USERPROFILE%\Documents\Custom Office Templates
   ```

   Press Enter after typing the address to view your templates.

7. **Select the template you want to attach to the document.**

8. **Click the Open button.**

   The Document Template item is updated in the Templates and Add-Ins dialog box.

9. **Click OK to assign the new template.**

You may not notice many changes. Reassigning a template doesn't remove any styles, text, or graphics associated with the original template. Styles from the new template are available to the document.

TIP

» If you simply want to remove a template, or apply the Normal template to any document, in Step 5 click in the Document Template text box and type **Normal**. Click OK.

» You can quickly summon the Templates and Add-Ins dialog box if the Developer tab is visible: In the Templates group, click the Document Templates button.

2

Go Graphical

Chapter 10

Text and Graphics Layout

Word processing isn't only about text. Word also tosses graphics into the mix. It features the capability to insert pictures, drawing objects, and special and unusual items into a document. That's nifty and fun, but it presents an interesting problem: How do text and graphics mix on a page? The solution is something called *layout,* which is a topic you should know about before you insert that first graphical whatzit into your text.

Where Text and Objects Meet

Early word processors had no more power than today's text editors. The notion of inserting an image into the text was blasphemy. Yet when that capability finally appeared, programmers had to figure out, and users had to discover, how to mix text and graphics.

Finding things to insert into a document

Non-text elements on a page aren't limited to pictures. Though pictures were first into a document. For layout purposes, each of these items is considered the same. Here's the short list:

Pictures: The traditional graphical item, a picture can be an image, some clip art, a photograph, an illustration, or one of a host of other graphical goodies you can insert into your document.

Shapes: A shape is a drawing object, or what the graphics designers call *line art*. Shapes can be applied as decorative elements, combined into complex structures, converted into text or picture boxes, and manipulated by a host of interesting commands.

SmartArt: Word's SmartArt gallery presents a selection of prebuilt shapes (drawing objects) with fill-in-the-blanks placeholders. This feature allows you to quickly add artwork to a document.

Charts: Rather than cobble together a pie chart or line graph, Word hosts a gallery of charts and graphs you can add as graphical elements to your document.

Text Boxes: Word features a specific text box command. It lists various text boxes, all designed and made to look pretty. This feature is truly a shortcut because you can convert any shape (drawing object) into a text box.

These items are all located on the Insert tab. Most are found in the Illustrations group. The text box appears in the Text group, though you can convert most drawing objects (shapes) into a text box. Figure 10-1 illustrates the locations on the Insert tab.

Graphics and graphic-like objects

FIGURE 10-1:
Graphical objects you can insert into a document.

 Other items are treated like graphics as well. The difference between these objects and other items, such as tables, is that these elements feature the Layout Options button, shown in the margin. See the later section "Setting layout options."

>> It's also possible to paste graphics in from another program. As long as the image is in a format Word recognizes, the process works like pasting in text, but the end result is an image in your document.

>> See Chapter 11 for specifics on shapes and text boxes.

>> Chapter 12 covers pictures and other graphics.

>> SmartArt and charts are covered in Chapter 13, along with other, nontraditional document objects.

Mixing text and objects

When word processors first allowed graphics and text to mingle, images were set at the same level as text; a picture was simply a large, single character. You could set it on a line by itself, center it as a paragraph, and call it all good. That trick worked for a while, but eventually word processing users demanded more.

Graphics can still exist in-line with text. That's the option Word chooses when you insert a picture, text box, or drawing object into your document. You can then free the object from the text, set it at a specific position, or wrap text around the object. These topics are covered elsewhere in this chapter, but before you dive into those settings, it helps to understand how Word structures elements on a page.

Figure 10-2 illustrates a page in a Word document. The base layer is the page itself, which could be the paper upon which a document is printed. Above the base layer comes any watermark, background color, or image. Above that layer is any graphical object set to float behind the text. The text itself exists at the next layer, along with any in-line graphics or graphics set with a wrapping option. Finally, the top level, the one "closest" to you, contains graphical objects floating in front of the text.

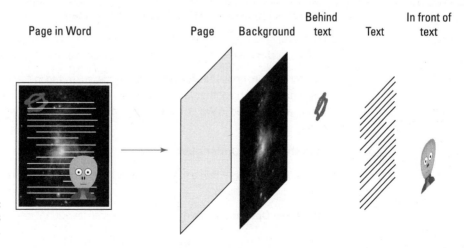

FIGURE 10-2:
Elements
on a page.

The layers illustrated in Figure 10-2 are relevant to layout options. You can position items in different layers to adjust appearances. Beyond these layers, when you apply drawing objects, they can be set in front of or behind each other — like layers within layers. But in the big picture, layout options are set as illustrated in Figure 10-2.

Layout Choices

The simplest layout choice involves setting an object on a line (in a paragraph) by itself. That's how Word instantly sets the layout when you insert an image or another object: It becomes part of the text. Simply set that item as its own paragraph, and center it. You're done. You probably want to do more with your document than that simple choice.

Setting layout options

The general method of inserting a graphic or another object in your text works like this:

1. **Position the insertion pointer at the location where you want the image to appear.**

    It doesn't matter if you're precise at this point. Graphics can be moved and arranged later, but first you need to get the thing into the text.

2. **Click the Insert tab.**

3. **Choose the item to insert, such as Picture or Shape.**

    Details for selecting items are found in Chapters 11, 12, and 13. For example, you might choose the Shapes command and select a rectangle from the menu.

    The item you insert is selected and appears, as illustrated in Figure 10-3. It might appear with another layout attribute, depending on which attributes you've already used in Word, but Figure 10-3 shows the In Line with Text layout option.

 4. **Click the Layout Options button.**

    The button appears when a graphical object is selected. If you don't see the button, click the object.

    The Layout Options pop-up menu lists the seven layout options available.

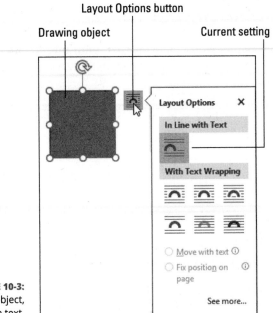

Drawing object

Layout Options button

Current setting

FIGURE 10-3:
A drawing object,
in line with text.

5. **Choose another layout option from the pop-up menu.**

The options are described throughout this chapter.

Beyond the layout options, you have the choice of how to position an object on the page. You can set an object at an absolute position or position it relative to a certain paragraph.

TIP

>> If the Layout Options button doesn't appear, the object you've selected can't be repositioned on the page.

>> Some objects, such as tables, can be inserted into a text box. In that instance, you can apply layout options to the object.

>> Layout options are also available on the Ribbon. After selecting an object, click the Format tab (Drawing Tools Format, Picture Tools Format, and so on). In the Arrange group, click the Wrap Text button and choose a layout option from the menu.

>> Layout options might also be located on a right-click shortcut menu: Right-click the object and choose Wrap Text from the pop-up menu. Layout options are shown on the Wrap Text submenu.

Using the Inline option

The traditional layout option is In Line with Text. With this setting chosen, the

To set this option, obey these directions:

1. **Click to set the insertion pointer at the location in your document where you want to object to appear.**

I recommend creating an empty paragraph and placing the object in that paragraph.

2. **Insert the object.**

Chapters 11, 12, and 13 offer specifics.

3. **Click the Layout Options button.**

4. **Choose the In Line with Text option.**

This layout setting directs Word to place the object in the text, just like other characters and words.

The object now moves with the rest of the text. You can use the mouse to drag it around, but it stays with the surrounding text. If you need to free it from the text, choose another layout option.

Wrapping text around an object

Four layout options allow you to wrap text around an object. Unlike the In Line with Text option, the object's position isn't locked into a paragraph's text. The four options are

Square: The object sits inside a rectangle, no matter what the object's shape. Text flows around the rectangle, keeping equidistance from the object.

Tight: This setting is similar to Square, though the text is closer to the object and matches its shape. So, if the object is a triangle, the "hole" in the text is shaped like a triangle.

Through: If the image's shape allows, text flows through the image, perhaps filling an interior space or a space between separate sides of the same object. When you choose this setting, you may have to edit the object's bounding box and position its wrap points to make the effect work. See the next section.

Top and Bottom: The image is held in a box with the top and bottom extending to the page margins.

Each of these settings is illustrated in Figure 10-4. In each instance, the object was selected, and the indicated wrapping option was selected from the Layout Options menu.

» The Tight option works best when the image is of an irregular shape, like a drawing object or a picture that features a transparent background. The triangle shown in Figure 10-4 (bottom left) was saved with the background set to transparent, which is why the Tight layout option looks good. (Well, it looks good on one side.)

» The Through example in Figure 10-4 works because the wrap points were edited to allow text to flow below the object. See the next section.

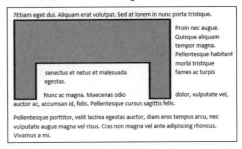

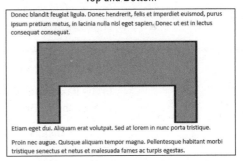

FIGURE 10-4:
Layout options
with text
wrapping.

Editing the wrap points

Both the Tight and Through layout options allow you to add more integrity to the polygon separating the object from the text. To hone the shape, you can edit the wrap points that define the polygon. This trick works only for the Tight and Through layout options.

Figure 10-5 illustrates an example of wrap points around a right triangle, though any irregularly shaped object would work.

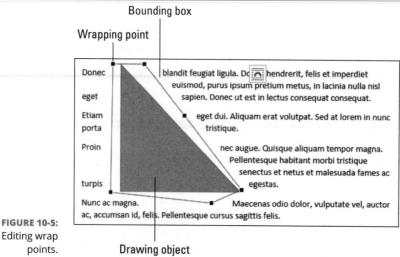

Bounding box

Wrapping point

Donec | blandit feugiat ligula. Dc ... hendrerit, felis et imperdiet euismod, purus ipsum pretium metus, in lacinia nulla nisl sapien. Donec ut est in lectus consequat consequat.

eget

Etiam porta | eget dui. Aliquam erat volutpat. Sed at lorem in nunc tristique.

Proin | nec augue. Quisque aliquam tempor magna. Pellentesque habitant morbi tristique senectus et netus et malesuada fames ac egestas.

turpis

Nunc ac magna. | Maecenas odio dolor, vulputate vel, auctor ac, accumsan id, felis. Pellentesque cursus sagittis felis.

FIGURE 10-5:
Editing wrap
points.

Drawing object

As an example of how to edit wrap points, follow these steps:

1. **Ensure that the document contains text so that you can play with the wrap.**

   If you're just goofing around, type **=lorem(10)** on a line by itself and press the Enter key to generate ten paragraphs of standard *Lorem Ipsum* placeholder text.

2. **Click the Insert tab.**

3. **In the Illustrations area, click the Shapes menu; in the Basic Shapes area, choose the Right Triangle item.**

   The basic shape is shown in the margin. Your job is to draw the triangle in the text.

4. **Drag the mouse down and to the right to create the triangle.**

   After releasing the mouse, you see size handles appear, as well as the Layout Options button. The Drawing Tools Format tab appears on the Ribbon.

5. **Click the Layout Options button.**

6. **Choose the Tight option.**

   The option is shown in the margin. After choosing this option, the text lines up very close with the triangle, which is the Tight layout option's default operation.

7. Click the Drawing Tools Format tab.

8. In the Arrange area, click the Wrap Text button.

9. Choose the Edit Wrap Points command.

A red line envelops the shape. Black squares on the line represent handles.

10. Adjust the wrap points.

Point the mouse at a wrap point. The mouse pointer changes, as shown in the margin. Drag the point to a new position to adjust the distance between the text and the object.

11. Add a wrap point.

To create a new wrap point, press the Ctrl key on the keyboard. The mouse pointer changes, as shown in the margin. Click on the bounding box (the red line) to drop a new wrap point. You can then drag that point to adjust the bounding box and set the distance between the text and the object.

12. Remove a wrap point.

To get rid of a wrap point, press the Ctrl key and point the mouse at a wrap point. The mouse pointer changes, as shown in the margin. Click the mouse to remove the wrap point.

13. When you're done editing the wrap points, click the mouse in the document's text.

The object is deselected, and you can return to editing text.

It's easy to get carried away with wrap points and editing the bounding box, but the results can look pretty sharp, especially when you have an object that Word doesn't wrap properly.

>> Most complex drawing objects on the Shape menu already feature detailed wrap points.

>> The triangle you draw in the text is preset with the line style and shading (fill) based on the current document theme.

>> Yes, you use a Ctrl+click to add *and* remove wrap points.

>> You can also edit wrap points when the Through layout option is chosen. (Refer to Step 6 in this section.)

Setting the image's position

Pictures, illustrations, and other objects are often related to the surrounding text. For example, that image of a cake best sits on a page with its recipe. To help you make this association, Word anchors objects to a paragraph. As the document changes, the image shifts with its anchored text. That way, you don't end up with the image on one page and its reference on another.

To confirm that an image is anchored to a paragraph, obey these directions:

1. **Click to select the image.**

2. **Look for the Anchor icon in the page's left margin.**

The Anchor icon is shown to the left. It's positioned next to the start of a paragraph to which the object is attached, but only if that option is selected.

3. **Click the Layout Options button.**

4. **Ensure that the option Move with Text is selected.**

When the Move with Text item is chosen, the graphic moves with the paragraph as you edit or add text to the rest of the document.

The other option on the Layout Options button menu is Fix Position on Page. This option frees the image's position from the text. When it's chosen (in Step 4), the object stays at the same location on the page regardless of how text is edited. The Anchor icon still appears.

If you want to be precise about where an object appears, click the More command in Step 4. The Layout dialog box appears. On the Position tab, you can set the Absolute Position options for the object's Horizontal and Vertical locations. In Figure 10-6, I've set the object's location one inch in from the page's top and left edges.

The page position affects all layout options except for In Line with Text.

» The In Line with Text option is automatically anchored to the paragraph in which it sits.

» The floating options, Behind Text and In Front of Text, can also be anchored to text or set to a specific position on the page. See the next section.

Floating an object in front of or behind text

Two layout options free the graphical object from the confines of your document's text. The object can float in front of the text or behind the text, and rest at any absolute position on the page. Earlier, in Figure 10-2, you see two such objects, one floating in front of text and the other behind the text.

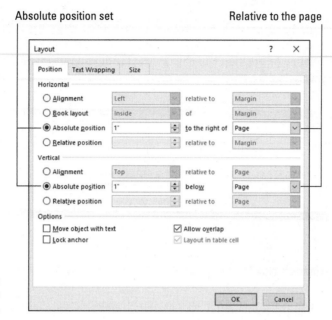

Absolute position set

Relative to the page

FIGURE 10-6:
Setting absolute page position.

To set an item's layout in front of or behind text, click the object and choose either item from the Layout Options pop-up menu.

- ❯❯ Of the two choices, I prefer to float objects in front of text. For example, if I'm creating a cover page with a text box for the title, I release the text box and set its layout to float in front of the text. That way, I can position the object exactly on the page.

- ❯❯ It can be difficult to select and move an object placed behind text. You must keep pointing the mouse at the object until the mouse pointer changes to the four-way arrow thing, shown in the margin. Then you can click to select the object or drag it to a new position.

- ❯❯ Objects in front of or behind text can still be anchored to a paragraph or the page. Refer to the preceding section for directions on how to set these options.

Aligning objects on a page

A page in Word features invisible gridlines that you can use to help align images. These lines appear as you drag an image around. They represent the page's top, bottom, left, and right margins, a centerline down the middle of the page, and the top of each paragraph on the page.

To see the lines, drag a graphical object around on the page. As the object nears one of the margins, a green guideline appears, as illustrated in Figure 10-7. Use the guideline to position the object's center or its edges with the page or paragraph elements.

Page's left margin guideline   Top-of-paragraph guideline

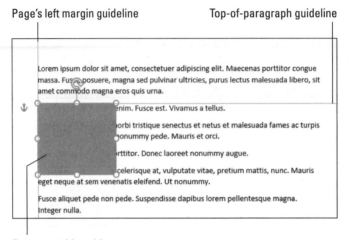

Lorem ipsum dolor sit amet, consectetuer adipiscing elit. Maecenas porttitor congue massa. Fusce posuere, magna sed pulvinar ultricies, purus lectus malesuada libero, sit amet commodo magna eros quis urna.

enim. Fusce est. Vivamus a tellus.

orbi tristique senectus et netus et malesuada fames ac turpis nonummy pede. Mauris et orci.

rttitor. Donec laoreet nonummy augue.

celerisque at, vulputate vitae, pretium mattis, nunc. Mauris eget neque at sem venenatis eleifend. Ut nonummy.

Fusce aliquet pede non pede. Suspendisse dapibus lorem pellentesque magna. Integer nulla.

FIGURE 10-7:
Setting an object's
position.

Drag to position object

The page's centerline appears whenever an object nears the center of the page. Position that guideline with the center handles on the object to ensure that it's centered left-to-right on the page.

Page layout artists are persnickety about text and graphics lined up on a page. Lining up an image with a page margin, or just the top of a paragraph, helps give the document a professional look, even though few readers notice the effort put into that task.

TIP

Chapter 11

Drawing Objects

t's just a simple button, located on the Insert tab in the Illustrations group. Yet the Shapes command opens a door to what would be considered a capable and full-functions drawing program right within Word. The shapes can be sized, colored, filled with text or graphics, combined, arranged, and aligned to build interesting illustrations and create custom graphics in a document. Or you can be childish and draw crude cartoons. Really, it's up to you.

Shapes and Such

On the Insert tab, in the Illustrations area, the Shapes button hosts a delightful menu chock-full of interesting *line art*. That's the official term for the drawing objects you find on that menu. You can find an assortment of basic shapes, lines, arrows, symbols, and all sorts of fun stuff to divert you from your writing duties.

Inserting a drawing object

No matter which shape you decide the document needs, the technique for insert-

1. **Scroll to the part of your document where you want to set the shape.**

You don't need to position the insertion pointer specifically; just have the page upon which you want the shape set visible on the screen.

2. **Click the Insert tab.**

3. **In the Illustrations area, click the Shapes button.**

A long menu unfurls, listing a smorgasbord of shapes.

4. **Click on the shape you desire.**

The mouse pointer changes to the Plus icon, indicating that you're in drawing mode. Your task is to drag the mouse on the screen to create the shape.

5. **Drag the mouse down and to the right to create the shape.**

The location and size are approximate at this point; you can adjust everything later.

When you release the mouse button, the shape appears in your document, similar to what's shown in Figure 11-1. You also see the Drawing Tools Format tab on the Ribbon, which helps you further modify or mangle the shape.

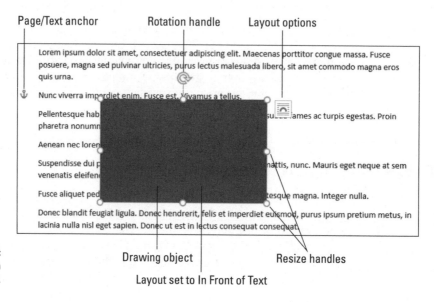

FIGURE 11-1:
A shape in a document.

If you choose a line in Step 4, you don't really need to drag through the document. You can, but if you just click the mouse, the line is set and ready for editing.

>> Just as you can copy and paste text, you can copy and paste objects: Click to select an object, and then press Ctrl+C. Every time you paste (Ctrl+V), you insert a new copy of the selected shape.

>> The shape's color reflects the document's current theme. Or, if you've already set a shape's color and line style, new shapes use those attributes.

>> Shapes are given the In Front of Text layout position. Refer to Chapter 10 for information on graphics layout.

>> The shape's layout also includes an anchor to a paragraph of text. See the later section "Changing the object's position."

Drawing a freeform shape

Every drawing object on the Shapes menu represents some type of polygon or other interesting object. The exception is the scribble tool, shown in the margin. When you choose that "shape," you become an artist and can draw a custom object over your text.

Follow these steps to effectively use the Scribble shape:

1. **Click the Insert tab.**

2. **In the Illustrations group, click the Shapes button.**

3. **Choose the Scribble tool.**

   The tool is found on the far right in the Lines area.

4. **Drag the mouse to draw a free-form shape in your document.**

   The mouse pointer changes to the Pencil icon as you drag and draw.

5. **Close the shape.**

   Ensure that you drag the mouse over the shape's starting position.

This step is the most important! When you're done dragging, loop around to the shape's starting point, like tying a knot in a string. If you don't close the shape, it will be ugly and I shall frown upon you incessantly.

>> If you screw up, try again: Delete the shape (press the Delete key or Ctrl+Z to undo).

>> The reason for closing the shape (refer to Step 5) is to ensure that you can apply a fill color or style. Otherwise, the shape becomes a contorted line. That's still a valid shape, but limited in its application.

>> See the later section "Editing a shape" for the necessary editing of any free-form shape.

TIP

>> Seriously, if you need a freehand shape, I recommend that you use a drawing program to create the shape. Using the Scribble tool in Word is a great diversion, but it rarely creates something you'd like to see in a professional document.

Changing the object's position

Shapes you slap into a document are anchored to a paragraph, but otherwise their layout is set to float atop the text. To move the shape to another position, heed these directions:

1. Point the mouse at the shape.

The mouse pointer changes to a four-arrow thing, shown in the margin. That's the drag-me cursor.

2. Drag the shape to a new position on the page.

As you drag, you may discover green guidelines that appear over the text. These lines help you position the object relative to the page's margins, the tops of paragraphs, and the centerline down the middle of the page.

For precise relocation of an object, you can use the Position button. Follow these steps:

1. Click to select the object.

2. Click the Drawing Tools Format tab.

3. In the Arrange group, click the Position button.

A menu appears with various locations described. The bottom nine locations position the object in the text with text wrapping layout (Square) chosen, illustrated in Figure 11-2.

4. Choose an item from the Position button menu.

As you point the mouse at each item, the object relocates to give you a preview of what its new arrangement looks like. Click an item to select that position.

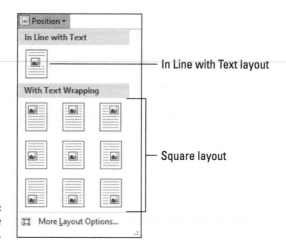

In Line with Text layout

Square layout

FIGURE 11-2:
Selecting the
object's position.

If you don't like the object's new location, repeat the steps in this section. If you want the object to float in front of the text again, follow Steps 1 and 2, but in Step 3 click the Wrap Text button. Choose the command In Front of Text.

TIP

>> If it helps, consider using the Zoom control on the status bar to resize the page in the document window. That way, you can properly see how the shape relates to the rest of the text.

>> Refer to Chapter 10 for more information on the green guidelines you see when moving an object on a page, as well as graphics layout options.

**TECHNICAL
STUFF**

>> Even more precise positioning of the object is possible if you use the Layout dialog box. Repeat the steps in this section, but in Step 4 choose More Layout Options. In the Layout dialog box, use the Position tab to set the object to an exact location on the page.

Resizing the shape

The simplest way to change a shape's size is to use the mouse to drag one of its eight handles in or out. The more complex-yet-precise way is to follow these steps:

1. **Click to select the object.**

2. **Click the Drawing Tools Format tab.**

3. **In the Size area, use the Shape Height and Shape Width gizmos to specify an exact size for the object.**

   The gizmos are illustrated in Figure 11-3. As you adjust the size, the object changes to reflect the new values.

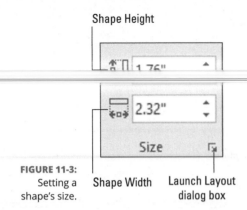

Shape Height

2.32"

Size

FIGURE 11-3:
Setting a
shape's size.

Shape Width   Launch Layout
dialog box

If you click the Launcher icon (refer to Figure 11-3), you see the Size tab in the Layout dialog box. The Height and Width items in that dialog box reflect the same values shown on the Ribbon. The dialog box does, however, contain a Scale feature. So, if you need to double the object's size, type **200%** in both the Height and Width boxes and click OK.

» Not every shape is a perfect rectangle, so what the size gizmos do is set the shape's bounding box.

» Use the top and bottom handles to change the object's vertical size; use the left and right handles to change the object's horizontal size.

» To resize in two directions at one time, grab one of the corner handles. If you hold the Shift key as you drag a corner handle, you maintain the object's aspect ratio.

» Shapes with rounded corners may feature an additional handle, a yellow one positioned next to the curve. This handle adjusts the shape's curved edge. Drag it left or right to set the curve depth.

» In the Layout dialog box, on the Size tab, you can select the Lock Aspect Ratio option to ensure that the percentage-size changes you make are equal for the object's height and width.

Rotating the shape

To spin a shape around, follow these steps:

1. **Point the mouse at the Rotation handle.**

The Rotation handle is found at the top center of the object. (Refer to Figure 11-1.) When you find the sweet spot, the mouse pointer changes, as shown in the margin.

2. **Drag the mouse to spin the object around.**

If you want to rotate an object in 90-degree increments, follow these precise steps:

1. **Click to select the object.**

2. **Click the Drawing Tools Format tab.**

3. **In the Arrange group, click the Rotate Objects button.**

4. **Choose Rotate Right 90° or Rotate Left 90° to rotate the object in that given increment.**

   You can repeat this step to continue to rotate the object.

For additional rotation control, choose the command More Rotation Options in Step 4. You see the Layout dialog box with the Size tab forward. Use the Rotation gizmo in the Rotate area to set a specific rotation amount. Click OK.

TIP

>> Also available on the Rotate Objects menu are options to flip the object along the vertical (up-down) and horizontal (left-right) axis.

>> In the Layout dialog box, a value of 0° sets the object "upright," or in its original orientation when you first drew the object. Setting the value to 0° effectively undoes any weird rotation angle you've applied.

Setting the objects' colors, line styles, and effects

Beyond the design, all drawing objects have three basic attributes:

>> Fill color

>> Line color, weight, and style

>> Effects

These items are all controlled from the Drawing Tools Format tab, in the Shape Styles group. The command buttons are Shape Fill, Shape Outline, and Shape Effects, as shown in Figure 11-4.

Also appearing in Figure 11-4 is the Shape Styles gallery. You can use that list to select a shape design that includes preset colors, designs, and effects.

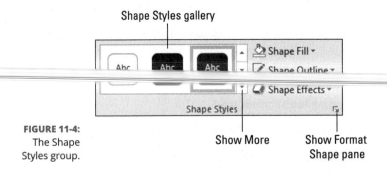

Shape Styles gallery

Shape Fill ▾

Shape Outline ▾

Shape Effects ▾

Shape Styles

FIGURE 11-4:
The Shape
Styles group.

Show More   Show Format
                   Shape pane

For an example of formatting an object, pretend (because you wouldn't actually do this in your right mind) that you need an orange box with a thick, purple dotted line and a drop shadow. Follow these steps to create such a thing:

1. Click the Insert tab.

2. Choose Shapes.

3. Select the rectangle shape.

4. Press the Shift key and drag the mouse in the document to create a square.

Don't worry about the square's location.

5. Click the Drawing Tools Format tab.

6. In the Arrange group, click the Position button.

7. Choose the Top Left position.

The object is placed at the top left corner of the page, and Square text-wrapping is applied.

8. In the Shape Styles group, click the Shape Fill button.

9. Choose an orange color.

The box's fill color changes to orange.

10. In the Shape Styles group, click the Shape Outline button.

11. Choose a purple color.

12. Click the Shape Outline button again and choose Weight ⇨ 6 pt.

13. Click the Shape Outline button again and choose Dashes ⇨ Round Dot.

The Round Dot choice is the second from the top in the submenu.

14. In the Shape Styles group, click the Shape Effects button.

15. Choose Shadow ⇨ Perspective Diagonal Lower Right.

You don't have to choose exactly this option; any shadow will do.

Behold your creation! Mine appears in Figure 11-5, albeit in grayscale because the publisher didn't want to print this book in color.

Outline at 6 pt, dotted, purple

Shape fill orange

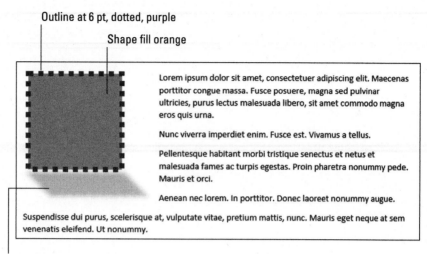

Lorem ipsum dolor sit amet, consectetuer adipiscing elit. Maecenas porttitor congue massa. Fusce posuere, magna sed pulvinar ultricies, purus lectus malesuada libero, sit amet commodo magna eros quis urna.

Nunc viverra imperdiet enim. Fusce est. Vivamus a tellus.

Pellentesque habitant morbi tristique senectus et netus et malesuada fames ac turpis egestas. Proin pharetra nonummy pede. Mauris et orci.

Aenean nec lorem. In porttitor. Donec laoreet nonummy augue.

Suspendisse dui purus, scelerisque at, vulputate vitae, pretium mattis, nunc. Mauris eget neque at sem venenatis eleifend. Ut nonummy.

FIGURE 11-5:
An object is colored, styled, and slapped with a drop shadow.

Perspective drop shadow

Any effect can be removed by simply replacing it with a new effect. The best way to manage multiple effects is to click the Launcher icon (refer to Figure 11-4) and use the Format Shape pane to control all settings: fill, line, effects, size, and so on.

TIP

>> The easiest way to style a shape is to select a preset option from the Shape Style gallery.

>> For a text box, the fill color is often set to the value No Color, which makes the text box transparent.

>> When a text box is used on a cover page, its fill color and line color are both set to the No Color value.

>> The color pallets shown on the Shape Fill and Shape Outline menus are related to the document theme. You see the theme colors first and then a palette of standard colors. See the nearby sidebar "Creating a new color" for more colorful choices.

>> The Gradient item on the Shape Fill menu lets you choose more than one color for the fill. The colors blend to form a gradient pattern. You can choose a preset gradient from the submenu or select the More Gradients item to build your own gradient fill.

>> In addition to fill colors, you can set a fill pattern: On the Shape fill menu, choose Texture. Select a pattern from the Texture submenu.

your document, Word lets you craft your own colors. To do so, choose the More Colors command from any color palette menu. You see the Colors dialog box with two tabs: Standard and Custom.

Use the Standard tab to choose a color from a matrix. You can also select transparency values.

Use the Custom tab to set a specific color. Choose a color from the grid, or set individual Red, Green, and Blue values. Set the darkness slider. Set the transparency. You can use the model to create over 16 million different colors.

The color you create is applied to whatever object is selected.

>> Also see the later section "Adding a picture to a shape," for information on using any image as the fill, or background, for a shape.

>> To change the document theme colors, click the Design tab and choose a new theme from the Colors menu.

>> Click the Shape Effects button to see a menu of effects categories, such as Shadow and Reflection. Choose a category to see a submenu full of specific effects. Each submenu features a command (at the bottom) that lets you view the effects portion of the Format Shape pane, where you can make further adjustments. The options are quite extensive.

WARNING

>> Be careful when selecting a preset shape from the Shape Styles gallery. Those thumbnails featuring *Abc* indicate that the format that's applied also transforms the shape into a text box.

>> To remove an effect, choose the effects category and then select the top item in the submenu. The item is named Remove, followed by the specific effect name.

Editing a shape

If you're not happy with a shape, don't delete it! Word allows you to reset a shape without the bother of deleting and replacing. This command is handy because it maintains the shape's color, line, effects, size, and position.

To swap one shape for another, follow these directions:

1. **Click to select the shape.**

2. **Click the Drawing Tools Format tab.**

3. **In the Insert Shapes group, click the Edit Shape button.**

   The button's icon is shown in the margin.

4. **Choose Change Shape.**

   A submenu of shapes appears.

5. **Select the new shape from the list.**

   The new shape replaces the old shape without altering the shape's style or position on the page.

You can take changing a shape one step further and edit a shape's points. These points define the shape itself, so you can add or remove points to build new shapes. To waste time with this activity, follow these steps:

1. **Click to select an existing shape.**

2. **Click the Drawing Tools Format tab.**

3. **In the Insert Shapes group, click the Edit Shape button and choose Edit Points.**

   Black squares appear on the shape's line, or *path*, indicating where an anchor point is set. You can move those points, add new points, or remove points.

4. **To move an anchor, point the mouse at the black square and drag it elsewhere.**

   When you point the mouse at a square, the cursor changes as shown in the margin. It's your clue that you can relocate the anchor point.

5. **To add a new anchor point, press the Ctrl key and click on the line (path) that defines the shape.**

   When you point the mouse at the line, the cursor changes as shown in the margin. Hold the Ctrl key and click the mouse to set a new point. You can then drag the point to a new location to build the shape.

6. **To remove an anchor point, press the Ctrl key and click on the black square.**

   When the square disappears, the anchor point for the shape goes away. This effect drastically alters the shape.

Some shapes feature curve handles on their anchor points, as illustrated in Figure 11-6. When you click on the black square, you can not only move the square — you can also adjust each of the curve handles to reshape the path.

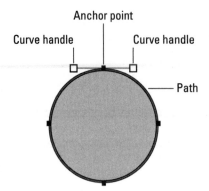

Anchor point

Curve handle   Curve handle

Path

FIGURE 11-6:
Editing a curve.

In Figure 11-6, the curve handles extend horizontally from the anchor point at an equal distance right and left. This distance and the handles' locations are what set the curve's path that creates the ellipse in the figure.

WARNING

>> If you remove too many points, you may "undefine" the shape; its size grows immeasurably small or large. If that happens, try to undo your edits, or delete the shape and start over.

>> The techniques for setting and moving anchor points are similar to the techniques for setting and moving the text-wrapping bounding box for the Tight and Through layout settings. Refer to Chapter 10.

TECHNICAL STUFF

>> The line creating a shape is known as a *path*. The handles that create a curved point on the path are known as *Bézier* curve handles. Adjusting the curve handles is a visual thing, but what you're effecting is far more technical and dictates how the path is drawn.

Shapes in Groups

When a single shape doesn't create the art you want, you can combine shapes. For example, in Figure 11-7, I created a crude figure by slapping down a few shapes; setting their locations, rotations, and colors; and arranging the shapes.

FIGURE 11-7:
Let's play ball!

Word features commands that let you work with shapes in groups. These commands help resolve interesting problems, such as which shapes appear in front of or behind others and how the shapes are aligned. Word also lets you group shapes so that when you waste time drawing a ballplayer, you can easily move him around in one piece.

Arranging shapes in front or behind

As far as layout is concerned, shapes can float behind text, mix with text, or float in front of text. Within those layers, however, the shapes stack up one atop the other.

The first shape you stick into a document is on the bottom of the stack. If you draw a new shape, that shape appears to be on top of the previous shape. The more shapes you draw, the deeper the stack. Some shapes can obscure others.

To arrange shapes, follow these steps:

1. **Click the shape you want to move forward or backward.**

   For example, a shape, such as the right arm shown in Figure 11-7, might be in front of the torso. If so, you select the right-arm shape.

2. **Click the Drawing Tools Format tab.**

3. **In the Arrange group, click the Send Backward or Bring Forward buttons.**

   The buttons rearrange the order of the selected image, moving it up or down the stack.

4. **Repeat Step 3 until the image is behind, or in front of, the other images.**

Both the Bring Forward and Send Backward buttons host menus. You can choose the Bring Forward or Send Backward commands to inch the selected object one layer at a time, or you can choose the Bring to Front or Send to Back command to

» If you set the shape's fill to the No Color setting, you can see through the shape, and stacking doesn't matter.

» The Bring Forward, Send Backward, Bring to Front, and Send to Back commands don't affect the object's layout. See Chapter 10 for details on layout options.

» Though you could set layout options to adjust an image's appearance, I recommend that you instead use the techniques presented in this section. The Behind Text and In Front of Text layout options are not designed for arranging or ordering shapes and other graphics objects.

Aligning shapes

Eyeball all you want and drag shapes around with the mouse, but when you really need objects to line up perfectly, you must surrender to Word. It features some basic alignment commands that can help you arrange shapes in a neat and clean manner.

The key to aligning objects is to use the Align button menu. It's found on the Drawing Tools Format tab, in the Arrange group, and it's illustrated in Figure 11-8. The commands can affect single objects or multiple objects you select.

To align a single object with the page margin or the edge of the page, follow these steps:

1. **Click to select the object.**

2. **Click the Drawing Tools Format tab.**

3. **In the Arrange group, click the Align button.**

4. **Choose Align to Margin.**

    The Align to Margin setting directs Word to use the page margins as a reference.

5. **Click the Align button and choose an alignment object.**

    For example, if you choose Align Center, the object is centered between the left and right page margins.

Alignment options

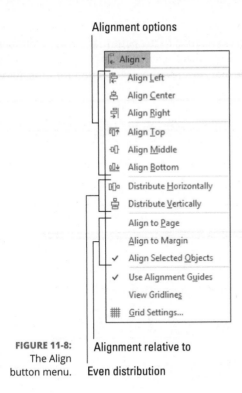

FIGURE 11-8:
The Align
button menu.

Alignment relative to

Even distribution

6. **If needed, repeat Step 5 to choose another alignment aspect.**

   For example, choose Align Top after choosing Align Center to place the object at the top center of the printed page.

To align two objects with each other, obey these directions:

1. **Click to select the first object.**

2. **Ctrl+click the second object.**

   Press and hold the Ctrl key as you click the mouse.

3. **Click the Drawing Tools Format tab.**

4. **In the Arrange group, click the Align button.**

5. **Choose Align Selected Objects.**

   This option directs Word to align the objects with each other, not relative to the page margins.

6. **Click the Align button and choose an alignment object to arrange the two shapes.**

   For example, if you choose Align Center, both shapes are centered (from left to right) relative to each other.

If you further want to align the objects relative to the page margins, I recommend that you next group the objects to keep their relative alignment and then align grouped objects relative to the page margins. See the next section for information

When more than two shapes are selected, you can distribute them in an even manner. That way, their position is evenly set, as shown in Figure 11-9.

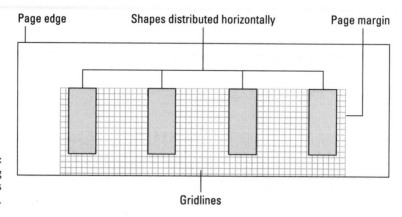

FIGURE 11-9:
Distributing
objects across
a page.

To distribute objects, heed these steps:

1. **Create and select multiple objects.**

   You must select at least three shapes to use the Distribute commands.

2. **Align the objects, as required.**

   For example, in Figure 11-9, I aligned all objects with the top page margin.

3. **Click the Align button and choose Distribute Horizontally or Distribute Vertically.**

   Either command separates the objects by an equal distance, either left to right or up and down. In Figure 11-9, the objects are distributed horizontally.

You can make further adjustments if the distribution isn't to your liking. In Figure 11-9, I displayed the gridlines to help further adjust objects. To view the gridlines, click the Align button and choose the View Gridlines command. Choose the command again to hide the grid.

REMEMBER

>> Object alignment is set relative to the page margins, to the page edge, or to the shapes themselves. Choose that relative option *first,* before you align one or more objects.

>> The Align to Page option sets objects relative to the page's edge. That means the objects may be outside the printable area and won't completely show up when the document is published.

>> To place an object in the upper left corner of a page, select the shape and choose these items (in order) from the Align menu: Align to Margin, Align Left, and then Align Top.

>> To place an object dead-center on a page, select the shape and choose from the Align menu: Align to Page, Align Center, and then Align Middle.

>> The Alignment Guides option (refer to Figure 11-8) is what sets those green lines you see when you drag a shape around on a page. They represent the page's margins, tops of paragraphs, as well as the centerline.

Grouping multiple shapes

After you have shapes arranged and aligned, my advice is to lock them together as a group. That way, they become a single object that you can move or manipulate as a single unit.

To set multiple objects into a group, follow these steps:

1. Click to select two or more objects.

Click the first object to select it. Then Ctrl+click additional objects to add them to the selection.

2. Click the Drawing Tools Format tab.

3. In the Arrange group, click the Group button.

The button is shown in the margin.

4. From the Group button menu, choose the Group command.

The selected objects from Step 1 are corralled into a single unit.

When you select any object in the group, you select the entire group. You can still select individual objects and adjust them: First click to select the group, and then click again to select and manipulate an individual shape.

To ungroup the objects, repeat the steps in this section, but in Step 4 choose the Ungroup command.

>> Once shapes are grouped, you can apply the same color and styles to all objects in the group.

>> Layout options chosen for a group affect all shapes within the group as a unit.

>> The group can be moved forward or back in the stack of shapes on a page. Refer to the earlier section "Arranging shapes in front or behind."

Using the drawing canvas

If you plan to create a group of shapes or some other interesting artwork, you can direct Word to insert a drawing canvas, a playground upon which you can create graphics. The canvas works similarly to setting objects in groups, except that you start out with a space in which shapes and other items can be placed.

To add a drawing canvas to your document, follow these steps:

1. **Click to set the insertion pointer at the spot where you want the drawing canvas to appear.**

The drawing canvas is inserted with the layout option In Line with Text. You can reset this option later, but the default setting means that the insertion pointer's location is relevant to the process.

2. **Click the Insert tab.**

3. **In the Illustrations group, click the Shapes button.**

4. **Choose the New Drawing Canvas command.**

The drawing canvas appears in the document at the insertion pointer's position.

A good next step would be to click the Layout Options button and choose the In Front of Text setting. That way, the drawing canvas and its objects appear like other shapes in the document.

>> The drawing canvas can be resized like any object.

>> Individual objects can be moved inside the drawing canvas without affecting the drawing canvas' location.

>> To move the drawing canvas, point the mouse at its edge. Then drag it to a new position.

>> You can apply a fill color, line styles, and other attributes to the drawing canvas.

>> The drawing canvas cannot be rotated. You can, however, group objects inside the canvas and rotate the group.

>> The alignment options covered in the earlier section "Aligning shapes" also apply to a drawing canvas.

>> The drawing canvas is a throwback to an earlier version of Word. For some reason, Microsoft changed the way Word 2000 worked with shapes and pictures, requiring you to first create a drawing canvas and then insert a graphic. I suppose that too many people were frustrated with that process, so in the next release of Word (2002), the drawing canvas was inserted automatically. Then, in the following release of Word (2003/XP), the drawing canvas was optional, as it is now in Word 2016.

Text and Graphics in Boxes

A shape can be a splash of color surrounded by a line. It can also serve as a frame. Inside that frame you can place text or an image. In fact, the text box is a common tool that Word uses to help you arrange text on a cover page or create a callout.

>> A *callout* is a fancy name for a text box in the middle of a page. It often quotes text found on the page, so another term for the callout is a *pull quote*.

>> See Chapter 14 for information on cover pages.

Inserting a text box

The simple way to pull in a text box is to yank a predesigned model from the Text Box gallery. Obey these directions:

1. **Go to the page in your document where you desire a text box.**

   You don't need to be specific; you can move the text box later.

2. **Click the Insert tab.**

3. **In the Text group, click the Text Box button.**

4. **Choose a text box from the gallery.**

   The text box is placed on the page you set in Step 1.

The text box is placed into the text layer on the document. Square wrapping is applied as the layout, so you can drag the box around to position it elsewhere on the page.

>> You can manipulate a text box in the same way you manipulate a shape: It can be resized, moved, rotated, and so on. Various sections throughout this chapter explain the details.

>> The preset text boxes are nicely designed and help you get a good start, but keep in mind that any middle school kid can do the same trick. If you want your documents to look better, I strongly recommend that you further

Converting a shape into a text box

When you want to get beyond the mundane, you can build your own text boxes. All you need to do is put a shape into a document and then convert the shape into a text box. You might have already gone through this process, without even knowing it.

To change a shape into a text box, follow these steps:

1. Insert a shape into the document.

Refer elsewhere in this chapter for details.

2. Right-click the shape and choose the Add Text command.

The cursor blinks in the middle of the shape, indicating that you can type. The text format is paragraph-centered and aligned with the middle of the shape.

3. Press Ctrl+L if you want the text left-aligned inside the shape.

4. On the Drawing Tools Format tab, in the Text group, click the Align Text button.

5. Choose the Top command to align the text with the top of the shape.

6. Type the text that goes into the box.

The text color may not match to your desires; the color that's selected depends on the document's theme. You can click the Home tab and set a new text color so that the results meet with your approval.

7. Click outside the box when you're done typing text.

If the Add Text command doesn't appear on the shortcut menu (refer to Step 2), the shape cannot accommodate text.

>> You can resize the box to better accommodate the text. Or, if the box needs to be a certain dimension, you can link the leftover text into another text box. See the next section.

>> Text inside a shape is formatted just like text anywhere else in Word. You can even use the Ruler to set indents and tabs, though that's a bit extreme for a text box.

TIP

>> When a shape features text, you must click the mouse on the shape's edge to select the shape or to drag it around. If you click inside the shape, you're clicking inside the text.

>> If you have trouble accessing the text in a shape, right-click inside the shape and choose the Edit Text command.

>> You cannot reverse the shape-to-text-box transformation, but you can delete all the text inside a shape.

Linking text boxes

When you have a text box overflowing with text, you can link that overflow into another text box. The effect is that two (or more) boxes contain the same flow of text. To link text between two shapes, obey these steps:

1. **Create both shapes and fill the first shape with text.**

Refer to the preceding section for information on converting a shape into text.

Not every shape accepts the text conversion.

REMEMBER

2. **Click to select the first shape, the one that contains the overflow text.**

3. **Click the Drawing Tools Format tab.**

4. **In the Text group, click the Create Link button.**

The mouse pointer changes to something that looks like a bucket spilling out letters, as shown in the margin.

5. **Click on the second shape.**

Text flows from the first shape into the second shape.

You can repeat these steps to make overflow text from the second shape flow into a third shape.

>> The second shape must be configured as a text box before you can flow text into the shape. Refer to the preceding section.

>> If you've already flowed text into a shape but want to use another shape instead, change the shape. Refer to the earlier section "Editing a shape."

>> The surefire way to screw up text links is to delete a shape. When you do, you essentially need to start over again: Delete all linked shapes.

» To unlink shapes, click on the original (or previous) shape and click the Break Link button. The Break Link button replaces the Create Link button in the Text group on the Drawing Tools Format tab. After you click the button, the text no

Adding a picture to a shape

Setting a picture into a shape is more of a background fill operation, but a lot of Word users take advantage of this feature from the opposite perspective: Instead of using the picture as the shape's "fill color," you're using the shape to create a special frame for the picture.

To use a shape as a picture frame, follow these steps:

1. **Add a shape to your document.**

   It must be a shape suitable for framing a picture.

2. **Click to select the shape.**

3. **Click the Drawing Tools Format tab.**

4. **In the Shape Styles group, click the Shape Fill button.**

5. **Choose the Picture command.**

   The Insert Pictures dialog box appears.

6. **Choose From a File.**

   You can also choose a Bing image search or search for files directly on your OneDrive cloud storage.

7. **Use the Insert Picture dialog box to hunt down an image.**

8. **Click to select the image, and then click the Insert button.**

   The image is placed in the shape. An example is shown in Figure 11-10.

You can modify the shape — for example, to choose a new border.

To adjust the picture, right-click inside the shape and choose the Format Shape command. The Format Picture pane appears, illustrated in Figure 11-11. Click the Picture icon heading, and use the controls in the Format Picture pane to further adjust the image.

FIGURE 11-10:
A picture
in a shape.

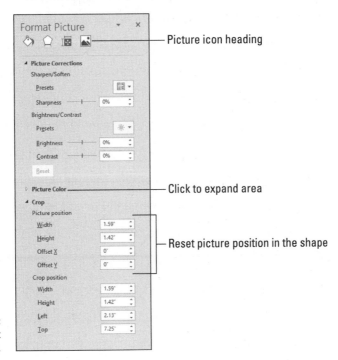

Picture icon heading

Click to expand area

Reset picture position in the shape

FIGURE 11-11:
The Format
Picture pane.

For example, to help adjust the image within the shape, manipulate the Picture Position controls.

REMEMBER

» See Chapter 12 for information on cropping an image inside a shape.

» Just as not every shape can contain text (see "Converting a shape into a text box"), not every shape can hold a picture as its fill "color."

Chapter 12

Pictures and Illustrations

Word makes it cinchy to stick a picture, an illustration, or another type of graphic into your document. It's almost *too* easy. Because of the simplicity, Microsoft added an armada of picture-editing tools, commands, features, and options. So, sticking a photo of Uncle Earl into your essay on the "olden says" isn't just a three-click operation. No, you're faced with dozens of options and diversions that can transform a rudimentary operation into a complex ordeal that you might eventually enjoy more than actually writing text.

>> All of Word's layout options apply to images you insert into your document. Refer to Chapter 10 for details.

>> Many of the arrangement and order commands for drawing objects (shapes) also apply to pictures in a document. See Chapter 11.

>> If you get serious about mixing text and pictures, I recommend obtaining a desktop publishing (DTP) program. That software is designed specifically to manage text and graphics across large documents. Word can do the job in a

One Thousand Words

Nothing brings up the level of sophistication in a document like a well-placed photograph, piece of art, or scribble that you just made in the Paint program while you were yabbering on the phone. As long as the image complements your text, add it.

>> The more pictures you add to a document, the more sluggish Word can become. This effect is most notable on slower PCs.

>> Pictures don't show up in Draft view. That's not an issue, however, because the act of inserting a picture switches the document view from Draft to Print Layout.

Adding an image

To shove a picture into your document, follow these steps:

1. **Set the insertion pointer to the spot where you want the image to appear.**

   Pictures are inserted with the In Line with Text layout option selected. You can change this option, as described in Chapter 10.

2. **Click the Insert tab.**

3. **In the Illustrations group, click the Pictures button.**

   The Insert Picture dialog box appears. It works like an Open dialog box, though it's configured to show only pictures and images you can stick into a Word document.

4. **Work the dialog box to locate the image file.**

   Use the controls to navigate to the proper folder on your PC's storage system where the image is buried.

5. **Select the image and click the Insert button.**

   The image appears in the document's text, at the spot where you set the insertion pointer in Step 1.

After the image sits in your document, you might want to adjust it and perhaps apply formatting or a figure caption. To assist you, the Picture Tools Format toolbar appears. Other sections in this chapter describe how to use the commands on that toolbar.

>> You can drag the image around in the text, but if you want to position it precisely, you need to reset the layout options. Refer to Chapter 10 for details. Specifically, you'll want either the Square or Tight setting. You can also read in that chapter how you can line up the image with the page margins.

>> Word reads most common graphics file formats. These include the PNG, JPEG, and GIF file formats popular on the Internet, as well as Windows BMP files and TIF files used by professionals.

>> The Picture Tools Format toolbar appears only when a picture is selected.

>> A picture can be applied to the page background or watermark. See Chapter 14 for information.

Copying and pasting an image

One of the easiest ways to get an image into a document is to copy and paste. It's such a simple operation that people forget this trick. Heed these kindergarten steps:

1. **From any other program, select and copy an image.**

   Click to select an image. On a web page, you can right-click and choose the Copy Image (or similar) command.

2. **In Word, set the insertion pointer to the location where you want the image pasted.**

3. **Press Ctrl+V.**

   The image appears in the document.

The only time this trick doesn't work is when the image is of an incompatible format. For example, you're using a specific graphics program or an older piece of software where you can copy the image but Word won't let you paste.

>> If you don't choose the command to copy an image from a web page, you end up copying a link to the image.

>> It's also possible to drag an image from a program window into the Word document. This method may not be completely successful due to overlapping windows and incompatible file formats.

Adding an image from the web

Thanks to image search, the web is often the first place people go to find images ~~for a document. Word is able to comply. Follow these steps:~~

1. **Position the insertion pointer to the location where you want the image to appear.**

   You can move the image elsewhere, primarily by resetting its layout options, as covered in Chapter 10.

2. **Click the Insert tab.**

3. **In the Illustrations group, click the Online Pictures button.**

   The Insert Pictures dialog box lists several online sources for finding images. The only one you want to see, Google Image Search, isn't there.

4. **Click in the search box by Bing Image Search, type an image description, and press Enter.**

   For example, type **waterfalls** to find an image of a waterfall. The dialog box changes to show search results from the Internet.

5. **Select an image and click the Insert button to add it to your document.**

   The image is downloaded, placed into the document, and selected. At this point, you can modify the image, change its layout, and do other thrilling things, as described throughout this chapter.

If the results (after Step 4) don't meet your needs, use the Search box to refine your search text. Or click the Cancel button.

>> At present, you cannot add Google Image Search to the list of options presented in the Insert Pictures dialog box. However:

>> You can use any search engine to locate an image, save that image to your PC, and then insert the image per the directions in the earlier section "Adding an image."

WARNING

>> Just because you find an image on the Internet doesn't mean that you have the right to use it. The image must be flagged as public domain, free to use, "copyleft," or otherwise specifically made available for anyone to use. Always assume that *all* Internet images are copyrighted.

>> The copyright laws do allow what's called *fair use* for educational, research, and other purposes. This exception doesn't grant you immunity. If you are preparing a document for any professional purposes, for profit, for marketing, or to promote services, then standard copyright law applies.

>> The Bing Image Search results are set to show Creative Commons copyrighted material. You can use the information, subject to certain restrictions. For example, your use requires that you cite the author's name. You are responsible for determining which Creative Commons rights are attached to an image and for respecting those rights.

Replacing an image

If you have an image positioned, formatted, and captioned but find a better image later, please don't start over! You can swap out the image while retaining its location and layout. Follow these thrilling steps:

1. **Select the image.**
2. **Click the Picture Tools Format tab.**

3. **In the Adjust group, click the Change Picture button.**
4. **Choose a source from the Insert Pictures dialog box, such as From a File.**

   At this point, the picture is selected and inserted into the document as described in the earlier section "Adding an image."

Unlike adding a new image, the picture you choose takes on the existing image's size and location in the document. If any image effects or styles were added to the original image, they are not applied to the replacement.

Removing a picture

To pull a picture from your document, heed these short steps:

1. **Click to select the image.**
2. **Press the Delete key.**

   The image is gone.

If you made a mistake, gasp audibly, and then press Ctrl+Z to undo.

Image Adjustment

Thanks to a selection of interesting and useful tools, Word pretends to be somewhat of a graphics manipulation program. You can add some fine-tuning to an image, apply special effects, and perform basic operations such as cropping the image, resizing, and rotating. The goal is to make the image look good in your document so that people don't notice your horrible writing.

offers tools necessary to help you finish the job.

>> Information on picture resizing and rotating is found in Chapter 11. The information there applies to both pictures and shapes.

>> The commands in this section affect an image directly. See the later section "Picture Frame Formatting" for information on how to control the appearance of an image's frame in a document.

Cropping an image

Cropping isn't the same thing as resizing. When you resize an image, you change its dimensions, but not its content. Cropping is like taking a pair of scissors to an image and slicing away a chunk. Follow these steps to crop an image:

1. **Click to select the image with an unwanted chunk.**

Refer to Figure 12-1 for an example.

2. **Click the Picture Tools Format tab.**

3. **In the Size group, click the Crop button.**

The button hosts a menu, so if you click the menu, choose Crop ⇨ Crop. The image changes to grow cropping bars, as illustrated in Figure 12-1.

4. **Adjust the cropping bars to slice out one or more parts of the image.**

Drag the bars inward to slice out a portion of the image. As you drag, the portion to be removed is shaded in dark gray.

5. **Press the Enter key to lock in the changes.**

The image is cropped, which affects its overall size.

That's the basic crop operation, but the Crop command button features additional commands designed to confound and confuse you. Here's the rundown:

Crop to Shape: Choose a shape from the submenu to instantly crop the image to that given shape. For example, to place the picture into an oval, choose the Oval shape from the Crop to Shape submenu.

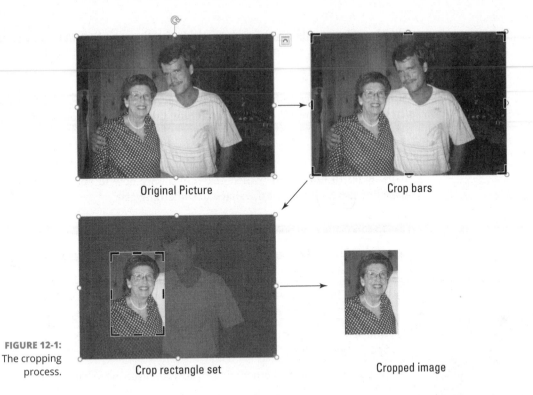

Original Picture

Crop bars

Crop rectangle set

Cropped image

FIGURE 12-1:
The cropping
process.

Aspect Ratio: Select an aspect ratio from the submenu to resize and crop the image to match the horizontal-to-vertical ratio. Keep in mind that the ratios are organized in portrait and landscape orientations. Press Enter after choosing the ratio to complete the crop.

The next two Crop menu items affect only pictures placed in shapes. Figure 12-2 shows some examples.

FIGURE 12-2:
Cropping an
image in a shape.

Original picture inside a shape

Fill crop

Fit crop

Fill: The Fill crop adjusts the picture inside the shape so that most of the image fills the shape. This setting crops away more of the image than the Fit option, as shown in Figure 12-2.

Fit: This setting tries to fit the entire picture into the shape, even if that means part of the shape doesn't contain the picture. Choose the Fit crop when you want to see more of the image inside the shape.

When the Fill and Fit crops don't meet with your desires, consider changing the shape. Refer to Chapter 11, which covers not only how to stick a picture into a shape but also how to reset the shape to something else.

>> To cancel the crop operation, press the Esc key.

>> After cropping is complete, press Ctrl+Z to undo. You may have to press Ctrl+Z a few times to back out of the entire operation.

>> The Crop to Shape command is really just a handy shortcut for inserting a shape and adding a picture as the background. Refer to Chapter 11.

>> One option to account for the Fit crop is to remove the picture's background. See the next section.

>> It's quicker to grab the corner cropping tools to resize in two directions at once.

TIP

Removing the background

If you don't want a background for the picture — even a plain white background — then the best way to address the issue is to use an image editing program: Remove the background and save the image with the background set to Transparent. The TIFF, PNG, and GIF file formats support this feature.

When it's not possible to create an image with a transparent background, you can use the Remove Background tool in Word in an attempt to clean up a picture's background image. Obey these completely safe steps:

1. Click to select the picture.

It should have a plain, or otherwise uniform, background.

2. Click the Picture Tools Format tab.

3. In the Adjust group, click the Remove Background button.

Word examines the image. It sets pink highlights to areas that it believes to be the background. If you're good with Word's choices, skip to Step 6.

4. **Adjust the bounding box to help Word determine what portion of the image to keep.**

   The bounding box works like the Crop command, but in this instance you're corralling off the portion of the image that's not in the background. After moving the handles, Word adjusts the pink highlight. If you're pleased, skip to Step 6.

5. **Use the Mark Areas to Remove button to draw out portions of the background.**

   Drag the mouse over a portion of the image that should be in the background.

   If you get to this point, you might have exceeded Word's capabilities to remove the background.

6. **Click the Keep Changes button.**

   Word removes the background, making that portion of the image transparent.

Word replaces the picture background with a transparent layer. At this point, you might want to crop the image and adjust the layout to account for the new shape.

Making corrections

For some quick adjustments to an image, use the Make Corrections command. It adjusts the brightness, contrast, and focus on pictures inserted into a document. Obey these directions:

1. **Click to select the picture.**

2. **Click the Picture Tools Format tab.**

3. 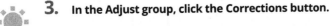 **In the Adjust group, click the Corrections button.**

   The Corrections button menu shows a grid of image thumbnails and displays how the picture (chosen in Step 1) is affected by the various focus, brightness, and contrast settings, similar to what's shown in Figure 12-3.

4. **Choose a thumbnail from the menu.**

   The effect is applied to the image.

You may need to repeat these steps a few times to get both sharpness and brightness/contrast settings correct. If not, in Step 4, choose the command Picture Correction Options. You see the Format Picture pane with specific controls presented to adjust the sharpen/soften settings, brightness, and contrast.

If somewhere down the road you don't like the changes you've made and you want to restore the image, see the later section "Restoring an image (removing effects)."

Adjusting the image's color

You may not know it, but many photographers and image editors subtly adjust the colors presented in an image. They want to bring out the best colors and highlight certain parts of the image. They claim that it's to make the picture look its best, but it's all just lies! You can practice the same type of mendacity for photos in Word.

To adjust color in a picture, heed these devious directions:

1. **Click to select the picture.**

2. **Click the Picture Tools Format tab.**

3. **In the Adjust group, click the Color button.**

   A menu of color choices appears as thumbnails, detailing how each option affects the selected image.

4. **Choose a thumbnail from the Color gallery to apply that color effect to the image.**

As an example, you need to make a color image monochrome. If so, select the Grayscale effect. It's located in the Recolor area — first row, second column.

If you point the mouse at one of the Color gallery's thumbnails, you see a preview of the effect on the image in your document. It may take a moment for that effect to preview, so wait for it. The color isn't set until you click the mouse.

To remove any color effects, see the later section "Restoring an image (removing effects)."

Adding artistic effects

If you want to get all fancy with your images, you can add some cheesy artistic effects. No, these aren't special effects, like you'd see in a movie. They're image effects, and they're cheesy because people use them not to add anything but because it's fun to apply. Follow these fun steps:

1. **Click to select the picture.**

The nifty thing about the cheesy artistic effects is that the worse the picture, the more effective the effects. So don't be shy with that cheese.

2. **Click the Picture Tools Format tab.**

3. **In the Adjust group, click the Artistic Effects button.**

Behold a palette of thumbnails detailing how the various effects apply to the selected image.

4. **Click to select a thumbnail and apply that effect to the image.**

The effects are pretty static; they can't be adjusted. The command at the bottom of the menu, Artistic Effects Options, doesn't really offer any more control over the effects as they're presented.

It's easy to confuse Artistic Effects with Picture Effects. The key difference is that Picture Effects apply more to the frame around the image than to the image itself. See the later section "Applying a frame effect."

Restoring an image (removing effects)

The Undo command, Ctrl+Z, is your first recourse when you mess up image adjustment. After a while, however, whacking Ctrl+Z repeatedly is counterproductive. A better solution is to reset the image, which converts it back to its original state, before you applied all the corrections and effects.

To peel away image modifications, heed these steps:

1. **Select the picture.**

~~Click.~~

2. **Click the Picture Tools Format tab and, in the Adjust group, click the Remove Effects button.**

   The picture is restored.

The Remove Effects button is a menu. From the menu, you can choose Reset Picture, but also the command Reset Picture & Size. When you choose that option, any resizing you've done to the image — including cropping — is removed as well.

Picture Frame Formatting

A picture in your document need not sit near your text with only a buffer of empty space for comfort. No, you can apply to the image a frame. That's my term for it. What Word calls the frame falls under the category of Picture Styles. These are different effects than those covered in the earlier section "Image Adjustment." These effects apply to the picture and the space around it.

Selecting a picture style

The quickest way to frame a picture is to choose a preset style from the Picture Styles gallery. Heed these steps:

1. **Click to select a picture.**

2. **Click the Picture Tools Format tab.**

3. **In the Picture Styles group, choose a preset picture style from the gallery.**

   Or you can click the More button, illustrated in Figure 12-4, to display a whole slew of styles.

4. **Choose a picture style from the gallery.**

   If you point the mouse at the style, you see a preview of how it affects the image inside the document. Click the style to apply it to the picture.

Though this method is quick, it's also what most other people use when they desire to frame or modify a picture. You can mix up the effects, as covered in the next two sections. That should help make your pictures look unique.

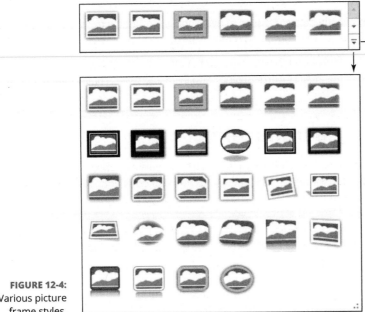

———— More button

FIGURE 12-4:
Various picture
frame styles.

Adding a border

The simplest form of picture frame is a border or line applied around the picture. You can apply a specific color, weight (thickness), and style to the line in whatever manner complements the image. Follow these steps:

1. **Select the image.**

2. **Click the Picture Tools Format tab.**

3. **In the Picture Styles group, click the Picture Border button.**

   The Picture Border menu lists various colors, plus submenus to adjust the border thickness and line style.

4. **Choose a color from the palette presented.**

   The colors are based on the document theme, and they will change if you select a new document theme. To choose a specific color, pluck one from the Standard Colors list or choose More Outline Colors.

If you need to set the line thickness or create a dashed line, repeat these steps but choose Weight and Dashes from the menu.

To exercise full control over the border, choose Weight ⇨ More Lines to view the Format Picture pane. The settings in the Line area offer more control over the line color, type, style, corners, and joins.

>> To remove the border from an image, choose No Outline from the Picture Border menu. This command removes the border color, thickness, and style.

>> Border colors are related to the document theme. If the document theme is changed, the image's border colors, and even line styles, could change as well.

Applying a frame effect

To add a complex frame effect to your picture, you can choose one of the preset borders from the Picture Styles gallery, or you can craft your own, custom border. To do so, use the various items on the Picture Effects menu.

The Picture Effects button is found on the Picture Tools Format tab, in the Picture Styles group. Its menu is divided into multiple categories, each of which features a submenu of different designs.

To add a frame effect, obey these directions:

1. **Click to select the image.**

2. **Click the Picture Tools Format tab.**

 3. **In the Picture Styles group, click the Picture Effects button.**

4. **Choose a category, and then choose an effect.**

The effect is applied to the picture.

As with other picture manipulation tools, you can point the mouse at an effect to preview what it does to the image in your document. You can also double up on effects — add perhaps soft edges as well as a reflection.

To remove all effects, use the Picture Reset button, as described in the earlier section "Restoring an image (removing effects)."

Caption That Picture

Not all pictures in a document need to have captions. An initial image of a map of Africa may help introduce the reader to your subject (assuming the subject is Africa). If you need to reference the picture, however, it helps to have a caption. That way, you can write *See Figure 1* and the reader knows where to look.

Here's the secret: A caption is really just a text box. It's set at the same width as the picture (or other object). In Figure 12-5, you see such a text box set below a picture. To create such a caption, you first insert the picture and then add the text box and format it.

Picture   Objects grouped

Jonah at the Independence Day Parade, 2013

FIGURE 12-5:
A caption below
a picture. Text box

Follow these steps to place a text box below (or above) a picture in your document:

1. **Click to select the text box.**

   After you select it, you can see the picture's bounding box, which helps you draw the text box.

2. **Click the Insert tab.**

3. **In the Text group, click the Text Box button and choose the Draw Text Box command.**

   This step saves time over drawing a shape and converting it to a text box. It also formats the text box to a black-and-white color scheme.

4. **Drag the mouse below the selected picture to set the location and size of the text box.**

5. **Type and format the figure caption inside the text box.**

   All text and formatting commands apply in a text box. In Figure 12-5, I pressed Ctrl+E to apply center paragraph alignment and Ctrl+B to create boldface text.

6. Click the Drawing Tools Format tab.

7. In the Shape Styles area, click the Shape Outline button and choose No Outline from the menu.

This step removes the outline around the text box. If you want to keep the outline, skip this step. Likewise, if you want to shade the text box or apply other effects (which I don't recommend), use the tools in the Shape Styles group. Refer to Chapter 11 for specifics.

8. Set the text box layout to match the picture layout.

In both cases, I recommend something other than In Line with Text. For example, click on the picture and click the Layout Options button to view the layout. Then click on the text box, click its Layout Options button, and choose the same option, such as Square or Tight.

9. Click to select the picture, and then Ctrl+click to select the image.

Both items are now a unit.

10. Click the Drawing Tools Format tab.

11. In the Arrange group, click the Align button and choose Align Center.

12. In the Arrange group, click the Group button and choose the Group command.

The picture and its caption (text box) are now aligned and grouped into a single unit.

Now that both the picture and caption are lined up and grouped and the proper layout applied, you can move them around in your text and they stay together. Thanks to the layout option, text flows around both items.

>> Captions also explain what's going on in the image, name people who are pictured, and describe other details that are helpful to the reader.

>> Word has a caption-tracking reference feature, which inserts captions below pictures, tables, and other items in the text. This feature helps you build a list of figures in a document. See Chapter 21 for details on how Word's Insert Caption command works.

>> Beyond pictures, you can use the techniques in this section to add a caption to a table or any of a number of objects you can stick into a document.

>> Refer to Chapter 10 for layout options.

>> Refer to Chapter 11 for information on converting shapes to a text box.

Chapter 13

Insert Objects Weird and Amazing

What are the limits of the things that Word can stick into a document? Text is understandable. Pictures are fun and interesting, and Word does a fair job of managing their layout and effects. Beyond those items, Word lets a document host various other objects. These include specific items that solve particular puzzles, but also just weird stuff, like the entire Excel program.

Objects Beyond Mere Mortal Text

If Word were a meal, every day would be a Thanksgiving feast. That variety doesn't mean you need to stuff yourself; having the basics is good enough for most people. I mean, just because they have both the pink stuff and the green stuff doesn't mean that you need to consume both. Still, a document does not live by text alone. For some specific document duties, Word hosts ample tools to help make the job easier.

Having fun with WordArt

I think WordArt was the first graphical toy to be included in Word. It was actually

WordArt! And like anything people love, they overused it, so today WordArt is considered rather trite.

To stick WordArt into your document, obey these tiresome steps:

1. **Click the Insert tab.**

2. **In the Text group, click the WordArt button.**

   A menu appears, listing various WordArt styles.

3. **Choose a style from the list.**

   A WordArt object appears in the document. It's formatted with the layout option In Front of Text. The Drawing Tools Format tab appears, with the WordArt Styles group visible.

4. **Type the WordArt text into the box.**

   WordArt is commonly used for headings or special titles. It's more of a graphical element than a text element.

5. **Make further adjustments to the WordArt object.**

   You can choose another style from the WordArt Style gallery, adjust the color fill, line style, and effects, and position the WordArt object on the page.

WordArt can be edited like any text in a text box: Click the WordArt object and edit the text. The fancy formatting may vanish while you edit, but it returns when you're done.

Curiously enough, Word's Find command locates WordArt text. Even so, I don't recommend using WordArt as a title or section heading.

Adding SmartArt

If you're in the process of organizing multiple shapes to express something in your document, such as a flowchart, take a look at the SmartArt feature instead.

SmartArt is a collection of multiple shapes, arranged in common and useful ways. Adorning some of the shapes are text boxes, which further helps save time over creating all that nonsense yourself.

To slap SmartArt into a document, follow these slappy steps:

1. **Click the Insert tab.**

2. **In the Illustrations group, click the Smart Art button.**

   The Choose a SmartArt Graphic dialog box appears. It lists categories on the left, examples in the middle, and descriptions on the right, as illustrated in Figure 13-1.

SmartArt categories   SmartArt examples   Description

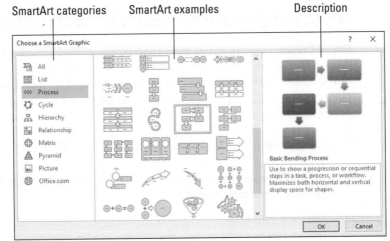

3. **Choose a category.**

   For example, choose Process to create a type of flowchart.

4. **Select a SmartArt design from the center portion of the dialog box.**

5. **Click OK.**

   The selected SmartArt is placed into your document.

6. **Continue working on the SmartArt object.**

Nothing is perfect. Your next task is, at minimum, to add text to the SmartArt. Any text boxes contain placeholder text, which you can replace with your own text, including any formatting.

The SmartArt object itself is a drawing canvas, inside of which are placed shapes. You can move the shapes around within the canvas. You can even change the shapes' coloring and styles.

To complete the SmartArt operation, click on the drawing canvas border to select the entire object. At that point, you can apply layout settings so that text wraps around the artwork or floats in front of the text.

>> Refer to Chapter 11 for details on the various shapes that comprise the SmartArt object. You can also read there about the drawing canvas.

>> Layout options are covered in Chapter 10.

Inserting a whole 'nuther Word document

One of the less obvious things you can stick into a Word document is another Word document. Rather than open both documents and copy-and-paste, you can quickly shove text (and formatting and everything else) from one document into your current document. This may save you time, and it's one method of boiler-plating common text.

To insert text from one document into another, follow these steps:

1. **Set the insertion pointer at the location where you want the other document's text to appear.**

2. **Click the Insert tab.**

3. **In the Text group, click the Object button.**

4. **Choose Text From File.**

   The command says *text,* but the entire contents of the document are placed inside the current document. Those contents include all formatting and any graphics.

5. **Use the Insert File dialog box to hunt down the Word document you want to insert.**

6. **Click to select the document icon, and then click the Insert button.**

   The document appears at the insertion pointer's location (refer to Step 1), complete with formatting, styles, and any graphics or other objects.

If your desire is to collect several documents to create a single document, such as a novel or long report, consider using Word's Master Document feature instead. See Chapter 20.

Summing up equations

Word's Symbol command hosts a variety of mathematical operators. You can employ the Math AutoCorrect feature to let you type complex equations. But when you really want to nerd out, you can don your set of Vulcan ears and use the Insert Equation function.

Don't fret when you don't know any good equations. Word supplies a whole gallery to choose from. Obey these logical steps:

1. **Click the Insert tab.**

2. **In the Symbols group, click the triangle by the Equation command to display the Equations gallery.**

3. **Choose a preset equation from the list.**

   There! You're smarter already.

When the equation materializes in your document, similar to what's shown in Figure 13-2, you see the Equation Tools Design tab. Yes, the tab looks like a final in a physics class you wandered into drunk. My guess is that if you know about equations, you'll figure out what's up.

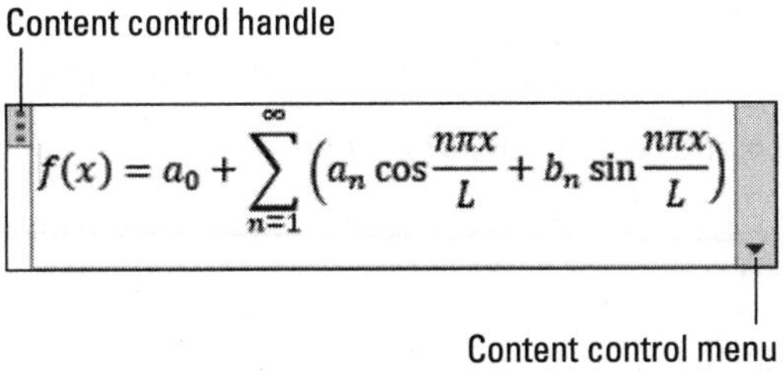

Content control handle

$$f(x) = a_0 + \sum_{n=1}^{\infty} \left(a_n \cos \frac{n\pi x}{L} + b_n \sin \frac{n\pi x}{L} \right)$$

FIGURE 13-2:
An equation content control.

Content control menu

Seriously, the Equation Tools Design tab lets you pluck out equation placeholders to build a larger sequence of characters that somehow holds significance among the propeller-heads.

>> Equations fit into a content control, which is like a tiny container for special text in a document. See Chapter 27 for information on content controls.

>> The Equation keyboard shortcut is Alt+=. That command sticks an equation content control into your document, selects its text, and displays the Equation Tools Design tab so that you can start solving problems.

>> To convert the content control to document text, click its menu button and choose the command Change to Inline.

>> I believe that the equation shown in Figure 13-2 transmutes lead into gold.

Putting a video in your document

I really don't want to write about this topic, because it's not really about writing text and video mixed. Still, inserting a video into a document is something Word is capable of doing. I'm just reluctantly capable of writing about it.

If you really want to see what a video looks like in a document, follow these steps:

1. **Click to place the insertion pointer at the spot where you want the video to appear.**

2. **Click the Insert tab.**

3. **In the Media group, click the Online Video button.**

    The Insert Video dialog box appears.

4. **Click in the search box by a video source, such as YouTube.**

5. **Type search words to locate your video.**

    If you know the title, type the title.

    After a moment, a range of videos appears in the Insert Video dialog box.

6. **Select a video and click the Insert button.**

    The video's visage is inserted as an object into your document at the insertion pointer's location.

To play the video, click it. The Word document goes dim, and then an overlay on the window plays the video.

>> The object's original layout is In Line with Text. You can change this layout option, as described in Chapter 10. You can also resize the video and drag it around. You can add a frame to it, or use the tools on the Picture Tools Format tab to adjust the video; refer to Chapter 12.

>> No, the video doesn't print. All you see is a static image on paper.

>> In secret, the video is a hyperlink embedded in the document. Don't tell anyone! See Chapter 30 for details on hyperlinks.

TECHNICAL STUFF

Where Word Meets Excel

Sometimes a table isn't good enough. Especially if you've already done the work in Excel, why bother re-creating your efforts in Word? Or perhaps you need Excel's power within a table inside Word. All these things are possible, providing you know the forbidden secrets of how Word and Excel mingle.

Pasting part of an Excel worksheet into a document

The most obvious way to get data from Excel into your Word document is to copy-and-paste the table. This process involves some legerdemain with regard to showing two program windows on the screen at once. Carefully heed these directions:

1. **Open both Excel and Word.**

2. **Create the document and work on the spreadsheet.**

Perform whatever magic you need in both programs to get ready to copy from one to the other.

If possible, keep the windows overlapping to where you can access both easily, as illustrated in Figure 13-3.

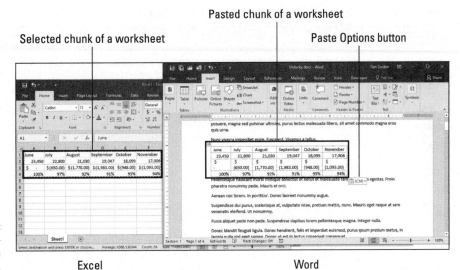

Pasted chunk of a worksheet

Selected chunk of a worksheet

Paste Options button

FIGURE 13-3: A copy-and-paste from Excel to Word.

Excel

Word

3. **Select the cells you want to copy in Excel.**

Drag the mouse over the cells to select them.

4. **Press Ctrl+C to copy.**

5. **Switch to the Word window.**

6. **Position the insertion pointer where you want the table to be pasted.**

For now, consider that the copied portion of the worksheet becomes a table in Word.

7. **Press Ctrl+V to paste.**

The cells appear as a table inside your document.

As with any item you paste, a Paste Options button appears in Word, as shown in Figure 13-3. This button has a higher level of importance when pasting between Excel and Word than it does otherwise. The choice you make from the Paste Options button menu must be done carefully.

To keep the Excel data as a table, click the Paste Options button and choose either the option Keep Source Formatting (K) or Use Destination Styles (S). The difference between the two is whether the table contains Excel's styles (K) or Word's styles (S).

The other choices available on the Paste Options menu are illustrated in Table 13-1.

TABLE 13-1   ## Excel Worksheet Pasting Options

Icon	Shortcut	Command	Description
	K	Keep Source Formatting	A table is pasted using Excel's text format.
	S	Use Destination Styles	A table is pasted using Word's text format.
	F	Link & Keep Source Formatting	A linked table is inserted using Excel's text format.
	L	Link & Use Destination Styles	A linked table is inserted using Word's text format.
	U	Picture	A graphical image is created of the Excel data and is pasted into the document as a picture.
	T	Keep Text Only	The cell's data is pasted in as tab-separated text.

If you just want the text from the worksheet, tap Ctrl and then the T key to choose the Keep Text Only option. The text is pasted in with each cell separated by tab characters.

The Picture option takes the worksheet chunk and pastes it in as a static image. As with any picture in a Word document, you can flow text around the object, resize it, and so on. The picture, however, doesn't update if you change the worksheet in Excel.

The Link options, which parallel the style/formatting paste options, are covered in the next section.

>> When you choose the paste options described in this section, the table in Word contains only plain text, not formulas. The formulas are retained in the Excel worksheet.

>> If you want the table to update in Word when you work in Excel, you need a linked worksheet. See the next section.

Copying and linking a worksheet

The standard copy-and-paste operation is static. Once you paste your Excel worksheet, it becomes a table in Word — or it's plain text or a graphic. When you next update your worksheet, you need to repeat the operation: copy and paste, as described in the preceding section. That is, unless you paste and link.

To paste and link, choose one of the two linking options from the Paste Options menu, shown in Figure 13-4: Link & Keep Source Formatting or Link & Use Destination styles. Both options paste a link to the worksheet, which can keep the data fresh. The difference lies in which styles are used — Excel's or Word's, respectively.

Paste and link commands

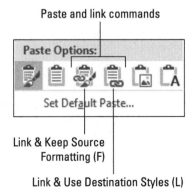

FIGURE 13-4:
Paste link choices on the Paste Options menu.

Link & Keep Source Formatting (F)

Link & Use Destination Styles (L)

To paste and link, follow these directions:

1. Create the spreadsheet in Excel and the document in Word.

Save both documents before you proceed. If you don't save the worksheet, the linking operation might not be successful.

2. Select from the spreadsheet the cells that you want to copy and link.

3. Press Ctrl+C.

4. Switch to the Word window.

If you can see the window, click on it. You can also click on the Word document's button on the taskbar or use the Alt+Tab keyboard shortcut to switch to the proper window.

5. Click to position the insertion pointer at the location in the document's text where you want the Excel data to be pasted.

When you link the data from Excel, it appears in Word as a table. My advice is to place the table in a paragraph by itself — on a blank line.

6. Press Ctrl+V to paste.

7. Tap the Ctrl key and press the L key.

Pressing the L key keeps Word's styles. You can also press the F key to keep the Excel styles. Either key pastes the table as a link to the Excel worksheet.

The rows and columns of cells from the worksheet appear as a table in your document. The data, however, is linked to Excel, so the table's text looks more like a field than plain text. For example, when you click in the table, the entire table becomes highlighted, just like a field.

>> The best part is that if you change the Excel worksheet, those updates are reflected in Word. To refresh the pasted table, right-click its text and choose the Update Link command. The table is refreshed to reflect the current Excel data.

>> When both Excel and Word are open at the same time, with the linked data appearing in both program windows, you don't need to click the Update Link button. As you work in Excel, any changes are instantly reflected in Word.

>> If you need to edit the data, don't bother opening Excel. Instead, right-click in the table and choose the command Linked Worksheet Object ⇨ Edit Link. Excel opens, displays the worksheet, and lets you modify the data.

>> See Chapter 24 for information on fields.

>> The Alt+Tab keyboard shortcut displays a list of open windows. Hold the Alt key down while you tap the Tab key to cycle through the windows. This shortcut is known as the "cool switch."

Opening an Excel worksheet inside of Word

One of the quirkiest things you can do in Word is open an Excel object inside a document. The effect is that you transform Word into Excel without opening Excel directly. This operation has boggled the minds of Word users for centuries.

To transmogrify Word into Excel — a procedure that avoids the need to open Excel and copy-and-paste — continue with these meticulous steps:

1. Save your Word document.

Saving often is a proper thing to do, especially when you're superstitious.

2. Place the insertion pointer on a blank line.

The embedded Excel object works like a table in Word. Tables are best set on a line by themselves.

3. Click the Insert tab.

4. In the Text group, click the Object button and choose Object.

The Object dialog box appears. The items listed in the dialog box use the Object Linking and Embedding (OLE) feature introduced in Office 95. Each one can be inserted "live" into your Word document.

5. Select Microsoft Excel Worksheet.

6. Click OK.

A snippet of an Excel worksheet roosts in Word, as illustrated in Figure 13-5. The Excel Ribbon replaces Word's Ribbon. At this point, you're effectively using Excel within Word.

7. Create the worksheet.

Use Excel to place fun and interesting items into the worksheet's cells, manipulating them in a manner that involves all the thrills and danger of whatever it is that spreadsheets do best. I wouldn't know; I'm a writer.

You don't need to save the worksheet. In fact, when you're done doing whatever in Excel-in-Word, click the mouse outside of the worksheet's heavily armed border. At that point, Word recovers, and you can continue to work on your document.

The Excel object resembles a table in Word. It's not a graphical object, so it remains in-line with the rest of the document's text. To edit the worksheet, double-click on its object. Excel takes over the Word window again, and you can modify the

TIP

If you find the experience of Excel-in-Word to be jarring, refer to the preceding section and use the paste-link option instead.

Excel's Ribbon

FIGURE 13-5:
An Excel object, embedded in a Word document.

Embedded Excel object   Word document

Whipping up a chart

Another way that Excel and Word mix it up is with the Chart command. This command allows you to build a graphic inside a document, similar to the way Excel creates charts. Or, I should put it, exactly the way Excel makes charts because, once again, Excel is called upon from within Word to help you build a chart.

To add a chart graphic to your document, follow these richly illustrated steps:

1. Click the Insert tab.

2. In the Illustrations group, click the Chart button.

The Insert Chart dialog box appears. It lists a wide variety of chart types, and specific examples of each chart type, as illustrated in Figure 13-6.

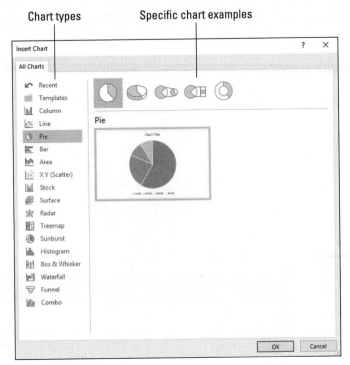

FIGURE 13-6:
The Insert Chart
dialog box.

3. Choose a chart category.

4. Select a specific chart type.

5. Click OK.

A chart sample is inserted into the document. You also see the Edit Data window, which looks like an Excel worksheet. (It is.) The worksheet is preset with labels and values, which are reflected in the sample chart, as illustrated in Figure 13-7.

6. Edit the chart data.

Click the mouse in the Edit Data window to modify the labels and corresponding data for your chart.

If you need to add a row, type it into the mini-worksheet. The row's data instantly appears in the chart.

If you need to remove a row, click the row number and press the Delete key. The row is removed and the chart is updated.

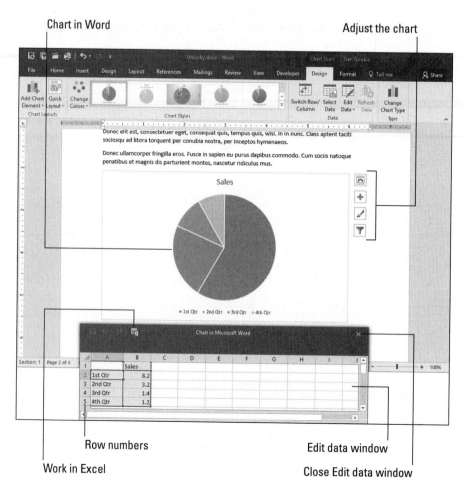

Chart in Word

Adjust the chart

FIGURE 13-7:
Creating
the chart.

Row numbers

Edit data window

Work in Excel

Close Edit data window

7. Close the Edit Data window when you're done editing the data.

The chart object stays selected, and you can continue to customize it, adjust its layout, and so on. Or click elsewhere in the document to continue editing.

If you need to update the chart or change the data, right-click in the Chart and choose the command Edit Data ⇨ Edit Data. The Edit Data window appears again, and you can modify the values.

The buttons to the right of the chart object help you adjust the chart's layout and appearance.

 Use the Layout Options button to set how the chart interacts with the text. The In Line with Text option is chosen by default, but you can reset this option so that text wraps around the chart or the chart floats in front of or behind text. Refer to Chapter 10 for more information on object layout.

 Click the Chart Elements button to set appearance options for three chart elements: Title, Labels, and Legend. On the button, submenus direct which parts of each element show up, or not.

 The Style button allows you to reset the chart's look. You can't reset the chart type, such as bar graph to pie graph, but you can scroll the list and apply a new style or appearance to the existing chart.

 Use the Filter button to customize how values and names are used in the chart. You can choose which portions of the chart to highlight and where and how the names or labels appear.

To directly change the chart's fill or outline color, right-click the chart. The Mini Toolbar shows Fill and Outline buttons, from which you can select new colors.

If you really want to change the chart type, right-click the chart and choose the Change Chart Type command. Choose a new chart style and layout from the Change Chart Type dialog box, and then click OK to apply those changes. The data remains the same; only the chart's appearance changes.

To remove a chart, click to select it, and then press the Delete key.

3

Word at Work

Chapter 14

Beyond Routine Documents

When you're done writing, formatting, and sprucing up a document and you have the time and (more importantly) the skills, you can add some final touches to truly make your document shine. These are items that go beyond the basics and the routine, and they're often required for professional documents in a business setting.

Cover Pages

The first page of a document is important. That page is called the *cover page* or *cover sheet*, and it serves as an introduction, like a handshake. You can use Word's Cover Page command to quickly add a preset introduction to your document, or you can craft your own cover sheet that may fit in better with your document's design.

easier to create it first, but not necessary to do so.

>> If possible, I recommend setting a cover page as its own document section. Refer to Chapter 6.

>> A document's header and footer are affected by the cover sheet. Generally, you don't want to extend the existing header or footer to the cover page. Refer to Chapter 7 for details on headers and footers.

>> Also see the section "Setting a page border," later in this chapter, if you want to put a border around the cover page.

Selecting a preset cover page

Word features a slate of cover pages you can instantly slap into your document. The Cover Page feature inserts the page, many of which feature designs and various fill-in-the-blanks items. The feature also suppresses any existing headers and footers so that the cover page shows up clean.

To add a preset cover page to your document, follow these steps:

1. **Save your document.**

   Adding a cover page is a perfect point in time to celebrate the fact that you haven't saved your document in a while.

2. **Click the Insert tab.**

3. **In the Pages group, click the Cover Page button.**

   A gallery of cover page samples appears, similar to what's shown in Figure 14-1.

4. **Click a cover page thumbnail.**

   The cover page is automatically inserted as the document's first page. The page isn't set in a new section, but the header and footer for that page are suppressed.

5. **Click on any content controls to add custom text to the cover page.**

   The content controls describe which text best goes on the cover page. For example, the Document Title control is replaced with your document's title. If you don't plan on using one of the suggestions, click to select it and then press the Delete key to remove the preset text.

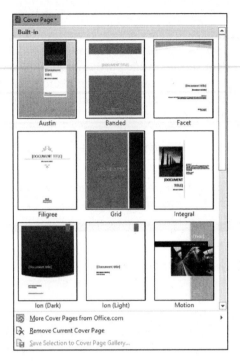

FIGURE 14-1:
Various
cover pages.

When you're displeased with the selections offered on the Cover Page menu, choose the item More Cover Pages from Office.com. (Refer to Step 3.) Choose an item from the submenu.

>> The fill-in-the-blanks items on Word's preset cover pages are content controls. See Chapter 27 for details.

>> You can repeat the steps in this section to select a different cover page. Just choose the new page in Step 3, and the current page is replaced along with any text items you've set or edits you've made to the old cover page.

>> To remove a preset cover page, repeat Steps 1 and 2, but in Step 3 choose the command Remove Current Cover Page. The cover page is excised, restoring your document to its original state.

Designing your own cover page

Word's preset cover pages are okay, but they may not be as perfect as you desire. You can use a preset cover page and then customize it, but if you're going to make that much effort, you might as well take a stab at designing your own cover page.

The *cover page* is the first page in your document, but it must be treated as a special element, separate from the document's text. I recommend that the cover page end in a hard page break or section break. Further, it must be separated from the

to meet these goals. Rather than bore you with all of them, I offer the following steps to add a cover page to a document:

1. **Press Ctrl+Home to move the insertion pointer to the tippy-top of the document.**

   You can add a cover page before or after you write the document's text. I'll assume that you're doing so after writing the text, though the same steps apply, either way.

2. **Click the Layout tab.**

3. **In the Page Setup group, click the Breaks button.**

4. **Choose Next Page.**

   The Next Page break is a section break. It creates a new section in your document. This step isn't required; you could use a standard page break, but the section break makes it easier to control headers/footers and page numbers.

   The insertion pointer is at the second page of the document, in Section 2. The cover page is ready for festooning with whatever decorations you desire, and the following two sections offer some suggestions. The next task before you begin working on the cover page is to further separate it from the rest of the document.

5. **Click the Insert tab.**

6. **In the Header & Footer group, click the Header button and choose Edit Header.**

   The document window changes to reveal the Section 2 header, illustrated in Figure 14-2. The Header & Footer Tools Design tab appears.

7. **In the Navigation group, click Link to Previous to deselect that item.**

   The Link to Previous setting copies the header/footer from the previous section to the current section. You don't want that setting active.

8. **You can edit the header now, adding a title or a page number reference or whatever other material is necessary for the rest of the document.**

   Next, you need to repeat these steps, but for the document's footer.

9. **Click the Go to Footer button.**

Unlink from cover page   Separate cover page

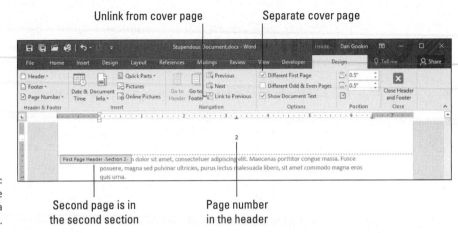

FIGURE 14-2:
Editing the
header for a
cover page.

Second page is in   Page number
the second section   in the header

10. Click the Link to Previous button.

11. Click the Close Header and Footer button.

You're done separating the header and footer from the cover page.

Well, maybe you're not completely done with the header and footer. If you plan to insert a page number into the header or footer, see the next section. Otherwise, you're done.

At this point, you can edit the cover page. You can add text, graphics, and other fun design derring-do. That page is separate from the rest of the document, so changes made elsewhere don't affect it.

REMEMBER

>> These steps assume that the cover page is in its own section. If you set a hard page break (refer to Step 4), extra steps are required in order to remove the header and footer from the cover page. Rather than bother with those steps, just obey my directions in this section.

>> The section break looks like a page break in Print Layout view. In Draft view, the section break appears as a double dotted line across the page with the words *Section Break (Next Page)* in the center.

Resetting the page number

For a professional document, it's odd to number the cover page. In fact, the cover page isn't even counted in the document's page count. So the second physical page in the document would be numbered starting with 1 and not 2. To effect that change, you must direct Word to renumber the document's pages.

The following steps assume that a page number reference is set in the document's header or footer. In Figure 14-2, you see the page number 2 in the header. That reference must be reset to 1. Heed these directions to make that change:

1. **Edit the header or footer containing the page number.**

    Click the Insert tab, and in the Header & Footer group, click the Header button and choose Edit Header. Or you can choose the Footer button and then Edit Footer.

2. **Right-click the page number.**

3. **From the shortcut menu, choose the Format Page Numbers command.**

    The Page Number Format dialog box appears, as shown in Figure 14-3.

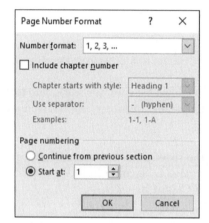

FIGURE 14-3: The Page Number Format dialog box.

4. **At the bottom of the dialog box, choose Start At and set 1 as the value.**

5. **Click OK.**

    The pages in the document are renumbered so that the first page after the cover page is now page 1.

6. **Close the document header when you're done making changes.**

    Click the Close button, or click the mouse in the document's text.

This change is possible because the header is held in its own section, if you follow my advice earlier in this chapter. The second page of the document starts in a new section. Effectively, you reset the page number values for the second section in the document; the first section (the cover page) lacks page number references.

Centering a page from top to bottom

Word features plenty of text and paragraph formatting tools to help you craft a marvelous document title for the cover page. The only tools that aren't readily available are those that let you set the title in the middle of the page, centered top-to-bottom. To achieve that feat, you must set the page's vertical alignment. The feature isn't easy to find.

In Figure 14-4, you see two versions of a title page. Both dwell in their own section at the start of a document. On the left, a title appears centered as a paragraph but aligned at the top of the page. The same title appears on the right, but with vertical page alignment applied. Follow these steps to duplicate this effect:

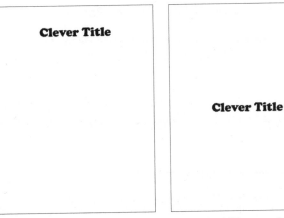

FIGURE 14-4:
Vertically
aligning a page.

Vertical Alignment Top   Vertical Alignment Center

1. **Write and format text on the title page.**

   The text is written in paragraphs, just like normal text. You can apply paragraph alignment, if you like, because it doesn't affect vertical alignment.

   If you're using text boxes for the title, they remain unaffected by vertical alignment. See the next section.

2. **Click the Layout tab.**

3. **In the Page Setup group, click the Launcher icon.**

   The Launcher icon appears in the lower right corner of the group, as illustrated in the margin.

4. **In the Page Setup dialog box, click the Layout tab.**

5. **In the Page area, choose Center from the Vertical Alignment menu.**

6. **From the Apply To menu, choose This Section.**

   You want center vertical alignment to apply only to the cover page, not to every page in the document. Again, this is ~~what~~ setting the cover page in its own section.

7. **Click OK.**

   The page's contents are centered, from top to bottom, as illustrated on the right in Figure 14-4.

If you find that these directions don't meet to your liking, your next best option is to place the text into boxes and position them on the page. See the next section.

Using text boxes for titles

For the most precise control over cover page elements, place text into boxes. The boxes can be arranged and positioned *just so*, making the cover page layout exactly what you want.

The following steps apply a generic approach to using text boxes on a cover page. For more detail on text box formatting and layout, refer to Chapter 11.

1. **Click the Insert tab.**

2. **In the Text area, click the Text box button.**

3. **Choose the Draw Textbox command.**

   The mouse pointer changes to a plus sign, as shown in the margin.

4. **Drag the mouse on the cover page to create a text box.**

   Don't fret over the size just yet. You can resize the box after you add text.

5. **Type the title into the Text box.**

   If the title has a subtitle, you can type it as well, though it might be a better idea to place the subtitle into its own box.

6. **Format the text.**

   All text and paragraph formats work inside of the text box. Choose the font, size, and other attributes. You probably want to apply center justification for the paragraph format.

7. **Resize the text box to accommodate the text.**

   Drag one of the handles to stretch or shrink the box, as illustrated in Figure 14-5.

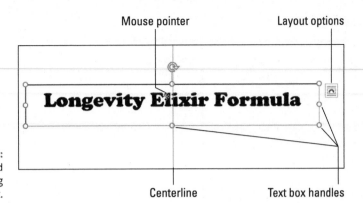

Mouse pointer   Layout options

Longevity Elixir Formula

Centerline   Text box handles

FIGURE 14-5:
Resizing and
positioning
the text box.

8. **Point the mouse at the text box so that the mouse pointer changes to a four-way arrow.**

Refer to Figure 14-5 as well as to the margin. When the mouse pointer changes, you can drag the box to a different location on the cover page.

9. **Drag the text box to line it up with page elements.**

When you near the top, left, right, or bottom edges of the page, or when you drag the box over the centerline, you see a green guideline on the screen. It's your clue that the text box is properly aligned with the page. In Figure 14-5, the centerline appears, lining up with the center of the text box.

10. **Right-click on the box's edge.**

A special pop-up menu appears.

11. **Click the Outline button and choose No Outline.**

The text box's outline vanishes, leaving only the text. (The outline shows up when the text box is selected; click elsewhere to preview the box.)

12. **Click the Layout Options button.**

The Layout Options palette appears. The In Front of Text layout option should be selected as illustrated in Figure 14-6. If not, click that option.

13. **Select the option Fix Position On Page.**

This option ensures that none of the text on the page affects how you've positioned the text box.

14. **Click the X Close button to dismiss the Layout Options palette.**

15. **Repeat Steps 2 through 14 to create additional text boxes.**

The final cover page can sport as many text boxes or other graphical elements as needed, but don't overdo it.

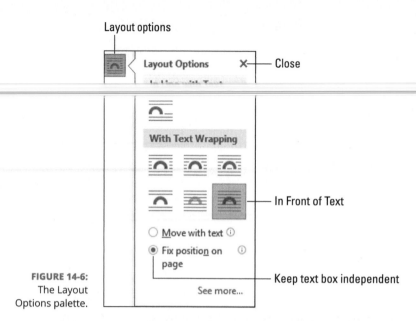

Layout options

Layout Options ✕ —— Close

With Text Wrapping

—— In Front of Text

○ Move with text ⓘ
◉ Fix position on ⓘ
   page

—— Keep text box independent

See more...

FIGURE 14-6:
The Layout
Options palette.

TIP

You can create all the boxes at once and then use the Zoom tool on the status bar to zoom out and arrange the boxes precisely. That reduced image of the cover page helps you ensure that items are organized just the way you want.

» I recommend placing cover-page text elements each into their own text boxes. If you need another element — specifically, a subtitle, an author, an address, or even another line of text in a different style — use another text box.

» As you manage the text boxes, Word switches between graphics mode and editing mode. When you point the mouse at the box's edges, you can manipulate the box as a graphical element. When you click in the text, you edit the text.

» You don't have to dispense with the text box outline. You can even add a background color. Chapter 11 discusses the options.

Word's Phony Watermarks

A *watermark* is a feature found on fancy paper. You might not be able to see it directly. In most cases, you hold up the paper to a bright light and you can see the watermark, which could be an image or some text embedded in the paper. Watermarks exist to impress.

Word has the capability to simulate a watermark — a phony watermark. The effect is similar to a true watermark, but instead of being embedded in the paper, Word's watermark is really nothing more than a faint background object. It's not used to impress, but it's another way to identify a document as a draft or copy. This use of the watermark is common in office environments.

Adding a watermark

To stick a watermark on the background of all pages in your document, heed these directions:

1. **Press Ctrl+Home to position the insertion pointer at the start of a document.**

2. **Click the Design tab.**

3. **In the Page Background group, click the Watermark button.**

    You see the Watermark gallery and menu, as shown in Figure 14-7. A scrolling list of preset, commonly used watermarks appears.

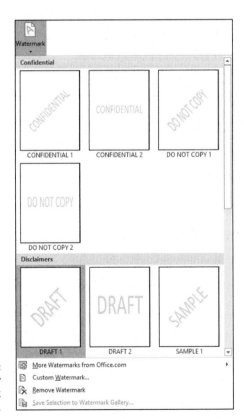

FIGURE 14-7: Word's phony watermark gallery.

4. **Choose a watermark from the list.**

   For example, DRAFT appears to be popular in windy offices.

The watermark is applied to all pages in the document. If you don't see it, ensure that you're using Print Layout view; you cannot see the watermark in Draft view.

TECHNICAL STUFF

>> A document can have only one watermark. If you choose another watermark (for example, to set it on one page only), all the watermarks are changed in the document.

>> I've witnessed funky behavior after applying the watermark when the insertion pointer is not at the start of the document. I've seen the watermark apply to only one page or to a group of pages. To ensure that the watermark is applied to all pages in the document, follow the steps as outlined in this section.

>> The watermark prints with the rest of the document. If not, see the later section "Printing background objects."

>> If you can't get the watermark to work properly, follow the steps in the next section, which might work better.

Customizing the watermark

The most common watermark I see in Word is Draft. Other preset watermarks are useful, including Copy and Sample. Lamentably, a TOP SECRET watermark isn't available. Word doesn't let you create your own text as a watermark, but you can use an image as a watermark. The secret is to access the Printed Watermark dialog box, shown in Figure 14-8.

To customize the watermark, follow these steps:

1. **Click the Design tab.**

2. **In the Page Background group, click the Watermark button.**

3. **Choose the Custom Watermark command.**

   The Printed Watermark dialog box shows up.

To change the watermark's color, click the Color menu and choose a new color. If you keep the Semitransparent check box selected, the watermark fades into the background. When that option is deselected, the watermark appears as a solid color.

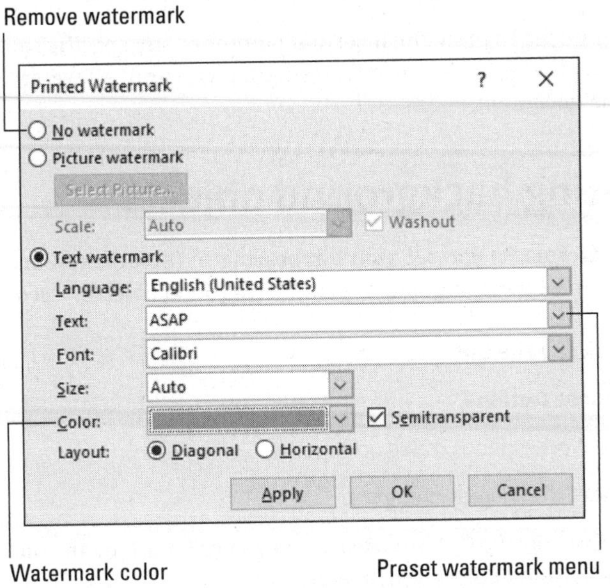

Remove watermark

FIGURE 14-8:
The Printed
Watermark
dialog box.

Watermark color   Preset watermark menu

Choose Picture Watermark to set an image as the watermark. Use the Select Picture button to find an image. This is the technique you use in Word to set a background image on a page. Keep the Washout item selected, or else the image overwhelms the document's text.

TIP

Before you finish making your settings, click the Apply button. The watermark effect is added to the document window, which you can preview behind the Printed Watermark dialog box. If you need to make further adjustments, do so. Click the OK button when you're satisfied.

Not that I'm an expert, but I believe that creating a company logo watermark in Word would be tacky. If that's your desire, I recommend that you pay a stationer some money and have them print up some custom watermarked paper.

Removing the watermark

To banish the watermark from your document, follow these steps:

1. **Click the Design tab.**

2. **Click the Watermark button and Choose the Remove Watermark command.**

You don't have to place the insertion pointer at any specific spot in the document. Once you choose the Remove Watermark command, all watermarks are banished from the document.

Printing background objects

If the watermarks you set aren't appearing in the printed document, ensure that Word is properly configured to print background objects. Heed these directions:

1. **Click the File tab.**

2. **Choose Options.**

   The Word Options dialog box appears.

3. **Select the Display category.**

4. **In the Printing Options area, place a check mark by the option Print Background Colors and Images.**

5. **Click OK.**

Try printing the document again to see whether the watermarks print.

Document Tricks

Word's selection of document tricks is as extensive as items you'll find up a magician's sleeve. Like several dozen handkerchiefs, some doves, and a few playing cards, not all tricks are particularly useful. Still, they may amaze you.

Writing a return address

This trick isn't really a secret, but too many Word users have difficulty typing out a return address — or any document element where the lines must be set close together.

As an example, in Figure 14-9, you see three return addresses, side by side. The first uses Word's standard paragraph line spacing of 1.08. The second uses single-spacing, which is practically identical to 1.08 line spacing. The third example (on the far right), uses a soft return, or line break.

Sherlock Holmes	Sherlock Holmes	Sherlock Holmes
221B Baker Street	221B Baker Street	221B Baker Street London, England
London, England	London, England	
1.08 Line Spacing	Single Line Spacing	Soft Returns

FIGURE 14-9:
Paragraph
line-spacing
effects.

To insert a soft return, press Shift+Enter at the end of a line.

The soft return doesn't start a new paragraph. It merely splits the line, causing text to continue at the left paragraph indentation. Line spacing attributes are ignored when you use a soft return.

>> Beyond addresses, you can also use the soft return to split a long document title or heading. The soft return keeps the text together, just as it does for a return address, which looks better on the page.

 >> Word doesn't display the soft-return character, just as it doesn't display the paragraph mark. You can use the Show/Hide command to reveal the soft-return character, shown in the margin.

Adding page color

It's possible in Word to apply a background color to pages in your document. I see no reason to apply such a page attribute. Frankly, if you want to print on colored paper, buy colored paper. But if you want to add a background color — which is really more like a block of color — obey these directions:

1. **Click the Design tab.**

2. **In the Page Background group, click the Page Color button.**

3. **Choose a page color from the list.**

   The color is applied instantly.

The Page Color command affects the entire document. It's not hindered by section breaks.

>> To change or remove the page color, repeat the steps in this section, but choose a new color from the list in Step 3. Choose No Color to remove the page color.

>> Choose the Fill Effects command from the Page Color menu to apply gradients, textures, patterns, and pictures to the page color. For example, you can apply a gradient sepia tone that makes the page looked weathered and worn. (As does printing on special paper, but I digress.)

>> Page effects and background images don't look as professional as selecting quality paper with such effects designed into the page.

>> On some printers, the ~~~~~~~

page. That's because some printers require approximately half an inch of space to pull the paper through the printer. If you see such a strip of colorless paper in the printed document, blame the printer, not Word.

Setting a page border

Page borders can be tricky. That's because sometimes they show up and sometimes they don't. It could be a printer issue, but I have a solution, either way.

To surround the page with a border, similar to how borders are applied to paragraphs, heed these steps:

1. **If you want to apply the border only to the cover page, click the mouse on that page.**

   This step assumes that the cover page is set in its own section.

2. **Click the Design tab.**

3. **In the Page Background group, click the Page Borders button.**

   The Borders and Shading dialog box appears. The Page Border tab is selected, as shown in Figure 14-10. It works exactly like the Borders tab, though the effects are added to the entire page, not just to one or more paragraphs. Also, an Art menu shows up, which I believe was added for comic relief.

4. **Choose a setting, such as Box.**

   The Box setting is the most popular. It encloses the entire page.

5. **Choose a line style from the Style list.**

   Scroll the list to peruse the various styles.

6. **Set a color.**

   The Automatic color is usually black, though it could be different, depending on the document theme.

7. **Set the line width.**

   Use the Preview window to see how the border is applied to the page.

8. **Use the Apply to menu to set whether the border is applied to every page in the document or only in the current section.**

For example, if the cover page is its own section and that's the only part of the document to which you want to apply the page border, choose This Section from the menu.

9. **Click OK to apply the page border.**

The border appears in Print Layout view. You can also see it on the Print Preview screen just before you print.

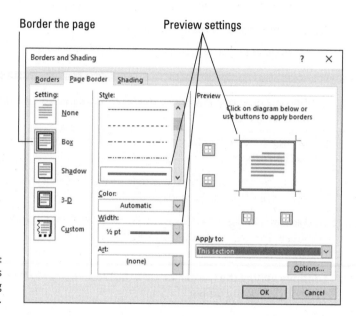

FIGURE 14-10:
The Borders
and Shading
dialog box.

To remove the border, repeat Steps 1 through 3. In Step 4, choose None and then click OK. The border is removed.

TIP

» If the border doesn't print, you can make one modification that might help: In the Borders and Shading dialog box, click the Options button. In the Border and Shading Options dialog box, click the Measure From menu and choose Text. Click OK (twice) to close the dialog boxes. With this setting change, the page border is moved inward a tad, which may help it to show up when printed.

» If you split your document into sections, choose This Section from the Apply To menu in Step 8. Refer to Chapter 6 for more information on document sections.

» This book doesn't specifically cover the paragraph border format. For details on applying that format, I recommend the title *Word 2016 For Dummies* (Wiley).

Putting the filename in a header or footer

To help identify a printed document's location in the digital realm, many office

if you follow these steps:

1. **Click the Insert tab.**

2. **In the Header & Footer group, click the Header button.**

3. **Choose Edit Header from the menu.**

   The document's header is revealed.

   You could also choose Edit Footer if you prefer the filename located in the footer.

4. **Position the insertion pointer to the location where you want the filename to appear.**

5. **On the Header & Footer Design tab, in the Insert group, choose Document Info ⇨ File Path.**

   The document's full filename is inserted into the header. If you want the file's name, choose File Name instead of File Path.

TECHNICAL STUFF

   The File Path or File Name command inserts the FILENAME field into the document. The File Path command adds the \p switch, which directs Word to display the full pathname. See Chapter 24 for details on fields.

6. **Continue editing the header, or click the Close Header and Footer button to return to the document.**

Filenames routinely appear on draft documents, but not on the final version. Follow Steps 1 through 3 in this section and delete the FILENAME field to remove the filename from the document's header.

>> A *pathname* is a document's full name but also describes its location on the local storage system. It starts with a drive letter, and then all parent folders, and then (finally) the filename and the filename extension.

>> Refer to Chapter 7 for details on editing headers and footers in your document.

REMEMBER

>> The document header is affected by sections. If you want to ensure that the filename appears in all sections, you must link the sections, as described in Chapter 7.

Printing for three-ring binding

Whether you print on three-hole-punch paper or punch the holes yourself, you notice something: Your document's text could scoot over a notch to accommodate the holes. You probably wish you would have thought of that before printing.

Don't mess with the page margins or paragraph indents! Word accommodates three-ring binders as it does any binding. The secret is to create a binding area in the page format. This area is known as the *gutter*. Follow these steps to add a gutter to your document:

1. **Click the Layout tab.**

2. **In the Page Setup group, click the Launcher icon.**

The Page Setup dialog box appears.

3. **Click the Margins tab.**

The Margins area is located at the top of the dialog box, illustrated in Figure 14-11. The *gutter* is an extra margin, as illustrated in the figure. Its position is set to the left or top of the page, depending on the binding.

Margins area   Gutter size   Gutter location

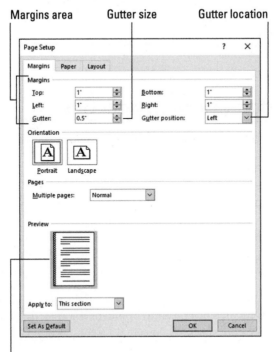

FIGURE 14-11: The Page Setup dialog box.

Binding area (gutter)

4. **Set the size in the Gutter box.**

   For three-ring binding, I add an extra half-inch for the gutter.

   As you set the Gutter value, you see the Preview part of the dialog box adjust to accommodate the binding.

5. **Set the Gutter Position box to Left or Top.**

   The top option would be chosen if you were using the three-hole punch on the short end of the paper, such as if you used the Landscape page orientation. (Refer to Figure 14-11.)

6. **Click OK.**

   When Word is in Print Layout view, you can see the wider space on the left side of the page. This space is the combined page margin and gutter.

The gutter affects all your document's pages. If you're printing on both sides of the page, the gutter is applied left and right, depending on how the document lays out. This setting is made automatically when you print the document.

>> The gutter and page margin combine to set the paragraph indentation. See Chapter 2 for details on the paragraph indentation format.

>> Gutter is an apt description. When you open a book, the place where the left and right pages meet (near the binding) is narrow and useless for text. That's why it's referred to as a gutter.

Setting document properties

You can round up the information stored with a document in several ways. This data, collectively known as a document's *properties*, is accessed from the Info screen in Word. Follow these steps:

1. **Click the File tab.**

2. **Choose Info.**

   Info is chosen by default, but I wanted to show at least two steps here to keep my editors happy.

The document's Properties list appears on the right side of the screen. You may consider it trivia, but in a business environment it's an activity record.

To print the document's properties, follow these steps:

1. **Press Ctrl+P.**

   The Print screen appears.

2. **Click the first button below the Settings heading.**

   The button might say Print All Pages. It's the Print What button, though no label appears nearby.

3. **Choose Document Info from the menu.**

4. **Click the Print button.**

   A single sheet prints, listing the document's properties, similar to what's shown in Figure 14-12.

Filename: Stupendous Document.docx
Directory: C:\Users\Dan\Dropbox\screenshots
Template: C:\Users\Dan\AppData\Roaming\Microsoft\Templates\Normal.dotm
Title:
Subject:
Author: Dan Gookin
Keywords:
Comments:
Creation Date: 4/20/2016 8:17:00 AM
Change Number: 2
Last Saved On: 4/20/2016 9:56:00 PM
Last Saved By: Dan Gookin
Total Editing Time: 1,458 Minutes
Last Printed On: 4/21/2016 8:47:00 AM
As of Last Complete Printing
    Number of Pages: 1 (approx.)
    Number of Words: 874
    Number of Characters: 5,153 (approx.)

FIGURE 14-12: A document's properties sheet.

To set more of the properties, such as the empty Title and Subject lines, shown in Figure 14-12, obey these directions:

1. **Click the File tab.**

   The Info screen appears.

2. **Click the Properties heading**

   A single-item menu is available.

3. **Choose Advanced Properties.**

   The document's Properties dialog box shows up.

   4. ~~Fill in the various fields in the dialog box.~~

   Supply as much information about the document as you want, such as the title and subject. (Word doesn't glean that information from the document itself.)

5. **Click OK to set the document's properties.**

Any items you add are printed as described in this section. They also stick to the document, even if you copy the document's file to another computer. In fact, some might consider the information to be a security risk. See Chapter 28 for information on document inspection.

Creating a digital signature object

In the real world, you grab a pen (not a pencil) and sign a document. That method of verification has been valid for centuries — even when someone illiterate drew the cross of St. Andrew and kissed it. That's the origin of the X signature line, and also why *X* signifies a "kiss" in popular culture.

You can add a digital signature line to your document, which allows someone to sign it. This feature isn't that common, because Adobe offers a better solution in its PDF documents. If you want to add a digital signature to your Word documents, follow these steps:

1. **Place the insertion pointer at the position where you want the digital signature to appear.**

   The signature is an object similar to a graphical element, but minus layout options. Figure 14-13 illustrates a digital signature object in a document.

2. **Click the Insert tab.**

3. **In the Text group, click the Add Signature Line button.**

   If the menu appears, choose the command Microsoft Office Signature Line.

   The Signature Setup dialog box appears.

4. **Fill in the Suggested Signer box.**

   This box contains the name of the person signing, such as Al Capone, shown in Figure 14-13.

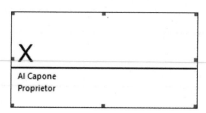

FIGURE 14-13:
A digital
signature object.

5. **Fill in the Suggested Signer's Title.**

   The text you type appears below the signer's name. In Figure 14-13, the text *Proprietor* appears.

6. **Fill in the Email field, if desired.**

   I leave this one blank.

7. **Click OK.**

   The digital signature object is inserted into the document.

You can drag the digital signature object around, or you can adjust its size: Use the mouse to drag one of the handles.

» To sign the document, the user clicks the digital signature object. If a digital signature isn't on file, a web page opens that instructs the user how to configure a digital signature and sign the document.

» To edit the signature, right-click on it and choose the Signature Setup command.

» You can remove a digital signature as you would any object: Click to select, and tap the Backspace key.

Chapter 15

Different Document Types and Printer Control

The text you write in Word is just a team of bits glowing inside your PC's innards. The text doesn't actually become a document until you save it. That process copies the bits into a more formal and permanent arrangement. As you work, you save, and the saved copy of your document is updated and kept fresh. That's the big picture for document creation and storage.

File management in Word involves two key commands: Save and Open. These commands not only lord it over the stuff you create in Word, but they also play host to other documents, and even nondocument files, you may encounter. Also playing a role is the printer, which is the escape hatch for all electronic documents, transforming your text from those glowing bits on the screen into ink on paper.

>> Documents you create in Word are saved as files on your PC's storage system or on the cloud. The files are not saved in Word; they are unique and separate items.

>> Managing files falls under the reign of Windows, the PC's operating system. You use Windows to copy, move, delete, and organize document files.

Save Documents in Strange Formats

Word's document file format is officially known as just that: the Word *document file format.* It's an organized set of data stored inside a computer that, when read properly, becomes a lovely document. Word isn't the only program that uses a specific format. And, just to be kind, Word has the capability to save documents in other formats.

Understanding document formats

In the computer world, thousands of document formats exist. A few of them are really popular and well-known, such as Word's document format, the Adobe Acrobat format (PDF), the HTML or web page format, and others. Some document formats are less popular, and not just because they're ugly. These could be file formats abandoned by programs long gone or highly specific file formats used only in certain industries or markets.

Most programs generate their own, unique document format. Most major pieces of software also understand other file formats, including common file formats like Word's document file format. When different programs access these alien file formats, they allow for the efficient exchange of information. That way, you can save a document in a generic file format and be assured that someone else can read it or even edit it and save it again in that same format or in another format.

Common document file formats are listed in Table 15-1. These are the types of documents from which Word can read and to which Word can write.

When you save to one of these alien file formats, I recommend that you first save your work in Word's native format. After that you can save in the other format as directed by whatever source you're using. For example, you save your résumé in Word and then save it as a PDF document for uploading to some potential employer.

TABLE 15-1 ## Common Document File Formats

Format	Filename Extension	Description
Acrobat	pdf	The Adobe Acrobat file format, known as the Portable Document Format, or PDF.
OpenDocument	odt	A document saved from the OpenOffice suite.
Plain text	txt	A document that contains only text and no formatting or other information.
Rich Text Format	rtf	A plain-text document, but with formatting information included. When read by Word, the RTF format displays as formatted text.
Web page	htm, html	A plain-text document with HTML coding for layout and other web goodies.
Word document	doc	An older Word document file format.
Word document	docx	A Word document file format; Word versions 2007 to present.
WordPerfect	wpd, doc	A word processing document generated by the WordPerfect program.
XML	xml	A text document created in the eXtensible Markup Language, which is similar to HTML.
XML Paper Specification	xps	A shareable file format that no one uses; designed by Microsoft to compete with PDF.

In many programs, the art of saving information in another file format is called *exporting.* In Word, you use the standard Save As command.

TIP

>> Generally speaking, you'll be prompted which format to use. For example, the submission guidelines for your online article may say to upload your proposal as an RTF file.

>> Word's document format is considered one of the standard file formats. Many other programs and applications can read and write Word's document files.

>> When a program dies, or is absorbed by another software developer, its file format becomes a legacy format. Sometimes the format is retained and used by other programs, but most of the time it's neglected. I have hundreds of such files in my archives. They represent documents and graphics files from old books. I have no software that can read to translate the data. Still I can recover text from those files; see the section "Recovering text from any old file," later in this chapter.

>> Graphically speaking, Word can read any of the common graphics file formats. Most of today's graphics editing programs and apps can save in, or export to, these file formats. Refer to Chapter 12 for information on which graphics file formats Word prefers to use.

>> For information on saving in the htm, html, or web page file format, see Chapter 30.

actually the extension that describes the file type to Windows, not any information gleaned from elsewhere. The extension determines which program opens the file and which icon represents the file. The stupid part is that you can freely edit the filename extension, which effectively changes the file type. That's why Windows doesn't show the filename extension in a File Explorer window. See the nearby sidebar, "Showing the filename extensions."

Saving a plain-text document

When you're required to save your document as plain text, you're kissing adieu all the formatting and just about everything else special in the document. In fact, text editors exist for the purpose of creating plain-text files. Still, Word can skinny down any document, reducing it to the basic text.

SHOWING THE FILENAME EXTENSIONS

If you really want to view filename extensions, you must direct the File Explorer program in Windows to reveal them to you. It's not that difficult of a trick to pull off. Follow these steps in Windows 10:

1. Press Win+E to summon a File Explorer window.

2. Click the View tab.

3. Place a check mark by the item File Name Extensions.

In Windows 7, the steps are more bizarre:

1. Open the Control Panel and choose Appearance and Personalization.

2. Click the Folder Options heading.

3. In the Folder Options dialog box, click the View tab.

4. Remove the check mark by the item Hide Extensions for Known File Types.

The primary reason Windows hides the filename extension is that it doesn't want you to change the extension when you rename (or save) a file. If you can see the extension, avoid the temptation to change it.

Follow these steps to save a copy of your document as a plain text, or ASCII, file:

1. **Save the document one more time.**

It's best to keep a Word document file of your text file.

2. **Click the File tab.**

3. **Choose Save As.**

The file's original name is retained in the File Name box. You can change it, if you like:

4. **If necessary, choose a folder for the file.**

I recommend keeping the file in the same folder as the Word document. You can copy it later.

5. **Type a new name for the file.**

The text file may require a special name, or special consideration such as underlines instead of spaces. Some text files might have very short names for compatibility with older software.

6. **From the File Type menu, choose Plain Text (*.txt).**

7. **Click the Save button.**

The File Conversion dialog box appears, similar to what's shown in Figure 15-1. This dialog box allows you to hone options for the text file, which may seem odd, yet different formats for text files exist.

Set the end-of-line character

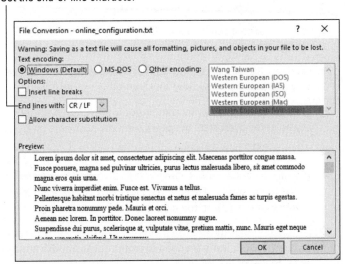

FIGURE 15-1:
Setting options
for a text file.

8. **Set options in the File Conversion dialog box.**

The most important option is the End Lines With menu. Despite their ubiquity,

~~the~~ ~~enter key press. In Windows, it's~~ CR/LF, which means carriage return and line feed characters — two characters. On Unix systems, it's LF (line feed) only.

9. **Click OK to save the file.**

The plain-text file is created and saved in the folder you selected.

10. **Close the text document: Press Ctrl+W.**

Believe it or not, the document appearing in Word is now a text file, not a Word document. Check out the title bar, which may show the text document's filename. When you close the document, you remove any risk of attempting to add nontext elements to the document.

The plain-text document isn't a Word document. In Windows, plain-text documents are associated with the Notepad program (unless another program is selected). If you double-click the text document's icon, it opens in Notepad, not Word. You can open the document in Word: See the later section "Choosing a specific document format."

>> It's okay to have two files of the same name in the same folder, as long as the files are of different types. If so, the files have different filename extensions, which means that the names aren't the same.

>> A text file contains only letters, numbers, symbols, and a few special characters such as space, tab, and Enter.

>> The plain-text filename extension is txt.

>> Many documents are required to be plain text, including many computer configuration files.

>> Plain-text files are also known as *ASCII* files. By tradition, these text files use only the basic ASCII symbols and codes, numbered 0 through 127.

TECHNICAL STUFF

>> Technically, a plain-text file contains only the ASCII characters, which would banish any accented characters or special symbols, such as © or €, from the document.

>> You may see the term *ASCII* used instead of *text file.*

>> The carriage return (CR) character is ASCII code 13. Its function is to return the cursor to the start of the line. The line feed (LF) character is ASCII code 10. It advances the cursor to the next line.

>> Computer programmers use plain-text files to create programs and apps. Even so, special text editors are used to write code instead of a major-horsepower word processor like Word.

Saving in the old Word document format

A few people still use Word versions prior to Word 2007. Microsoft has tried to accommodate them, but some stubborn folks never change. You can help them out by saving a document in the older, original doc file format. Heed these steps:

1. **Save your document one more time in the current Word document format.**

When you save in Word's current format, docx, you ensure that all the new features are available to that document.

2. **Click the File tab.**

3. **Click Save As.**

4. **Change the filename, if necessary.**

It's possible to keep both current and older Word documents in the same folder with the same filename. The extensions are different, but I suggest that you consider shortening or modifying the name just to keep your own sanity. For example, change Chapter15 to Chapter15-old when you save.

Figure 15-2 illustrates the differences between the two icons and their filename extensions as they appear in a File Explorer window.

FIGURE 15-2:
New and old
Word icons.

Chapter01.docx
(New document file icon)

Chapter01.doc
(Old document file icon)

5. **From the File Type menu, choose Word 97-2003 Document (*.doc).**

6. **Click the Save button.**

The document is converted to Word's older format — unless it contains any incompatible elements. These are features available in the current version of Word that cannot translate to the older document file format. If so, you see the Microsoft Word Compatibility Checker dialog box, similar to what's shown in Figure 15-3.

In Figure 15-3, you see two items flagged in the document: a content control and SmartArt graphics. The dialog box describes how both are converted, should you elect to continue. This side effect of saving in an old document format is why I directed you to save the original document in Step 1.

7. **Click the Continue button to proceed with saving the document, given the changes listed in the Microsoft Word Compatibility Checker dialog box.**

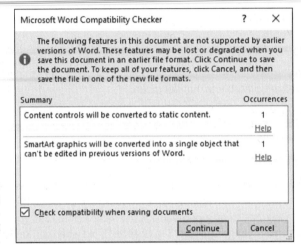

FIGURE 15-3:
The Microsoft
Word Compatibil-
ity Checker dialog
box.

The document is saved. It stays in the Word program window. Its name on the window's title bar is appended by the text [Compatibility Mode]. That's your clue that the document sports the older file format. It can no longer host some of the new Word features.

8. **Close the document: Press Ctrl+W.**

TIP

My advice is to close the document; don't edit it further. If you need to edit the document, use the original version that you saved in Step 1.

Once the older document has been saved (and closed), you can copy it to another location, a thumb drive, or cloud storage or attach it to an email message.

>> Beyond content controls and SmartArt objects, another important item missing from the older doc format are document themes. After you save, click the Design tab and observe the disabled buttons on the Ribbon. These features aren't available to older Word documents.

>> To update an older Word document to the current format, see the later section "Converting a document from Compatibility Mode."

>> Refer to Chapter 13 for information on SmartArt objects. See Chapter 28 for details on content controls.

Creating a PDF

Perhaps the most compatible form of document available today is the Adobe Acrobat Portable Document Format file, also known as a *PDF*. This format is the best way to distribute your Word documents; just about any computer hosts the Adobe Acrobat Reader program, which opens and displays PDF documents.

To save your document in the PDF format, obey these steps:

1. **Save your document.**

   I recommend saving your work as a standard Word document before you export to the PDF format.

2. **Click the File tab.**

3. **Choose Export.**

   Unlike saving in other file formats, to create a PDF format you don't use the Save As command in Word.

4. **Choose Create PDF/XPS Document.**

5. **Click the button Create PDF/XPS.**

   The Publish As PDF or XPS dialog box appears. It's a modified version of the Save As dialog box, but in this instance the type is chosen as PDF.

6. **Type a name for the file.**

   I recommend changing the name from the Word file, though doing so isn't necessary. Both the PDF and Word document can share the same names, but sport different file types and icons.

7. **Click the Publish button.**

8. **Choose a program to open the PDF, if prompted.**

   When you haven't yet set a program to open the PDF file, you'll be prompted. If Adobe Acrobat Reader is on the list, choose it.

After you save the PDF file, the program set to read Acrobat documents opens and displays the result. You can peruse the PDF, or close the program and return to Word. The original document remains open and ready for editing or whatever.

And in the now-he-tells-us category: Look for the Microsoft Print to PDF "printer" on the Print screen in Word. See the later section "Printing a PDF."

>> PDF documents render the content consistently on all computers and devices. That's why they're so popular.

>> Few people use the XPS document format. Those files are limited to folks who already have Microsoft Office, so if that's your target audience, you might as well just give them a Word document.

>> You can obtain a free copy of the Acrobat Reader from get.adobe.com/reader.

>> See the later section "Reading a PDF" for information on opening a PDF document in Word.

Saving an RTF document

The most common file format for exchanging documents between word processors is probably Word's own document file format. Coming in second would be the web page document. That topic is covered in Chapter 30, which is specific to web page publishing. Still, most word processors today can read the web page document, or HTML, file format.

For compatibility with ancient word processors or other programs that can't read Word's document file format, I recommend the RTF file format. RTF stands for Rich Text Format. It's a plain-text document, but one that encodes text formatting and other nontext elements.

To save your Word document in the RTF format, follow these directions:

1. Save the document one more time in Word's native, docx file format.

Press Ctrl+S.

2. Click the File tab.

3. Choose Export.

4. Choose Change File Type.

5. On the right side of the window, choose Rich Text Format (*.rtf).

6. Click the Save As button.

The traditional Save As dialog box appears, with the File Type menu showing the Rich Text Format (*.rtf) file format.

7. Click the Save button to save the file.

The file is saved, but the current document in Word becomes an RTF document. You see the text [Compatibility Mode] appear on the title bar. You probably don't want to continue editing the RTF document, so:

8. Press Ctrl+W to close the document.

If you need to further edit the original document, open the one you saved in Step 1.

You can now send the RTF file to the other computer, where the antique software program can open it and convert its contents to whatever oddball format that program uses.

Word opens RTF documents for editing. In fact, you can work in the document if you like, save it, and close it. To convert an RTF document to a Word document, see the later section "Converting a document from Compatibility Mode."

Open Documents from Strange Formats

Perhaps you're like me and you have archives from generations back. These files include documents created by word processing programs long since discarded in the bit dumpster of technology. That's a sad story, but it has a happy ending: Word does its best to not only open documents saved in unusual formats but also recover text from just about any file. That's an amazing trick.

Recovering text from any old file

It amazes me which antique word processing files Word recognizes. For example, I used WordPerfect 5.1 to write *DOS For Dummies* in 1991. I still have those documents. Word 2016 opens those files, no problem. Follow these steps to attempt that feat, albeit with your own antique word processing files:

1. **Press Ctrl+O.**

   The Open screen appears.

2. **Click the Browse button.**

   The Open dialog box shows up, which is a far better tool than the Open screen for hunting down files.

3. **In the Open dialog box, choose All Files (*.*) as the file type.**

   The File Type menu restricts the files listed in the Open dialog box to only those types specified. The All Files (*.*) type lists all files, which includes formats Word may not recognize. For example, the old WordPerfect (for DOS) file type.

4. **Choose the file to open.**

5. **Click the Open button.**

   The file opens in Word, translated from whatever file format Word recognizes into a document.

If the file type isn't recognized, Word displays the File Conversion dialog box, similar to what's shown in Figure 15-4. Work the controls in that dialog box to see whether you can massage the text into a digestible format. If so, click the OK button. If not, click Cancel and accept that the file can't be opened.

File you're attempting to open in Word

File Conversion - pyramid (2015_06_21 14_39_31 UTC).png

Select the encoding that makes your document readable.
Text encoding:
◉ Windows (Default)   ○ MS-DOS   ○ Other encoding:

Wang Taiwan
Western European (DOS)
Western European (IA5)
Western European (ISO)
Western European (Mac)

Preview:

Use the preview to check the results

FIGURE 15-4:
Word attempts to translate an unknown file.

>> I'll be honest: The controls in the File Conversion dialog box are rather limited. If you don't see what you want immediately in the Preview window, give up.

>> In Figure 15-4, I attempted to open a graphics file. The proper way to insert graphics into a document is to use the Insert Pictures command. Refer to Chapter 12.

>> Word's capability to recover text from older files is one reason I keep my old word processing files around.

>> See Chapter 29 for information on resetting the Ctrl+O command to bring up the traditional Open dialog box. Or just remember that somehow the Ctrl+F12 keyboard shortcut automatically summons the Open dialog box.

TECHNICAL STUFF

>> Word once had a feature called Recover Text from Any File. It appeared on the File Type menu in the Open dialog box. When that option was chosen, Word attempted to open the file and, if it had trouble, display the File Conversion dialog box. (Refer to Figure 15-4.) This feature is now built into the All Files (*.*) file type, as described in this section.

Choosing a specific document format

The key to opening a document in a strange format from a strange program developed on a strange planet by strange alien nerds is to know the file format. You have two approaches: First, you could direct the Open dialog box to list only those files of a certain format or file type. Second, you could use the approach covered in the preceding section to open any old file. I'll assume you know the file type.

For example, you need to open a plain-text document in Word. Follow these steps:

1. Press Ctrl+O.

2. On the Open screen, click the Browse button.

The good ol' Open dialog box appears.

3. From the File Type menu, choose Text Files (*.txt).

The Open dialog box displays only text files.

4. Navigate to the folder containing the text file you want to open.

5. Click to select the file.

6. Click the Open button.

The text file is opened and ready for action in Word.

Some plain-text files don't show up in the Open dialog box. For example, a log file is plain text and might use the filename extension log. If so, you need to choose All File (*.*) as the file type and browse for the log file (or whatever file) that way.

REMEMBER

» A plain-text, or any other type of document format, is not the same as a Word document. You can edit such a document in Word, but you may see a warning dialog box when you attempt to save. That's because Word desires to save the text as a Word document, not a plain-text file.

» To save a file as plain-text, refer to the earlier section "Saving a plain-text document." Then I recommend saving your edited document as a Word document.

» I could recommend that you use a text editor to create plain-text documents. That's a good choice, but Word offers the advantage of document proofing, a feature often missing from plain-text editors.

Reading a PDF

Just as Word lets you save a document in the common PDF file format, you can also open a PDF document in Word. You aren't really editing the PDF document, but you can extract the text and even graphics from the PDF to create a Word document. Follow these directions:

2. Click the Browse button.

3. Locate a PDF file in the Open dialog box window.

For some reason, the PDF file is considered a Word document file. So, ensure that All Word Documents is chosen as the file type. You could also choose the PDF Files (*.pdf) file type, if you want only PDF documents to show up in the Open dialog box.

4. Select a PDF file.

5. Click the Open button.

An info dialog box appears (the *i* on the left side of the dialog box means *info*), explaining that the conversion may take some time and might not be as pretty as the original PDF.

6. Click the OK button.

The PDF file is translated into a Word document.

7. Save the result as a Word document.

Use the Save As command to save the document in Word's document file format: Click the File tab and choose Save As. Give the file a name and click the Save button.

I recommend saving the results as a Word document to avoid any compatibility issues later.

TIP

If you really want to create PDF files, obtain the Adobe Acrobat DC program. It works like a printer, in that you "print" your Word documents to Acrobat as you would send a document to a printer. The Acrobat DC program has the benefit of letting you customize the PDF, add fill-in-the-blanks fields, set options for a digital signature, and more. It's the proper tool for the job if you need to create PDF files on a regular basis. To obtain Acrobat, visit acrobat.adobe.com.

Converting a document from Compatibility Mode

When you work with an older Word document file, or perhaps load up a word processing document from another source, you may see the text [Compatibility Mode] on the document window's title bar. That text reminds you that, although you can edit the document, certain features are disabled. These features include the capability to update a document's formats in real time, document themes, content controls, SmartArt objects, and more.

To update a document for the current version of Word, follow these steps:

1. Click the File tab.

2. On the Info screen, click the Convert button.

A dialog box may appear, explaining the conversion process. If you click the Do Not Ask Me Again box, you don't see the dialog box again.

3. If prompted, click OK in the dialog box.

The document is updated; the text [Compatibility Mode] vanishes from the title bar.

You still have to save the document. For some older documents, you may see the Save As dialog box again. If so, choose the Word Document (*.docx) file format.

Printer Tricks

Printing is a basic activity, something I really don't need to expound upon. I, however, can think of a few printer tricks I'd like to impart.

>> Ensure that the printer is on, ready to print, and stocked with paper and ink before you print.

>> Windows is in charge of adding and configuring printers. The process is automatic, especially for network printers. The list of printers available in Windows appears on the Print screen in Word.

>> If you desire more information about printers and printing, refer to the book *PCs For Dummies,* which I wrote (Wiley).

Printing a PDF

The classic way to create an Acrobat or PDF document is to print to it. That sounds like a weird step, but not every printer needs to be a physical device. If you have Adobe Acrobat installed, you may find it on the printer list. Otherwise, you can use the Microsoft Print to PDF "printer." Follow these steps:

1. Save your document one last time.

2. Press Ctrl+P.

The Print screen appears.

3. Click the Printer button.

See Figure 15-5 for the location of the Printer button as well as other interesting items on the Print screen.

4. Choose Microsoft Print to PDF.

If you've installed Adobe Acrobat, choose it as the printer.

5. Click the big Print button.

Because you're not really printing, the next thing you see is the Save Print Output dialog box; you're saving as a file what would otherwise be a printed document.

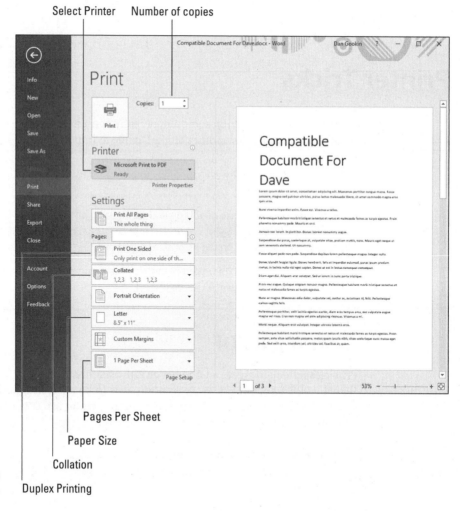

Select Printer   Number of copies

Pages Per Sheet

Paper Size

Collation

FIGURE 15-5:
The Print screen.   Duplex Printing

6. **Work the dialog box to choose a location for the PDF file.**

7. **In the File Name box, type a name for the PDF document.**

8. **Click the Save button.**

   The PDF document is created and saved in the location you specified. (Refer to Step 6.)

The document can be opened in Word, per the directions in the earlier section "Reading a PDF," but you'll most likely use the Acrobat Reader to view the document.

Refer to the earlier section "Creating a PDF" for additional Word document-to-PDF details.

Printing multiple copies

When you need to print a copy of the report for everyone on the board, how do you want it printed? Your options are to print one copy at a time — say, pages 1 through 8 over and over. Or you can print a dozen copies of page 1, and then a dozen of page 2, and so on. These options are known as *collated* and *uncollated*.

On the Print screen, use the Copies gizmo to set the number of copies, such as 6 or however many people attend the meeting. Then use the Collation button (refer to Figure 15-5) to choose whether you want to print copies collated or uncollated. I would choose Collated so that you don't have to shuffle all the pages after you print.

REMEMBER

The only problem with the collation options is that you frequently remember to set the option *after* you start printing.

Printing on both sides of a sheet of paper

I'm surprised how many of today's printers feature *duplex* printing. That's the fancy term for a printer's capability to print on both sides of a sheet of paper. Word is happy to accommodate this printer feature, but you, the human, must remember to activate it.

Before you print, click the Duplex Printing button on the Print screen; refer to Figure 15-5. Available options depend on the printer. If the printer isn't capable of duplex printing, you see only the Print One Sided option and perhaps the Manually Print on Both Sides option. Otherwise, choose the binding side, long edge or short edge, as shown in Figure 15-6.

Binding on the sides

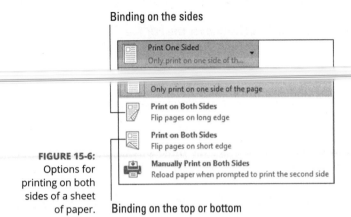

FIGURE 15-6:
Options for
printing on both
sides of a sheet
of paper.

Binding on the top or bottom

The Long Edge and Short Edge options must match where you've set the page gutter — if you've set a page gutter. Refer to Chapter 14 for information on page gutters, which is covered under the topic of three-ring binding.

The Manually Print on Both Sides option is used on printers without duplex capability. You print in two batches: First, the odd-numbered pages are printed. Then Word prompts you to reinsert the printing pages into the printer. Use the proper orientation (flip the pages over) so that you don't print twice on the same side of the sheet. Then proceed to print the even-numbered pages. This technique is a pain, but it works.

Printing more than one page per sheet

The page-per-sheet concept might be alien to you. That's okay; it's not something you do every day. After all, documents are organized by page in Word. But what is a page? And what is a sheet of paper? They're both concepts, like responsible drinking.

On the Print screen, you can set how many of Word's pages to print on a single sheet of paper. In Figure 15-5, the value 1 Page Per Sheet is selected. That button features a menu that lists other options, from 2 pages per sheet on up to 16 teensy-tiny pages per sheet, as shown in Figure 15-7.

TECHNICAL STUFF

If it's your desire to print two pages per sheet and have it look good, my advice is to reset the paper size to half a standard sheet of paper and then print two pages per sheet. This layout option looks better than Word's attempt to shove two Word-size pages onto a single sheet of paper. Follow these steps:

1. **Click the Layout tab.**

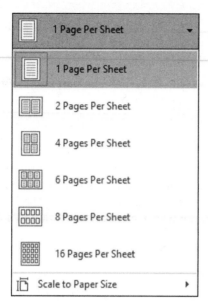

FIGURE 15-7:
Setting pages per
sheet.

2. **In the Page Setup group, click the Launcher icon.**

   The icon is located in the lower right corner of the group.

   The Page Setup dialog box appears.

3. **Click the Paper tab.**

   The Paper Size menu should show the default paper size, Letter. The width is equal to 8.5 inches, and the height is set to 11 inches.

4. **Click the Paper Size menu and choose Custom.**

5. **In the Width box, type** 5.5.

   This value is half the height of a sheet of standard US sheet of paper, at 11 inches.

6. **In the Height box, type** 8.5.

   This value is the width of a standard sheet of paper, which is now the height.

7. **Click OK.**

   In Print Layout view, you see the new page size reflected in your document. It's half a sheet of paper, if the standard sheet of paper were oriented horizontally and split down the middle.

8. **Press Ctrl+P.**

   On the Print screen, you see that the Paper Size menu shows Custom Paper Size.

9. **From the Pages Per Sheet menu, choose 2 Pages Per Sheet.**

Lamentably, the Preview window doesn't show two pages per sheet. That

10. **Click the Print button.**

The document prints two pages per sheet, horizontally, but with sufficient margins to be readable. You can also staple or bind the sheets and still be able to read the text.

I've used these settings to print out a novel at two pages per sheet and then bind the results so that people could read the printed result. The final product saved lots of paper and presented the text in a format more akin to a paperback novel than a full sheet of manuscript paper.

Chapter 16

Collaboration and Sharing

You might consider writing to be a solitary art. That might be true, but the publishing process involves more than a single person. It's good for any writer to get feedback on their text. This process involves more than one set of eyes — hopefully, a competent editor and copy editor. For a project in a business or office setting, several people might contribute to the final document — even Jared in shipping, who is probably high on something all the time.

Word's collaboration tools help you interact with others during the document creation process. You can provide feedback and comments, track who-changed-what, and even collaborate in real time on the Internet.

Here Are My Thoughts

Teachers and editors have historically demanded that primitive, typewritten documents feature ample margins and double, or even triple, line spacing. The reason was simple: Room was required in order to write comments and make corrections.

If you plan on printing a document, consider adding space for scribbled feedback. In the digital realm, however, tools are available for providing feedback inside the document.

Highlighting text

The basic feedback tool is the Text Highlight Color attribute, also called the highlighter tool. Like it's real-world counterpart, the Text Highlighter Color command applies a background shade to text. Follow these steps to mark up a document:

1. **Click the Home tab.**

2. **In the Font group, click the Text Highlight Color tool.**

If you've already chosen the tool, this step deactivates it. Otherwise, you're ready to start highlighting text.

3. **Drag the mouse over the text to apply the highlight color shown on the tool's command button.**

While the tool is active, the mouse pointer changes, as shown in the margin. You can drag over any swath of text to apply the highlight.

>> To deactivate the Text Highlight Color tool, press the Esc key or click the Text Highlight Color button a second time.

>> To remove highlighting, rehighlight the text. As long as the highlight is the same color, it's removed.

>> To change the highlight color, click the menu button next to the Text Highlight Color button. Choose a color from the list.

>> Different editors and reviewers may want to use different highlighter colors.

TIP

>> The Text Highlight Color feature isn't a text formatting attribute; you cannot use the Clear All Formatting command (Ctrl+spacebar) to remove it. Instead, you must rehighlight the same text in the same color or choose the No Color option from the Text Highlight Color button's menu.

>> Highlighting is good to reference material without the need to add a comment for each item. For example, repeated words or phrases can be highlighted as well as commented.

Inserting a comment

The traditional way to comment on someone else's document was to scribble text in the margin. When word processing, editors use a special style or text color to make comments. That's okay, but it runs the risk of accidentally leaving that text in the final document. A better solution is to use Word's comment tools.

To add a comment into a document, obey these steps:

1. **Select a chunk of text.**

   The text is the subject of your comment.

2. **Click the Review tab.**

3. **In the Comments area, click the New Comment button.**

   A comment area appears on the right side of the document, in the Word program window. Your name appears in a comment bubble, as illustrated in Figure 16-1.

4. **Type the comment text.**

   Be brief. Be descriptive. Be supportive.

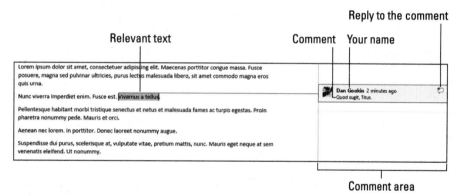

FIGURE 16-1:
A comment.

After you make the comment, you can continue working through the document. After you click back in the text, the box around the comment disappears, but the comment area stays open and the text you selected remains highlighted.

TIP

>> It may be tempting to select large chunks of text, but keep the selections brief. I would never select more than a sentence at a time.

>> To quickly select a sentence of text, press Ctrl and click the mouse in the sentence.

>> When multiple people comment on your text, a different color presents each person's comments.

>> It's possible to comment on a comment: Click on a comment to show its rectangle, and then click the Reply button, illustrated in Figure 16-1.

>> In Draft view, comments appear in the Revisions pane. Comments in the text remain highlighted, and are suffixed by the commenter's initials and a comment number.

Showing and hiding comments

Word uses a complex system to determine whether the comment area appears on the right side of a document, or whether comments show up at all. The system involves three command buttons on the Review tab: Show Comments, Display for Review, and Show Markup, all illustrated in Figure 16-2.

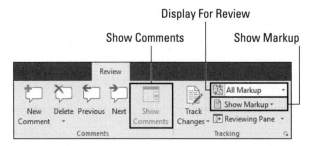

FIGURE 16-2:
Coordinating whether you see comments.

The Show Comments button is disabled in Figure 16-2. It's enabled only when you choose the Simple Markup command from the Display for Review button menu.

The Display for Review button hosts a menu of four items. Comments are visible when the items Simple Markup and All Markup are chosen.

The Show Markup button lists items to reveal, depending on the choices made from the Display for Review button's menu. If the Comments item on Display For Review menu is enabled (if it features a check mark), the comments are visible.

>> If comments are hidden, the Comment icon hangs in the right margin. This icon indicates that a comment lurks somewhere in the text. Hover the mouse over this icon to see which parts of the text are commented on. Click the icon to view the comments.

>> The Comment icon doesn't appear in Draft view, though the comments remain highlighted and tagged with the commenter's initials.

>> Also see the later section "Showing or hiding revisions," which discusses in more detail how the Display for Review and Show Markup buttons affect what appears in your document.

Reviewing comments

With the comment area visible, it's easy to peruse what others have written about your text. An easier to way is to page through the comments one a time, which is a good choice for a particularly long document.

The comment review buttons are found on the Review tab in the Comments group. The two you want to mess with are Previous Comment and Next Comment, but probably not in that order.

Click the Next Comment button to hop to the next chunk of commented text in your document. If the comment area is hidden, a card appears with the comment, including any replies.

Click the Previous Comment button to review comments between the insertion pointer and the start of the document — to "go back" if you're paging forward through the comments.

Marking a comment as Done

As you review comments, you can accept them by marking them Done: Right-click the comment text and choose Mark Comment Done from the pop-up menu.

A comment marked as Done still appears, though its text is faded. The commented portion of the text remains highlighted, but the color is more transparent.

>> The purpose of marking commented text as Done is to confirm that you've read the comment. The comment remains visible.

>> You can choose the Mark Comment Done command a second time to restore the comment.

Deleting comments

The best way to vent your anger at a comment is soak the computer in molten lead. A more productive thing to do is to delete the comment. Heed these directions:

1. **Click the Review tab.**

2. **In the Comments area, click the Previous or Next buttons to locate a comment.**

3. **Click the Delete Comment button.**

The comment is gone.

The Undo command restores deleted comments, in case you make a mistake.

Look What They Did!

Some editors aren't nice enough just to make comments. No, they see fit to edit your text with reckless abandon. Imagine the nerve! Then again, they could either tell you what's wrong or fix it. The issue is knowing what was changed. To best determine where and how text was modified, Word offers the Track Changes feature.

Activating the Track Changes feature

Before some weirdo or editor (is that redundant?) begins hacking away at your text, implore that person to activate Word's Track Changes feature. It's simple, and regardless of what you think about the other person, you will thank them for employing this useful feature.

To activate the Track Changes feature, follow these steps:

1. **Click the Review tab.**

2. **In the Tracking group, click the Track Changes button and choose Track Changes.**

The Track Changes button becomes highlighted.

3. **Begin editing the document.**

As you edit, type, delete, or reformat the text, the changes appear highlighted on the screen.

The highlighting you see on the screen depends on the setting chosen from the Display for Review menu, as well as whether you're using Print Layout view or Draft view. See the later section "Showing or hiding revisions" for details.

And now, the shortcut: The status bar hosts the Track Changes button. It's called Track Changes, and it's followed by the word *On* or *Off*, depending on the current state of the command. Click the button to turn on the feature; click again to turn it off. See Chapter 18 for more information about the status bar.

>> The Track Changes feature covers all changes to the document. These modifications include both the addition and removal of text, as well as formatting changes.

>> In addition to the Track Changes feature, Word offers the Compare Versions tool. See the later section "When Revision Marks Are Forgotten."

Disabling Track Changes

To deactivate the Track Changes feature, click the Track Changes button a second time. (Refer to the steps in the preceding section.) The Track Changes button returns to normal (its highlight disappears), and the status bar reports the message Track Changes: Off if you've set the status bar to display the Track Changes setting.

REMEMBER

>> Any document modifications made when the Track Changes feature is inactive are not marked as such by Word. Any existing revision marks are shown, but nothing new is marked.

>> No, you don't just turn off Track Changes when you're done. You peruse the changes and then choose whether to accept or reject each one.

>> See the later section "Accepting or rejecting changes" for information on how to deal with the revisions.

Locking the changes

Oh, why bother being nice? Before you hand off a document, you can activate and lock the Track Changes feature. Obey these directions:

1. **Click the Review tab.**

2. **In the Tracking group, click the Track Changes button and choose Lock Tracking from the menu.**

   The Lock Tracking dialog box appears.

3. **Type a password twice.**

   The same password is typed twice to ensure that you know the password.

4. **Click OK.**

   The Track Changes button is dimmed; the feature can no longer be deactivated.

To remove the lock, repeat the steps in this section, but in Step 3 type the password. Click OK to unlock the Track Changes feature.

WARNING

The Lock Tracking feature is not a document security tool. The only thing it prevents is anyone from disabling the Track Changes feature. See Chapter 28 for information on document security.

Showing or hiding revisions

How revision marks appear in your document depends on your preferences. If you want to see every dang detail, that option is available. If you want to see only hints or nothing at all, you can choose those settings. The secret is to access the Display for Review menu. Follow these directions:

1. **Click the Review tab.**

2. **In the Tracking group, click the Display for Review button.**

   The button's icon is shown in the margin.

The Display for Review button shows the current option for revision marks. Four choices are available:

Simple Markup: A vertical line appears in the left margin next to altered paragraphs.

All Markup: In addition to the vertical line, revision marks appear in the text. Added text is underlined. Removed text is shown as strikethrough. The revisions are color coded, so if the document was assaulted by more than one editor, each has his own color.

No Markup: All revisions are hidden in the text. They still exist, but you don't see them. I find this option best for editing the text because the revision marks don't get in my way.

Original: The changes are all hidden, and the document is presented as it was before the Track Changes feature was activated.

To see who did a revision, point the mouse at the revision. A pop-up bubble appears with the editor's name, the time of the edit, and a description of what was changed.

TIP

If you want to see a summary — which can get quite lengthy — activate the Reviewing pane. Follow these steps:

1. **Click the Review tab.**

2. **In the Tracking group, click the Reviewing Pane button.**

   The Revisions pane appears, showing a summary of all the document's changes since the Track Changes feature was activated.

Click on an item in the Revisions pane to instantly hop to that location in your document.

REMEMBER

>> With All Markup chosen, text inserted into the document appears with the underline text attribute active. The underlined text indicates new text added.

>> With All Markup chosen, text removed from the document appears with the ~~strikeout text attribute~~ active. The strikeout text was removed.

>> The underline and strikethrough text indicate revision marks. These are not attributes applied to the text.

>> The Revisions pane shows up no matter which option you've chosen from the Display for Review menu.

>> If you click the Reviewing Pane button, you see a menu from which you can choose whether the Revisions pane appears horizontally or vertically.

>> Yeah: Don't ask me why the command is called Reviewing Pane, but the actual gizmo is called the Revisions pane.

Accepting or rejecting changes

Those revision marks need not linger in your document, the embarrassing blemishes of a failed grammar school education. Seriously, the Track Changes feature is designed to show suggestions, not mortal changes. As the document's author, it's your choice whether to accept or reject the changes.

Obey these steps to approve or disapprove revisions:

1. **Press Ctrl+Home to visit the tippy-top of your document.**

2. **Click the Review tab.**

3. **In the Change group, click the Next Change button.**

Word moves the insertion pointer to the location in your document where the next change occurred.

4. **Click the Accept button to agree with the change; click the Reject button to dismiss the change.**

No matter which button you choose, the revision mark is removed. If you choose Accept, the change becomes part of the text. If you choose Reject, the change is removed.

5. **Continue to click the Accept or Reject buttons to move through the document.**

You no longer need to click the Next button as you accept and reject revisions.

If you're impatient, or just angry, you can employ two shortcuts to expedite the process: From the Accept button's menu, choose Accept All Changes. Or, from the Reject button's menu, choose Reject All Changes. Poof! The document review is complete.

You can also choose the variation on those commands: Accept All Changes and Stop Tracking, or Reject All Changes and Stop Tracking. In both cases, the document is scoured and the Track Changes feature deactivated.

WARNING

» It's easy to get confused! When you click the Accept button for a deletion, you are deleting the text. When you click the Reject button for an insertion, you are removing the inserted text. Sometimes, you might find yourself clicking Reject when you meant to accept a deletion.

» The revision marks stay with your document until you accept or reject them.

When Revision Marks Are Forgotten

Your document has made the rounds, and even Delores in Accounting got her hands on it. She'll never get over that night you stood her up, even though you had a damn good excuse. Anyway, no one bothered to activate the Track Changes feature. Now you're faced with two copies of your document: the original and the mangled version. What to do, what to do?

Fret not! Word features a Document Compare tool. It automatically applies revision marks to show you the exact differences between two documents. To use the tool, you must have two copies of the document available: the original and the copy. You must know both filenames. Once you're set, follow these steps to compare the documents:

1. **Click the Review tab.**

It doesn't matter which document is currently open. You could be working with a blank document; Word doesn't care.

2. **In the Compare group, click the Compare button and choose Compare.**

The Compare Documents dialog box appears, as shown in Figure 16-3. Your goal is to specify the original document and the copy or revised document as illustrated in the figure.

Summon the Open dialog box

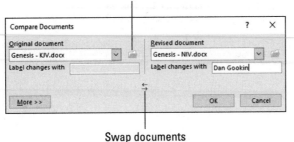

FIGURE 16-3:
The Compare
Documents
dialog box.

Swap documents

3. **Click the Original Document menu and choose the original document.**

You must choose the name even if the original document is currently shown in the Word document window. The menu lists all documents in the current folder. Click the folder icon if you need to access files in another folder.

4. **Click the Revised Document menu and choose the updated document.**

This document is the one that has the changes. The revision marks shown in the final document display what the revised document has added or removed.

TIP

If you get the original and revised documents reversed, click the Swap icon in the Compare Documents dialog box. (Refer to Figure 16-3.)

5. **Click OK.**

Word opens both documents, compares the original with the revised version, and displays a new document with the changes shown in revision marks.

Figure 16-4 lists the changes between the two documents listed in Figure 16-3. The combined document appears in the center pane. A list of items changed is shown in the Revisions pane (on the left). The two source documents are shown on the right.

The documents are synchronized, so that they scroll together. This feature allows you to peruse all three to see what was changed.

At this point, you can proceed as described in the earlier section "Accepting or rejecting changes." Peruse the revision marks to see which to keep or which to toss out.

When you're done, save the compared result document as you would any other document.

>> The Compare command is unavailable if the document has been protected. See Chapter 28 for information on text editing restrictions.

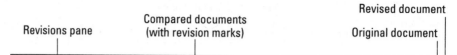

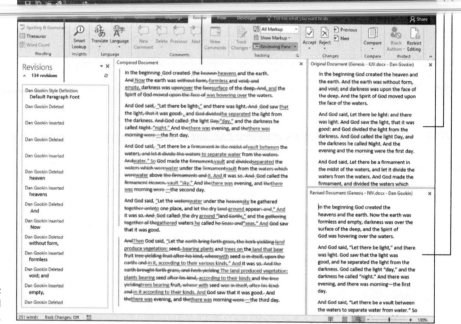

FIGURE 16-4:
The compared
documents.

>> If you accidentally close one of the document panes (shown in Figure 16-4),
use the Compare button menu on the Review tab to restore it: Choose
Compare ⇨ Show Source Documents ⇨ Show Both.

>> The Display for Review menu is set to All Markup for the compared document.
Refer to the earlier section "Showing or hiding revisions" for information on
changing the view, which might make the compared document more
readable.

**TECHNICAL
STUFF**

>> The Compare button menu also features a command called Combine. Its
effect is nearly identical to the Compare command, but its purpose is to
gather changes from multiple revised copies. So when more than one
document already has revision marks, use the Combine command in Step 2
and repeat the steps in this section for all marked-up document copies
(choosing Combine in Step 2) to create a single revised copy.

Online Collaboration

The ultimate form of collaboration is to have multiple people working on the same document at the same time. This insanity need not involve one PC with several keyboards. Instead, you share a document online and host several contributors, each making edits and suggestions at once. It sounds crazy, but it can be quite productive.

Sending out invitations

The part of online collaboration involves gathering a virtual group of people to edit or view the same document. Just as you might send out invitations to a party, you send out invitations to work on the document. Cake and balloons are optional.

To invite online humans to participate in your document's creation and editing, heed these steps:

1. Open the document you plan on sharing.

The document must be saved to your OneDrive account. If it hasn't been, you'll be prompted to save a copy there before you can proceed.

2. Click the File tab.

3. Choose Share.

If you haven't yet saved the document on your OneDrive storage, you'll be prompted to do so now.

Also, if you're not logged into your Microsoft account, you'll be prompted to do so.

4. Choose Share With People, and then, on the right side of the window, click the Share with People button.

You're returned to the document. A Share pane appears on the right side of the window. Your job is to send out email invites to people to join you and work together on the document.

5. Type the email address of a friendly collaborator or evil editor.

You can click the Address book icon to pull in contacts from Outlook — provided that you have Outlook configured on your PC.

After you type the address, the Share pane changes, as illustrated in Figure 16-5.

6. Select how the other user can affect the document.

Your options are Can Edit or Can View. An editor has full control over the document.

Type additional addresses

FIGURE 16-5:
The Share pane.

7. **Add more people, if desired: Type additional email addresses into the Invite People box.**

   The setting chosen in Step 6 affects everyone with whom you share the document.

8. **Click the Share button.**

   The email invite is broadcast to various recipients. The recipients are listed in the Share pane pending their acceptance of the invite.

The email message received shows a Word file icon, the filename, and a View In OneDrive button. When the recipient clicks the button, he can edit the document, either on the web or in his own copy of Word. See the next section.

TIP

>> If you're concerned about keeping the original document, share a copy: After Step 3 in this section, save the copy to a new location or under a new filename on your OneDrive storage.

>> You can click the Share tab found near the top right corner of the window to quickly skip over Steps 2 through 4 in this section.

>> Email invites are sent from your Microsoft account, which is why you must be logged in to that account to use the Share feature.

Working together on a document

Users you invite to work on a document can view that document on the web or in their own copy of Word. Normally, the OneDrive link opens in a Word on the Web page. This web page presentation is a look-only thing; the other users can read the document.

If the user is allowed to edit the document, he can click on the Edit in Browser button on the web page. At that point the browser screen changes to reflect the online copy of Word. And if the user has Word installed on his PC, he can click the OPEN IN WORD link to begin editing the document in the full version of Word.

When other users can edit your document, and they start doing so, you'll see a pop-up in the Word window, similar to what's shown in Figure 16-6. Click the Yes button to let other online editors to view the changes made to your document.

As the other users work on the document, you see different highlights representing text selected or perhaps a cursor location. If any changes are made, they are reflected by an Update icon appearing in the document's margin, as shown in Figure 16-7. Save the document to update the text and highlight what was changed.

>> Sharing works better while you're communicating. Word presently lacks any real-time chat mode for editing, so I assume you'll be on the phone or chatting with some app while you collaborate on the document.

FIGURE 16-6:
Viewing a shared web document online.

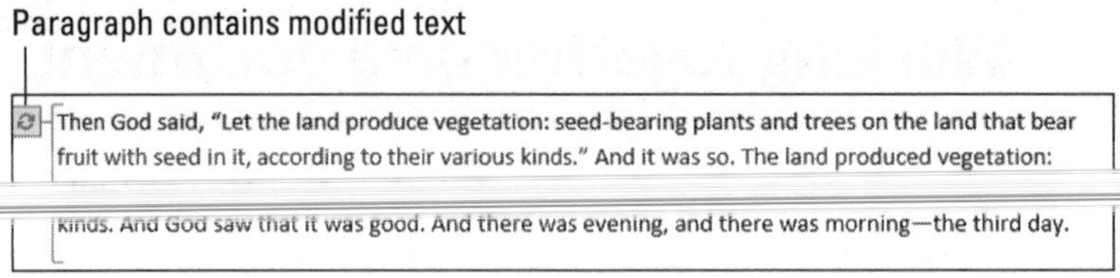

Paragraph contains modified text

FIGURE 16-7:
Changes made
online are
pending in this
paragraph.

> Then God said, "Let the land produce vegetation: seed-bearing plants and trees on the land that bear
> fruit with seed in it, according to their various kinds." And it was so. The land produced vegetation:
>
> kinds. And God saw that it was good. And there was evening, and there was morning—the third day.

>> Don't bother activating the Track Changes feature while a document is shared; it won't work. Instead, you can compare the document after it's shared with an original copy. Refer to the earlier section "When Revision Marks Are Forgotten."

>> See Chapter 29 for information on using Word on the web.

Ending collaboration

To end document sharing, close the document: Press Ctrl+W. The Sharing link expires and your collaborators receive a notice saying that the document is no longer shared. Any further edits a collaborator makes can be saved to a new document on that computer, but not to your copy.

Chapter 17

Word for Lawyers and WordPerfect Converts

I have a reason why this chapter combines information about using Word in a legal setting as well as converting from WordPerfect: Lawyers adore WordPerfect. To the software developers' credit, they found a market and catered to it brilliantly. But over time, the move from WordPerfect to Word became an inevitability, for not only lawyers but normal people as well.

Line Numbers on the Page

I'm not an attorney, but I know that one thing required in the legal profession is a document with line numbers marching down the page. This feature is also used in radio scripts, just in case you're a lawyer who moonlights reading midnight radio drama.

Adding line numbers

Line numbering can start at the top of each page or be continuous for the entire

1. **Click the Layout tab.**

2. **In the Page Setup group, click the Line Numbers button.**

A menu appears, from which you can choose line numbering options. All Word documents are preset with the None option chosen, for no line numbers.

3. **Choose Continuous to number all lines in the document consecutively, or choose Restart Each Page to start the first line of the page at number 1.**

The lines in the document are numbered sequentially, top-down, in the left margin of the page, as shown in Figure 17-1.

Line numbers without paragraph spacing   Line numbers with paragraph spacing

TIP

To make the line numbers look good, format paragraphs without spacing before or after. It's okay to adjust the line spacing, but the space before or after a paragraph isn't numbered, so the line numbering down the side of the page looks uneven. Compare Figure 17-1 right and left to see examples.

Line numbering is affected by document sections. If you need only a portion of the document numbered, set those pages into their own section and apply the line numbering to that section only. In Step 3, choose Restart Each Section. Refer to Chapter 6 for information on setting sections within a document.

Formatting line numbers

If you desire to format the line numbers, you can bring up the Line Numbers dialog box to set some options, such as how far away from the text the numbers appear. Obey these directions:

1. **Click the Layout tab.**

2. **Click the Line Numbers button and choose Numbering Options.**

   The Page Setup dialog box appears.

3. **Click the Line Numbers button.**

   The Line Numbers dialog box appears, as shown in Figure 17-2.

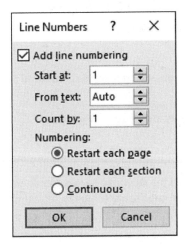

Most of the options you can set in the Line Numbers dialog box have preset commands on the Line Numbers menu, described in the preceding section. One item you can't set, however, is the From Text distance.

To set how far to the left of the page margin the numbers appear, enter a value in the box. For example, the value 0.5" sets the numbers half an inch from the left page margin. The Auto value sets the numbers about ¼-inch from the page margin.

WARNING

Avoid setting line numbers closer than ½-inch to the page edge. That's because not every printer is capable of printing information toward the edge of the paper.

See Chapter 2 for information about page margins and paragraph indents.

Removing line numbers

To zap all line numbers from a document, follow these steps:

1. **Click the Layout tab.**

2. **In the Page Setup group, click the Line Numbers button and choose None.**

   The line numbers are gone.

If your document is split into sections, the preceding steps remove line numbers from the current section only.

To remove line numbering from a single paragraph, follow these steps:

1. **Click to place the insertion pointer in the given paragraph.**

   You can also select a group of paragraphs.

2. **Click the Layout tab.**

3. **Click the Line Numbers button and choose the command Suppress for Current Paragraph.**

   The line numbering for the given paragraph(s) is skipped.

Numbering resumes at the following paragraph.

REMEMBER

The line numbering is suppressed for an entire paragraph. Even when each line of the paragraph is numbered, the command removes all numbered lines in the paragraph.

The Table of Authorities

A table of authorities is a list of legal references and sources, similar to a bibliography. Like the Bibliography, the Table of Authorities is one of Word's document reference tools. Most of these tools are covered in Chapter 21, but because a table of authorities is typically found in legal documents, it's mentioned here.

Marking citations

Word doesn't write the citations in a table of authorities for you; that's your job. It can help you organize and list them. To make that happen, you must mark the citations in your document. Obey these steps:

1. **Finish your document.**

   To best mark citations, it helps to have the document completed with all the citations written. Though you can mark citations as you go, it's more effective to finish the document first. Oh, and:

2. **Save your document.**

   Always save.

3. **Select a citation.**

   Select the first instance of a citation in the document. If the citation is inside parentheses, don't select the parentheses (though you can edit them out later).

4. **Click the References tab.**

5. **In the Table of Authorities group, click the Mark Citation button.**

   The Mark Citation dialog box appears, with the text you selected from Step 3 shown inside, as depicted in Figure 17-3.

Text selected in the document

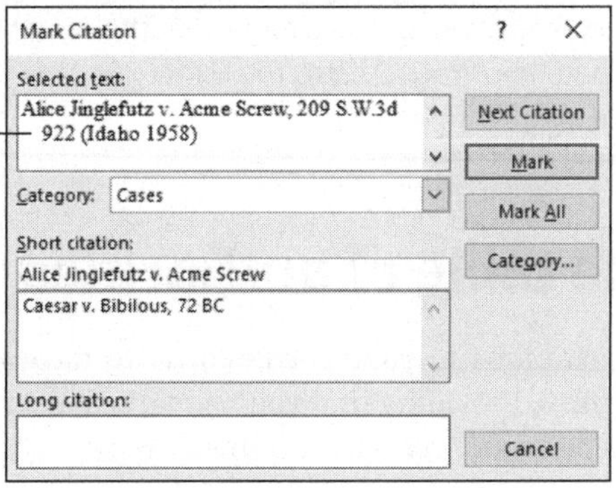

Mark Citation   ?   ×

Selected text:
Alice Jinglefutz v. Acme Screw, 209 S.W.3d   Next Citation
922 (Idaho 1958)
                                               Mark
Category: Cases   Mark All
Short citation:
Alice Jinglefutz v. Acme Screw   Category...
Caesar v. Bibilous, 72 BC

Long citation:
                                               Cancel

FIGURE 17-3: The Mark Citation dialog box.

6. **Choose a category, such as Cases or Statutes.**

7. **If a longer citation is required, type it in the Long Citation text box.**

8. **Click the Mark button to mark the citation, or click Mark All to mark all instances of the citation in the document.**

   The Mark All button directs Word to track the pages on which the same citation appears. Those pages are referenced in the table of authorities.

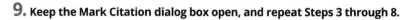

9. **Keep the Mark Citation dialog box open, and repeat Steps 3 through 8.**

If you click the Next Citation button, Word hops forward in the document to the next bit of text it believes to be a citation.

10. **When you're done marking citations, click the Cancel button.**

The dialog box goes away.

A side effect of using the Mark Citation tool is that Word activates the Show/Hide feature, revealing the document's codes. Specific to the citations, you see a field displayed "in the raw" next to the citation text. That's okay! Don't delete the field, though you can turn off the Show/Hide feature: See the later section "Revealing the codes."

>> To remove a citation, erase its text.

>> Editing a citation is tricky. You can't just re-mark it — you just activate the Show/Hide command to reveal the citation's secret text. Delete that secret text, contained between the curly brackets. Then mark the citation again as described in this section.

>> Marking citations is similar to marking items for inclusion in an index. In fact, creating an index is similar to creating a table of authorities: You mark text for inclusion in a list, and then Word creates the list for you. See Chapter 21 for information on creating an index.

Inserting the table of authorities

The goal of marking citations in your document is to have Word automatically build a table of authorities. Providing that you've marked all citations and done all that other attorney–type stuff, proceed with these steps:

1. **Place the insertion pointer on the page where you want the table of authorities to start.**

I would recommend starting the page with a hard page break or even a section break. See Chapter 6 for details.

You might also consider setting a title on the page — something clever, like *Table of Authorities.* If you want that text included in a table of contents, ensure that you use the Heading 1 or similar style for the title.

2. **Click the References tab.**

3. **In the Table of Authorities group, click the Insert Table of Authorities button.**

The Table of Authorities dialog box appears. It shows a preview of what the table looks like, as shown in Figure 17-4.

Preview

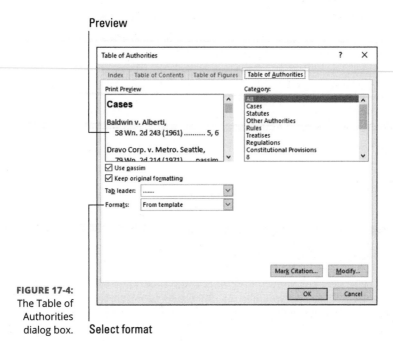

Select format

4. **Choose an item from the Formats menu.**

As you select items, the Preview window updates to reflect how the table of authorities appears.

You can also choose an underline style from the Tab Leader menu. Again, the Preview window updates to show you the Table of Authorities style and presentation.

5. **Click OK to insert the table of authorities into your document.**

Take a moment to look at it. If it's not correct, press Ctrl+Z to undo and start over at Step 3.

The table of authorities is actually a document field. You don't edit it; Word creates it for you, based on the text you've marked as citations. (Refer to the preceding section.)

>> To edit the table of authorities, right-click in the table's text and choose the Edit Field command. In the Edit Field dialog box, click the Table of Authorities button. You see the Table of Authorities dialog box (refer to Figure 17-4), where you can make changes to the format or layout.

>> Yes, you can add more citations to the table at any time: Refer to the preceding section for details on marking citations. You need to update the table of authorities after you add or change citations.

>> The Use Passim setting in the Table of Authorities dialog box substitutes the word *passim* for a citation that has multiple references throughout the document. If you'd rather see the specific page numbers, un-check the Use

>> To update the table of authorities, right-click in the table's text and choose the Update Field command. You must perform this step after marking new citations or editing your document. It ensures that any changes are included in the table.

>> See Chapter 21 for more information on document references. Chapter 24 covers fields.

Other Legal Considerations

I've scoured the Internet as well as my email inbox for questions from law offices regarding specific issues with Microsoft Word. I have a bunch of them, and many of the answers are addressed in this book — specifically, in this chapter. Two additional topics are left-right block indent and text redaction.

>> Also see Chapter 15 for information on saving Word documents in other file formats. These formats might be required for electronic submission of documents.

>> Information on footnotes and endnotes is found in Chapter 21.

Setting a left-right block indent

The *left-right block indent* is a paragraph format, frequently found in legal documents. Also known as a *block quote*, this style involves increasing a paragraph's left and right indentations by equal values. Figure 17-5 illustrates how such a format might look.

To scrunch in a paragraph's left and right indentation, follow these steps:

1. **Place the insertion pointer in the given paragraph or select a group of paragraphs.**

2. **Click the Layout tab.**

3. **In the Paragraph group, type** 0.5 **in the Left Indentation box.**

4. **Type** 0.5 **in the Right Indentation box.**

The paragraph's left and right indentations move toward the center of the document, setting that text aside from the text above and below it.

Paragraph's left indentation   Paragraph's right indentation

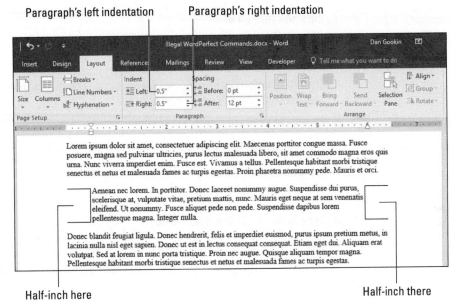

FIGURE 17-5:
Indenting a
paragraph.

Half-inch here   Half-inch there

You can set a value other than half-an-inch in Step 3. Set whatever looks good.

TIP

>> Word features a "half-inch indent" command: Press Ctrl+M. This keyboard shortcut affects only the paragraph's left indentation.

>> If you plan on using the left-right block indent frequently, I recommend that you create a block indent style and include that style with your document templates.

>> Paragraph indentation is not the same thing as adjusting a page's margins. In Word, page margins and paragraph indents are two separate things.

>> Refer to Chapter 2 for all the details on paragraph formatting.

Redacting text

When you need to remove information from a document, I recommend that you create and apply a Redaction style. This style doesn't remove text, and it doesn't blank it out. Instead, it sets the text's foreground and background colors to black. The end result is that the text doesn't show up in the document, similar to what's shown in Figure 17-6.

FIGURE 17-6:
Redaction in
action.

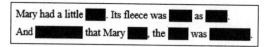

To create a Redaction style in Word, follow these steps:

1. **Click the Home tab.**

2. **In the Styles group, click the More button in the lower right corner of the Style Gallery.**

   The More button is shown in the margin. Upon success, you see the rest of the Style Gallery, plus a few commands.

3. **Choose the Create a Style command.**

   The Create New Style from Formatting dialog box appears.

4. **Click the Modify button.**

   The dialog box expands to show more options, similar to Figure 17-7.

5. **Type** Redaction **in the Name box.**

6. **From the Style Type menu, choose Character.**

7. **In the Formatting area, click the Font Color button and choose black.**

   On the color menu, the blackest black color is located below the first *e* in the word *Theme.*

8. **Click the Format button and choose Border.**

9. **Click the Shading tab in the Borders and Shading dialog box.**

10. **Click the Fill button.**

    You see a color menu similar to the one you saw in Step 7.

11. **Choose black as the fill color.**

    Choose the same black, the one located below the first *e* in the word *Theme.*

12. **Click OK.**

13. **If you want to add the Redaction style to the template, place a check mark by the item New Documents Based On This Template.**

    This style is probably something you'll use again and again, so it makes sense to add it to the template.

14. **Click OK to create the Redaction style.**

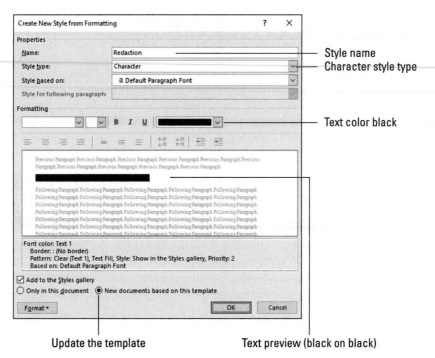

Style name
Character style type
Text color black

FIGURE 17-7:
Building the
Redaction style.

Update the template

Text preview (black on black)

To apply the style, select text in your document and then choose the Redaction style from the Home tab's Style gallery or from the Styles pane.

» Your inclination might be to simply set the text's foreground and background colors to black, which can be done in Word: The text color is set in the Font dialog box, and the background color is part of the Borders and Shading command. Instead, I urge you to build a Redaction style, as recommended in this section.

» The automatic font color is usually black, but when you create the Redaction style, you want to assert a true black color. That's because if you later edit the default text color or style, the Automatic option may change to a color other than black. That change would render text visible in the Redaction style.

» By setting both the text color and background shading to black, you not only redact the text but also prevent someone from selecting that chunk of text and viewing its contents "inversed" in the selected block.

» Refer to Chapters 8 and 9 for information on styles and templates, respectively.

Hello, WordPerfect User!

I admit that I, too, am a WordPerfect refugee. I made the conversion a long time ago, back when WordPerfect was a DOS (text mode) program. It was my beloved word processor, the first I had ever used that actually respected me as a writer. Then I was offered a King Kong-size pile of cash to write about Microsoft Word, and, well, my loyalties changed.

Converting your WordPerfect documents

Word has the capability to open WordPerfect documents. That's where your enthusiasm for the conversion must halt. Once the document is open, I strongly urge you to save it in the Word document format: Retain the old file, but work only on the new, Word document.

To open a WordPerfect document in Word, follow these steps when using Word:

1. **Press Ctrl+O.**

   The Open screen appears.

2. **Click the Browse button.**

   The traditional Open dialog box, which you were expecting in Step 1, finally appears.

3. **Click the File Type menu and choose All Files (*.*).**

4. **Browse to the folder containing the WordPerfect document file.**

5. **Select the file you want to open, and then click the Open button.**

   Word converts the WordPerfect document as best it can, displaying it in the Word program window.

6. **Don't do anything!**

   Don't edit the document, don't critique the translation, don't marvel at your text.

7. **Click the File tab.**

8. **Choose Save As.**

   The Save As screen appears.

9. **Ensure that Word Document (*.docx) is chosen from the File Type menu.**

10. **Optionally, change the file's name.**

    You don't need to change the filename, but if the new name helps you to distinguish it from the original WordPerfect document, all the better.

11. **Click the Save button.**

You can now work on the document.

Word lacks a feature to massively update all your WordPerfect documents. As someone who's made the conversion, I don't recommend that you do so. Instead, keep those older documents. Word can open them as necessary. At that time, if you need to continue working on the document, save it first as a Word document and then proceed.

Revealing the codes

Perhaps the command WordPerfect users miss the most is Reveal Codes. It was one of my favorites when I used WordPerfect ages ago. Don't bother looking for a similar command in Word; it doesn't exist. That's because Word doesn't really use formatting codes in the same way as WordPerfect.

The closest approximation to the Reveal Codes command is the Show/Hide command. It exposes hidden or nonprintable items in the document. To turn on this feature, obey these steps:

1. **Click the Home tab.**

¶ **2.** **In the Paragraph group, click the Show/Hide button.**

The button is shown in the margin.

Once active, the document is beset with various symbols representing nonprintable characters or hidden document elements, such as fields. Table 17-1 lists the variety of what you might see.

TABLE 17-1   **Hidden Characters**

Symbol	Represents	Description
{}	Field	A document field, with text held between the braces
·	Space	The space character
→	Tab	The tab character
¬	Optional hyphen	A line break used at the end of a line, but hidden otherwise
¶	Paragraph	The location where the Enter key was pressed to end a paragraph of text
a̶b̶c̶	Hidden text	Text with the hidden attribute applied, which doesn't appear in the document

Another apology for not having the Reveal Codes command is the Reveal Formatting command. The only thing it shares with Reveal Codes is the word *reveal*. Otherwise, it's not helpful to a WordPerfect convert.

To use the Reveal Formatting command, press Shift+F1. The Reveal Formatting pane appears. It lists all sorts of details about the current text format, from font to paragraph to section, as illustrated in Figure 17-8.

You can click on an item in the list to change the formatting, such as Indentation, shown in Figure 17-8, in which case the proper dialog box or location in Word appears. At that point, you can change the specific formatting element.

Formatting details

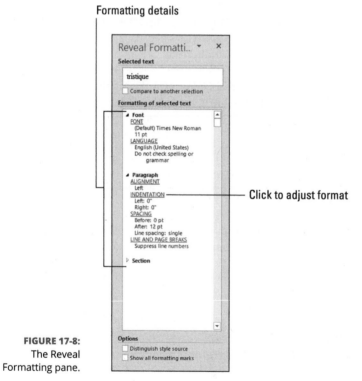

Click to adjust format

FIGURE 17-8:
The Reveal
Formatting pane.

Yeah, that's not *really* the same as Reveal Codes.

» The keyboard shortcut for the Show/Hide command is Ctrl+Shift+8. Use the 8 key above the U and I keys, not the 8 key on the numeric keypad.

» Tabs are covered in Chapter 3. It's important in Word to distinguish between the tab character and a tab stop.

- » The line break symbol represents an optional hyphen. Refer to Chapter 2 for details on hyphenation in Word.

- » The topic of hidden text is uncovered in Chapter 1.

- » See Chapter 31 for information for information on always displaying hidden characters in a document.

Understanding Word's oddities

Here are some final thoughts and suggestions for making the WordPerfect-to-Word transition go down a little easier:

- » Word's formatting is shown right on the screen. If the text is *italic*, it prints in *italic*. Word doesn't conceal any formatting properties, even in Draft view.

- » If you use Draft view (which I do), don't be surprised when some features, such as inserting graphics, switch you to Print Layout view.

- » Text formatting applies only to a chunk of text. You typically format text by selecting and then formatting. If you activate a feature, such as italics or bold, that feature applies only to new text you type, not from the current position to the end of the document.

REMEMBER

- » Word looks at a document as sections, pages, paragraphs, and characters. These are the formatting elements.

- » It's best to use styles in Word, which are more useful than WordPerfect's styles. Word's styles come in handy when applying formatting changes to vast swaths of text. Refer to Chapter 8.

- » Word uses both page margins and paragraph indents, which are not the same thing. Refer to Chapter 2 for details on the differences.

- » Consider activating the option to display the paragraph marks in your text. See Chapter 31 for information on showing the ¶ character.

- » Learn about templates, and use them. They are real time-savers. Chapter 9 covers templates, though more basic information is found in the book *Word 2016 For Dummies* (Wiley).

- » WordPerfect's macros are similar to three concepts in Word: AutoText, AutoCorrect, and document building blocks. See Chapter 23.

- » Definitely learn about Word's macros, which are more about augmenting commands and automating processes than automatically typing text. See

Chapter 25. Design your own macros to emulate your favorite WordPerfect functions. Then create your own tab on the Ribbon to host those command buttons.

>> See Chapter 34, which lists Word's function keys and command equivalents. Word lacks an onscreen reference for its function-key equivalents.

One final piece of advice: Use Word. It's your word processor now. Get comfortable with it. Learn and appreciate its quirks. Any piece of software takes time to get used to. Allocate yourself a few months. After a while, you may not adore Word as much as you adore WordPerfect, but you'll tolerate it more than you do now.

4

Word for Writers

Chapter 18
Tools for Every Author

Word hosts an abundance of features to succor the budding scribe. It won't encourage you to write every day, help meet your quota, or reward you when your text is brilliant. Word will, however, help you locate spelling errors and fix common grammatical blunders, and it offers tools to assist any wordsmith with their writing duties.

TIP

Word's digital tools are no replacement for a second set of eyes on your text. Nothing helps a writer like a good editor, even an amateur editor. If you truly want to become a professional writer, you will welcome the opportunity for others to read and judge your prose.

Behold! The Document Window

Word's document window is a flexible thing. You can direct Word to show you lots of controls and options, or you can configure the window to be as reserved as a haiku.

Figure 18-1 illustrates the two ways I prefer to work in Word. The window setup on the left shows Draft view. This is how I work when writing technical books, such as this one. On the right is Print Layout view, which I prefer when writing

Navigation pane   Ruler   Style pane   Ribbon   Status bar

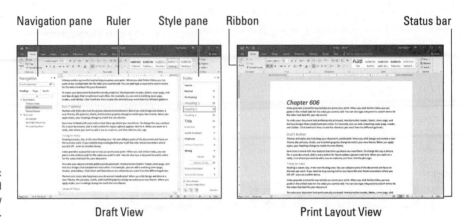

FIGURE 18-1:
Two Word
window
configurations.

Draft View   Print Layout View

The difference between the setups is in which items are shown in the document window and how they appear. These items are the Ribbon, the document view, the optional panes that can appear left and right of the document, and the status bar.

Another item to consider placing in the document window is the Ruler. See Chapters 2 and 3 for information about the Ruler.

Showing or hiding the Ribbon

For pure writing tasks, you don't really need to see the Ribbon hanging at the top of the document window. To hide it, click the up-pointing chevron, as illustrated in Figure 18-2 (left). The Ribbon's tabs remain, which you can click to view the Ribbon and its various graphical groups and command buttons.

To keep the Ribbon visible at all times, click the Pin icon, shown on the right in Figure 18-2. When the Ribbon is hidden, first click a tab, such as the Home tab, and then you can access the Pin icon.

TIP

The Ribbon menu (refer to Figure 18-2) contains two items that expedite the hide/pin process: Choose Show Tabs and Commands to keep the Ribbon visible; choose Show Tabs to hide the Ribbon.

Ribbon menu

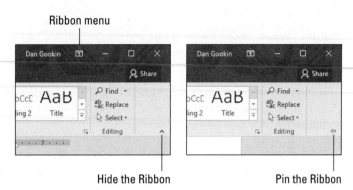

FIGURE 18-2:
Showing and
hiding the
Ribbon.

Hide the Ribbon   Pin the Ribbon

Going full-screen

If you're a fan of absolutely no clutter when you write, you can direct Word to fill the screen with the document window and hide the Ribbon. The end effect is a blank sheet of paper floating on the screen.

To activate full-screen mode, follow these steps:

1. **Click the Show Ribbon menu button.**

Refer to Figure 18-2 for its location. The button is found in the upper right corner of the document window.

2. **Choose Auto-Hide Ribbon.**

To access the Ribbon in full-screen mode, tap the Alt key. Or you can click on the three horizontal dots located in the upper left corner of the screen.

To exit full-screen mode, click the Ribbon menu (found in the upper right corner of the screen) and choose either Show Tabs and Commands or Show Tabs.

If the window is *maximized* (fills the screen), click the Restore icon, shown in the margin and found in the upper left corner of the screen, to resize the document window.

Setting the document view

Word offers five ways to view a document in its window. Three of the ways are popular enough to find a spot on the status bar; the rest are accessed from the View menu, found in the Views group. Here are all five views:

Read Mode: Best for reading text, but not editing. This icon, shown in the margin, is found on the status bar.

Print Layout: Good for editing text, especially when you need to view document formatting, graphics, tables, and other items. This icon is also found on the status bar.

Web Layout: Shows how the document would look if presented on a web page instead of on a sheet of paper. This icon is the third view icon found on the status bar.

Outline: Used for organizing topics, as covered in Chapter 19.

Draft: Great for writing, but not for final document preview or layout.

Of the five modes, the two used most frequently by writers are Print Layout and Draft. Of those two, I prefer Draft over Print Layout. Only when I'm crafting a document with graphics, tables, or other nontext elements do I use Print Layout. Even then, Word automatically switches to Print Layout view when you manipulate certain objects.

>> The view is maintained when you switch to full-screen mode, as covered in the preceding section.

>> No matter which mode you prefer (for me, it's Draft), Word opens documents in either the Print Layout or Web Layout view, depending on which view you last used.

>> If these shortcut icons for Read Mode, Print Layout, and Web Layout views don't appear on the status bar, choose View Shortcuts from the status bar's shortcut menu, as described in the later section "Controlling the status bar."

Adding useful panes

Some Word features present themselves as floating windows or panes to the left and right of the document window. These panes come and go, depending on what you're doing in Word. If not, you can dismiss them by clicking the X (Close) button in the pane's upper right corner.

Two panes I find handy for writing are the Navigation pane and Styles pane. Refer to Figure 18-1 for an example of how these panes can appear in the document window.

The Navigation pane hosts three tabs: Headings, Pages, and Results.

Headings: The Headings tab lists your document's headings, like a mini-outline. The headings match the heading styles and indent themselves accordingly. This tab allows you to see a quick overview of your document. You can also click on a heading to instantly hop to that location.

Pages: The Pages tab presents your document as a column of thumbnails. If you use Draft view (see the preceding section), the Pages tab lets you see the document layout in context.

Results: The Results tab appears when you use Word's Find command; press Ctrl+F to see it. Search results appear on the tab as well as highlighted on the screen.

The Styles pane lists the document's current styles or those styles associated with the document's template. I find it much more convenient than using the Home tab's Style gallery. Follow these steps to show the Styles pane:

1. **Click the Home tab.**

2. **In the Styles group, click the Launcher icon in the lower right corner.**

   The icon is shown in the margin.

3. **If you want the Styles pane docked to the side of the window, drag it until the mouse pointer is at the left edge of the document window.**

4. **Place a check mark by Show Preview to see the styles in context.**

   The Show Preview option is found at the bottom of the Styles pane.

To undock the Styles pane, use the mouse to drag the top part of the pane left or right.

TIP

>> I prefer that the Styles pane show only those styles related to the current document. Refer to Chapter 8 for information on setting that option, as well as more details on a document's styles.

>> Refer to Chapter 9 for details on document templates.

TECHNICAL STUFF

>> The Navigation pane's Headings tab is similar to the Document Map feature, available in very old versions of Word.

Controlling the status bar

The *status bar* lurks at the bottom of the Word document window, and it can be your friend — as long as you don't overload it with too much junk.

The key to too much junk, not enough junk, and Goldilocks junk is found on the status bar menu: Right-click the status bar to see the full list of items available. Figure 18-3 illustrates the menu, along with the items I recommend as useful for a writer.

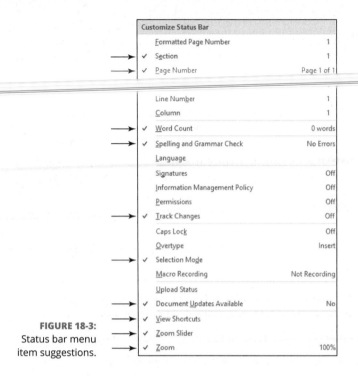

To add an item to the status bar, follow these directions:

1. **Right-click the status bar to display its menu.**

   Refer to Figure 18-3.

2. **Click to choose an item to add.**

   Added items appear with a check mark to their left.

3. **Click elsewhere in the document window or press the Esc key when you're done adding items.**

To remove an item, choose it from the status bar menu to remove its check mark. (Refer to Step 2.)

The items shown in Figure 18-3 are merely my suggestions. I activate Line Numbers and Macro Recording items on the status bar, but that just reflects my preferences.

Count Your Words

Anyone who's written articles for a magazine or a letter to the editor knows about *word count.* It's a limit you don't want to surpass. For professional writers, word count is the way you get paid; the first article I sold paid me a nickel a word. Pulling a word count is a common activity, and Word does the job for you automatically.

TIP

>> Publishers deal in word counts, not page counts. Page count varies depending on layout and design choices.

>> Word count is set as a maximum value, such as 1,000 words or 2,500 words.

>> Novels typically run between 40,000 and 100,000 words.

>> The best way to get a letter-to-the-editor published is to be brief. If the newspaper suggests "200 words maximum," keep your dispatch to 200 words or fewer.

Checking the word count

To see how near you are to that maximum word count, follow these steps:

1. **Click the Review tab.**

2. **In the Proofing group, click the Word Count button.**

   Behold the Word Count dialog box, similar to Figure 18-4, which lists text statistics beyond the total number of words.

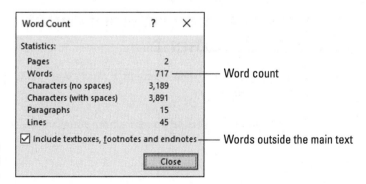

FIGURE 18-4:
The Word Count
dialog box.

REMEMBER

The total number of words, such as 717 in Figure 18-4, includes any individual text tidbit, such as the title at the top of the document, and even footnotes and endnotes if you select the check box. (Refer to the figure.)

See Chapter 21 for information on footnotes and endnotes and why their word counts should or should not be included in the document's total.

Adding the word count to the status bar

A better way to check your document's current word count it to place that value on the status bar. That way, it's always updated and visible, similar to what's shown in Figure 18-5.

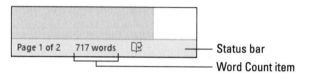

Page 1 of 2   717 words ——— Status bar
———— Word Count item

To add the word count to the status bar, refer to the earlier section "Controlling the status bar." Choose the Word Count item from the status bar menu.

TIP

>> Not only does the status bar's Word Count item show the current word count, but you can also click it to quickly access the Word Count dialog box.

>> If you select text, the word count on the status bar shows values for the selected text as well as the document's total word count.

Inserting the current word count into your document

Follow these steps to insert the document's word count value when submitting your article or column:

1. **Click to position the insertion pointer where you want the value to appear.**

For example, after the text *word count =.*

2. **Click the Insert tab.**

3. **In the Text group, click the Quick Parts button and choose Field.**

   The Quick Parts button is illustrated in the margin.

4. **In the Field dialog box, from the Categories menu, choose Document information.**

5. **From the Field Names list, choose NumWords.**

6. **Click the OK button.**

The field shows the document's current word count, not including the field's text (which adds one to the count).

REMEMBER

>> If you edit the document, you must update the field: Right-click the word count and choose the Update Field command.

>> See Chapter 24 for further details on document fields.

Viewing readability statistics

I remember an editor admonishing me to "write at a sixth grade level!" How do you know at which grade level to peg your writing? And what does that mean?

Reading level refers to whether your text is easy or difficult to read. It has to do with objective items such as word choice and sentence length. The document's topic also plays a role, but as far as Word is concerned, the Flesch-Kincaid readability tests are used to judge your text. Two values are supplied: Reading Ease and Flesch-Kincaid Grade Level index.

To gauge your document's readability, you must activate Word's Readability feature:

1. **Click the File tab and choose Options.**

   The Word Options dialog box appears.

2. **Choose Proofing from the left side of the dialog box.**

3. **Place a check mark by the item Show Readability Statistics.**

4. **Click OK.**

To check the statistics, you must perform a manual spell check on your document. See the later section "Proofing your document manually." At the end of the check, a summary dialog box appears, similar to what's shown in Figure 18-6.

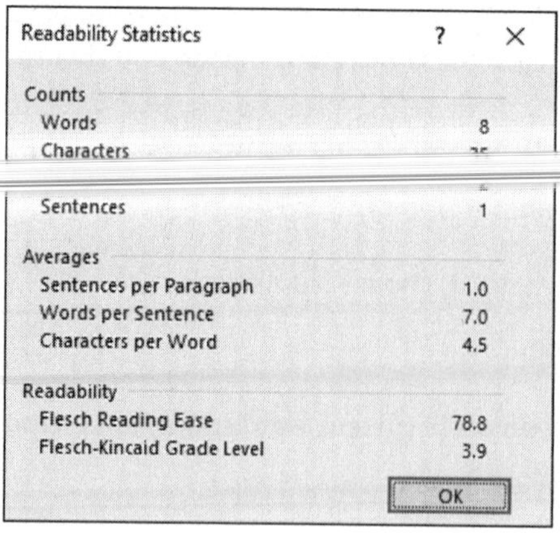

Readability Statistics	?	X
Counts		
Words		8
Characters		35
Sentences		1
Averages		
Sentences per Paragraph		1.0
Words per Sentence		7.0
Characters per Word		4.5
Readability		
Flesch Reading Ease		78.8
Flesch-Kincaid Grade Level		3.9
	OK	

FIGURE 18-6:
Readability score for a short story.

>> The *Reading Ease* is a score between 0.0 and 100.0, with values above 50.0 indicating easy-to-read text and values closer to 0.0 indicating rather difficult text. College-level text, considered difficult to read, is scored at 30.0 and below.

>> The Flesch-Kincaid Grade Level value represents the grade school level where a student would find reading your text easy. For example, a score of 5.0 would indicate that a fifth-grader would have little problem reading your stuff.

>> This chapter has a Reading Ease score of 66.1, with a grade level of 7.2.

Document Proofing

Fortunately for me, one of the qualifications for being a good writer is not the ability to win a spelling bee. I'm a horrid speller; most writers are. In the old days, editors corrected spelling errors. Since version 7, Word does the spell checking job automatically as you type. Soon afterward, grammar checking was added, though I'm not an enthusiastic fan of that feature.

>> Improperly spelled words appear with a red zigzag underline.

>> Improper grammar or word usage appears with a blue zigzag underline.

>> To correct a spelling error, right-click the word and choose the proper spelling from the shortcut menu. If the correct word isn't found, take another stab at spelling and try again. If all else fails, grab a dictionary.

>> To fix a grammar error, right-click the blue-underlined word and choose a replacement. If the grammar is fine, which happens often, choose the Ignore Once command.

>> When you're really stuck on spelling, open a web browser and type the word into Google's Search text box. Google might suggest the proper spelling or suggest a better word.

>> You must know the old adage by now: A spell check isn't the same as proofreading. Words can be spelled properly but used inappropriately. Nothing beats having that second set of eyes look at your text.

TIP

>> To increase your English grammar kung fu, I strongly recommend that you read a copy of Strunk & White's *The Elements of Style*. It's an excellent book, short and pithy. It will help you understand and use English grammar far more than anything you've forgotten since high school.

Disabling on-the-fly proofing

Maybe you don't like to see the red zigzag underline of shame. Or the blue zigzags flag for incorrect grammar, but the usage is acceptable in your prose. If you prefer, you can forbid Word from performing on-the-fly proofing, which may help you concentrate more on writing and less on correcting your text.

To disable automatic spell checking, grammar checking, or both, follow these steps:

1. **Click the File tab and choose Options.**

   The Word Options dialog box appears.

2. **On the left side of the dialog box, choose Proofing.**

3. **Remove the check mark by the item Check Spelling As You Type.**

4. **Remove the check mark by the item Mark Grammar Errors As You Type.**

5. **Click OK.**

Once disabled, Word refuses to show a proofing command's red or blue zigzag underlines. You can still proof your document, but it's a process you must do manually. See the next section.

Proofing your document manually

When on-the-fly proofing is disabled, the task falls upon your shoulders: You

1. **Click the Review tab.**

2. **In the Proofing group, click the Spelling & Grammar button.**

    The Spelling pane appears, similar to what's shown in Figure 18-7. Each
    misspelled word is displayed one at a time.

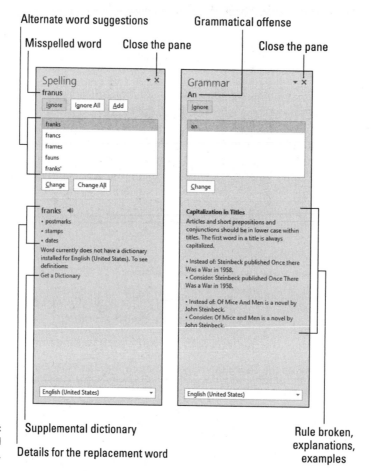

Alternate word suggestions   Grammatical offense

Misspelled word   Close the pane   Close the pane

FIGURE 18-7:
The Spelling and
Grammar panes.

Supplemental dictionary

Details for the replacement word

Rule broken,
explanations,
examples

3. **Deal with the issue.**

    The options presented on the Spelling and Grammar panes differ, depending
    on the issue at hand. Among your choices are

Ignore: Direct the spell check to forgive that one word flagged as misspelled, or the grammar checker to let the problem sneak by.

Ignore All: Direct the proofer to ignore all instances of the improperly spelled word or grammatical issue.

Add: Place the word that's flagged as misspelled into the dictionary. See the later section "Working with the dictionary."

Change: Replace the misspelled word with an alternative word from the list (refer to Figure 18-7), or replace a grammatical issue with something more acceptable.

Change All: Replace all instances of the misspelled word with the word chosen from the list.

Though it's not a command, you can also click in your document to temporarily suspend proofing and make corrections. Click the Resume button to continue proofing from that point.

4. **Keep proofing until you see the dialog box informing you that the spell check is complete; click OK.**

   If you've enabled the Readability Statistics option, you see that dialog box when proofing is complete. See the earlier section "Viewing readability statistics."

TIP

Manual proofing is done on the entire document, from top to bottom. If you need to proof only a word or another document chunk, mark that chunk of text as a block, and then work through the steps in this section.

>> Click the Spelling and Grammar Check icon on the status bar (see the next section) to quickly start proofing your document.

>> To cancel manual proofing, click the X button to close the pane. (Refer to Figure 18-7.)

>> You can perform a manual proof even when on-the-fly spell check is active. If words are misspelled or items are flagged as grammatically incorrect and they've been ignored, the Spelling or Grammar pane still appears. Otherwise, you see the spell-check-is-complete dialog box or the Readability Statistics dialog box, if that feature is enabled.

Understanding the spell check icon

The status bar features a Spelling and Grammar Check icon, which works as not only a shortcut to initiate proofing your document but also an indicator of whether your document has been proofed. Figure 18-8 illustrates the different ways the icon is presented.

FIGURE 18-8:
Incarnations

and Grammar
Check icon.

proofed

Proofing
in progress

Document
needs
proofing

A quick glance at the icon tells you whether the document has been proofed (and errors acknowledged or ignored), is being proofed, or needs proofing, as illustrated in Figure 18-8.

See the earlier section "Controlling the status bar" for information on adding the Spelling and Grammar Check icon to the status bar.

Working with the dictionary

When a word is flagged as improperly spelled but you know for certain that it's a legitimate word, you can add the word to your personal dictionary:

1. **Right-click the word flagged as misspelled.**

2. **Choose Add to Dictionary.**

   The word is added to the dictionary. It's no longer flagged as being misspelled.

If you goof and mistakenly add a word to the personal dictionary, you can remove it. To do so, you must edit the dictionary. Follow these steps:

1. **Click the File tab and choose Options.**

2. **In the Word Options dialog box, choose Proofing.**

3. **Click the Custom Dictionaries button.**

   The Custom Dictionaries dialog box appears.

4. **Ensure that the personal dictionary named RoamaingCustom.dic (Default) is chosen.**

5. **Click the Edit Word List button.**

   The dictionary's word list appears.

6. **Click to select the word to remove from the scrolling Dictionary list.**

7. **Click the Delete button.**

8. **Click OK to close the personal-dictionary dialog box.**

   You can close the other dialog boxes as well.

To manually add an entry to the custom dictionary, after Step 5 type the word into the Word(s) text box, and then click the Add button.

>> If you use Office 365, the personal dictionary contains words you add from each of your Word or Office installations.

>> The personal dictionary is not the same as the supplemental dictionary you can obtain from the Office Store. See the nearby sidebar, "Another dictionary for Word."

Undoing an ignore proofing command

Proofing your document is not for the impatient. When you're careless, you may choose to ignore a word that you didn't mean to ignore. When that happens, you must undo the operation and direct Word to start over with document proofing. Follow these steps:

1. **Click the File tab and choose Options.**

2. **Choose Proofing from the left side of the Word Options dialog box.**

3. **Click the Recheck Document button.**

4. **Click the Yes button to confirm.**

The end effect is that any and all misspelled words you've chosen to ignore, or grammatical blunders you've forgiven, are once again flagged as incorrect.

ANOTHER DICTIONARY FOR WORD

You may notice some text in the Spelling pane indicating that Word lacks a dictionary. (Refer to Figure 18-7.) That *Get a Dictionary* text might make you ponder how Word can check your spelling without using a dictionary. It does, of course. What the text refers to is obtaining another dictionary from the Office Store, such as the *Merriam-Webster* free digital dictionary. Having such a dictionary adds its definition to the text you see in the Spelling pane.

To add a free dictionary to Word, in the Spelling pane click the Get a Dictionary link. Click the Download button for the dictionary you want, such as *Merriam-Webster*. That dictionary is then referenced in Word whenever you need to check a word's definition or usage.

Adjusting the grammar checking sensitivity

Say that you value the grammar check, just not all its suggestions. For example, ~~that two spaces should follow a period.~~ To direct Word to ignore your stubborn adherence to typewriter rules, follow these steps:

1. **Click the File tab and choose Options.**

   The Word Options dialog box appears.

2. **Choose Proofing.**

3. **By the Writing Style item, click the Settings button.**

   The Grammar Settings dialog box appears. It lists the specific items the grammar checker looks for.

4. **Remove the check mark by a specific item to disable that proofing feature.**

   For example, the Spacing item.

5. **Click OK to dismiss the Grammar Settings dialog box, and then click OK again to banish the Word Options dialog box.**

You can also disable on-the-fly grammar checking, as described earlier in this chapter.

REMEMBER

Tools for a Wordsmith

During typewriter times, and even in the early computer era, writers kept handy various references to help them craft the best text. Chief among the references were a dictionary and thesaurus. Also recommended were a book of quotations, foreign phrases, a rhyming dictionary — even the full-on encyclopedia. The modern computer provides alternatives to those references, but I must confess that reference books still look handsome on a shelf.

Choosing a better word

Every writer tends to use the same words over and over. To spice up your text, consider using Word's Thesaurus to pluck out a better term. Heed these directions:

1. **Right-click a word you want to improve.**

   The best word choices are adjectives.

2. **Choose Synonyms from the pop-up menu.**

3. **Select a better word from the list.**

To explore additional synonyms in detail, choose Thesaurus in Step 3. You see the Thesaurus pane appear, similar to what's shown in Figure 18-9.

The Thesaurus pane shows far more word choices than the shortcut menu, including antonyms or words that describe the opposite of the selected term.

The only drawback to the Thesaurus pane is that to stick a replacement word into your document, you must right-click that word and choose the Insert command. Otherwise, if you click a term, you see additional synonyms.

REMEMBER

>> Another way to view the Thesaurus pane is to click the Review tab and then click the Thesaurus button.

>> Not every word features a synonym.

>> The dictionary definition shown in Figure 18-9 is provided by a supplemental dictionary. Refer to the sidebar "Another dictionary for Word," earlier in this chapter.

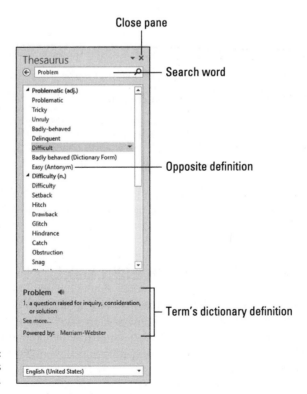

FIGURE 18-9:
The Thesaurus pane.

Translating some text

It sounds as though Word's Translate commands might help you spice up some text by adding a foreign flair to your prose. That would be crummy. If you want to use foreign words in your text, learn another language or buy a book full of foreign phrases. Otherwise, Word's language tool works best when translating text from another language into your own.

For example, you might use the term *bon mot* in your text. To confirm that it means what you intend, follow these steps:

1. **Select the foreign language text.**

2. **Right-click the selected text and choose Translate.**

3. **Click the Yes button to confirm that it's okay to send a chunk of text out to the Internet.**

   Word uses tools on the Internet to translate your text.

4. **In the Research pane, ensure that the proper languages are chosen in the From and To fields.**

   In the *bon mot* example, the From language is French and the To language is English.

5. **Click the arrow by the Search For box (the one that contains the foreign phrase) to summon the translation if it doesn't appear automatically.**

   Refer to Figure 18-10 for the arrow's location as well as the translation results.

6. **Close the Research pane when you're done.**

As you can see from Figure 18-10, only the word *bon* is translated. The full meaning of *bon mot* is "good word." It refers to a witty comment. So I would say that Word's Translate feature has some room for growth.

REMEMBER

Computer translation is a nifty tool, but it remains crude. It's okay for forming an idea of how text would translate, but as humorous examples on the Internet prove, it's far from perfect.

Ignoring a span of foreign text

If you're clever enough to add foreign text to your document, you'll note that Word flags the text (some or all) as obnoxiously misspelled. *Quel ridicule!* That red zigzag stain remains below the phrase, despite it being accurate in another language. Rather than ignore the words, you can direct Word to not proof that text. Here's how:

Term to translate

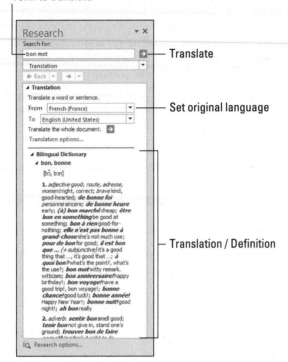

Translate

Set original language

Translation / Definition

1. **Select the foreign-language text, or any text you want the proofer to ignore.**

2. **Click the Review tab.**

3. **In the Language group, click the Language button and choose the Set Proofing Language command.**

   The Language dialog box appears.

4. **Place a check mark by the option Do Not Check Spelling or Grammar.**

   The setting applies only to selected text, not to the rest of the document.

5. **Click OK.**

   The selected text, which may have been flagged as misspelled, is cleared of any proofing marks.

These steps affect only the selected text; the rest of the document continues to be proofed.

You can also direct Word to use a foreign-language proofer on the selected text: In Step 4, choose the language from the scrolling list, such as French (France). If the foreign-language dictionary is installed in Word, the text is proofed in that

to not proof the text, as described in this section.

REMEMBER

>> If the word is spelled correctly, add it to the dictionary. If the word is okay for the document, choose Ignore. Use the steps in this section only for text you don't want proofed, such as foreign-language text or quotes.

>> See sections earlier in this chapter for information on ignoring proofing or adding words to the dictionary.

Chapter 19

From Brainstorm to Outline

I'm certain that some guy once sat down and instantly wrote, from front to back, a wonderful story. It was all in his head, and then he wrote it down. Such a person is amazingly rare. For most writers, organization is required before anything is written. From a complex novel about aliens, zombies, and the Russian revolution to a technical book on the intrigues of the Document Object Module, outlining is the vital first step taken by any serious writer.

The Outline Thing

If you've never used an outline program or even a stack of 3-by-5 cards to create an outline, you're really missing out. Outlining tools aren't just for writers. They help you organize anything, from a simple shopping list to the complex-but-legal process whereby major political parties ignore election results.

The outlining process works like this:

1. **Jot down your ideas.**

   Start writing a quick list, in any order. This is the brainstorming step.

2. **Continue to add ideas and organize them.**

   Organization is when you determine which ideas are bigger than others and which come first. It's quite common when outlining to rearrange topics, move them, or eliminate them as the outline develops.

3. **Finish the outline.**

   When you start writing content instead of ideas, you're done outlining.

Outlining is a process that continues even after you start writing. The changes may not be major, but they come as your thoughts solidify. When I write, I keep the outline document window open all the time. That way, I can reference other parts of the book or jot down new information, relevant elsewhere, that may pop into my head. My outlines aren't complete until the book is done.

REMEMBER

» Items in an outline are called *topics*.

» Topics are set at various levels, from major topics to specific topics.

» It's possible for an outline to contain notes, though when you reach that level of organization, you need to start writing and stop outlining.

» The outline is for you, the writer. It doesn't need to follow any rules or guidelines. An outline is simply a tool to help you organize your thoughts.

Word's Outline View

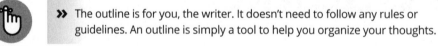

A long time ago, an outliner was a program separate from your word processor. For my early books, I used an outliner called Acta on the Macintosh. On the PC, I used GrandView. Word incorporated outlining as a feature back in the early 1990s, so you no longer need to obtain special software. You do, however, need to know how to work with Outline view in Word.

Activating Outline view

To switch to Outline view, follow these steps:

1. **Click the View tab.**

2. **In the Views group, click the Outline button.**

Word's document window changes. Handles appear to the left of each paragraph in the document. The handles let you organize the paragraphs, determine whether a topic has subtopics, and expand or collapse topics. The variety of handles is shown in Figure 19-1.

Topic with subtopics

Topic without subtopics

FIGURE 19-1:
Paragraph (topic)
handles in
Outline view.

Narrative (text) topic

Also visible in the window in Outline view is the Outlining tab. See the next section.

>> You can switch between Outline view and any other document view in Word. Outline view is simply a presentation, one that works best for arranging and organizing paragraphs of text.

>> In the big picture, an outline is just another Word document: Save it as you would any Word document. When you open an outline, it opens in either Print Layout or Web Layout view, depending on which view you used last. You must then switch to Outline view, as described in this section.

Exploring the Outlining tab

When Outline view is active, the Outlining tab appears, joining other tabs on the Ribbon. The tab features controls to help you manipulate the outline, as illustrated in Figure 19-2. Though the controls are handy, it's often faster to use keyboard shortcuts to manipulate your outline, as discussed elsewhere in this chapter.

One item on the Outlining tab that comes in handy is the Show Level menu. It allows you to quickly view the outline from any level, from major topics down to detailed topics. See the later section "Collapsing and expanding outline topics."

The Close Outline View button exits Outline view and restores Print Layout view. You can use this button, or you can click the View tab, to select a specific view for the document, such as Draft.

Outline view controls

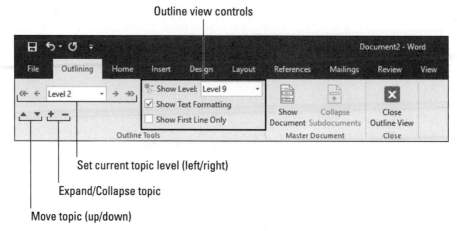

Set current topic level (left/right)

Expand/Collapse topic

FIGURE 19-2:
The Outlining tab.

Move topic (up/down)

Using heading styles

To make Outline mode work, Word uses its built-in heading styles: Heading 1, Heading 2, and so on. Each heading style represents a topic level in the outline. Heading 1 is the top level; Heading 2, the next level; and so on.

The built-in heading styles present themselves visually in Outline view. The top-level Heading 1 style is larger and heavier than Heading 2. Each style gets smaller and has other unique attributes, which helps as a visual reference in your outline.

If you prefer to see the outline without text formatting, on the Outlining tab (refer to Figure 19-2), remove the check mark by the Show Text Formatting item.

Outline Construction

Building an outline is the part of the brainstorming process where you write down information. It begins haphazardly, as described earlier in this chapter. That's fine, so don't let an initially disorganized outline vex you. As brainstorming progresses, the outline takes shape and your ideas acquire an order.

Creating top-level topics

In Outline view, the lines you initially type in a document are given the Heading 1 style. Each line, or topic, features a handle on the left. Your job is at this point is to type topics, to brainstorm. Don't worry about organization — just type some items related to the overall topic, similar to what's shown in Figure 19-3.

No subtopics   Keep topic text short

⊖ Coffee is fun to drink
⊖ Coffee is hot
⊖ Coffee helps you to get up in the morning
⊖ Coffee comes in many varieties
⊖ Flavored Coffee
⊖ Decaf
⊖ Espresso
⊖ Iced Coffee
⊖ Coffee comes from beans
⊖ Coffee is made in machines
⊖ Coffee comes from beans

End-of-Document marker

FIGURE 19-3:
Top-level topics.   Catch duplicate topics later

>> Don't worry about topic order just yet.

>> Don't worry whether a topic should become a subtopic.

>> Don't make the topics too wordy.

>> If you need to add notes to a topic, see the later section "Adding narrative," though that step should come later.

>> That squat horizontal bar at the end of the outline marks the end of the document; it's not something you can edit or remove. The same bar appears when you edit a document in Draft view.

Moving topics

After brainstorming, you organize topics. The order depends on the subject. The order can be chronological, from best to worst, from important to least important, or whatever the subject demands. In Figure 19-4, I've ordered the top-level topics for my coffee brainstorm (refer to Figure 19-3). I used coffee production as the order.

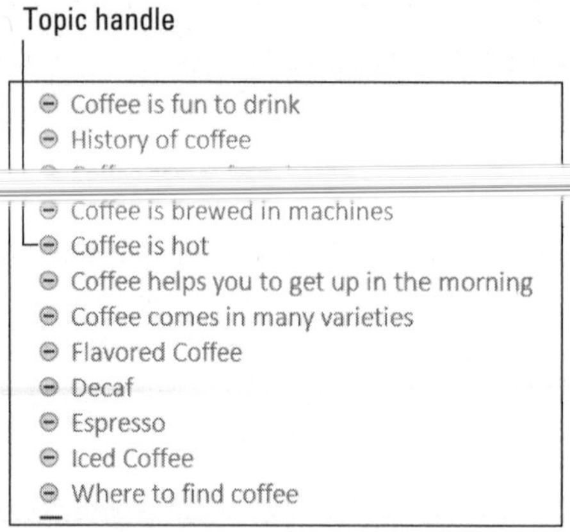

Topic handle

Coffee is fun to drink
History of coffee
Coffee is brewed in machines
Coffee is hot
Coffee helps you to get up in the morning
Coffee comes in many varieties
Flavored Coffee
Decaf
Espresso
Iced Coffee
Where to find coffee

FIGURE 19-4:
Organizing topics.

The easiest way to move a topic is to use the mouse: Drag the topic's handle up or down. See Figure 19-4.

On the Outlining toolbar, two command buttons move the current topic:

 Click the Move Up button to move a topic up.

The keyboard shortcut is Alt+Shift+↑.

 Click the Move Down button to move a topic down.

The keyboard shortcut is Alt+Shift+↓.

It's quicker to use the Move Down and Move Up keyboard shortcuts than to use the toolbar buttons.

As you move topics up or down, it's perfectly acceptable to add or remove topics. You can also catch duplicates. (Refer to Figure 19-3.) Also make subtle edits, if necessary. You'll find that moving topics might inspire you to create new topics.

>> To add a topic, type a new line as you normally would in Word. Topics exist as their own paragraphs.

>> To remove a topic, select the line and delete it, as you would any paragraph in Word.

>> To split a topic, place the insertion pointer into the topic's text at the point where you want to split the topic. Press the Enter key.

>> When you're outlining a novel, the topics eventually become chapters.

» Moving a topic doesn't change its level. To change a topic's level, see the next section.

» The topic-moving keyboard commands can be used to move any paragraph of text in Word, whether Outline view is active or not: Press Alt+Shift+↑ to move the current paragraph up; press Alt+Shift+↓ to move the current paragraph down.

Demoting or promoting a topic

During your brainstorm, you may notice how some topics are related. If so, consider demoting those topics into subtopics. In Figure 19-5, the types-of-coffee topics are demoted and placed under a new topic, "Coffee comes in many varieties."

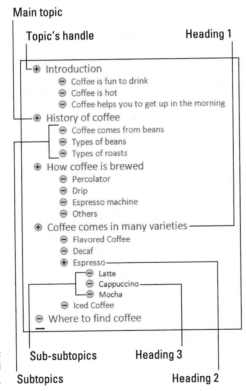

FIGURE 19-5: Topics and subtopics.

In Figure 19-5, every topic and subtopic is set at a certain indent in Outline view. The text style is based on the heading style. You can see in the figure how each indent sports its own style, which makes viewing the outline easier. Also see the later section "Collapsing and expanding outline topics."

Promoting and demoting a topic are the official terms for moving a topic left or right in an outline.

(move it right one notch), click the Demote button on the Outlining toolbar.

The keyboard shortcut to demote a topic is Alt+Shift+→.

To promote a topic (move it left one notch), click the Promote button on the Outlining toolbar.

The keyboard shortcut is Alt+Shift+←.

One other button on the Outlining toolbar lets you move a topic: The Promote to Heading 1 button shifts a topic all the way up to a top level. This button has no keyboard shortcut.

Finally, you can use the Outlining tab's Outline Level menu to set a topic to any level:

1. **On the Outlining tab, click the Outline Level menu.**

   Refer to Figure 19-2 for its location.

2. **Choose a new topic level.**

   You can set any topic level; it doesn't have to be up a notch or below a notch, though I don't recommend you get all wacky with your outline.

As a bonus, the Outline Level menu shows the current topic's level. So if you're working deep down in a vast outline, you can check the level by glancing at the Outline Level menu.

>> Topic, or Heading style, indents show up only in Outline view.

>> When you demote a topic, you create a subtopic for the topic (line of text) just above the current topic.

>> You need a subtopic when two or more same-level topics are similar. When that happens, demote those topics into subtopics below a new, higher-level topic.

>> People who know more than I do claim that you can't have a topic with only one subtopic. If so, eliminate the subtopic, add a second subtopic, or promote the subtopic.

TIP

» For a novel, you want to organize chapters as main topics. Subtopics within a chapter could cover what happens in that chapter, a list of characters involved, and so on.

» The keyboard shortcuts to promote and demote topics are available in any Word document. Use them to convert text to the header style or to change from one header style to another.

Moving topics and subtopics together

Whether you're moving a topic up or down or promoting or demoting that topic, only the topic itself — the single line of text — moves. Any subtopics remain in their same positions. To move a topic and all its subtopics, you have two options.

First, you can collapse the topic. See the later section "Collapsing and expanding outline topics." Once collapsed, all subtopics move with the topic.

Second, you can select the topic and its subtopics as a block. This type of selection works differently in Outline view than in Word's text-editing views. To move the topics, follow these steps:

1. **Click the topic's handle.**

The topic and all its subtopics are selected as a block.

2. **Move, promote, or demote the topic and subtopics as a group.**

You can use any of the commands mentioned in the preceding two sections to move the group. You can also use the mouse to drag the group in any direction, though that technique is a bit tricky to master.

You can also select multiple topics to promote or demote or move them as a group. Drag the mouse over the topics to select them.

WARNING

Text selection in Outline view works differently than in other Word document views. It's possible to select part of a topic's text, but you cannot select parts of text from two topics. When you select two or more topics, the full lines for both topics are selected. If you need to do fancy text selection, switch to Print Layout view or Draft view, manipulate the text, and then switch back to Outline view.

Adding narrative

When the urge to write something hits you in Outline view, do so: Write narratives when you feel compelled. The key is to set the paragraph's format to Normal.

That way, it's treated differently in Outline view than the heading-formatted topics.

~~will as body text. I prefer the term~~ *narrative* because the keyboard shortcut to convert a topic to body text is Ctrl+Shift+N.

In Figure 19-6, you see narrative text added to the coffee outline. A narrative paragraph sits below any topic level. You can even add a narrative paragraph as the first part of the outline.

Collapsed topic

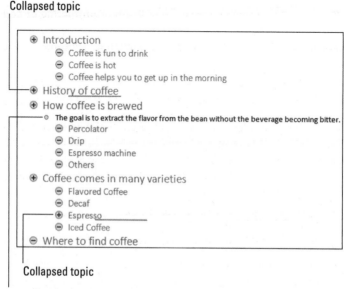

FIGURE 19-6:
Narrative text in
an outline.
Collapsed topic

Narrative text (Body Text)

 In addition to the Ctrl+Shift+N keyboard shortcut, you can click the Demote to Body Text button, shown in the margin. The button is found on the Outlining tab in the Outline Tools group. (Refer to Figure 19-2.)

>> A *narrative* is any text in an outline that adds more information or lets you jot down non-topic thoughts.

>> Narratives can be moved up or down or anywhere in the outline. See the earlier section "Moving topics."

>> To convert a narrative to a topic, promote or demote the paragraph. See the earlier section "Demoting or promoting a topic."

Outline Presentation

The goal of an outline is to eventually organize your thoughts and then do something with the results. To help you meet that end, Word offers various ways to present the outline on the screen, on the page, or even in mini-outline view in any document.

Collapsing and expanding outline topics

Complex outlines, brimming with detail and information, are wonderful things. I finished writing the book *WordPerfect For Dummies* in only three weeks because I had spent months building a marvelously detailed outline. In fact, much of the final book's text was included in the outline's narrative text. Make your outlines just as detailed and you too will be equally blessed.

The problem with a detailed outline is that it consumes a lot of screen space. Scrolling a long outline becomes tedious and distracting. The job is made easier when you collapse portions of the outline.

To collapse a topic and all its subtopics, double-click the mouse on the topic's handle. The keyboard shortcut is the minus key on the numeric keypad. You can also use the Collapse button found on the Ribbon's Outlining tab.

Collapsed topics appear with a fuzzy underline to the right of the topic's text. Refer to Figure 19-6 for examples of collapsed topics.

To expand a collapsed topic, double-click the mouse on the collapsed topic's handle. You can also press the plus key on the numeric keypad. On the Outlining tab, click the Expand button to expand a topic.

As an example, the outline to your book might show *Parts* as the top (Heading 1) level and *Chapters* as the next (Heading 2) level. To quickly see an overview of your book's table of contents, choose Level 2 from the Show Level menu. The outline is collapsed, hiding any Level 3 (Heading 3) topics and below.

>> To quickly expand all topics throughout the outline, choose All Levels from the Show Level menu on the Outlining toolbar.

>> The keyboard shortcut for showing a specific level in an outline is Alt+Shift+*n*, where *n* is a number 1 through 9. To show all topics, use the shortcut Alt+Shift+N (the letter *N*).

>> When you move a collapsed topic, you also move all the topic's subtopics.

>> Another way to shorten an outline is to place a check mark by the option Show First Line Only, found in the Outline Tools group on the Outlining toolbar. When active, this setting truncates long topics and narratives, ~~the same as collapsing topics, but~~ it does tighten the outline's presentation.

Printing the outline

An outline prints like any other Word document. All the document's text prints, even when you've collapsed topics or chosen to show only the first line of text for a topic or narrative. That's because when you use Word's Print command (Ctrl+P), the document view is changed from Outline to Print Layout. You can skip that step to print only visible topics in an outline, but you must know the secret.

The secret: If you want to print only visible topics in an outline, you need to enable the Quick Print button on Word's Quick Access toolbar. Follow these steps:

1. Click the down-pointing arrow by the Quick Access toolbar.

Use Figure 19-7 as your guide.

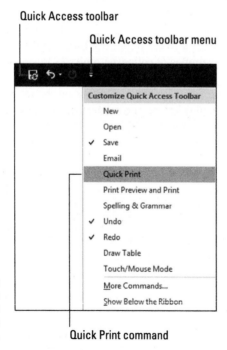

Quick Access toolbar

Quick Access toolbar menu

Quick Print command

FIGURE 19-7:
Adding the Quick Print icon to the Quick Access toolbar.

2. **Choose Quick Print.**

The Quick Print icon is added to the Quick Access toolbar.

 To print the outline showing only visible topics, first arrange the outline so that it shows only what you want to print. Refer to the preceding section for information on expanding and collapsing topics. On the Quick Access toolbar, click the Quick Print button, shown in the margin, to print only the visible topics.

Using the navigation pane

I keep my manuscript's outline open in a separate window while I work. For the current document, however, you can summon a mini-outline that's far easier to use. It's called the Navigation pane, shown in Figure 19-8.

Headings tab is active

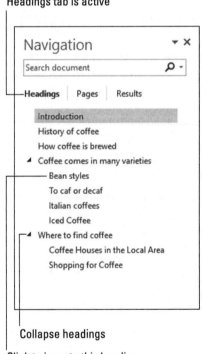

FIGURE 19-8:
The Navigation
pane. Collapse headings

Click to jump to this heading

The Navigation pane works best in Print Layout and Draft views. To summon the pane, follow these steps:

1. **Click the View tab.**

2. **In the Show group, place a check mark by the Navigation Pane item.**

The Navigation pane, Headings tab, shows a list of headings in your document ~~in the Heading Styles (or their equivalents). The pane isn't designed for~~ organizing your thoughts; instead, it's best put to use as a way to jump around your document: To use the Navigation pane, click a heading. Word instantly shows you that specific part of your document.

>> Click the triangle next to a document heading to collapse or expand any of its sections. Refer to Figure 19-8.

>> The Navigation pane appears when you use the standard Find command. In that case, the Results tab is shown. Click the Headings tab, illustrated in Figure 19-8, to view the document outline again.

OUTLINE-MANIPULATION SHORTCUT KEYS

The best way to manipulate an outline is to use the keyboard. Of all Word's weirdo key combinations, it may behoove you to use and memorize the following:

Key Combo	What It Does
Alt+Shift+→	Demotes a topic
Alt+Shift+←	Promotes a topic
Alt+Shift+↑	Moves a topic up one line
Alt+Shift+↓	Moves a topic down one line
Ctrl+Shift+N	Adds a narrative (body text) to the outline
Alt+Shift+1	Displays only Heading 1 (top-level) topics
Alt+Shift+2	Displays only Heading 1 and Heading 2 topics
Alt+Shift+N	Displays Heading N topics
Alt+Shift+A	Displays all topics
Numeric keypad +	Expands the topic, showing all subtopics and narratives
Numeric keypad –	Collapses the topic
Numeric keypad *	Shows all topic levels

Chapter 20

Humongous Documents

No upper limit exists for a Word document's size, not a maximum page count or word count or any other text measurement. I don't know whether or not anyone is crazy enough to test that claim. The longest single document I ever created was over 240 pages long. Word seemed to deal with it well, but the document was just text — no graphics or fancy formatting. Though you may never write a document that long, you may someday desire to write a book or some other long manuscript. When you do, you'll find several ways to deal with all that text in Word, none of which are obvious.

Write That Novel!

Sit down, crack your knuckles, and be prepared to type the Great American Novel. Comfy? Good! Because you'll be sitting there a while. The typical novel is between 40,000 and 100,000 words. Pages? Don't worry about pages. Instead, worry about how to best manage such a tremendous task on your word processor.

» The actual length of a novel depends on whom you ask; I've never seen any hard-and-fast rules.

» Anything shorter than 40,000 words is considered a *novella*. Some novellas can be as short as 7,500 words.

» Magazine articles run anywhere from 1,000 to 10,000 words, with 2,500 the average, depending on the publication.

» Some publishers are reluctant to accept, let alone read, a first novel greater than 100,000 words. The topic must be truly compelling for the word count to go higher.

» *The Great Gatsby*, written by F. Scott Fitzgerald, is considered the epitome of the Great American Novel. It clocks in at about 50,000 words.

Building one, long manuscript

Your first instinct when writing a long document is to put all the text into one file. That approach makes sense because Word trains you to see one written document as equal to one Word document file. For some manuscripts, this approach works best and might even be required. For others, the long–document method adds unforeseen complications.

Pros

» With a single document, you can set formatting for the entire manuscript. This includes headers, footers, page numbers, chapter titles, and other page-level formatting.

» A long document gives you a complete word count.

» Many publishers request that the manuscript be submitted as a single document.

» An eBook must be formatted and submitted as one file.

» It's easier to create hyperlinks in an eBook when you're working with a single document.

» Creating a table of contents or an index is simple.

» Managing one document file is easier than managing multiple documents (one per chapter). For example, reorganizing your book is a matter of copy-and-paste as opposed to renaming a slew of files.

Cons

>> The longer the document, the more difficult it is to move around within the document. See the later section "Splitting the window."

>> It's easier for a single file to become damaged, corrupted, overwritten, or lost. Efforts can be made to mitigate that problem; always back up your computer files.

>> Though it's easier to copy-and-paste to reorganize chapters, if you screw up, it's more difficult to undo the mistake.

>> If you decide to cut something, such as a chapter, it's gone unless you save that chunk in another document. When you cut a chapter as a document, you can use Windows to recover the deleted document.

>> At some point, Word slows down as the document grows. Especially if you add graphics, tables, and other objects, a long manuscript may tax the computer's abilities to run Word.

Writing one chapter per document

The first book I wrote (unpublished) was a single document. It was murder working with such a long document. Since that time, I've split my books into separate documents, one for each chapter. Most professional writers work this way.

Pros

>> Shorter, chapter-size documents are easy to work on and quicker to search, and take less time to finish.

>> It's simple to track your progress, because the manuscript's folder shows more files (documents) as your writing progresses.

>> Working on multiple chapters at the same time is easy because each chapter naturally exists in its own document window.

>> You can add lots of graphics, tables, and other items to the document and not worry about their addition affecting Word's performance.

>> If you cut a chapter, you can save it in a backup folder. That way, you can quickly recover some or all of the chapter's text should you decide to do so in the future.

>> You can still generate a single document as the final result of your efforts. See the later section "The Master Document."

Cons

>> If you reorganize your book, you need to rename the document files as well as

why I recommend creating a good outline to start; refer to Chapter 19.)

>> Publishers may require you to consolidate the chapters for submission. eBook publishers require that you submit a single document.

>> Word's document-wide references, such as the table of contents, work only when you've combined the separate chapters into a master document.

>> To print the manuscript, you must open and print each individual chapter document. Ditto for converting the documents' file format.

>> You can never obtain an overall word count or page count unless you examine each chapter document individually and tally the totals or you create a master document.

One Long Manuscript

Huge documents can just happen; they grow like bamboo. Or perhaps you have set out to write your manuscript as one long document on purpose. Either way, as you work, you may encounter some difficulties that the folks who follow the one-chapter-per-document method don't encounter. To help remedy those issues, consider a few helpful tricks, such as adding bookmarks and splitting or creating a new document window.

Bookmarking your text

Word's Bookmark command can help you locate a specific spot in a long document. For example, you can bookmark a chunk of text that needs more work so that you can return to it later. Or you can bookmark a passage of text that's quoted elsewhere in the book. Using a bookmark in this manner is more effective than writing yourself a note in the text, which you can forget about or not notice later.

To bookmark a chunk of text, follow these steps:

1. **Select the relevant chunk of text.**
2. **Click the Insert tab.**

3. **In the Links group, click the Bookmark button.**

   The Bookmark dialog box appears.

4. **Type the bookmark name.**

   Bookmark names cannot contain spaces, so use underlines instead. Be descriptive! For example, *Fix_this_description* or *Belindas_confession*.

5. **Click the Add button.**

   The bookmark is set in the document. It has no visual feedback.

To use the bookmark, refer to the next section.

>> Bookmarks are used to create hyperlinks in eBooks. See Chapter 22.

>> Bookmarks also come into play for certain document fields and cross-references. See Chapter 24 for information on fields; Chapter 21 covers cross-references.

>> You can also use Word's comment feature to write yourself notes, though you may find that approach a bit distracting. See Chapter 16.

>> When Word starts, it flags the previous location where you last edited. You see a tag near the vertical scrollbar, saying "Welcome back." Click that tag to return to the last spot you edited in the document.

>> To hop between the last few edits you've made, use the Shift+F5 keyboard shortcut.

TIP

Visiting a bookmark

To use a bookmark, you summon the Find and Replace dialog box. It lists all bookmarks in your document and lets you hop to any specific bookmark location. Follow these steps:

1. **Press Ctrl+G.**

   Ctrl+G is the shortcut for the Go To tab in the Find and Replace dialog box, shown in Figure 20-1.

2. **Choose Bookmark from the Go to What list, as illustrated in Figure 20-1.**

3. **Click the menu button to choose a bookmark.**

4. **Click the Go To button to visit the bookmark's location in your document.**

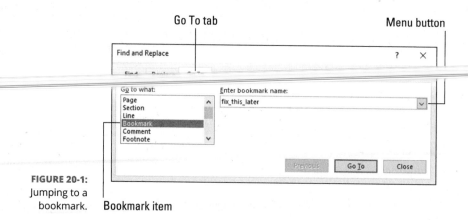

Go To tab　　　　　　　　　　　　　Menu button

FIGURE 20-1:
Jumping to a
bookmark.　　Bookmark item

Setting and visiting bookmarks doesn't guarantee that you'll remember them. Therefore, I suggest that you commit to memory the Ctrl+G keyboard shortcut and use it frequently to review any bookmarks you've set for editing purposes.

REMEMBER

Removing a bookmark

Bookmarks aren't edited like regular text. You can't see them in Draft view. And it's difficult to accidentally delete one. To best remove a bookmark, return to the Bookmark dialog box by following these steps:

1. **Click the Insert tab.**

2. **In the Links group, click the Bookmark button.**

3. **Click to highlight the bookmark you want to remove.**

   All the document's bookmarks appear in the scrolling list portion of the Bookmark dialog box.

4. **Click the Delete button.**

5. **Repeat Steps 3 and 4 to peel away additional bookmarks.**

If you forget to remove bookmarks, it's no big deal. They don't show up in the text, unlike comments you may write to yourself in the body of the manuscript.

Splitting the window

One of the regrets of working on a 200-plus-page manuscript is that it's more difficult to work on two different parts of the document at once. The quick way to review or edit another location in your document is to split Word's window into two panes. Obey these directions:

1. **Click the View tab.**

2. **In the Window group, click the Split button.**

The document portion of the window splits in twain, as shown in Figure 20-2. You can scroll each portion above or below the split; click on one side or the other to control what appears there.

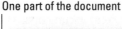

To adjust the size of the split, point the mouse at the split bar, as illustrated in Figure 20-2. When the mouse pointer changes as shown in the margin, drag the mouse up or down.

One part of the document   Split bar

FIGURE 20-2:
A split window.   'nuther part of the document

To remove the split, double-click the split bar. The top portion of the split remains.

Opening a second window

A split window is fine for a quick edit or fact-check. When you really need to hop ~~around in a long document,~~ the best trick is to open a second document window. The end result is that you have two Word document windows open, but each shows a different part of the same document.

To open a second window and view a different part of a long document, follow these steps:

1. **Click the View tab.**

2. **In the Window group, click New Window.**

   A second Word document window appears, showing the same document as the first window.

You can open as many windows for the current document as you need; just repeat the steps in this section. Each window works independently of the other, showing a specific portion of the document. It's the same document in every window, so edits in one window are updated in the others.

TIP

The window's title bar reflects which window you're viewing. The document's filename is suffixed with a colon and a number. The number references the window as opened in sequence.

Close the extra windows as you would any window. The main difference is that Word warns you to save an unsaved document only when you close the final window.

The Master Document

My preferred method to organize big writing projects is to craft one chapter per Word document. My publisher prefers this method as well; this chapter was born in Word document 20.docx, which is how it was finally submitted to the publisher.

When you opt to write your Great American Novel one chapter per document, you may find it necessary to eventually stitch everything together. In Word, that process is referred to as creating a master document.

The master document is built upon a collection of subdocuments — specifically, those chapter documents for your manuscript. The individual documents are referenced inside the master document, which then becomes the final, long manuscript with consistent headers, footers, page numbers, word count, and so on.

>> The master document becomes another Word document in your manuscript's folder.

>> Individual documents you place into the master document are referred to as *subdocuments*.

>> The master document references and uses the subdocuments. Do not delete them!

>> With a master document, you can work on the individual document files or in the master document itself. Changes in one place affect both files.

TIP

>> It's important that all the subdocuments use the same document template. This choice provides consistency for the master document and saves you lots of headaches later.

>> Refer to Chapter 9 for information on templates.

Creating the master document

After you've honed all the individual chapter documents and deemed them ready to bring together, you begin the process of creating a master document. Follow these steps:

REMEMBER

1. **Start a new document in Word.**

Ensure that you use the same template used by the chapter documents.

2. **Save the master document.**

Press Ctrl+S and assign the document a suitable name in the same folder as your chapter documents.

I use the name Master Document. As long as it's in the same folder with my chapter documents, I know what it is and to which book it belongs.

3. **Click the View tab.**

4. **In the Views group, click the Outline button.**

5. **In the Master Document group, click the Show Document button.**

The button serves two purposes. When you're done creating the master document, it displays the full-length manuscript. At this stage, however, the button reveals the remaining commands in the Master Document group.

6. **Click the Insert button.**

The Insert Subdocument window appears. It functions like an Open dialog box.

7. **Choose the first chapter to insert into the master document; click the Open button.**

The d̶o̶c̶u̶m̶e̶n̶t̶ ̶i̶s̶ ̶i̶n̶s̶e̶r̶t̶e̶d̶

Each subdocument-paragraph sports a handle, a feature of Outline view. (Refer to Chapter 19.)

8. **Click the Insert button again.**

9. **Choose the next chapter document to insert into the master document.**

If the master document isn't using the same template as its subdocuments, you see a warning at this point. My advice: Start over and set the same template for each document. Refer to Chapter 9.

10. **Repeat Steps 8 and 9 to insert all remaining subdocuments.**

11. **Save the master document.**

The end result looks pretty gross, but that's because you're viewing the document in Outline view. Choose Print Layout view to see a more realistic picture of what the master document looks like.

 To get an idea of what the master document *really* looks like, click the Collapse Subdocuments button. (The button is located on the Outlining tab in the Master Document group.) Each document appears as a link, separated by a continuous section break.

> ❯❯ One way to put the Collapse Subdocuments tool to work is to ensure that every subdocument has been inserted in the proper order. If they haven't, see the next section on how to rearrange subdocuments.

> ❯❯ If you prefer not to have changes in the master document updated in the subdocuments, you can unlink the two. See the later section "Remove a subdocument" for details on unlinking subdocuments.

REMEMBER

> ❯❯ The master document automatically inserts a continuous section break between subdocuments. This type of section break asserts that each new chapter starts at the top of a page. You don't need to add a page break or section break to the end of your individual chapter documents. You may need to fix headers and other formatting. See the later section "Edit text."

> ❯❯ Also see Chapter 6 for information on section breaks.

Working with the master document

After all the subdocuments are added to the master document, you can complete your manuscript. This process involves checking the document format, page numbers, and headers and footers and then creating document references, such as the table of contents, the index, and other lists.

Edit text

I recommend that you proof the master document just as you proofed the individual chapter documents. Read the thing! Ensure that the subdocuments are expanded. Obey these directions:

1. Click the View tab.

2. Choose Outline view.

3. Click the Expand Subdocuments button.

The links in the master document are updated to reflect the contents of the individual chapter files.

REMEMBER

Any edits you make in the master document are reflected in the individual chapter documents. These edits also include formatting changes.

Also give an eye to the document's layout. How does it look as one big chunk? Follow these steps:

1. Click the View tab.

2. Choose Print Layout view.

3. Use the zoom slider on the status bar to zoom out so that a single page fits in the document window.

4. Page through your document to check formatting, headers and footers, page numbers, and other items.

If you notice that the headers and footers don't flow, you need to edit the master document. See Chapter 7 for details. To keep the headers and footers consistent, you must ensure that the Link to Previous option is set.

Add a subdocument

Don't despair if you need to add another chapter at the Master Document stage of your project. Word lets you insert new subdocuments into a master document at any time. Heed these steps:

1. Save the master document.

2. Click the View tab and choose Outline.

3. **If the subdocuments are *collapsed* (listed as links), click the Expand Subdocuments button.**

4. ~~Position the~~ ... ~~where you want to add the new~~ **subdocument.**

Between each subdocument in the master document, you see a blank line. In Outline view, the line features a single dot between the two boxes that contains the subdocument before and after. Figure 20-3 illustrates what to look for.

Preceding subdocument   Click here

FIGURE 20-3:
Where to put the
insertion pointer
to insert a
subdocument.

⊙ Inserting after here

⊙ ─────────────

⊞ ⊙ Inserting before here

Next subdocument

5. **On the Outlining tab, in the Master Document group, click the Insert Subdocument button.**

6. **Use the Insert Subdocument dialog box to locate the chapter file.**

7. **Click the Open button to insert the subdocument into the master document.**

You shouldn't have to follow these steps if you used an outline to organize your thoughts before you started to write. Refer to Chapter 19. Also, adding a subdocument after you've already added your manuscript's original chapters most likely means you were premature to create the master document.

Move a subdocument

Your editor has informed you that Chapter 15 should come before Chapter 16. Making that move in the master document is difficult. As an alternative, I suggest that you close the master document and then rename the individual chapter files: 15 to 16 and 16 to 15. When you rename the files, you don't need to mess with the master document; it's updated the next time it's loaded and the subdocuments are expanded.

Remove a subdocument

Pulling a subdocument from the master document involves two steps. First you must unlink the subdocument, removing the coordination between the two files. Second, you remove the subdocument's text.

When you unlink a subdocument, you retain that document's text in the master document. Any updates to either document, however, aren't reflected in the other. Follow these steps to unlink a document in the master document:

1. **Click the Expand Subdocuments button.**

2. **Place the insertion pointer inside the text of the subdocument you want to remove.**

   You don't need to select all the text; just click the mouse inside that chunk somewhere.

3. **On the Outlining tab, in the Master Document group, click the Unlink button.**

   The subdocument text loses its border. If you collapse the subdocuments, the text doesn't condense into a link.

4. **Save the master document.**

5. **Remove the subdocument's text.**

   Select the text and delete it as you would any text in a document.

REMEMBER

If you removed a subdocument between two other subdocuments, keep a blank line between the remaining two subdocuments. Refer to Figure 20-3 to see what the blank line looks like. It's the same as the narrative paragraph (Normal style) in Word's Outline view.

Chapter 21

Document References

Not every manuscript is a magazine article or novel. Many professional documents are created in the educational world or for industry professionals. These papers require reference features not normally found in your typical office memorandum. The references include document features you most likely moaned about in college and high school, including a bibliography, notes, a glossary, and other text tidbits. The good news is that Word provides tools that generate these references, automatically — providing you know where to find the tools and how to use them.

Word can capably generate many different types of references for you, all automatically. It handles a lot of the details, providing that you jump through a few hoops — but nothing too obnoxious. The end result is an updated reference, such as a table of contents, a list of figures, notes, or other reference-style lists.

>> Word keeps its automatic reference-creation tools on the References tab: Click the References tab to view the different groups.

automatically as you change your text.

>> Some references work as document fields. If you modify your document, you must update the reference field. Examples are provided throughout this chapter. Also see Chapter 24 for more information on fields.

>> The References tab features the Table of Authorities group. The table of authorities is used primarily in legal documents. Refer to Chapter 17.

>> Those references Word doesn't create automatically must be built manually. Generally, these types of references are simple lists that don't link back to a document's text, such as a glossary. Word lacks tools specific to create these types of references.

Table of Contents

If you want to be one of the cool kids and pretend that you're part of the publishing industry, you refer to the table of contents as the *TOC*. Say "tea-oh-see." You can also say "tock," but "tea-oh-see" is what I hear more often. Once you know this secret, you can proceed with using Word's Table of Contents tool to add a nicely formatted, accurate, and effortless TOC to your document.

Understanding the TOC

In its most basic form, a *table of contents* is a list of chapter titles. It could also be a list of headings in a document, which includes main headings and subheadings. Word's Table of Contents tool lets you determine which level of heading the TOC represents, the layout of the TOC, and other aspects.

The key to making the Table of Contents tool work is to employ heading styles in your document. You can use Word's built-in heading styles, or you can create your own heading styles. If you create your own, ensure that the style's Paragraph Level attribute is properly set; otherwise, the Table of Contents tool doesn't work.

Refer to Chapter 8 for information on creating your own heading styles with the Paragraph Level attribute set.

Inserting a TOC

Your document's table of contents should go in its own section, or at least be separated by a hard page break before and after. The TOC is one of the first items in a manuscript, after the title page and copyright page.

To set your document's table of contents, follow these steps:

1. **Place the insertion pointer at the top of a page where you want the table of contents to appear.**

   If necessary, set a next page section break or a hard page break to start a new page. Refer to Chapter 6 for information on these types of page breaks.

2. **Type a page title for the table of contents.**

   My favorite title is *Table of Contents,* though I'm sure you can think of something more interesting.

   TIP

   Do not use a heading style to format the table of contents title unless you want the TOC to reference itself.

3. **Position the insertion pointer on the next line, below the TOC title.**

   Press the Enter key after typing the title to get a new, blank line.

4. **Click the References tab.**

5. **In the Table of Contents group, click the Table of Contents button.**

   You can choose a preset TOC from the gallery, but the dialog box offers you more control.

6. **Choose Custom Table of Contents.**

   The Table of Contents dialog box appears, as shown in Figure 21-1. It offers two views: one for printed documents and another for the web, which also counts for publishing eBooks.

7. **Configure the page numbers' appearance.**

   If you want page numbers in the TOC, place a check mark by the Show Page Numbers option.

   To right-justify the page numbers, place a check mark by the Right Align Page Numbers option. If you choose this option, you can set a tab leader from the Tab Leader menu.

   The preview in the top left area of the dialog box shows how the TOC appears based on the page numbering options you select.

Page number control

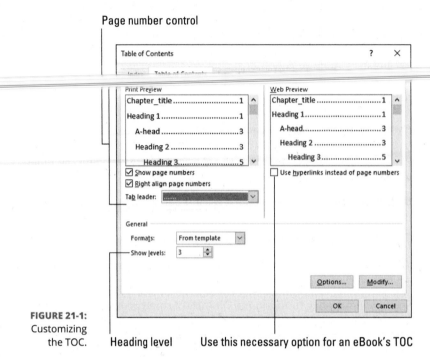

FIGURE 21-1:
Customizing
the TOC.

Heading level   Use this necessary option for an eBook's TOC

8. **Set hyperlinks for web or eBook publishing.**

If you plan to publish an eBook, place a check mark by the option Use Hyperlinks Instead of Page Numbers. eBooks don't use page numbers, but links come in handy.

You can remove the options for page numbers if you plan on publishing an eBook, but for eBooks that use the HTML (web page) format, that step isn't necessary in Word. See Chapter 22 for further details on eBook publishing.

9. **Determine how deep you want the TOC to go.**

The maximum number of levels you can choose depends on how you apply the Heading styles in your document. For my eBook manuscripts, I set the TOC to 2 levels. That setting includes the chapter heads and any subheads within the chapters.

10. **Click the OK button to insert the TOC into your document.**

11. **Examine the TOC.**

If you goofed, press Ctrl+Z (Undo) and start over again at Step 5.

12. **On the line after the TOC, set another hard page break or section break.**

By setting breaks before and after the TOC, you ensure that it appears on a page (or multiple pages) by itself.

TIP

If the TOC is empty, you failed to assign proper paragraph levels to your document's styles. Read Chapter 8 for details on how to fix that problem, though you can use the Options button in the Table of Contents dialog box to assign TOC levels to your document's existing styles.

Updating the TOC

REMEMBER

The TOC looks like text, but as with many of Word's automatic document references, it's actually a field. If you change your manuscript, move a chapter or two, or add information, you must remember to update the TOC. Obey these directions:

1. **Right-click the mouse somewhere in the TOC's text.**

2. **From the shortcut menu, choose the Update Field command.**

 The TOC is refreshed.

WARNING

Do not attempt to edit the TOC. You can try, but to properly present the table of contents, follow my advice for setting document heading styles and refresh the TOC field.

Footnotes and Endnotes

Footnotes and endnotes are frequently lumped together. They're similar concepts — just presented at different locations in the document: A footnote is a reference at the bottom of the page; endnotes appear at the end of a document. In both cases, a superscripted note number appears by the reference in the text.

>> For both the footnote and endnote, the superscripted number is sequential. You don't have to add it yourself.

>> Word automatically formats and places footnotes and endnotes. It also manages the reference numbers.

>> Choose either footnotes or endnotes for your document. Don't use both.

TIP

>> To see a footnote's or endnote's text, point the mouse at the superscripted number in the document's text. The note appears in a pop-up bubble.

>> Typographers refer to both footnotes and endnotes as *notes.* The only difference between the two is their location in the document.

Adding a footnote

A *footnote* is a chunk of text that further explains something in the text or that has ~~removed from the text so as not to be distracting.~~ It presents itself more immediately than an endnote, which isn't necessarily on the same page.

To set a footnote in your document, follow these steps:

1. **Place the insertion pointer just after the word or phrase the footnote will reference.**

   You can also select the text if you have trouble placing the insertion pointer.

2. **Click the References tab.**

3. **Click the Insert Footnote button.**

   AB^1

   Instantly, Word superscripts a number by the text. You see the bottom of the page, where a horizontal line separates the text from the footnote(s). The same superscripted number appears, as shown in Figure 21-2.

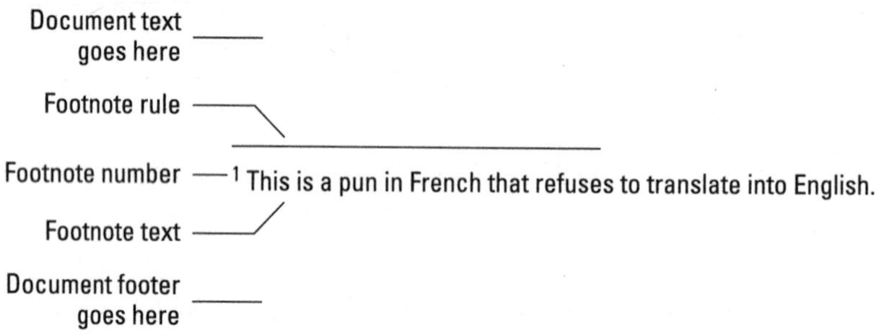

Document text
goes here

Footnote rule

Footnote number —[1] This is a pun in French that refuses to translate into English.

Footnote text

FIGURE 21-2:
A footnote.

Document footer
goes here

4. **Type the footnote text.**

5. **Click the mouse back in your document and continue editing.**

   You can press the Shift+F5 keyboard shortcut to return to the location you clicked in Step 1. This trick may not work if you've done extensive editing within the footnote.

These steps add a footnote anywhere in your document. You never need to worry about renumbering the notes; Word does that automatically.

>> If you're using Word to create an eBook or a web page, use an endnote instead of a footnote. Web pages and eBooks don't feature pages. Therefore, footnotes are irrelevant.

>> It's better to use footnotes, as opposed to writing multiple parenthetical references in the same paragraph.

>> The keyboard shortcut for the Insert Footnote command is Alt+Ctrl+F.

>> Footnotes renumber at the start of each page.

>> Word uses numbers to reference footnotes. You can change this option to use other symbols, such as the dagger (†) or whatever pleases you. See the later section "Setting note options."

TECHNICAL STUFF

>> A document's word count usually doesn't include footnotes. Some scholars use this exception to exceed the number of words allowed in their manuscripts; they place excess verbiage into the footnotes. Try to avoid using that sneaky trick. Refer to Chapter 18 for information on Word's word count command.

Creating an endnote

Endnotes work just like footnotes. Both are created in a similar manner, so if you're gifted with footnote talent, your endnote skills will closely follow.

To add an endnote to your document, obey these steps:

1. **Click the mouse to set the insertion pointer just after a word or phrase.**

   The superscripted endnote reference appears at that location, but Word creates it for you automatically.

2. **Click the References tab.**

3. **Click the Insert Endnote button.**

4. **Type the endnote text.**

5. **Click the mouse back in your document and continue editing.**

The endnote is placed after the last paragraph in the document, below a horizontal rule similar to the one shown for a footnote in Figure 21-2.

>> The keyboard shortcut to insert an endnote is Alt+Ctrl+D.

>> Word uses lowercase Roman numerals to number endnotes. This choice can be changed. See the later section "Setting note options."

>> Endnote numbers are cumulative throughout your document. Word manages the numbers, so you don't need to manually renumber endnotes as you create more, remove some, or edit text in your document.

>> If you're using endnotes for citations, you can save time by writing *Ibid* for an endnote reference that's identical to the preceding reference.

information applies to endnotes.

Reviewing notes

Footnotes and endnotes appear in the document window just as they print — unless you're working in Draft view. Either way, you can quickly review a document's notes. Follow these directions:

1. **Click the References tab.**

2. **In the Footnotes group, click the triangle next to the Next Footnote button.**

   A menu appears, with four options.

3. **Choose the command to view the next or previous footnote or endnote.**

   Word whisks you to the spot in your document where the footnote's or endnote's superscripted reference appears in the text.

To view the note's text, point the mouse at the superscripted reference.

Changing notes

To edit a footnote or endnote, first locate the note's superscripted reference in your text; see the preceding section for the quick way to find these references.

Double-click the superscripted reference to edit the note. Word shows the note at the bottom of the page, or in a special pane when you've selected Draft view. Edit the text as you would any text in Word; all formatting rules apply, though I don't recommend that you go nuts with styles in notes.

To remove a note, follow these steps:

1. **Select the note's superscripted reference.**

2. **Press the Delete key on the keyboard.**

   The note is gone.

Any remaining notes in the document are renumbered to account for the change.

Setting note options

To control various note options, summon the Footnote and Endnote dialog box, shown in Figure 21-3.

Choose note format

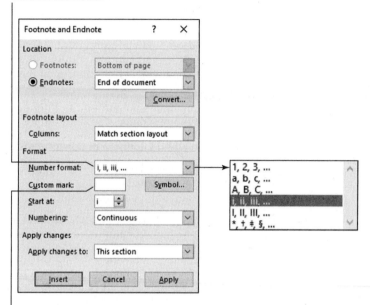

FIGURE 21-3:
The Footnote and
Endnote dialog
box.

Set custom symbol

Follow these steps:

1. **Click the References tab.**

2. **In the Footnotes group, click the dialog box launcher.**

The most common thing you'll likely change in the dialog box are the symbols used to reference the notes. To change them, choose a new scheme from the Number Format menu. (Refer to Figure 21-3.)

To set a custom symbol, click the Symbol button. Use the Symbol dialog box to pluck out a special character to apply to the notes.

REMEMBER

Click the Apply button when you're done setting options in the Footnote and Endnote dialog box. If you click the Insert button, you're adding a new footnote or endnote, depending on which option is selected at the top of the dialog box.

Converting between footnotes and endnotes

when you goof and you need an endnote when you have a footnote, or vice versa, follow these steps to convert between the two:

1. **Double-click the note's superscript.**

   Refer to the earlier section "Reviewing notes" to help quickly locate notes in your document.

   When you double-click the superscript, you're taken to the note itself.

2. **Right-click on the note.**

   You can click anywhere on the note's text.

3. **Choose the command Convert to Endnote or Convert to Footnote.**

   The note is converted.

I recommend that you repeat these steps for each note in your document. Though it's technically possible to mix footnotes and endnotes in Word, it's not something your reader will expect.

Citations and the Bibliography

Scholarly works and dreaded term papers frequently include citations and a bibliography. These references help attribute a source, such as Søren Kierkegaard, who wrote several books that college students even today pretend to read. Word manages those sources for you to make automatic tasks of placing citations and including a bibliography.

Creating citations

A *citation* is a reference to another published work. It appears within the body of the text, with the author's name and year enclosed in parentheses. For example, I once wrote that there is no logic in the computer industry (Gookin, 1989). The citation is what appears in parentheses. It also implies that additional information is available later in the document, appearing in an organized bibliography.

Follow these steps to create a new citation:

1. **Click the mouse where you want the citation to appear in the text.**

2. **Click the References tab.**

3. **In the Citations & Bibliography group, click the Insert Citation button.**

4. **Choose Add New Source.**

The Create Source dialog box appears.

5. **Fill in the text fields relevant to the citation.**

Important are the Name, Title, Year, and possibly Publisher fields. If you need more fields, place a check mark by the option Show All Bibliography Fields.

6. **Click the OK button to create the source and insert the citation into the text.**

The citation is inserted at the spot you clicked in Step 1.

The citation looks like text, but it's not. Word uses a content control to present the citation's text. When you click on the text, you see the control's features, as illustrated in Figure 21-4. Use the menu on the content control to adjust the citation, as illustrated in the figure.

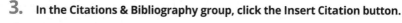

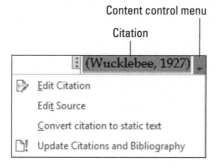

FIGURE 21-4:
A Citation content control.

>> Determining how much information to include for the citation depends on the type of document. Some periodicals and journals require more information than others.

>> Some editors prefer that you use endnotes for citations. Refer to the earlier section "Creating an endnote."

>> The Reference tab's Table of Authorities group sports a Mark Citation button. This button is not the same as the Insert Citation button, referenced in this section. The Mark Citation button is used for preparing legal documents. Refer to Chapter 17.

WARNING

>> The beauty of the content control is that, should you change the citation (choose Edit Source from the menu shown in Figure 21-4), you update all citations in your document as well as the bibliography.

>> See Chapter 27 for more information on content controls.

Inserting existing citations

After you create a new citation source, you can quickly summon that same citation again. This process saves oodles of time when you need to re-reference a citation in your manuscript. To do so, follow these steps:

1. **Click in the text where you want the citation to appear.**

2. **Click the References tab.**

3. **Click the Insert Citation button.**

4. **Choose the citation from the list.**

The citation's content control is inserted into your document.

Building the bibliography

The endgame for the citations in your document is a *bibliography*, which lists the full details for each source cited. Like most document references, the bibliography appears at the end of your manuscript, after the document's text and before the index. Word creates the bibliography automatically, based on the document's citations.

To insert the bibliography into your document, obey these steps:

1. **Start a new page for the bibliography.**

   You can set a new hard page break or a section break. Refer to Chapter 6 for information on the differences.

2. **Click the References tab.**

3. **Click the Bibliography button.**

4. **Choose a bibliography style from the menu.**

   A formatted bibliography, including the title, appears in your document. The bibliography's text lists, in alphabetical order, all citations you created.

If you prefer to create your own bibliography, type **Bibliography** on a line by itself after Step 1. Format that line as a top-level heading style so that it's included in the document's table of contents. Work Steps 2 and 3, but for Step 4 choose the Insert Bibliography command. The citations are inserted, which you can then format to match the document's text.

As with the citations, the bibliography is a content control. To update the bibliography, click the control and choose the Update Citations and Bibliography command.

Automatic Captions

Word can insert and track captions for your document's figures, tables, and equations. The caption text and sequence are tracked so that all captions are numbered sequentially. You can use the automatic captions to build a list of figures and page numbers as a document reference.

You need to use Word's Caption command only when you plan to build a list based on the captions, such as a list of figures. If so, Word builds the list automatically, as described in this section. Otherwise, you can caption figures as shown in Chapter 12.

Adding a caption

Word's Caption feature affixes caption text to specific items in a document. These items include graphics (pictures), equations, and tables. The caption goes above or below the item. Word supplies the caption label — Figure, Equation, or Table — and adds a sequential number. You type the caption text or description.

Follow these steps to add a caption to a figure, a table, or an equation:

1. Click to select the object: picture, table, or equation.

You can stick a caption anywhere in your text, but by definition a caption must go next to something that needs captioning.

2. Click the References tab.

3. In the Captions group, click the Insert Caption button.

The Caption dialog box appears, as shown in Figure 21-5.

Whether the label is removed or replaced, the sequential number remains. You cannot delete the number, which is the whole point of using the Insert Caption command to sequentially number items in a document.

Choose preset label text

Label (supplied by Word)

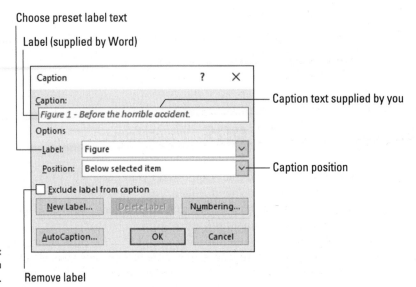

Caption text supplied by you

Caption position

FIGURE 21-5:
The Caption
dialog box.

Remove label

4. **Type the caption's text.**

   The text is placed after the caption label.

5. **Set the caption's position, either above or below the item.**

   The two options are chosen from the Position menu.

6. **Click OK to set the caption.**

Word uses its built-in Caption style to format the caption. You can select another style after the caption is inserted or modify the built-in style.

>> If the item you've captioned uses the Inline Text layout, the caption appears as a paragraph of text below the object. Otherwise, the caption is placed inside a text box. I recommend that you group the caption with the picture (or object) so that they work together for layout purposes. Refer to Chapter 11 for text box details.

>> The AutoCaption option (refer to Figure 21-5) directs Word to automatically summon the Caption dialog box anytime you insert a picture into your document. Choose the image file type from the AutoCaption dialog box, set the basic caption options, and then click OK.

>> You can add chapter numbers to the figure text. To do so, click the Numbering button in the Caption dialog box. In the Caption Numbering dialog box, place a check mark by the option Include Chapter Number, and then set which style your document uses for the title-level heading.

>> The caption text is simply a paragraph of text, though the caption number is a field. See Chapter 24 for information on fields.

>> Chapter 4 covers tables, including how to select an entire table.

>> Equations are covered in Chapter 13.

Inserting a list of captions

After you've set a document's captions, you can smack the whole list of them into your document with a single command. That's the point of having Word set the captions, as opposed to creating them manually.

Like many document references, a list of figures (or list of tables or list of equations) is part of the back matter, located at the end of the document before the index. Follow these steps to insert a list of captions into your document:

1. **Start a blank page at the end of your document.**

Refer to Chapter 6 for directions on setting a hard page break or a next-page section break.

2. **Type a heading for the list of captions.**

If you want the list of captions to appear in the document's table of contents, use a level 1 heading style to format the paragraph.

3. **Press the Enter key after typing the heading, so that the list of captions starts on a new line.**

4. **Click the References tab.**

5. **In the Captions group, click the Insert Table of Figures button.**

The Table of Figures dialog box appears. It shows a preview of the list and includes options for page numbers and hyperlinks.

If you're including the list of figures in an eBook or a web page document, don't bother with the page numbers: In the Table of Figures dialog box, remove the check mark by the Show Page Numbers option. Ensure that the Hyperlinks Instead of Page Numbers option is selected instead.

6. **Click the OK button to insert the list of captions.**

You may additionally want to end the list with a hard page break or section page break. Add that break to keep the list of captions separate from the document's other end matter.

REMEMBER

Like most automatic references in Word, the list of captions is a field. If you edit, add, or remove any captions, you need to update the field: Right-click in the list of captions and choose the command Update Field.

Cross-References

Word's Cross-Reference command lets you insert references to other spots in your document. Unlike when you type static text *see page 6*, the cross-reference is anchored to a specific item in the text. That way, the page reference maintains accuracy.

A cross-reference can point to a variety of different items in a document: heading, bookmark, figure, footnote, or table. As long as the cross-reference refers to one of these items, follow these directions to create it:

1. Click the mouse where you want the cross-reference to appear.

The reference can appear in a number of ways. It can be a page number or the text from a heading. Word sticks the reference into your text at the point where you click the mouse.

2. Click the References tab.

3. In the Captions group, click the Cross-Reference button.

The Cross-Reference dialog box appears.

4. Choose what you want to reference from the Reference Type menu.

For example, to reference a bookmark, choose Bookmark. To reference a specific document heading, choose Heading. To reference a figure, you must reference a set caption for the figure, as covered earlier in this chapter.

5. Select the item from the large list in the center of the dialog box.

Choose a specific heading, a bookmark, or whatever else appears in the list.

6. Choose how to reference the item from the Insert Reference To menu.

For example, to reference a heading's text, choose Heading Text. To reference the page number where the heading is found, choose Page Number.

7. **If you're composing an eBook or a web page, place a check mark by the item Insert As Hyperlink.**

REMEMBER

Page number cross-references make no sense in an eBook. That's because eBooks lack pages.

8. **Click the Insert button to place the cross-reference.**

The cross-reference text appears at the insertion pointer's location (from Step 1).

Also see Chapter 22 for more information on hyperlinks in eBooks.

Glossary

A *glossary* is frequently included in more technical documents; it provides a list of terms and definitions. The terms appear in the text, but the glossary doesn't reference specific page numbers. Because of this missing link, Word lacks a specific command to build a glossary. Instead, you must manually create it.

I recommend starting the glossary on a page by itself. Place it in the back of the manuscript, after the text but before the index. Title the page *Glossary* and use one of the document's heading styles if you want the glossary included in the table of contents.

Each glossary entry is a word followed by a definition. No specific format is recommended for this type of presentation, but I recommend keeping the word and definition in the same paragraph. Figure 21-6 lists a few options for paragraph formats. You can also present the glossary as a 2-column list.

Franistat. The thing in the machine that needs adjusting when nothing needs adjusting.

Regular Paragraph

Franistat. The thing in the machine that needs adjusting when nothing needs adjusting.

Hanging Indent

FIGURE 21-6: Different glossary-entry formats.

Franistat   The thing in the machine that needs adjusting when nothing needs adjusting.

Tab Indent

Index

table of contents. It's the way printed documents let you perform a topic or subject search, but it works only when the term you're looking for is referenced and that term is found in the context you desire.

REMEMBER

>> An index is not the same as a glossary of terms. It should also not merely repeat the table of contents.

>> You don't need an index for an eBook. eBook apps feature a Search command, which negates the need to add an index. Also, eBooks don't have page numbers, so an index reference would be useless anyway.

TECHNICAL STUFF

>> In the United States, authors are responsible for creating their books' indexes. Most of the time, however, the author or publisher hires a professional indexer to do the job. So don't complain if you're contracted to write a book and the publisher requires that you create the book's index.

Marking entries for the index

The key to building a strong index is to tag words and phrases in your document that you figure someone may want to reference. For example, a cookbook may have an index that references various ingredients, styles of cooking, or food categories such as desserts.

To make an index entry, follow these steps:

1. **Select the text to include in the index.**

   You need to select only a single word; double-click the word to select it. Select more than one word when you want all that text to appear in the index.

2. **Click the Reference tab.**

3. **In the Index group, click the Mark Entry button.**

   The Mark Index Entry dialog box appears, similar to what's shown in Figure 21-7. This dialog box stays open so that you can continue to mark index entries without having to repeat Steps 2 and 3.

4. **Click the Mark button.**

When you mark an index entry, Word activates the Show/Hide command to reveal some of the document's formatting. Refer to Chapter 17 for details on the Show/Hide command. In this instance, the index-marking field appears in the document next to the word you marked. It looks similar to this:

```
{·XE·"whisky"}
```

Don't delete that reference! It's flags the word *whisky* for inclusion in the document's index. Step 7 explains how to hide the reference.

Optional subentry

Selected text

Mark Index Entry	?	X

Index

Main entry: mucus

Subentry: from nose

Options

○ Cross-reference: *See*

◉ Current page

○ Page range

Bookmark:

Page number format

☐ Bold

☐ Italic

This dialog box stays open so that you can mark multiple index entries.

[Mark] [Mark All] [Close]

FIGURE 21-7:
The Mark Index
Entry dialog box.

Create index reference

Finish adding words to the index

5. **Continue working through your document, selecting text and clicking the Mark button or Mark All button in the Mark Index Entry dialog box.**

The dialog box stays open, and you can work on your document without closing it; slide it off the document window if its location bugs you.

6. **When you're done marking entries, click the Close button in the Mark Index Entry dialog box.**

them, you use the Show/Hide command:

7. **Click the Home tab, and then click the Show/Hide button to deactivate that feature.**

The Show/Hide button is shown in the margin.

You can stop and start the index process at any time while you work on your document. You don't need to hurry up and finish after one swipe. In fact, I recommend creating the index after your first draft and then looking for index items again just before you finish the final draft.

TIP

» To save time, click the Mark All button to index every occurrence of the word or phrase in the document.

» You can edit the text in the Main Entry text box. If the word you select isn't precise, you can make it so. For example, if you selected the text *Swiffer type of mop,* you can edit it to read *Swiffer mop* in the Mark Entry text box.

» To create a useful index, you need to view your manuscript topically. Consider terms or phrases that someone might want to search for in your text.

» The Subentry text box in the Mark Index Entry dialog box helps readers locate more specific information related to a main topic. For example, you can index the word *email* and then offer subentry text to include topics like sending, receiving, forwarding, attachments, and so on. Especially for common topics, consider adding subentries.

» How thorough should an index be? Well, hopefully, it's not larger than the document it's indexing. As a seasoned technical-book author, I can tell you that people complain about indexes being inaccurate and incomplete. Your Word document's index will be accurate. Whether or not it's thorough depends on how well you mark up your text.

Inserting the index

After you feel that you've sufficiently marked plenty of index entries, you can insert the manuscript's index. Obey these directions:

1. **Position the insertion pointer to the location where you want the index to appear.**

   The index is located at the end of a document. Of all a document's references, the index appears last. I can find no rule to verify that the index is always last. Some publishers may add other material after the index, but not additional appendixes or references.

2. **Insert a hard page break or a next-page section break.**

   You want the index to start on its own page. See Chapter 6 for information on setting the various types of page breaks.

3. **Type the word** Index.

   If your manuscript features a table of contents, set the text style to the top-level heading. That way, the index appears in the TOC.

4. **Press the Enter key to start the index text on a new line.**

5. **Click the References tab.**

6. **In the Index group, click the Insert Index button.**

   The Index dialog box appears, shown in Figure 21-8.

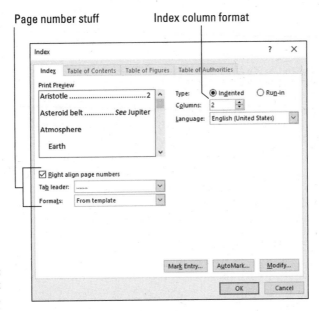

7. **If you want the page numbers to appear right-justified, place a check mark in the box by Right Align Page Numbers.**

If you don't right-align the page numbers, the numbers appear right by the index entry. Use the Print Preview window to gauge the differences.

8. **Set the number of columns for the index.**

Because indexes are generally brief, Word presets two columns per page for the index. (Refer to Figure 21-8.) If you prefer one column, use the Columns gizmo to specify 1 instead of 2.

9. **Click the OK button to add the index to your document.**

10. **If any pages follow the index, add another hard page break after the last line in the index.**

The index reflects the items you marked in your document, each with its appropriate page number. Any subentries appear indented below the main entry.

TECHNICAL STUFF

Word adds a continuous section break above and below the index's text (the field). This type of section break is what allows the index to be formatted into multiple columns. A continuous section break, however, does not force the index to reside on its own page, only within its own section. Refer to Chapter 6 for more details on sections.

Updating the index

Similar to other Word references, the index is a field. It looks like static text, but it's not. Because it's a field, it's necessary to update the index after you edit your document. That way, any page renumbering is reflected in the index, as well as any new entries you may have marked.

To update the document's index, heed these steps:

1. **Right-click the mouse inside the index.**

2. **Choose Update Field from the shortcut menu.**

The index is refreshed.

The index is a field. When you click the mouse inside of the field, the text grows a gray background. See Chapter 24 for more information on document fields.

Chapter 22

eBook Publishing

t's all the rage these days: Skip over the arduous process of obtaining an agent and shopping a book to the various publishing houses. Screw 'em! That's because you can take your work and self-publish it electronically and it costs you nothing. Millions of mobile device users can then buy your literary efforts, transforming you into an overnight success! That's the dream, anyway.

The eBook Process

Whether you want your book to be published traditionally or electronically, the process remains the same: Sit your butt in a chair and write! The content of your book is independent of the format, though you do have some specific items to take into consideration. These are based on the eBook's presentation, which is digital, not on paper.

>> Word is fully capable of producing your eBook, including references, pictures, or whatever you want in the book. You do not need separate desktop publishing software to make an eBook.

>> Any Word document can be converted to an eBook. If you specifically set out to create an eBook, however, you can save yourself some time by minding the advice listed in this section.

>> An eBook is not simply a PDF copy of your book. eBooks use a special document format that can be read only by eBook reader software.

Writing the manuscript

I recommend that you write your eBook as a single document in Word. You can write separate chapters if you like, as mentioned in Chapter 20. If so, create a master document when you're done: Eventually, you'll want all your eBook's text in a single Word document. That step is required for the final conversion into the eBook file.

To start a new chapter in your eBook document, or to bring any element to the top of a page, insert a page break. Use a hard page break. The next page section break also works, but because the document lacks any meaningful page formatting (see the next section), there's no point in breaking up your text into sections.

>> Document elements separated by a hard page break include the cover page, front matter, chapters, and any back matter, including a glossary or an index. See the nearby sidebar, "Front matter and back matter."

>> Refer to Chapter 6 for details on page breaks in Word.

>> You can copyright your own work. Write the word *Copyright* followed by the copyright symbol and the date, as in © 2016. In Word, type **(C)** and those three characters are autocorrected into the copyright symbol.

>> You do not need to register your text with any official department or agency. Any individual can issue a copyright. Please don't pay to have your own work copyrighted.

>> A *foreword* (not *forward*) is text appearing in the front matter and written by someone other than yourself. It serves as an introduction to the work, usually by a professional or another well-known person. Not every book needs a foreword.

>> A *preface* is written by the author. It serves as extra narrative for the book, to explain the topic or provide background. Like the foreword, a preface is optional.

>> The *introduction* is written by the author. It's more formal than a preface and typically found in technical and trade books.

>> Refer to Chapter 21 for information on adding the table of contents, glossary, bibliography, and index to your eBook.

FRONT MATTER AND BACK MATTER

The official publishing name for pages of text that appear at the start of a book is *front matter*. The front matter can include the book's title page, a copyright page, the table of contents (TOC), a foreword, a preface, and an introduction. Of these items, a title page is a must. The book's title and author should sit on a page by themselves at the start of your eBook. Most eBooks also include a copyright page, with information about the book, the publication date, and details about the publisher and author. Also include the eBook version number.

Back matter is any information that follows the main body of the text. Examples include a glossary, appendixes, a bibliography, endnotes, and — in print books — an index. The final thing in any book can be marketing material, as described in this chapter.

Formatting your eBook document

REMEMBER

Perhaps the most important thing to remember when you write an eBook is that page size, page count, or anything having to do with a page is irrelevant: eBooks don't have pages!

If you like, you can format the document as it might present itself on an eBook reader. This special page formatting doesn't translate to the eBook reader software, but it can help visually remind you of the text's final appearance. Follow these steps:

1. **Click the Layout tab.**

2. **In the Page Setup group, click the Margins button.**

3. **Choose Wide.**

   The Wide option isn't specifically an eBook reader format, but it's narrow enough that you get the idea how text might look on a mobile device.

Even when you adjust the margins, what you see in the document window may not approximate what a reader sees; that's because most eBook readers allow the user to reorient the device from vertical to horizontal, which reformats the eBook's text accordingly.

» Don't bother with headers or footers in your manuscript. They won't show up in the final eBook.

» Don't bother with page numbers.

>> Don't fuss over choosing a special font. Many eBook reader programs let the reader choose the typeface and font size.

>> ~~when~~ using special characters. Basic characters and symbols translate well into the eBook format, but some characters may appear as tiny squares (unknown characters). You might even see unpredictable characters, depending on what you're trying to do and how the eBook reader app interprets the text. The only way to know for certain is to use the app's preview software, as described later in this chapter.

>> Text color transfers to the eBook reader app, though specific colors may not. I would just avoid using special colors in your text.

>> Paragraph formatting still applies to an eBook — specifically, the spaces before and after a paragraph as well as left-right indents and first-line indents. Line spacing might translate to the final eBook, though some eBook apps let the user adjust line spacing.

TIP

>> Though eBooks don't feature page counts, your readers might want to know the *word* count; refer to Chapter 18. Another relevant eBook attribute is the final file size. That topic is covered later in this chapter.

Using pictures or graphics

Do you love to spice up your book with clever illustrations, photos, or even festive dingbats between the chapters? Don't. One thing eBooks can't handle well are graphics.

The problem isn't with Word, which can deftly manipulate pictures and other nontextual elements. The problem is with the eBook software, which inconsistently translates the images in the final, published work. As with some formatting issues, the only way to know how pictures look in a final eBook document is to preview the document before you publish.

>> Unlike printing on paper, in an eBook the graphic's dimensions in pixels plays a role in how large or small the image appears in an eBook reader app. Don't be surprised if one image is quite large and the next image — formatted the same in Word — appears tiny in the eBook.

TIP

>> If you can, try to be consistent with the image resolution as measured in pixels, horizontally and vertically. Pixel depth is also important; an image set to 72 pixels will appear smaller than an image set to 300 pixels.

>> Ensure that you know which file format the eBook publishing software uses before you create the images. Some eBook publishers may limit their documents to specific file types, such as JPEG and not PNG.

>> When formatting the images, I recommend you use the inline-with-text layout option. Keep the images on a line by themselves, centered from left to right. Any fancy layout options you attempt may not translate to the final document.

>> See Part 2 of this book for details on how to work with graphical objects in Word.

Creating hyperlinks

When you need to reference another part of your eBook, insert a hyperlink into your document. People who read eBooks are accustomed to tapping a link as opposed to flipping pages. It's natural.

A hyperlink is inserted directly, or it can be added as a cross-reference. I recommend inserting the links directly. Follow these steps:

1. **Select the text that you want to appear as a link.**

2. **Click the Insert tab.**

3. **In the Links group, click the Hyperlink button.**

   The Insert Hyperlink dialog box appears, as illustrated in Figure 22-1.

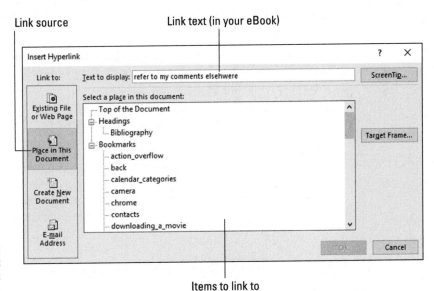

Link source

Link text (in your eBook)

Items to link to

4. **From the Link To list, choose Place in This Document.**

The center portion of the Insert Hyperlink dialog box changes to ~~list~~ ~~document. These include~~ bookmarks as well as text formatted in Word's heading styles. Of the two, I recommend setting bookmarks as the target for your eBook's hyperlinks.

5. **Scroll through the list to find an item, a heading, or a bookmark to link to.**

In my eBooks, I use bookmarks, which I find more flexible than Word's heading styles.

6. **Click the OK button to create the link.**

The text stays linked to the bookmark or heading in the document. Even if you modify the text, the link remains valid. Only when you delete the heading or bookmark does the link cease to function.

The link appears in the document as blue underlined text. In Word, Ctrl+click the mouse on the link to follow it. When the document is published as an eBook, the user can click or tap the link to jump to another part of the text.

>> Refer to Chapter 20 for information on creating bookmarks.

>> Word can create automatic hyperlinks for its references, such as a table of contents. See the next section.

>> The keyboard shortcut for inserting a hyperlink is Ctrl+K. Follow Step 1 in the preceding step list, and then press Ctrl+K to summon the Insert Hyperlink dialog box.

>> Right-click on a hyperlink to change its target. Choose the Edit Hyperlink command, and then use the Insert Hyperlink dialog box to make any necessary modifications.

>> To erase a hyperlink, right-click on the blue underlined text. Choose the Remove Hyperlink command from the shortcut menu. This command doesn't delete the hyperlink text.

>> The Select a Place in This Document list (refer to Figure 22-1) shows headings and bookmarks. Only those headings formatted by using Word's built-in Heading styles appear in the list. If you've created your heading styles, they don't show up. That's another reason I recommend using bookmarks instead.

Adding document references

The number of references you place into your eBook depends on the topic. All eBook publishers, however, recommend that you place a table of contents in your document.

REMEMBER Chapter 21 covers creating a table of contents. Refer there for specific directions on adding a TOC to your eBook. Remember to use hyperlinks in the TOC, not page numbers.

Don't bother with an index for your eBook. Readers use the Search command to look for text in an eBook. Also, the lack of page numbers in an eBook render an index useless.

eBook Publishing Tips

In a way, an eBook publisher is more like a vanity press than a traditional publisher. The difference is marketing: A traditional publisher has a vested interest in selling your book. A vanity press doesn't care, because you're paying for everything. An eBook publisher provides the venue and markets its app or reading hardware, but it's still up to you to pull more weight as an author than you would when using a traditional book publisher.

Titling your tome

Crafting a proper title for a book is an art form. It's a lot tougher than you think. In fact, you might be surprised to discover that most authors don't title their own books. Even when they do, the publisher may devise a better title. And getting the title correct is highly important: The title is the first introduction to your book.

If an easy book-titling formula existed, I'd gladly pass it along. Yet even the big publishing houses struggle. To provide a suggestion, consider pulling text from your book — a quote or thought you find rather pithy. For example, *Outnumbered, Outsmarted, But Not Defeated* might be some text found in a book that the author would otherwise title *That Time Those Aliens Came to Earth and Nearly Killed Everyone*.

>> Pull a quote from poetry or another source if you lack inspiration. I can't imagine how many pieces of literature have been titled by taking quotes from Shakespeare's *Hamlet*.

>> Avoid starting your eBook's title with *How To*. The Library of Congress doesn't list any book that starts with *How To*. Also, it's not that creative. (Yes, I know about the musical *How to Succeed in Business Without Really Trying*, which is why I wrote *avoid* instead of *don't*.)

>> You cannot copyright your book's title. You might be able to trademark the title, which involves a legal process. Book series can be trademarked, or in the case of *For Dummies®*, a registered trademark is used.

>> To help confuse you further, rules for naming books always have exceptions, such as Abbie Hoffman's *Steal This Book*. Remember, the goal is to get someone to notice your Book.

Generating a cover

After you dream up the perfect title, another important-yet-difficult job is to apply that title to a festive book cover. In the real world, publishers pay graphics artists way too little money to dream up professional covers. Even when the publishers chicken out and buy stock photos, a lot of thought goes into the selection — or at least one would hope.

If you want the best cover for your eTome, hire a professional graphics designer to create one. A designer is far better at the task than you would be. Otherwise, keep the cover simple and attractive.

>> eBook publishers require that you upload a graphics file for the cover. This image is separate from the document, so you don't need to include the cover inside the manuscript's text, unless you really want to.

>> Check with the publisher to confirm the graphics file format. You can use whatever means available to create the image, but it must be uploaded in a specific format, such as JPEG.

WARNING

>> Most images on the Internet are copyrighted — even if the image doesn't say that it's copyrighted or have the © symbol, you still need permission to use it. *Fair use* doesn't apply to an eBook you plan on selling. Only when an image is flagged as being in the public domain can you use it.

>> A good source for public domain images is the government. NASA images are all public domain, though that may not help you design a cover for your 17th century romance novel.

Finding a publisher

Plenty of eBook publishers rim the online galaxy. That's good news! The only bad news is that many of them mandate exclusivity. So my advice is to pick one publisher and stick with it.

Any quick search of the Internet provides you with a list of eBook publishers. Of the lot, I believe that Amazon Kindle Direct Publishing (KDP) is the best choice. Kindle offers a wide exposure, and Amazon is a Goliath of the online retail world.

Each eBook publisher has its own procedures for submitting your manuscript. The directions are found on the eBook publisher's web page, and they're written with the best intentions. Still, the process can be intimidating. Don't worry if you screw up: You're given plenty of opportunities to preview the book and even to unpublish it.

WARNING

>> Amazon KDP requires exclusivity for a period of time, depending on which services you subscribe to. After that time, it's possible to submit your eBook to another publisher. Check with the terms of your Amazon publishing agreement before you do so.

>> You definitely do not need to pay a third party to prep and publish the book. Though some services might be worth it, offering marketing advice and such, most are completely unnecessary.

>> One of the beauties of eBook publishing is that it's very easy to submit a new edition of your book. If readers find mistakes, you can fix them and upload a better eBook to replace the one currently online.

>> Check with the eBook publisher to see in which formats it wants the material submitted. Word is capable of saving in a variety of formats, one of which is most likely what the publisher wants. Refer to Chapter 15 for information on saving a Word document in a special file format.

Publishing with Kindle Direct Publishing

Of all the online publishers, I believe Amazon's Kindle Direct Publishing (KDP) would be a good place for any budding eAuthor to start: Visit kdp.amazon.com to sign up.

After creating a KDP account, or using your existing Amazon account, obtain the Kindle Preview software for your computer. You'll find it in the area where content tools are located. You might also find a tutorial online that goes over the publishing process.

Kindle eBooks are submitted in the HTML or web page format. To convert your Word document into that format, follow these steps:

1. **Save your document.**

Ensure that your Word document is up-to-date before you make the conversion. Also, the book must be in a single file, as described earlier in this chapter.

2. **Click the File tab.**

3. **Choose Save As.**

The Save As screen appears.

4. **For the file type, choose Web Page Filtered.**

   The File Type menu appears below the file name ~~...~~

   ~~...~~ file manager or the traditional Save As dialog box.

5. **Click the Save button.**

   A warning appears. What it explains is a good thing: Word is awful at creating HTML documents, but the Web Page Filtered option removes a lot of the crap.

6. **Click the Yes button in the warning dialog box.**

   Your eBook is saved as a web page document. The view changes to Web Layout.

7. **Close the document.**

   And keep in mind that Word may open again in Web Layout view. Refer to Chapter 18 for information about changing document views.

The original manuscript still exists as a Word document. The web page document is saved in the same folder, but with the htm filename extension. If the eBook contained any images, those files are stored in a folder with the same name as the document.

The next step is to archive the document along with the image file folder, if present. Here's how to create such an archive in Windows:

1. **Open your manuscript's folder in Windows.**

   You see your Word document(s), plus the newly created htm (web page) file and a folder containing images, though if your eBook doesn't contain images, you don't see a folder. Both files and the folder have the same name.

2. **Select the web page (htm) file and the image folder.**

   Ctrl+click to select two files.

3. **Right-click one of the selected files.**

4. **From the pop-up menu, choose Send To ⇨ Compressed (Zipped) Folder.**

   Another file appears in the folder window. It's an archive (zip file) with the same name as the htm file or folder.

5. **Press the Enter key to lock in the archive filename.**

   It's the archive (zip) file that you upload to KDP to create your eBook.

The next few steps take place online, on the KDP web page. You fill in information about your book, including the title, your name, and so on. You upload the book's cover file. Then you upload the archive (zip) file you created.

See the next few sections for what to do next. These tasks include previewing the eBook and setting the price point.

Previewing the final eBook

Before you click the big Publish button and offer your efforts to digital libraries across the land, I strongly recommend that you download a preview of your eBook. All eBook publishers should offer this feature: On the web page where you describe and submit your document, an option is available to download the final product.

To view the eBook preview, you need eBook reader software. You can use a preview program, such as the Kindle Preview I mention earlier in this chapter. Use that software to see how your book looks in digital form.

Use the preview program to get the book's big picture. Ensure that the chapter breaks look okay. Check the layout and graphics, if you dared do anything fancy. You're not proofreading at this point, though it doesn't hurt.

If you see anything awry, fix it in the original Word document. Then follow the steps to convert and upload the eBook manuscript. This course of action is perfectly okay; not until you click the Publish button is the book available for purchase. Even then, the book may require approval by the publisher.

Setting the price

No one is an expert at determining what a book should cost. A book is worth what someone will pay for it, and no one can tell you what that price can be.

Generally speaking, an eBook is priced lower than its real-world copy. A $39 hardcover mystery novel may have an electronic cousin that retails for $14. How was that price calculated? Possibly by witchcraft. I just don't know.

Your best guess is to look at your competition to see what the prices are. That will help give you an idea. The goal isn't to get rich by selling one book, but rather to make a steady stream of money by selling many books at a reasonable price.

Related to the price, of course, is what you get paid. For each eBook sold, you receive a portion of the price or *royalty*. The eBook publisher offers various rates, depending on which ~~~~~~~~~~~~ and on other items, such as your book's file size. Foreign royalty rates are different from domestic.

>> Beware of pricing a book too low! Consumers often believe that a low price implies low quality.

>> In most cases, taxes on foreign sales are paid by the publisher. In the United States, you are responsible for reporting your royalties as income on your taxes.

>> The eBook's file size might also weigh in on the pricing. To determine your Word document's file size, click the File tab. On the Info screen, the document's file size is shown at the top left. To obtain the size of the file you upload to the publisher, you need to use Windows and view the zip (archive) file's size in a folder window.

Marketing your eBooks

I'm sure that eBook publishing has met with a lot of success for many authors, but take with a grain of salt the stories of people who made a fortune. Few people stroll out of the eBook casino winning big with one pull at the lucky slot machine. Most successful eBook authors arrived at their position because of one word: marketing.

Welcome to the final phase of eBook publishing, the one where pretty much every author fails. That failure makes sense: Authors write, marketers market. Some authors are great at marketing (and lousy at writing, but that's another story), but most don't give it another thought.

Give marking another thought.

You must push and sell your book. The publisher might have tools available to assist you, or services you can subscribe to. The onus is on you, however, to make the effort and let people know about your book. You can advertise, make the circuit attending self-publishing conferences, speak at libraries, and just do the whole PR routine.

>> One of the first pieces of marketing regarding your eBook, whether you know it or not, is the title. Refer to the earlier section "Titling your tome."

>> Always end your eBook manuscript with a list of your other titles. Place that page near the end of your eBook. Set the page title style so that it appears in the table of contents.

TIP

5
Document Automation

Chapter 23

AutoCorrect, AutoText, and AutoFormat

W ord tries its best to help you with the writing task. When you goof, mistakes are corrected. When it looks like you meant to type a special character, Word inserts the proper character for you. Formatted lists and paragraphs can also appear automatically. Some of these features save a lot of time, and some you may find get in your way. Together, these tools form what I call the Autos.

Know Your Autos

that use the name Auto. They're all automatic, they serve comparable functions, and they have annoyingly similar names. Here's the Big Picture:

AutoCorrect: This function corrects common typos and capitalizations. It also inherited many of the old AutoText features from previous versions of Word.

AutoText Building Blocks: This function lets you insert preset chunks of text. It's not the same as the old AutoText feature.

AutoFormat: This feature lets you format your document in one operation. It's a holdover from earlier versions of Word. The AutoFormat command isn't even found on the Ribbon. I list it here because it's easily confused with the AutoFormat As You Type command.

AutoFormat As You Type: This function deals with formatting text, applying similar paragraph styles (bullets, numbers, and so on), and converting individual characters to their proper equivalents (such as ½ for 1/2).

Two Auto commands you might be familiar with, that aren't in this list, are Auto-Complete and AutoText. These commands were popular in older versions of Word, but are unavailable in Word 2016.

Don't let yourself become confused over the sloppy way the Auto commands are organized, or how some of them are familiar yet no longer available. If you've used Word for any length of time, you might find that confusion oddly comfortable. As a consolation, all these commands are headquartered in the same dialog box, as illustrated in Figure 23-1.

To summon the AutoCorrect dialog box, shown in Figure 23-1, follow these steps:

1. **Click the File tab.**

2. **Choose Options.**

   The Word Options dialog box appears.

3. **Choose Proofing from the left side of the Word Options dialog box.**

4. **On the right side of the dialog box, click the AutoCorrect Options button.**

   Behold the AutoCorrect dialog box.

Of the five tabs shown in the AutoCorrect dialog box, you need to concern yourself with only two: AutoCorrect and AutoFormat As You Type. (Refer to Figure 23-1.)

AutoCorrect tab　　　　　　　AutoFormat As You Type tab

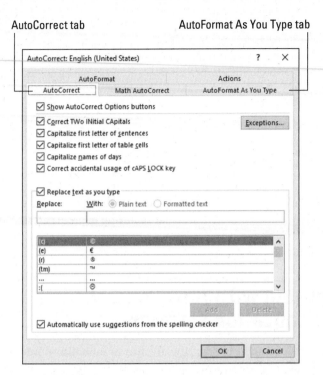

FIGURE 23-1:
Auto Central
in Word.

>> Later sections in this chapter require that you access the AutoCorrect dialog box. As a shortcut, look for the AutoFormat Options or AutoCorrect Options icon in your text. You can quickly access AutoFormat or AutoCorrect settings from that icon.

>> The Math AutoCorrect tab provides an extension to the AutoCorrect (old AutoText) entries — specifically, to conjure mathematical symbols. If you understand symbols such as $\cap$ and $\cong$, click the tab to review its repertoire.

>> Options on the Actions tab are normally disabled. They can be used to provide extra commands on Word's right-click shortcut menu. The commands appear on the Additional Actions submenu. For example, you can right-click on a date and choose Additional Actions ⇨ Schedule a Meeting.

>> The biggest question most people ask is why are two AutoFormat tabs available in the AutoComplete dialog box? The AutoFormat tab relates to Word's AutoFormat command. Don't bother looking for that command on the Ribbon; it's not there. So you can ignore the AutoFormat tab. The one you want to pay attention to is AutoFormat As You Type.

>> If you miss the old AutoText feature, see the later section "Pretending that AutoCorrect is AutoText."

» Word 2016 lacks an AutoComplete function. It was removed a few versions ago. In its place you create an AutoText building block, which works just like the old AutoComplete. See the later section "Creating an AutoText building block."

AutoCorrect the Boo-Boos

Word's AutoCorrect feature supplements the spell check proofing tool. Basically, AutoCorrect lets you avoid the shame of having to proof certain words in your text. When AutoCorrect is active, common typos and capitalization errors are corrected automatically.

Working with AutoCorrect capitalization settings

It's not that you don't know how or when to capitalize words. No, the problem is that sneaky Shift key. When you're too late or too early with that key, or you dawdle too long, you create capitalization typos. The word may be flagged as misspelled, though it's just the uppercase/lowercase letters that are different.

The common capitalization errors are illustrated in Figure 23-2, which is a close-up of part of the AutoCorrect dialog box (the AutoCorrect tab). These five settings cover the most common Shift key boo-boos.

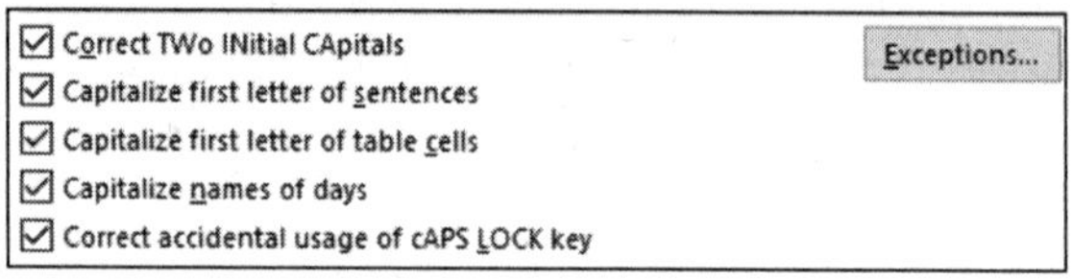

FIGURE 23-2:
AutoCorrect's
capitalization
settings.

☑ Correct TWo INitial CApitals   Exceptions...
☑ Capitalize first letter of sentences
☑ Capitalize first letter of table cells
☑ Capitalize names of days
☑ Correct accidental usage of cAPS LOCK key

To turn one or more of the capitalization settings on or off, obey these directions:

1. Click the File tab and choose Options.

2. Choose Proofing on the left side of the Word Options dialog box.

3. Click the AutoCorrect Options button.

4. Ensure that the AutoCorrect tab is selected.

5. **Remove or add check marks by the options you want to deactivate or activate, respectively.**

For example, if you don't want the first letter of a sentence capitalized in your poetry, remove the check mark by the option Capitalize First Letter of Sentences.

6. **Click the OK button when you're done, and click OK again to close the Word Options dialog box.**

Click the Exceptions button (refer to Figure 23-2) to direct AutoCorrect *not* to capitalize certain words. For example, AutoCorrect doesn't interpret the period after a common abbreviation as the end of a sentence. That's because those abbreviations are listed in the AutoCorrect Exceptions dialog box, shown in Figure 23-3.

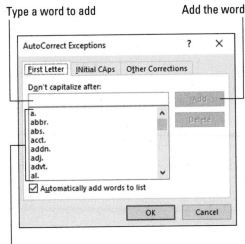

Type a word to add   Add the word

FIGURE 23-3:
Exceptions to AutoCorrect's capitalization rules.

Abbreviations

You can add your own abbreviations to the list: Type the text into the box (refer to Figure 23-3) and click the Add button.

The INitial CAps tab lets you set exceptions for proper words that require more than one initial capital letter. Click the tab to see one example: IDs, short for identifications.

The Other Corrections tab allows you to type any old jumble of lowercase and capital letters and add each word to a list. AutoCorrect then ignores those words. My advice is to create this list as you work on your document. If the capitalization IdaHO is required in your text, add that exact word as an exception in the Auto-Correct Exceptions dialog box.

Pretending that AutoCorrect is AutoText

AutoCorrect's second feature (after fixing capitalization errors) is replacing com-

AutoText feature, beloved by Word users from generations past.

The first set of corrections converts common text abbreviations into their appropriate symbols, such as (C) into the copyright symbol, ©. These symbols are located at the top of the list of Replace Text As You Type list, illustrated in Figure 23-4 (top).

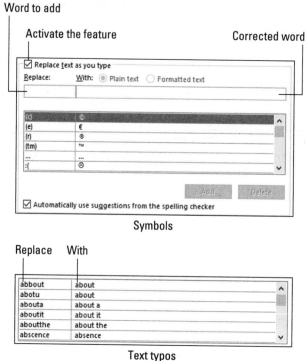

Word to add

Activate the feature

Corrected word

Symbols

Replace   With

FIGURE 23-4:
AutoCorrect's
replace-text list.

Text typos

Beyond symbols, AutoCorrect's replace-text list includes common typos, shown at the bottom in Figure 23-4. When you type one of the items on the left side of the list, Word automatically inserts the proper text on the right — providing that the Replace Text As You Type command is active.

To ensure that the feature is active, or to add another word to correct, obey these steps:

1. **Click the File tab and choose Options.**

2. **In the Word Options dialog box, choose Proofing on the left side.**

3. **Click the AutoCorrect Options button.**

   The AutoCorrect dialog box appears with the AutoCorrect tab up front.

4. **Ensure that there's a check mark by the option Replace Text As You Type.**

   When the check mark is present, the feature is active.

   To add another word, such as *break* to replace *braek*, continue with Step 5.

5. **In the Replace text box, type the word you frequently mistype.**

   For example, **braek**.

6. **In the With box, type the word to replace the mistyped word.**

   Such as **break**.

7. **Click the Add button.**

8. **Click OK to close the AutoCorrect dialog box, and then OK to close the Word Options dialog box.**

You can repeat Steps 5 through 7 to add a number of your favorite typos. Whenever the word you specify in Step 5 is typed, the word you enter for Step 6 replaces it automatically.

Undoing an AutoCorrect change

Every time AutoCorrect fixes capitalization, inserts a proper symbol, or corrects a typo, a small symbol appears in the document's text. You may not see it, so point the mouse at any word that is changed by AutoCorrect. Upon success, a small, blue rectangle appears in the text, as shown in Figure 23-5.

Point the mouse at the rectangle to see the AutoCorrect Options button, also shown in Figure 23-5. Click the button to reveal a menu, which allows you to do one of three things:

Undo: Choose the Change Back command to revert the change. You see the original word or characters listed in the menu, such as *becuase,* shown in Figure 23-5.

Stop correcting: Choose the Stop Automatically Correcting command to remove the word from the AutoCorrect list. If you select this command, the selected word will never be corrected again, not in any document.

View the AutoCorrect dialog box: Choose the bottom command on the menu to visit the AutoCorrect dialog box, and the AutoCorrect tab.

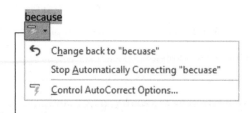

because   Point the mouse at the word
to see the rectangle

because   Point the mouse at the rectangle to

because

↩   Change back to "becuase"

    Stop Automatically Correcting "becuase"

⚡   Control AutoCorrect Options...

FIGURE 23-5:
The AutoCorrect
Options menu.

Click the AutoCorrect Options
button to see the menu

TIP

If you find yourself becoming annoyed with all the automatic corrections, disable the AutoCorrect Replace As You Type feature. Heed these directions:

1. **Click the File tab and choose Options.**

2. **Choose Proofing, and then click the AutoCorrect Options button.**

3. **In the AutoCorrect dialog box, on the AutoCorrect tab, remove the check mark by the item Replace As You Type.**

4. **Click OK to close the AutoCorrect dialog box.**

5. **Click OK to close the Word Options dialog box.**

If you merely want to disable the AutoCorrect Options button (refer to Figure 23-5), follow Steps 1 and 2, but in Step 3 remove the check mark by the option Show AutoCorrect Options Buttons.

>> The rectangle (refer to the top of Figure 23-5) appears only when you point the mouse at a corrected word. It sticks by the word until you close the document. When you open the document again, all AutoCorrect terms are fixed and cannot be reverted.

>> The AutoCorrect Options button is nearly identical to the AutoFormat Options button. See the later section "Undoing an AutoFormat change."

Instant Typing with AutoText Building Blocks

The AutoText feature was banished from Word many years ago. Also banished was the AutoComplete tool. In an effort to keep everyone confused, the AutoComplete tool was reinstated as something called an AutoText building block. It's a useful typing feature, but not one that's apparent or obvious.

Creating an AutoText building block

The AutoText building block is a typing assistant. You create building blocks for text you frequently type, such as your name, address, apologies, and so on. After you type the first few letters, Word pops up the AutoText building block bubble, as shown in Figure 23-6. Press the Enter key to have that text inserted automatically into your document.

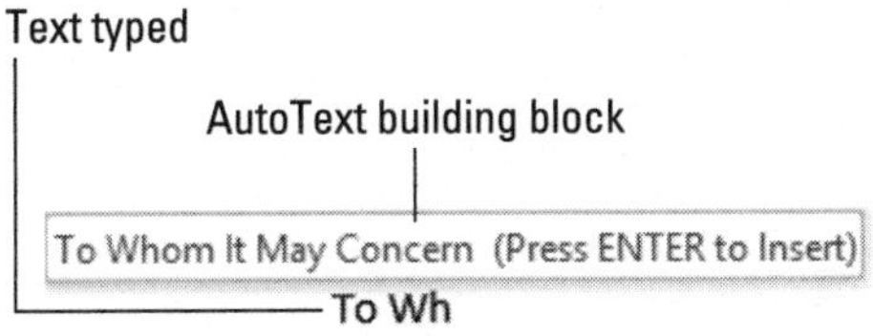

Text typed

AutoText building block

To Whom It May Concern (Press ENTER to Insert)

To Wh

FIGURE 23-6:
An AutoText building block in action.

Unlike the old AutoComplete function, the AutoText building block repertoire is pretty empty. That means you can get busy creating your own entries. Follow these directions:

1. **Type the text you want to stick into an AutoText building block.**

   For example, your name, street name, business, or any text you regularly type.

2. **Select the text.**

   If you want the building block to include the Enter keystroke at the end of a line, ensure that it's selected. If not, just select up to the last letter of the word you want in the building block.

3. **Click the Insert tab.**

4. **In the Text group, click the Quick Parts button.**

5. **Choose AutoText ⇨ Save Selection to AutoText Gallery.**

   The Create New Building Block dialog box appears, as illustrated in Figure 23-7.

The options in the Create New Building Block dialog box are set pretty much the way you need. If you're using a specific template, however, choose Normal. dotm (refer to Figure 23-7) so that the building block is available in all documents in Word.

6. **Click OK.**

   The selected text is added to the list of building blocks.

Building block name (not the building block text)

FIGURE 23-7:
The Create New Building Block dialog box.

Template where the building block is stored

To try out your invention, start a new line of text in a document and type the first few letters or words that you set as an AutoText building block. When you see the bubble appear (refer to Figure 23-6), press the Enter key to insert the text.

TIP

>> A faster way to insert a building block is to type the first few letters and press the F3 key. That way, you don't have to wait for the bubble to appear.

>> For more precise text-selecting, I recommend that you disable Word's word-selection feature. Instead, direct Word to select text one letter at a time. See Chapter 31.

>> If you have trouble *not* selecting the Enter key when you select the building block (refer to Step 2), type some text after the last word in the building block. That extra text prevents Word from automatically selecting the Enter key (paragraph character) at the end of a paragraph.

>> Use the Options menu in the Create New Building Block dialog box to set how Word inserts the text. Choose the option Insert Content in Its Own Paragraph to ensure that the building block is set as a line by itself.

» You can select multiple lines of text as a building block. For example, your return address.

» Keep the building block names unique, as well as the starting text for a building block. For example, if you create two building blocks that start with the same text, neither ever appears when you type text.

Reviewing building blocks

The building blocks you create are saved with a template file. If you don't choose a specific template, they're saved in the Normal.dotm template and made available to all your Word documents.

To review the building blocks, you've created, as well as other automatic document elements, you must summon the Building Blocks Organizer dialog box.

Obey these steps:

1. **Click the Insert tab.**

2. **In the Text group, click the Quick Parts button and choose Building Blocks Organizer.**

The Building Blocks Organizer dialog box appears.

AutoText building blocks appear at the top of the list. Other document elements are found in the list as well, which includes most of Word's built-in galleries.

You cannot edit your AutoText building blocks, but you can remove them: Click to select a building block in the Building Blocks Organizer dialog box, and then click the Delete button. You can then re-create the building block as discussed in the preceding section.

Close the Building Blocks Organizer dialog box when you're done poking around.

AutoFormat As You Type

Word's AutoFormat feature automatically applies character formats and paragraph styles to your text. It works similarly to AutoCorrect in that AutoFormat makes its changes on the fly. But of the two features, AutoFormat causes users more woe. It tends to make assumptions you may not agree with. That's okay! You can cheerfully disable the feature.

Understanding AutoFormat options

The AutoFormat function hosts a suite of routines, some of which might fall under ~~the AutoCorrect command~~... ~~though Microsoft~~ placed them under Auto-Format instead. The AutoFormat routines include

Replace As You Type: This feature converts some characters and text sequences into other characters, such as -- (two hyphens) into an — (em dash), or 1/2 into ½. Word also creates hyperlinks for web page addresses and network paths.

Apply As You Type: This feature converts text into formatted elements, including bulleted lists, numbered lists, tables, and so on. This is the AutoFormat feature most people find annoying.

Automatically As You Type: This feature copies special paragraph formatting to subsequent paragraphs, such as when you set paragraph indents or create a hanging indent list.

A summary of specific options for these features appears at the end of this section.

The AutoCorrect dialog box, on the AutoFormat As You Type tab, lists all the specifics for each of these categories, as illustrated in Figure 23-8.

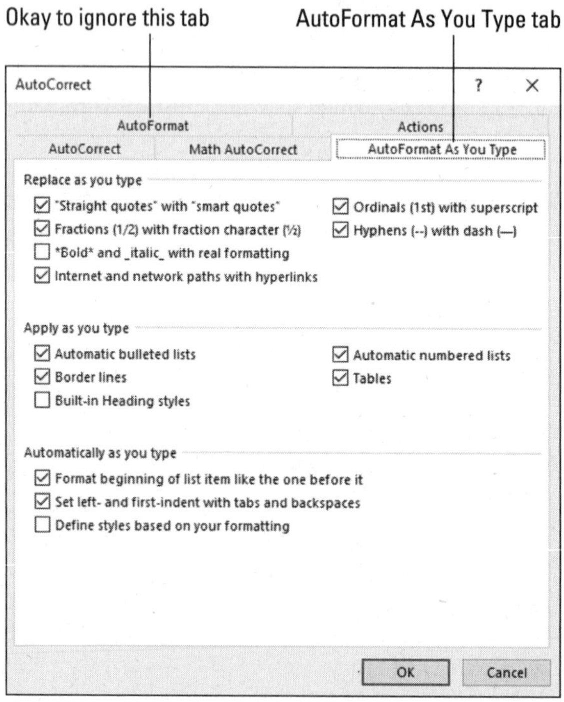

FIGURE 23-8:
The AutoFormat features.

Follow these steps:

1. **Click the File tab and choose Options.**

2. **Choose Proofing on the left side of the Word Options dialog box.**

3. **On the right side of the dialog box, click the AutoCorrect Options button.**

4. **Click the AutoFormat As You Type tab.**

   Don't click the AutoFormat tab. It shows similar items, but they apply to the all-at-once AutoFormat command.

To display the AutoCorrect dialog box, and the AutoFormat As You Type tab,

The actions listed in the dialog box affect text as you type. If something annoys you, which is frequently the case, you can undo the action or disable the feature. See the next section.

» Smart quotes are curved, "like this," as opposed to "like this." The apostrophe and single-quote characters are also affected by the Smart Quotes option.

» Not all fractions are affected by the Fractions setting. Only specific fractions feature single characters, such as ½ and ¾. Other fractions you can create manually: Superscript the nominator, and subscript the denominator.

» The dash (—) is known as an *em dash.* Its width is the same as the letter *M* in whichever font you're using. The keyboard shortcut for this character is Alt+Ctrl+- (hyphen). A longer dash is available: Press Shift+Alt+Ctrl+-.

» An automatic bulleted list is created whenever you start a line with an asterisk and a tab. Press the Enter key at the end of the paragraph to apply the bulleted list format.

» To create an automatic numbered list, start the paragraph with a number and a tab.

» To create automatic borderlines, type three hyphens on a line and press the Enter key.

» As an example of the Format Beginning of List feature, if you apply bold formatting to a word set aside in a hanging indented list, subsequent paragraphs automatically apply the bold format to the first word.

» The Set Left- and First-Indent with Tabs feature converts a tab at the start of a paragraph into a first-line indent format. This format is applied to all subsequent paragraphs.

Undoing an AutoFormat change

The AutoFormat command can be subtle, such as when straight quotes are con~~~~~~~~~~~~~~~~~~~~~~~~~~~~~~ ~~~~~ ~~ ~~~~ ~~ ~~~~~~~~~~ ~~~~~~~~ list is created for you.

For AutoFormat's Replace As You Type features, undoing a conversion works similarly to undoing an AutoCorrect change: See the earlier section "Undoing an AutoCorrect change." Also refer to Figure 23-5, which illustrates how the process works. The commands on the menu are subtly different, yet their actions are similar.

For more major text adjustments, you see the AutoFormat Options button, illustrated in Figure 23-9.

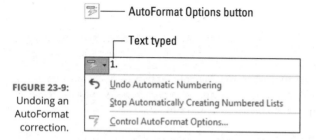

FIGURE 23-9:
Undoing an
AutoFormat
correction.

As an example, when you type 1. and then a tab, AutoFormat converts the line into a numbered paragraph, complete with indents. To undo that action, immediately follow these steps:

1. **Click the AutoFormat Options button.**

2. **Choose the Undo Automatic Numbering command.**

   You can also just press Esc, but you must be quick.

If you detest automatic paragraph numbering, choose the option Stop Automatically Creating Numbered Lists. That command directly dispenses with the feature.

Chapter 24

Document Fields

Text written in a word processor isn't the same as text "written in stone," but it's similar. Once you type a line or paragraph, that text is fixed. To change the contents, you must edit the line. To use a nerd term, the text is *static*.

A field provides for *dynamic* text, or text that changes based on conditions in your document. You can use fields to keep information fresh, reference changing items such as page numbers and bookmarks, and include other elements that add automated features to your document.

Field Philosophy

Word features an onslaught of different document fields. Many of them are employed by Word features, such as a table of contents, mail merge, or references in a header or footer. Beyond those uses, rare is the mortal Word user who bothers with fields. As evidence, I offer that the Field command button isn't the most obvious command to find on the Ribbon.

Inserting a field

All of Word's fields are accessed from the Field dialog box, illustrated in

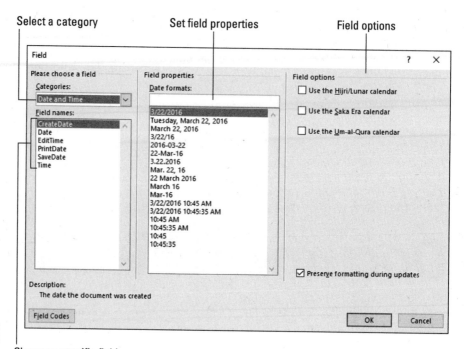

Select a category   Set field properties   Field options

Choose a specific field

FIGURE 24-1:
The Field
dialog box.

To summon that dialog box, and insert a field into your document, follow these steps:

1. Position the insertion point at the spot in your document where you want the field's text to appear.

The field is inserted like any other text. It can go inside the body of the document, into a header or footer, into a text box, or anywhere.

2. Click the Insert tab.

3. In the Text group, click the Quick Parts command button.

4. Choose Field.

The Field dialog box appears.

5. **Choose the field.**

   The dialog box is divided into three parts. (Refer to Figure 24-1.) It helps to choose a category first, such as Date & Time, and then select an individual field.

6. **Select the field properties.**

   Field properties don't appear for every field. In Figure 24-1, the date format is shown as a field property.

7. **Set field options.**

   As with field properties, not every field sports options.

8. **Click OK to insert the field into your document.**

   The field's text appears, though what you see is a dynamic field and not static text.

When you click on a field or move the insertion pointer inside a field, its text background becomes gray. That highlight confirms that the text is a field and, more importantly, that you shouldn't edit it. Though you can make changes, they will be discarded when the field is updated or when you reopen the document.

To remove a field, select it and then press the Delete or Backspace key twice. The extra key press is to remind you that you're removing a field and not static text.

Working with fields behind the scenes

Word's fields have two sides: a shiny, pretty side and a dark underside. Mostly you see the pretty side, which is the dynamic text the field generates — for example, the date shown at the top of Figure 24-2.

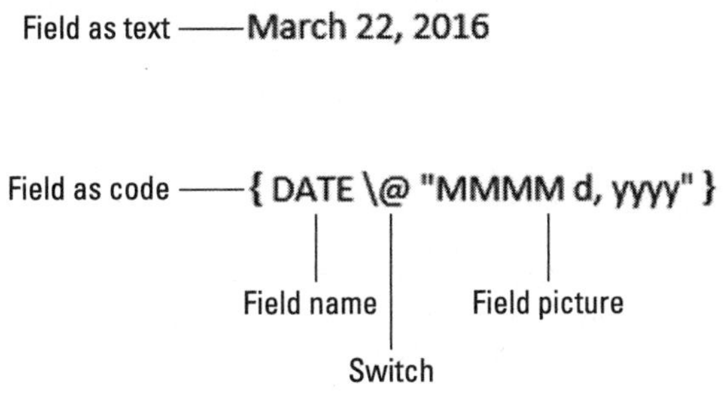

Field as text ——**March 22, 2016**

Field as code ——**{ DATE \@ "MMMM d, yyyy" }**

Field name | Field picture

Switch

FIGURE 24-2:
Two faces
to a field.

The ugly side has value in that you can access the field's innards. Further, you can edit the field directly, changing its output or format. That's entirely possible, providing you know what you're doing.

To switch between the field text and field codes, obey these directions:

1. **Right-click the field.**

2. **Choose Toggle Field Codes.**

   The field changes to code (refer to the bottom of Figure 24-2) or to text, the opposite of its current state.

Field codes appear between curly brackets. All fields start with a code name, written in all caps. That's followed by an optional switch, which is the backslash and another character, such as \@, shown in Figure 24-2. An optional field property appears in double quotes. Any further options appear after the field property, before the final curly bracket.

When the field's codes are revealed, you can edit them: Click in the field and type any changes. As an example, in Figure 24-3, the field property (or picture) shows "dd MMMM." That option directs Word to display the date field as day–month, as in 4 July. This choice isn't available directly in the Field dialog box; only by editing the DATE field's picture can you make the change.

FIGURE 24-3: An edited DATE field.

{ DATE \@ "dd MMMM" }

>> If you choose to edit the field directly, as shown in Figure 24-3, remember to update the field to reflect your changes. See the next section.

REMEMBER

>> See the later section "Using date-and-time fields" for specifics on date-and-time field properties, such as "dd MMMM."

>> To display codes for all fields throughout your document, press the Alt+F9 keyboard shortcut. Press Alt+F9 again to show the fields as text.

TIP

Updating a field

Fields are up-to-date when they're created. As you work with your document, the field's content may go stale. For example, a reference to page 4 might jiggle around to page 3, but the field may still show the number 4. To address this issue, fields must be updated.

To manually update a field, heed these steps:

1. **Right-click on the field text.**

2. **Choose the Update Field command.**

The field is generated anew, reflecting current document conditions.

TIP

» Some of Word's fields update when you close and reopen the document, but most don't. See the next section for tips on locating fields so that you can update them.

» To ensure that fields update before you print a document, open the Word Options dialog box: Click the File tab and choose Print. In the Display category, ensure that a check mark is set by the option Update Fields Before Printing.

Finding fields in a document

You can use the Find command to locate fields in your document. The only caveat is that the fields must be visible. Follow these steps:

1. **Press the Alt+F9 keyboard shortcut.**

   The forgettable Alt+F9 keyboard shortcut shows the codes for all fields in your document.

2. **Press Ctrl+F to summon the Navigation pane, and the Results tab.**

3. **Type ^d.**

   That's the caret character followed by a lowercase *D*. You do not need to press the Enter key.

   Instantly, all fields in your document are highlighted. Use the Previous or Next buttons on the Navigation tab to jump between the found fields in your document.

4. **Use the Up/Down buttons in the Navigation pane to review the fields in your document.**

   Unlike other times the Find command is used, text previews for fields may not appear in the Navigation pane.

To stop searching, you can close the Navigation pane. Press Alt+F9 again to transform all the document's fields back into text.

>> And now . . . the shortcut: To skip between fields in a document, press the F11 key. You're taken from one field to the next each time you press F11.

>> Want to cycle from b...

Building a field manually

If you find it tedious to access the Field dialog box to enter a document field, you can use a clever field-creation shortcut. You must know the field's code name, plus any optional switches or formats, but you may find this technique faster. Heed these secret directions:

1. **Position the insertion pointer where you want a field to appear in the document.**

2. **Press Ctrl+F9.**

   Word creates an empty field in your document and makes the code visible. You see two curly brackets, shaded gray. The cursor blinks between them, eagerly awaiting you to type field codes.

3. **Type the field code in all caps.**

   For example, type **PAGE** to set the current page number.

4. **Type any optional switches.**

   The switches vary, depending on which field you're using. A full list is available online, and this chapter lists a few of the codes.

5. **Type the field picture and other options as required.**

   The field's codes are visible, so the final step is to switch to the field's text view.

6. **Right-click the field and choose the Toggle Field Codes command.**

   You might also need to right-click on the field and choose the Update Field command.

The field looks and behaves like any other field in the document, though it was created manually.

>> The full list of fields and their codes can be found online at the Office.com support site. Visit https://support.office.com and search for *Field codes in Word*. (The direct web page address is too long to be useful as a reference here.)

>> Also see Table 24-1, elsewhere in this chapter, for DATE and TIME field references.

Field Cookbook

Most of Word's useful fields feature command buttons to directly insert the field. For example, on the Insert tab, in the Header & Footer group, you'll find the Page Number command. It's a shortcut to the various page number fields, all preformatted and preset for you. On that same tab, in the Text group, is the Date & Time button, which is a shortcut to insert a specific date or time field.

The advantage of using a field directly is that you can better customize its appearance. Further, if you know about fields, you can use the Page Number or Date & Time commands to insert the field and then right-click to edit the field exactly as you like.

Beyond page numbers and date/time fields, the majority of Word's fields relate to other, specific commands, such as Word's reference features, covered in Chapter 21. Still, a handful of useful fields remain, some of which can help automate your document and create useful dynamic text.

>> Word's Formula fields are used to manipulate rows and columns of data in a table. Refer to Chapter 4.

>> Many of Word's reference tools use fields to maintain information. These tools include the table of contents, the index, and cross-references. Refer to Chapter 21 for details.

Inserting page number fields

Page number references frequently find themselves in a document's header or footer. These fields can also go into any part of a document. So if you want to write "This is page 437" on page 437, you can do so.

REMEMBER

>> If you're writing an eBook, use hyperlinks instead of page number references. See Chapter 22.

>> Also see Chapter 7 for more information on fields that go into document headers and footers.

The current page number

The quick way to add the current page number to your document is to use the Page Number command button. Follow these steps:

1. **Click the Insert tab.**

2. **In the Header & Footer group, click the Page Number button.**

3. **Choose Current Position ⇨ Plain Number.**

   Word inserts a field into your document. To customize it, continue with Step 4.

   ~~the page number field and choose Edit Field.~~

   The Field dialog box appears.

5. **Choose a format from the list.**

6. **Click OK.**

The standard page number field is named PAGE.

Total page numbers

Your document's total page count is considered a document information field, not a numbering field.

1. **Position the insertion pointer at the spot where you want the document's total page count to appear.**

2. **Click the Insert tab.**

3. **Click the Quick Parts button and choose Field.**

   The Field dialog box appears.

4. **Choose Document Information from the Category menu.**

5. **Select the NumPages field.**

6. **Choose the page number format.**

7. **Click OK to insert the field.**

The total page number figure frequently follows the current page number in a footer. For example: 8/20 for page 8 in a 20-page document. In this example, you first insert the current page number field (PAGE), type a slash, and then insert the total pages (NUMPAGES).

Page numbers of other document elements

When you need to refer to another item in the document, such as a figure or quote, you can insert a page number reference to that item. The secret is to bookmark that item and then use the PageRef field to obtain the item's page number. Follow these steps:

1. **Bookmark the item you want to reference.**

   Select the item. On the Insert tab, in the Links group, click the Bookmark button. Type a unique name for the bookmark and click Add. (Refer to Chapter 20 for more details on creating bookmarks.)

2. **Click the insertion pointer where you want the page number reference to appear.**

3. **Summon the Field dialog box.**

   On the Insert tab, in the Text group, click Quick Parts and then Field.

4. **Choose the Links and References category.**

5. **Select the PageRef field.**

6. **Choose the bookmark name you set in Step 1.**

7. **Click OK to insert the field.**

The field references the bookmark's page number no matter where that item ends up in the final document.

Using date-and-time fields

Word's date-and-time fields reference not only the current date and time but also dates and times related to your document. For example, you can insert today's date or a date field that updates to reflect the current date. My favorite date field is the print date. And of all Word's fields, the date-and-time fields are perhaps the easiest to edit directly.

If you want the user to choose a document date, use the Date Picker content control. See Chapter 27.

TECHNICAL STUFF

The current date or time

The quick way to insert the current date or time is to use the handy Date and Time keyboard shortcuts:

The keyboard shortcut to insert the current date into your document is Alt+Shift+D.

The keyboard shortcut to insert the current time into your document is Alt+Shift+T.

These commands insert content controls, which work like fields, but they appear differently when you reveal their codes or click to select them. Still, they remain a handy way to get the date or time into a document. See Chapter 27 for more information on content controls.

The static date or time

If you only want to insert the date or time and not a field (or content control), follow these steps:

1. **Click the Insert tab.**

2. **In the Text group, click the Date & Time button.**

   The Date and Time dialog box appears. It lists common date-and-time formats,
   but doesn't allow you to create your own.

3. **Choose a format.**

   The format specifies whether the date or time or both are inserted into the text.

4. **Remove the check mark by the Update Automatically option.**

   When you remove the check mark, Word inserts text; otherwise, a field is inserted.

5. **Click OK.**

The document print date

The Print Date field is updated only when the document is printed. It's the field
I use at the top of my letter template to ensure that the date on the letter always
matches the date on which I print (and, hopefully, send) my correspondence.

Follow these steps:

1. **Position the insertion pointer where you want the print-date field to
   appear.**

   You can fuss on your own over whether it sits at the top right or top left of a page.

2. **Click the Insert tab.**

3. **In the Text group, choose Quick Parts ⇨ Field.**

4. **From the Category menu, choose Date and Time.**

5. **Select the PrintDate field.**

6. **Choose a format.**

7. **Click OK.**

Don't freak if you see the field display values *XXX 0,0000*. That bit of text appears
when you haven't yet printed the document. After the document is printed, the
field is updated automatically and printed with the rest of the text. In fact, the
next time you open the document, the previous print date appears. Again, Word
updates the date as you print the document.

A custom date or time field

Of all Word's fields, the DATE and TIME fields are the easiest to create on your own or to edit. The field name is DATE or TIME, followed by the \@ switch and a format string in double quotes.

Table 24-1 lists the characters referenced in the DATE and TIME field's picture or format string. If the format string is omitted, Word uses the default date and time presentations, which are *M/d/yyyy* for the date and *h:mm am/pm* for the time.

Case is important in a DATE or TIME field. The difference between *m* and *M* is significant.

Also refer to the earlier section "Building a field manually."

TABLE 24-1

Word's Date and Time Field Codes

Code	What It Stands For
am/pm	Suffix AM or PM after the current time
d	Day of the month
dd	Day of the month, two digits wide
ddd	Day of the week, three letters only
dddd	Day name
h	Hour, one digit wide, 12-hour format
H	Hour, one digit wide, 24-hour format
hh	Hour, two digits wide
HH	Hour, two digits wide
m	Minutes
mm	Minutes, two digits wide
M	Month number
MMM	Month name, three letters only
MMMM	Month, full name
s	Seconds
ss	Seconds, two digits wide
yy	Current year as two digits
yyyy	Current year as four digits

Adding document info fields

A *document info field* ~~saves~~ ~~the document~~ itself, its name, the ~~name, and~~ similar information. In fact, just about every aspect of a document can be stuffed into a field.

The document's author name

You may not remember, but Word (or Office) asked your name when you first installed the program. It knows your full name and initials. You can summon that information in a field so that a heading or another tag in the document can read *Author: Dan Gookin* (or whatever your name is).

1. **Position the insertion pointer where you want the document's author name to appear.**

2. **Click the Insert tab.**

3. **In the Text group, click the Quick Parts button and choose Field.**

4. **From the Categories menu, choose User Information.**

5. **Select the UserName field.**

   You can choose a format, though the (none) format just sticks the name into the document as is.

6. **Click OK.**

To review or reset your username in Word, open the Word Options dialog box: Click the File tab and choose Options. In the Word Options dialog box, in the General category, the User Name text box contains the author name associated with the document.

The document's filename

Your readers may not be thrilled to know the document's filename, but putting a filename in a header is something done often in professional and business environments.

Follow these steps:

1. **Click to place the insertion pointer where you want the document's filename to appear.**

2. **Click the Insert tab.**

3. **In the Text group, choose Quick Parts ⇨ Field.**

   The Field dialog box appears.

4. **From the Category menu, choose Document Information.**

5. **Select the FileName field.**

6. **Choose the text format from the Field Properties area of the dialog box.**

7. **If you want to include the full pathname, place a check mark by the Add Path to Filename option.**

8. **Click OK.**

When editing a header or footer, you can insert a filename from the Header & Footer Tools Design tab: In the Insert group, on the Document Info menu, choose the File Name command. This action inserts the FILENAME field, but only the filename is shown. If you want to include the full pathname, you must edit the field and then follow Step 7 (refer to the step list) in the Field dialog box.

>> To insert the document's file size, choose FileSize in Step 5. Choose a number format, and then specify whether the total should appear in kilobytes or megabytes.

>> You can display the document's template filename if you choose Template in Step 5. That's probably too esoteric of an info tidbit for most documents, but who knows?

>> Refer to Chapter 7 for more information on headers and footers.

Document editing information

When you need to justify your literary efforts, you can insert a field to show how long you've been working on a document.

1. **Summon the Field dialog box.**

   On the Insert tab, in the Text group, choose Quick Parts ⇨ Field.

2. **Select the Time and Date category.**

3. **Choose the EditTime field.**

4. **Ensure that you choose either (none) or 1, 2, 3 as the number format.**

   Any other format prevents the field from being rendered properly.

5. **Click OK.**

The EDITTIME field is expressed in minutes. So if you've been working on the document for two hours, the value 120 appears.

TECHNICAL
STUFF

The EDITTIME field represents the number of minutes a document is open on the screen. It doesn't indicate whether you were interacting with the document in any way.

Echoing text in a field

One bit of magic you can pull with a field is the ability to echo text from one part ~~...~~ So if you have a pithy quote in your term paper that you keep referencing, you don't have to search and then copy and paste when the quote changes; simply update all the reference fields.

To use a field to echo a chunk of text, obey these directions:

1. **Select the chunk of text to echo.**

Select all the text — whatever it is that you want repeated throughout your document. And keep in mind that the chunk of text you reference is the source. If it changes, that's the text you edit, not the copycat fields.

The next set of steps bookmark the text.

2. **Click the Insert tab.**

3. **In the Links group, click the Bookmark button.**

The Bookmark dialog box appears.

4. **Type a bookmark name and then click the Add button.**

Bookmark names cannot contain spaces.

REMEMBER

5. **Position the insertion pointer where you want the text echo to appear.**

This is the spot where you'll insert the reference field.

6. **Still on the Insert tab, in the Text group, click the Quick Parts button and choose Field.**

The Field dialog box appears.

7. **From the Categories menu, choose Links and References.**

8. **From the Field Names list, choose Ref.**

9. **Choose the bookmark name (from Step 4) in the Field Properties list.**

10. **Click OK to insert the field.**

The text is echoed in your document.

The magic of the REF field is that when you modify the original text, all the echoes are changed as well — but only after you update the fields. Refer to the earlier section "Finding fields in a document," which is the first step to updating. Once you locate a REF field, right-click it and choose Update Field to refresh its contents.

Refer to Chapter 20 for more information on setting bookmarks in Word.

Chapter 25

The Big Macro Picture

A macro is a shortcut. It provides a way to do many routine tasks with a quick, single action. In Word, you can create a macro to automate a repetitive task, create a new command, or build a custom document. Macros can also offer full programming power to Word, though you don't need to be a programmer to get the most from Word's macros.

» Macros are task-oriented. In Word, macros perform a specific task or a sequence of tasks.

» Generally speaking, any time you find yourself repeating the same sequence of commands in Word, you can create a macro to automate the process.

» *Macro* is short for *macro instruction*. That roughly translates as "a single directive that does multiple things." *Macro* is from the Greek word μακρύς, for *long*.

>> Word has featured a macro capability almost since its original version. The Macro command began as a simple keystroke/command recording and playback tool. With Word 97, Microsoft introduced Visual Basic for ~~A~~ ~~programming~~ language is still used in Word 2016.

Behold the Developer Tab

If you look real hard, you'll find the Macro command on the Ribbon's View tab. You could use that button to build macros and do all sorts of wondrous things, but instead I recommend that you unveil the normally hidden Developer tab. Follow these steps:

1. Right-click anywhere on the Ribbon.

2. Choose the Customize Ribbon command.

The Word Options dialog box appears, with the Customize Ribbon portion shown automatically. On the right side of the dialog box appears a list of all tabs that can appear on the Ribbon.

3. Place a check mark by Developer.

The check mark ensures that the Developer tab is visible.

4. Click the OK button.

The Developer tab appears on the far right tab on the Ribbon.

The Developer tab contains commands for automating Word documents. It hosts several groups to assist in that process. The Code group is where you'll find the Macro commands.

Keep the Developer tab open while you're reading this chapter, as well as the next few chapters, if you plan on further exploring document automation.

>> To hide the Developer tab, repeat the steps in this section, but in Step 3 remove the check mark.

>> I keep the Developer tab open all the time, not just for macros but also to access document protection and template commands.

>> See Chapter 31 for information on creating your own, custom tab on the Ribbon.

WARNING

>> Most of the tabs shown in the Word Options dialog box appear automatically when needed. That's why the list is extensive. For example, the Design and Layout tabs appear whenever a table is selected. The Format tab appears whenever a drawing object is selected. You don't need to mess with the check marks by these tabs to show or hide their contents.

Word Macro 101

Macros are immensely useful in that they help automate tedious tasks. They can be intimidating because of the VBA programming language, which isn't the friendliest thing to understand. Even the notion of a Developer tab implies a level of knowledge and sophistication to the process.

Ignore all that!

Instead, concentrate on the roots of a typical Word macro, which is the ability to record keystrokes and command choices and just about anything else you normally do in Word.

Understanding macros

At its simplest level, a *macro* is a series of commands or actions in Word, stacked together so that they run one after the other. Macros can become more complex, of course, but I would offer that the majority of Word's macros are really basic.

The process of creating a macro works like this:

1. **Know what you want the macro to do.**

   Look for repetitive tasks, processes you repeat often, or something you do where Word lacks a specific command. For example, you routinely must format the first three words of a paragraph in bold text. You must do this for many paragraphs in the document. That's the kind of repetitive task that a macro can make easier.

2. **Start the macro recording.**

   You give the macro a name and select other options before recording starts.

3. **Perform the desired actions.**

   When recording starts, all your keystrokes, command choices, and other actions are memorized by Word and stored in the macro.

4. Stop recording.

The macro is saved and made available to run again.

How you run the macro depends on how you assigned it when the macro was created: All macros can be run directly, as covered in the later section "Running a macro." For more direct access, you can assign the macro to a command button on the Ribbon or to a keyboard shortcut. Later sections in this chapter discuss the details.

>> Macros can be saved in the current document, in the Normal template, or in a specific template. You determine the location when the macro is created.

>> Most of the time, I recommend saving the macro in the Normal template, which is the best and simplest option.

REMEMBER

>> A Word macro need not be complex or sophisticated or involve programming skills to impress Bill Gates. It's merely a shortcut, designed to automate tasks. If you want to write a macro that swaps two letters, that's perfect.

Recording a macro

If you've never created a macro, a good way to start is to create a simple keystroke macro. This type of macro records some keyboard commands for quick playback when the macro is run.

As an example, the following steps create a macro that adds the bold text attribute to the first three words after the insertion pointer:

1. Ensure that you are editing a document that contains text and that the document has been saved.

You need some text to practice on to create any text-modification macro. If you simply want some throwaway text to use, on a new line, type **=rand()** and press the Enter key.

2. Position the insertion pointer in the document.

You can't assume anything when you create a macro, but for this example, set the insertion pointer at the start of a paragraph: Press Ctrl+↑.

3. Click the Developer tab.

Refer to the earlier section "Behold the Developer Tab" if you don't see it.

4. In the Code group, click the Record Macro button.

The Record Macro dialog box appears, as illustrated in Figure 25-1. At minimum, you need to name the macro. The other features of the dialog box are discussed elsewhere in this chapter.

Macro shortcut

No spaces

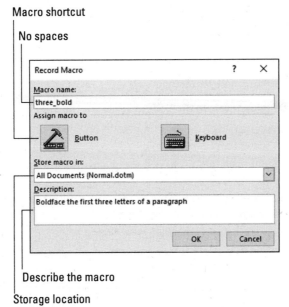

5. Type the macro's name.

Macro names cannot contain spaces; use the underscore character instead, as shown in Figure 25-1.

You can immediately assign the macro to a command button or keyboard shortcut in the Record Macro dialog box. Examples are provided later in this chapter.

The Save Macro In menu selects where Word keeps the macro's code. You can save in the current document, in a specific template, or in the Normal template. If you choose the Normal template, the macro is available to all Word documents, as shown in Figure 25-1.

6. Click the OK button to start recording the macro.

Word records your actions. The mouse pointer changes to show the Cassette Tape icon (which is a throwback to the 1990s) to remind you.

The changed mouse pointer is pretty much your visual clue that a macro is recording, though you might also see the Macro Recording item on the status bar. It appears as a gray square, the Stop icon. Refer to Chapter 18 for ~~information about the status bar.~~

7. **Type the keystrokes or click the commands to save in the macro.**

   In the example of making three words boldface, type the following:

   a. *Press the F8 key to enter Selection mode.*

   b. *Press Ctrl+→ three times to select three words.*

   c. *Press Ctrl+B to make the text bold.*

8. **On the Developer tab, in the Code group, click the Stop Recording button.**

   The macro is saved.

The next thing you need to do is to test the macro. See the next section.

>> If you've activated the Macro Recording option on the status bar, you see the Record Macro icon, shown in the margin. Click that icon to summon the Record Macro dialog box and begin recording a macro.

>> It's important to know where the insertion pointer needs to be when you record a macro and when you run the macro. If you're creating a macro only for yourself, that's not an issue. Just keep in mind where the insertion pointer needs to be; otherwise, the macro may not do what you want.

>> If a macro of the same name already exists, you're prompted whether to overwrite it. Overwriting existing macros is fine when you're modifying the macro to account for things you forgot when it was first recorded.

>> It's best to use keyboard commands for selecting text as opposed to mouse-selection. That's because:

>> Word macros don't record the mouse selecting text.

REMEMBER

>> To select text, use the F8 key shortcut. See the nearby sidebar, "The F8 key text-selection shortcut."

>> A recording macro cannot determine where you click the mouse in your text. Any clicks or double-clicks in your document are ignored.

>> Macros don't record any commands you select from a shortcut or right-click menu. Use commands on the Ribbon instead of right-clicking.

>> When you cannot access a command while recording a macro, the command must be manually inserted when you edit the macro. This step requires a bit more knowledge of macros, though documentation is available online. See Chapter 26.

TECHNICAL STUFF

>> The *=rand()* command (from Step 1 in this section) is a Word function that generates random text. Place a number between the parentheses to generate that many paragraphs of text. To set the number of paragraphs and lines per paragraph, use *=rand(p,l)* where *p* is the number of paragraphs and *l* is the number of lines per paragraph. The function *=rand.old()* generates the text "The quick brown fox jumps over the lazy dog" over and over. And the function *=lorem()* generates the traditional "Lorem ipsum" placeholder text.

Running a macro

The power of the macro lies in its capability to issue multiple commands at once. To make that power useful, macros are traditionally assigned to keyboard shortcuts or a command button. Even so, all macros can be run from the Macros dialog box.

To run a macro, heed these directions:

1. **Save your document.**

If the macro screws up, you don't want to lose anything. Save!

2. **If necessary, position the insertion pointer so that the macro can proceed.**

Some sophisticated macros ~~position the insertion pointer automatically.~~ For simple macros, you may have to click the mouse at a specific spot in the text, such as the start of a paragraph for the *three_bold* macro created in the preceding section.

3. **Click the Developer tab.**

4. **In the Code group, click the Macros button.**

The Macros dialog box appears, as shown in Figure 25-2. It lists all available macros, including those in the Normal template as well as any found in the current document or associated with the current document's template.

Available macros

Selected macro

Macros		? ✕
Macro name:		
three_bold		**Run**
Macro1		Step Into
swap_words		
three_bold		Edit
Update_all_fields		
		Create
		Delete
		Organizer...
Macros in:	All active templates and documents	
Description:		
Boldface the first three letters of a paragraph		
		Cancel

FIGURE 25-2: The Macros dialog box. Selected macro description

Where macros are found

5. **Select a macro to run.**

For example, the *three_bold* macro.

6. **Click the Run button.**

The dialog box vanishes. Word passes control to the macro, which does whatever it's supposed to do.

Most macros work quickly. In fact, it's difficult to tell that anything is going on, other than the macro's actions take place. Even so, you can't do anything with your document while the macro runs.

After the macro runs, you can continue working with the document: Write, save, edit, format, or do whatever.

>> A macro stops automatically after its final instruction.

>> If a macro runs amok, press Ctrl+Break to stop it. (Break and Pause share the same key on the PC keyboard, located above the cursor control keys.)

Deleting a macro

When you first set out to play with macros, you'll probably create a lot of macros named Macro1, Macro2, and so on. That's great! Practice is good. When you no longer need those macros or you want to remove any macro, follow these steps:

1. **Click the Developer tab.**

2. **In the Code group, click the Macros button.**

   The Macros dialog box appears.

3. **Select the macro you want to obliterate.**

4. **Click the Delete button.**

5. **Click the Yes button to confirm.**

   You can repeat Steps 3 through 5 to remove additional macros.

6. **Click the Close button when you're done.**

Macros are removed from their source. So, if they were saved as part of the Normal template (as most macros are), the macros are no longer available in any document. Otherwise, macros found in a single document are removed from that source.

REMEMBER

>> Deleting a macro from the Normal template removes its availability from all documents in Word.

>> A deleted macro may still sport a dead command button or an invalid keyboard shortcut. See the next section for information on macro shortcuts. See Chapter 31 for information on removing dead command buttons and invalid keyboard shortcuts.

Quick Macro Access

...............to the current document are listed the Macros dialog box. You can use the dialog box to run the macros, but that process is cumbersome. You have two options available to make accessing a macro more convenient. The first is to assign the macro to a Quick Access toolbar button. The second is to assign the macro to a keyboard shortcut.

Assigning a macro to a Quick Access toolbar button

A convenient way to access your macros is to place them as buttons on the Quick Access toolbar. You can create the macro's toolbar button before or after you create the macro.

In Figure 25-3, you see two macro icons assigned to the Quick Access toolbar. The one on the left uses the default Macro icon; the one on the right is assigned a custom icon.

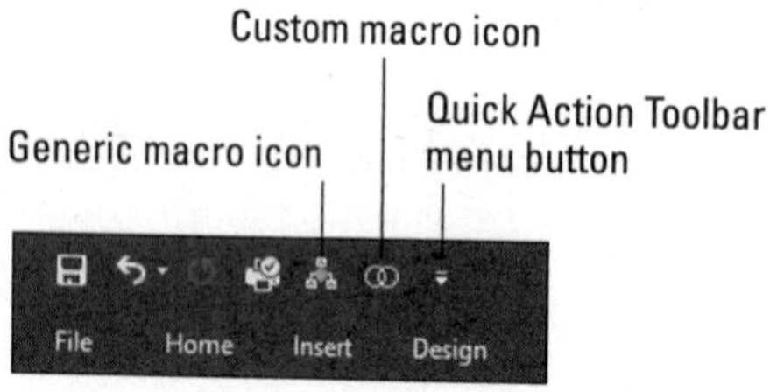

Custom macro icon

Quick Action Toolbar
menu button

Generic macro icon

FIGURE 25-3:
Macro icons
as Quick Access
toolbar buttons.

If you've already created a macro, follow these steps to assign it to a Quick Access toolbar button:

1. **Click the menu button to the right of the Quick Access toolbar.**

   Refer to Figure 25-3 for the menu button's location.

2. **Choose More Commands.**

   The Word Options dialog box appears, with the Quick Access Toolbar screen displayed.

3. **From the Choose Commands From menu, select Macros.**

   A list of all macros available to the current document appears, as shown in Figure 25-4.

4. **Click to select the macro you want to add to the toolbar.**

Select a macro

Buttons on the
Quick Access toolbar

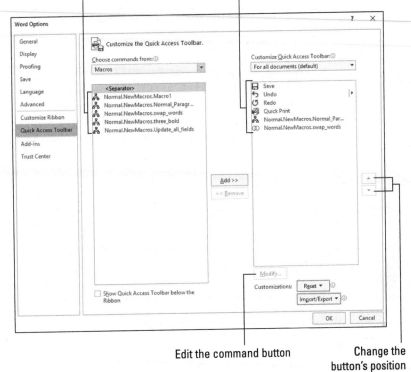

FIGURE 25-4:
Customizing the
Quick Access
toolbar.

Edit the command button

Change the
button's position

5. Click the Add button.

The macro is copied to the list of items currently on the toolbar, shown on the right side of the dialog box.

You can click the up- or down-arrow key to move the command, changing its order on the toolbar.

TIP

6. Click the Modify button.

The Modify Button dialog box appears.

7. Choose a new, better icon for the macro.

Your choices are rather limited, but I'm certain you can find something more interesting than the generic Macro icon (shown in the margin).

8. Type a shortcut name for the macro.

The macro's full, technical name appears in the Display Name box. Type a better name. That name appears in a pop-up bubble when you point the mouse at the button on the Quick Access toolbar.

9. **Click the OK button to lock in the new icon and name.**

10. **Click OK but close the Word Options dialog box.**

The icon can now be accessed quickly from the top of Word's document window.

You can assign a macro as a button on the Quick Access toolbar when the macro is created. To do so, click the Button button in the Record Macro dialog box (shown in Figure 25-1). At that point, follow along with Steps 4 through 10 in this section, though in Step 4 the macro you're creating is the only one that appears in the list.

REMEMBER

>> When you modify the Quick Access toolbar, you're making that change for all your documents.

>> Refer to the section "Recording a macro," earlier in this chapter, for more details on creating a new macro.

WARNING

>> If you delete a macro, any buttons you've assigned remain on the Quick Access toolbar. To remove the buttons, follow Steps 1 and 2 in this section. Select the macro on the right side of the Word Options dialog box. Click the Remove button (in the center of the dialog box). Click OK.

>> See Chapter 31 for information on the Quick Access toolbar.

>> When the Quick Access toolbar becomes too crowded, consider creating a custom tab on the Ribbon. This topic is also covered in Chapter 31.

Creating a macro keyboard shortcut

For macros I use frequently, especially those that manipulate text, I prefer to assign the macro to a keyboard shortcut. This assignment can be made when the macro is created, or you can set the macro's shortcut keys at any time.

To assign a keyboard shortcut to a macro you've already built and perfected, obey these directions:

1. **Right-click on the Ribbon and choose the command Customize the Ribbon.**

   No, you're not customizing the Ribbon, but that part of the Word Options dialog box that appears is where you build keyboard shortcuts.

2. **Click the Customize button.**

   The Customize Keyboard dialog box appears, as illustrated in Figure 25-5.

Choose Macros   Available macros

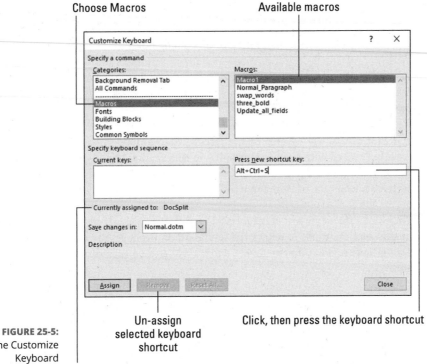

FIGURE 25-5:
The Customize
Keyboard
dialog box.

Un-assign
selected keyboard
shortcut

Click, then press the keyboard shortcut

Keyboard shortcut in use

3. From the Categories list, choose Macros.

The Macros category is located near the bottom of the list. When you select it, you see the list of available macros appear on the right side of the dialog box. (Refer to Figure 25-5.)

4. Click the mouse in the Press New Shortcut Key box.

You want to ensure that the box is selected.

5. Press the shortcut-key combination.

TIP

Many of the Alt+Ctrl+*letter* as well as Shift+Alt+*letter* key combinations are available to assign to macros. Try those first.

If a keyboard shortcut is in use, such as Alt+Ctrl+S, shown in Figure 25-5, select another key combination. I recommend that you don't alter any of Word's existing keyboard shortcuts.

When a keyboard shortcut isn't used by Word, you see the text *[unassigned]* in the Customize Keyboard dialog box.

6. Click the Assign button to lock in your choice.

7. **Click the Close button to dismiss the Customize Keyboard dialog box.**

8. **Click OK to banish the Word Options dialog box.**

Try out your new keyboard shortcut: Press the key combination you typed in Step 5. The macro runs, doing whatever marvelous thing you programmed it to do.

If you're clever enough to remember, you can assign a keyboard shortcut when you first create the macro. In the Record Macro dialog box, click the Keyboard button. Proceed with Steps 3 through 7 in this section to assign a key combination to the macro, and then continue recording the macro's commands. Refer to the earlier section "Recording a macro."

To remove the keyboard shortcut assigned to the macro, follow Steps 1 through 4 in this section. Click to select the keyboard shortcut in the Customize Keyboard dialog box (under Current Keys). Click the Remove button. Finish with Steps 6 and 7.

>> A macro can have both a keyboard shortcut and a toolbar button.

>> A keyboard shortcut can be assigned to any Word command, not just a macro. See Chapter 31 for information.

The Joys of Macro-Enabled Documents

I recommend saving your macros in the Normal template, which is where Word normally desires to put them. That way, they're available to all your documents, which is probably what you want.

When you need a macro to be specific to a single document, you must assign that macro to the document. This process involves creating a macro-enabled document, which is a special file type that's different from the standard Word document. You can also create macro-enabled templates, which provide a set of unique macros to the macro-enabled documents those templates create.

Saving macros with the current document

Saving a macro with a specific document involves two steps: First, you must choose the current document when you create the macro. Second, you must ensure that the document is saved as a macro-enabled document.

To create a macro in the current document, choose the document name in the Record Macro dialog box: Click the Store Macro In menu and choose the current document, as illustrated in Figure 25-6.

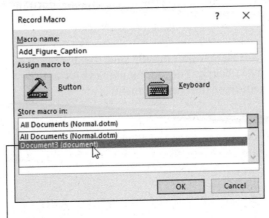

Select the current document

Create the macro as covered in the earlier section "Recording a macro."

After the macro is created (or even before), you must save the document as a macro-enabled file type. If you don't, and you try to save the document normally, a warning appears, as shown in Figure 25-7.

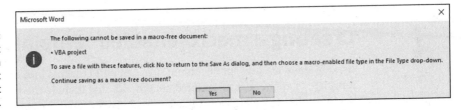

To save that document as a macro-enabled document when you see the warning message, follow these steps:

1. **Click the No button to dismiss the warning.**

   Refer to Figure 25-7, where the No button lurks. After clicking the button, you see the standard Save As dialog box.

2. **Click the Save As Type menu.**

3. **Choose the file format Word Macro-Enabled Document (*.docm).**

4. **Name the file, and work whatever other options you need to in the Save As dialog box.**

    ~~Include setting~~ a proper folder for the file.

5. **Click the Save button to save the macro-enabled document.**

    The macros are saved along with the document.

When you plan ahead, you can initially save the document as macro-enabled the first time you save: Click the File tab, choose Save As, and then select Word Macro-Enabled Document from the file type menu.

WARNING

When you open a macro-enabled document, a warning appears just below the Ribbon in the document window. Click the Enable Content button to allow the macros to run. Also see the later section "Dealing with a macro-enabled document."

>> Macro-enabled documents feature the docm filename extension.

>> Standard Word document files feature the docx filename extension.

>> The macros you create are available only in the macro-enabled document. Macros in the Normal template continue to be available.

TECHNICAL STUFF

>> The Normal template, which Word uses for all new documents and which contains all Word's default styles and settings, is actually a macro-enabled template. The full filename is Normal.dotm. This doesn't mean that all the documents you create are macro-enabled. See the next section.

Creating a macro-enabled template

In addition to the current document, you can build macros into a template. Use the template to create macro-enabled documents that include the template's macros. Saving such a template works like a cross between saving a template and saving a macro-enabled document. Heed these directions:

1. **Create the template as you would any template in Word.**

    Add styles, preset text, and any other options required by the documents that the template will create.

2. **Create or add the macros you want included with the template.**

    As you create the macros, choose the current document as the macro's location. See the preceding section.

3. **Save the template as a macro-enabled template.**

   Use the file type menu to choose Word Macro-Enabled Template (*.dotm).

To use the template, select it when you start a new document.

>> All documents you create by using the macro-enabled template can access the template's macros. These macros are in addition to any macros held in the Normal template.

>> If you copy the document to another computer, however, the template's macros aren't available in the document unless you create the document as macro-enabled. Refer to the preceding section.

>> See Chapter 9 for more information on templates.

Macro Security

Word's macros can be quite powerful. How powerful? In the late 1990s, the Bad Guys discovered that a Word file could contain a macro that automatically runs, pulls in information from the user's computer, and sends that information off to a website or generates spam or does a whole host of naughty things.

Since that time, several features have been added to Word to ensure macro security. Chief among them is the macro-enabled document, which sports a special file type in Word. Also available is the Trust Center, which is where you can set the security level for documents that run macros.

TECHNICAL STUFF

The Melissa virus (or worm) was one of the most infamous and successful examples of computer malware. Spawned in 1999, Melissa was a Microsoft Word macro. It spawned when the user opened an infected Word document. Without the user's knowledge, the macro read email addresses from Outlook Express and then sent copies of itself to every email account listed. At its peak, Melissa infected nearly one in five computers around the world.

Visiting the Trust Center

Macro security in Word is handled by a feature called the Trust Center. It deals with general security items, but one in particular controls how macros are handled when you open a document.

To visit the Trust Center, follow these steps:

1. Click the D...

2. **In the Code group, click the Macro Security button.**

   The Trust Center dialog box appears, as shown in Figure 25-8. The Macro Settings item is already chosen on the left side of the dialog box.

   Four macro security settings are available, as shown in Figure 25-8. They are

   Disable all macros without notification: No macros can run; they are disabled. This setting is the most restrictive and secure.

   Disable all macros with notification: You're alerted when a macro-enabled document is loaded. This is the default setting, as shown in Figure 25-8.

   Disable all macros except digitally signed macros: Only macros that have been registered or "digitally signed" are allowed to run.

   Enable all macros (not recommended; potentially dangerous code can run): The circus option, which you don't ever want to choose.

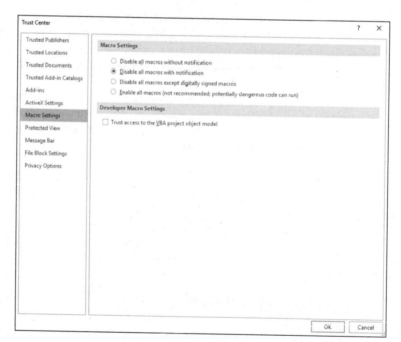

FIGURE 25-8: The Trust Center dialog box.

3. **Select a notification level, or leave it as is (which is probably best).**

4. **Click the OK button.**

The setting you choose is enforced when a macro-enabled document is opened. See the next section.

REMEMBER

>> Also refer to the earlier section "Saving macros with the current document," for details on creating a macro-enabled document.

>> If you choose to disable all macros without notification (the first option in the Trust Center dialog box), no macros saved in a macro-enabled document will run. Macros saved in the Normal template will still be available.

>> Digitally signed macros are created by individuals or developers who have obtained a digital certificate. To be valid, digital certificates must be installed into Windows. For a software developer, obtaining digital certification is a must. For an individual, it's possible to get a personal digital certificate, but such a thing isn't considered secure by the development community.

Dealing with a macro-enabled document

When you open a macro-enabled Word document, the settings made in the Trust Center take hold. (Refer to the preceding section.) When the option Disable All Macros with Notification is chosen (the default), you see a banner in the window, similar to what's shown in Figure 25-9. This is the notification referred to in the security setting.

FIGURE 25-9:
The macro
security warning
or notification.

Click to allow the
document's macros to run

Dismiss the warning
(Macros disabled)

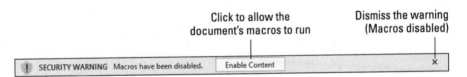

Click the Enable Content button to allow the document's macros to run. Otherwise, you can click the X button to dismiss the warning.

After it's enabled, you can run the document's macros. If you choose to close the banner, the macros won't run. To get the macros to run, close the document, open it again, and then click the Enable Content button.

Chapter 26

More Macro Fun

What fun can be had with macros? Tons! You can ably resist the draw to become a full-fledged VBA programmer yet still command a terrifying presence within the Word macro community. That's because it's relatively simple to cobble together a few complex macros without having to endure mind-numbing programming courses, read a 10,000-page book on macro programming, or wait for a full moon with a sharp knife and an unblemished goat. You just need to know a few tricks, plus where to look up quick answers to some common questions.

>> VBA stands for Visual Basic for Applications. It's the official name of the Word macro programming language.

>> If you're looking for a way to further explore Word macros, I recommend *Mastering VBA for Microsoft Office 2016,* by Richard Mansfield (Sybex). It's a doorstop, but it's thorough. And it looks impressive on the shelf.

The VBA Editor

~~macros. You can delete macros.~~ And, it's true: If you mess up, you simply re-record a macro and give it the same name. When the macro is really complex and you don't want to re-record it, or when you want to add some fancy programming pizazz, you use the Visual Basic for Applications editor.

Don't fret! You don't have to buy anything extra. You don't have to download something from the Microsoft mothership. As a part of the Microsoft Office suite, Word comes with the Visual Basic for Applications editor. It's included free! You just need to know how to fire it up.

Exploring the editor

The Microsoft Visual Basic for Applications editor's purpose is to help you craft intricate macros or explore VBA programming. Using the editor isn't required for building simple macros, but it does give you a peek into what a "simple macro" might actually look like, similar to what's shown in Figure 26-1.

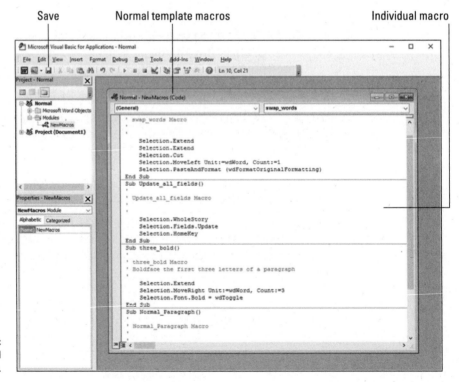

FIGURE 26-1:
The Visual Basic editor.

To open the Microsoft Visual Basic for Applications editor, which I call the *Visual Basic editor*, follow these steps:

1. **Click the Developer tab.**

2. **In the Code group, click the Visual Basic button.**

   The Visual Basic editor appears.

And now, the shortcut: Press the Alt+F11 key combination to open the Visual Basic editor.

In the editor window, you see any macros associated with the current document, which includes macros found in the Normal template (shown in Figure 26-1). If the document contains its own macros, they appear in a second subwindow.

Within each window, the macros are separated into individual boxes.

Like many programming editors, the Visual Basic editor offers features and options to sate the needs of the nerdiest of programmers. You don't need to use all the features or even know what they do, unless you plan to further explore VBA programming.

When you're done using the Visual Basic editor, close its window.

Reviewing macro code

Recording a macro is easy. You probably think to yourself, "Press F8. Press Ctrl+→ three times, and press Ctrl+B." That's great, and it's how you record a macro. The internal picture, however, is a bit different, especially when it comes to beholding a macro as it looks in the Visual Basic editor.

The keystrokes mentioned in the preceding paragraph were part of the *three_bold* macro, created in Chapter 25. That macro appears as follows in the Visual Basic editor:

```
Sub three_bold()
'
' three_bold Macro
' Boldface the first three letters of a paragraph
'
    Selection.Extend
    Selection.MoveRight Unit:=wdWord, Count:=3
    Selection.Font.Bold = wdToggle
End Sub
```

Flee not in terror, gentle reader!

This bit of VBA code represents the keystrokes F8, Ctrl... *three_bold* macro looks written out, in the raw. Here's the breakdown:

>> The first line identifies the macro. *Sub* is short for *sub*routine. It's followed by the macro's name and a set of empty parentheses.

>> The next four lines are comments. The apostrophe, or *single tick,* directs the VBA language to ignore the rest of the line. In this case, the comments title the macro and provide the Description text, originally typing into the Record Macro dialog box.

>> The next three lines are indented. These represent the keystrokes that you typed, encoded in the macro.

>> The last line is *End Sub,* which signals the end of the macro/subroutine.

Granted, a much better way to write the code would have been this:

```
Press F8
Press → three times
Press Ctrl+B
```

That code is much more readable, but it says the same thing as the three *Selection* lines in the earlier example. If you ever explore VBA in any depth, you'll grow to appreciate the subtleties of its strange ways. For now, just nod and keep reading.

REMEMBER

When you're done editing the macro, you can click the Save button in the Visual Basic editor and then switch back to the document window to try out your changes.

Editing a macro's VBA code

The point of the Visual Basic editor is to write or edit macro code. In that aspect, it works similarly to Word, which is used to write human language text. The Visual Basic editor, however, uses the VBA language. Also, it's more limited than Word, in that fancy formatting isn't necessary for writing macro code.

The code for the *three_bold* macro, shown in the preceding section, is created as an example in Chapter 25. If you haven't yet done so, visit that chapter to create the macro so that you have something upon which to practice editing. Then proceed with these steps:

1. **In Word, click the Developer tab.**

2. **In the Code group, click the Visual Basic button.**

   The Visual Basic editor displays all macros for the current document. For this example, locate the *three_bold* macro, which starts with the following line of text:

   ```
   Sub three_bold()
   ```

   The last line of code in the *three_bold* macro is a toggle:

   ```
   Selection.Font.Bold = wdToggle
   ```

   This command directs Word to flip the status of the bold font attribute; if it's on, the *wdToggle* directive turns it off, and vice versa. To change that condition so that the bold text attribute is always asserted, you need to edit the line.

3. **Change the *wdToggle* setting to *True*.**

   Edit the line to read as follows:

   ```
   Selection.Font.Bold = True
   ```

   With this modification, the macro always makes the text bold. If the text is already bold, it stays bold.

4. **Add a line to the code that removes text selection.**

   Insert this line into the macro, just before the *End Sub* line:

   ```
   Selection.MoveRight Unit:=wdCharacter count:=1
   ```

   This VBA code represents pressing the → key once. The effect is that the text is unselected after the bold attribute is applied.

5. **Save the macro, then switch back to Word to test it.**

   Run the macro to confirm that three words are set to bold type and then the text is unselected.

The final macro code should look like this:

```
Sub three_bold()
'
' three_bold Macro
' Boldface the first three letters of a paragraph
'
```

```
    Selection.Extend
    Selection.MoveRight Unit:=wdWord, Count:=3
    Selection.Font.Bold = True
    Selection.MoveRight Unit:=wdCharacter count:=1
  End Sub
```

You can close the Visual Basic editor.

If you find these steps too cumbersome, especially because you don't know the VBA language, don't worry! Instead of editing the macro, simply re-record it. The only code in this section that is unique to the VBA language is the word *True*, used to set the bold attribute.

Dealing with a macro boo-boo

If you mess around in the Visual Basic editor, you might encounter a situation that makes the editor angry. For example, you're poking around and testing commands and such, and then you see an error message when the macro runs, similar to the one shown in Figure 26-2.

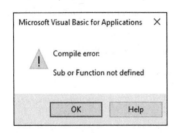

FIGURE 26-2:
Word warns you
of a macro
boo-boo.

When you encounter such an error, click the OK button. The Visual Basic editor opens and the offending macro *Sub* is highlighted, as shown in Figure 26-3. The specific issue may not be highlighted, as shown in the figure, but odds are good that whatever edit you last attempted is the root of the problem.

To fix the issue in the Visual Basic editor, obey these directions:

1. **Press Ctrl+Z to undo whatever you last did.**

This trick may not work. If not, try to manually undo your edits, remove additions, or add back in something you pulled out.

2. **Click the Reset button.**

The button, shown in the margin, is found on the Visual Basic editor toolbar. Click the button to reset the error condition, removing the ugly yellow highlight.

Error flag

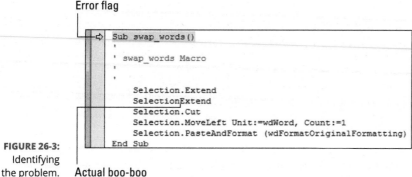

```
Sub swap_words()
'
' swap_words Macro
'
'
    Selection.Extend
    SelectionExtend
    Selection.Cut
    Selection.MoveLeft Unit:=wdWord, Count:=1
    Selection.PasteAndFormat (wdFormatOriginalFormatting)
End Sub
```

FIGURE 26-3:
Identifying
the problem.

Actual boo-boo

REMEMBER

It's often better simply to re-record the macro than to try and edit the thing. Only if you're comfortable with the VBA language, or you're familiar with programming and you can look up and implement what you want, should you bother trying to code a macro from scratch or edit an existing subroutine.

Beyond Mortal Macros

This book isn't all about Word's macros. I've allotted two chapters to the topic, but that's not nearly enough to cover the entire macro kingdom.

The deeper you go into VBA and Office programming, the more bizarre the journey. Chapter 33 offers a selection of useful macros you can explore. They touch upon several common topics, but above all, it's best to stick with macro automation based on recording keystrokes. If you want to go further into depth, this section explores some semi-advanced concepts you might find useful.

Processing an entire document

One of the tasks you might want to pursue in a macro is to work through all the text in a document. It's not the same as a search-and-replace. Say you want to apply bold text to the first word of every paragraph in a document. If so, you would code a macro that might look like this:

```
Sub first_word_bold()
'
' first_word_bold Macro
' Make the first word of every paragraph bold
'
```

```
      Selection.HomeKey Unit:=wdStory
      For i = 1 to ActiveDocument.Paragraphs.Count - 1
         Selection.MoveRight Unit:=wdWord, Count:...
         Selection.Font.Bold = True
         Selection.MoveDown Unit:=wdParagraph, Count:=1
      Next i
   EndSub
```

You can record the basic part of the macro, which is to move to the start of the document, press Ctrl+Shift+→, and then activate the bold attribute. Still, some editing would be required to reach the final code, just shown.

Here's how the statements translate into English:

The following statement is generated when you press the Ctrl+Home key to move the insertion pointer to the start of a document:

```
      Selection.HomeKey Unit:=wdStory
```

The following statement is a loop, which repeats the indented set of (three) statements:

```
      For i = 1 to ActiveDocument.Paragraphs.Count - 1
```

It repeats once for every paragraph in the document, which is the value that *Acti-veDocument.Paragraphs.Count* represents. The value 1 is subtracted from that total because the insertion pointer is already at the first paragraph in the document.

The following statement is generated when you press Ctrl+Shift+→, which selects the word to the right of the insertion pointer:

```
      Selection.MoveRight Unit:=wdWord, Count:=1, Extend:=wdExtend
```

The following statement sets the bold attribute of the selected text:

```
      Selection.Font.Bold = True
```

It's almost the equivalent of pressing the Ctrl+B keyboard shortcut. That shortcut specifies the word *wdToggle* instead of *True*, which was edited as just shown.

The following statement is the equivalent of pressing the Ctrl+↓ keyboard shortcut, which moves the insertion pointer to the start of the next paragraph.

```
      Selection.MoveDown Unit:=wdParagraph, Count:=1
```

And, finally:

```
Next i
```

This statement completes the *for* loop.

You can construct a similar Word macro that processes each paragraph in a document. To do so, first record the keystrokes you need to manipulate text in a paragraph. Then insert those keystrokes into a loop, as shown in the *first_word_bold* macro. Here's the code skeleton to use:

```
Selection.HomeKey Unit:=wdStory
    For i = 1 to ActiveDocument.Paragraphs.Count - 1
        '
        ' your code goes here
        '
        Selection.MoveDown Unit:=wdParagraph, Count:=1
    Next i
```

The first line moves to the top of the document. The *for* loop processes each paragraph in the document. You need the second-to-last line to "hop" the insertion pointer down to the next paragraph. As long as you replace the commented lines (starting with the tick mark) with your own macro code, the entire document is processed.

Entering a command that you cannot type

One of the frustrations you may find with the basic keyboard-recording macros is that some commands can't be accessed from the keyboard or found on the Ribbon. A shortcut might exist, but say that you're in a hurry or you're just unaware of the shortcut. In that case, you need to look up the command's VBA equivalent on the Microsoft Developer Network (MSDN) website:

```
https://msdn.microsoft.com/en-us/library/ee861527.aspx
```

On that site, you can search for a command name. Use Word's terminology, not your own, which helps improve the results. Even when you don't find the exact VBA statement or command, you might end up finding sample macro code that you can "borrow."

In Chapter 24, I refer to a macro that updates all fields in a document. It looks like this:

```
Sub update_all_fields()
'
' Update_all_fields Macro
' Refresh all of the document's fields
'
    Selection.WholeStory
    Selection.Fields.Update
    Selection.HomeKey
EndSub
```

The three lines in this macro carry out three tasks:

1. **Select all text in the document, which is the equivalent of Ctrl+A.**

2. **Update all the fields. Because the fields are selected with the document's text, the command affects all fields in the document.**

3. **Press the Home key, which moves the cursor to the start of the document (the selected text).**

When poking around on the MSDN website, I found another command that carries out all three tasks with only one line:

```
ActiveDocument.Fields.Update
```

That single line updates every field in the current document; no text need be selected.

I don't believe anyone could have the entire VBA language memorized, so it's not considered a cheat or a shortcut to look up a specific command or macro online. Often, that's the only way you'll find a command that you cannot type at the keyboard.

>> The VBA command *ActiveDocument.Fields.Update* is mapped to the F9 key in Word. So the macro could just record Ctrl+A and then F9, but that's not the point of this section: If you can't find a command button or keyboard shortcut, you can use the online reference to locate a specific VBA command.

>> No command on the right-click shortcut menu can be recorded in a macro.

>> The secret to accessing some commands is to create a Quick Access toolbar button shortcut for the command. Then you record the macro and click the

toolbar button to capture its essence. Afterward, you can remove the button from the Quick Access toolbar.

>> See Chapter 31 for details on working with the Quick Access toolbar.

Exploring VBA references

A great resource for obtaining more information about VBA and Word macros can be accessed directly from within the Visual Basic editor. Follow these steps:

1. Summon the Visual Basic editor.

Press Alt+F11.

2. Choose Help ⇨ Microsoft Visual Basic for Applications Help.

Your PC's web browser starts, opening the home page for VBA on the web.

Ensure that you choose the menu command in Step 2. The menu lists F1 as the command's keyboard shortcut, but the problem with pressing F1 is that it's contextual and doesn't take you directly to the VBA home page.

Chapter 27

Dynamic Templates with Content Controls

A *template* is a marvelous tool for rapid and consistent document creation: You can stuff into the template preset text, styles, graphics, and anything else that makes it easier to start your writing duties. To further bolster a template's power, you can add content controls.

A *content control* is a tiny box into which only a specific tidbit of information may reside. It allows you to help the user make specific choices with regard to a document's content. For example, you can create a fill-in-the-blanks field for a document title or have a preset image location where users can fetch their own graphics file. The content controls help the user create the document in the way you want it to look.

>> Some content controls can be quite complex, involving programming and other seriously advanced aspects of Word. This chapter covers only the more common and basic common content controls.

>> You can also use fields to automate document and template content. See Chapter 24.

The World of Content Controls

these steps:

1. **Right-click the Ribbon and choose Customize Ribbon.**

   The Word Options dialog box appears. Word's commands appear on the left side of the dialog box, with tabs on the Ribbon represented on the right.

2. **On the right side of the dialog box, place a check mark by Developer.**

   The check mark ensures that the Developer tab is visible.

3. **Click the OK button.**

   The Developer tab appears on the far right end of on the Ribbon. Content controls are located in the Controls group.

Content controls can go into any document, but they're most useful in document templates. That way, they can focus user attention on specific items that must be set in a proper manner, such as the document's title, an image, or any of the other wonderful things a content control can bring to a document.

Inserting a content control

The end result of a content control is that a specific item is placed into a document. That item is usually text, though a content control is available for adding graphics. The point is that a content control resides inside the document, just like text or a graphical image does. Before you add a content control, you need to know where it sits on the page.

As an example, you want to add a content control for a document's title. This is a fill-in-the-blanks content control, which serves as a placeholder for text. Follow these steps to insert the content control into a document:

1. **Position the insertion pointer where you want the content control to reside.**

   You can add some text and paragraph formatting, though formatting can come later.

2. **Click the Developer tab.**

   Refer to the preceding section for details on conjuring forth the Developer tab.

Aa

3. **In the Controls group, click the Rich Text content control.**

The icon is shown in the margin. After you click, the Rich Text content control appears in your document at the insertion pointer's location. It's selected, as shown on the left in Figure 27-1.

Handle

FIGURE 27-1:
The Rich Text
content control
in a document.

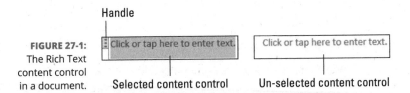

Selected content control   Un-selected content control

4. **Press the → key to deselect the content control.**

The content control appears as shown on the right in Figure 27-1.

The content control serves as a placeholder. Its text suggests that the user click or tap and then type something new. You can change the shading color (on the left in Figure 27-1) and format the text with the surrounding text. Though you cannot change the prompt from the default wording, *Click or tap here to enter text*, you can type text such as *Type the document title here* into the content control as a prompt.

Content controls are also found on the Insert tab. Those content controls insert document building blocks — specifically, information about the current document. Here's how to insert one of those document info content controls:

1. **Click the Insert tab.**

2. **In the Text group, click the Quick Parts button.**

3. **Choose Document Property and select an item from the submenu.**

The item you select, such as Author, is inserted into the document.

Though a Document Property item is a content control, I consider it to work more like a field than the other content controls discussed in this chapter. See Chapter 24 for information on fields.

>> To move the content control, click to select it; refer to the left side of Figure 27-1. Use the handle to drag the content control within your document's text.

>> The handle may change position when the content control has a title. It still looks the same (three vertical dots) and is located near the content control's upper left corner.

Changing the content control view

The standard way to view content controls is shown ~~early~~ ~~~~ the content control when the insertion pointer is inside, but transforms the content control into regular text otherwise. To better view content controls, and to see them at any time in your document, activate Design mode. Heed these steps:

1. **Click the Developer tab.**

2. **In the Controls group, click Design Mode.**

   The Design Mode button is a toggle; it's either on or off.

When Design mode is active, content controls become visible within the document, as shown in Figure 27-2. The content control shows its bounding box while selected (on the left in Figure 27-2), but when the insertion pointer is elsewhere in the document, the content control sports tabs to the right and left (shown on the right in Figure 27-2).

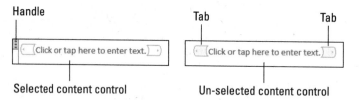

Handle   Tab   Tab

[Click or tap here to enter text.]   [Click or tap here to enter text.]

Selected content control   Un-selected content control

FIGURE 27-2: A content control in Design mode.

To deactivate Design mode, repeat the steps in this section.

The tab to the left of the control shows the title or is blank when a title hasn't been set.

You still have to click the content control to see the handle (on the left in Figure 27-2) to be able to drag and move the content control. You cannot use the left and right design-mode tabs to drag around the content control.

Setting a content control's properties

Word permits you to modify a few content control attributes, changing the way it appears in a document. Of the many things you can mess with, adding a title to a content control is about the most productive. To add or change a content control's title, follow these steps:

1. **Click to select the content control.**

   The content control's bounding box appears as well as its handle, shown on the left in both Figures 27-1 and 27-2.

2. **Click the Developer tab.**

3. **In the Controls group, click the Properties button.**

If you don't follow Step 1, the Properties window appears, which is a long, complex list of the document's options and current status. That's not what you want; start over.

If you followed Step 1, the content control's Properties dialog box appears, as shown in Figure 27-3.

Items in the Content Control Properties dialog box affect only the selected content control.

Content control appearance

Content control title text

| Content Control Properties | ? | × |

General

Title:

Tag:

Show as: Bounding Box ⌄

Color: 🎨 ⌄

☐ Use a style to format text typed into the empty control

Style: Default Paragraph Font ⌄

New Style...

☐ Remove content control when contents are edited

Locking

☐ Content control cannot be deleted

☐ Contents cannot be edited

OK   Cancel

FIGURE 27-3: The Content Control Properties dialog box.

Content control restrictions

Content control style

4. **Click the Title box and type a title for the content control.**

The title helps identify the control, and perhaps helps explain its function. The title appears next to the handle when the content control is selected.

5. **Click the OK button when you're done setting the content control's properties.**

The Show As drop-down menu (refer to Figure 27-3) allows you to set the content control's appearance, either as a bounding box, shown on the left in Figure 27-1, or a start/end tag, shown on the left in Figure 27-1.

The Style settings allow you to apply styles to the content control, though it can be formatted along with any text in your document.

The Content Control Cannot Be Deleted option allows the user to type text in the content control, but not to convert it into plain text or otherwise remove it.

See the later section "Converting a content control to text," for information on the Remove Content Control When Contents Are Edited option.

Removing a content control

You can delete text in a content control just as you can remove text anywhere in a document. Deleting the content control's text, however, doesn't remove the content control.

To rid the document of a content control, follow these steps:

1. **Click the content control to select it.**

2. **Click the content control's handle to *really* select it.**

Refer to Figures 27-1 and 27-2 for the handle's location.

3. **Press the Delete key or Backspace key on the keyboard.**

The content control is gone.

TIP

It's easier to delete a content control when Design mode is deactivated. Refer to the earlier section "Changing the content control view."

Converting a content control to text

Because content controls act like fill-in-the-blanks items for your document's users, you probably don't want to go through the bother of explaining how to convert the control's text into document text. The process isn't really necessary in that case because content controls behave just like any other text: They print, they can be formatted, and so on.

If you're curious, you can convert the content control into plain text. This process removes the control but keeps the content. Follow these steps:

1. **Right-click the content control.**

2. **Choose the Remove Content Control command.**

The content control's text or image remains.

Another way to effect this change is to summon the content control's Properties dialog box. Refer to the earlier section "Setting a content control's properties." In the Content Control Properties dialog box, place a check mark by the item Remove Content Control When Contents Are Edited. Click OK.

>> You don't want to convert the content control to text when it contains a prompt that you've written. In that case, you must use the default prompt: *Click or tap here to enter text.*

>> If you remove an empty content control, nothing remains. The gray placeholder text or image disappears.

Useful Content Controls

Content controls allow you to help out a user who opens a template. They can indicate where to type text and which text to type. You've probably seen these content controls in action if you've used any of Word's preset templates. It's relatively simple to add similar features to your document templates. Just follow the examples provided in this section.

REMEMBER

>> Content controls work best in a template. Remember to save your document as a template.

>> Refer to Chapter 9 for more information on document templates.

Setting up a fill-in-the-blanks item

Perhaps the most common and useful content control is the Rich Text content control, also known as the fill-in-the-blanks thing. It's the content control you see most often in Word's sample templates. It's also the content control most users want to use in their own document templates.

To add a Rich Text content control to your document, follow these steps:

1. **Position the insertion pointer.**

The content control works like text. It can sit in a line, on a line by itself, or anywhere on the page. You can format the text or apply a style.

2. **Click the Developer tab.**

3. **In the Controls group, click the Rich Text Content Control button.**

If you want the content control to disappear and its text remain, then continue with Step 4; otherwise you're done.

4. **In the Controls group, click the Properties button.**

The Content Control Properties dialog box appears.

5. **Type a Title for the content control.**

The Title can help users understand what they're typing, such as Your Name, Job Description, or Places Where You're Ticklish.

6. **Place a check mark by the option Remove Content Control When Contents Are Edited.**

This step is optional, though I prefer to convert the content control to text so that it doesn't distract me after I'm done with it. Do not place the check mark when you plan on presetting text inside the content control, such as "Your Name" or "Favorite snack."

7. **Click OK.**

The Rich Text content control is added to the document.

You can continue creating the template, adding more text, setting up styles, or throwing in a few more content controls.

>> The Rich Text content control works best for text items required in the final document.

>> The "rich text" part means that the text inside the control can be formatted by character, word, or some random chunk.

>> You cannot edit the placeholder text.

>> I use the Rich Text content control in my chapter document templates. The chapter number is a content control. It's also set to convert to text after I type the chapter number.

REMEMBER

Adding a multiline text field

For entering multiple lines of text, use a Plain Text content control. You might think that this content control doesn't allow the text to be formatted. That's incorrect. The text can be formatted, just not individual portions of the text. But the primary bonus from using the Plain Text content control is that the user can set its properties to allow for multiline input.

Follow these steps to add a Plain Text content control for multiline input:

1. **Set the insertion pointer to the location where you want to place the Plain Text content control.**

2. **Click the Developer tab.**

3. **In the Controls group, click the Plain Text Content Control button.**

    The Plain Text content control looks similar to the Rich Text content control, covered in the preceding section.

4. **In the Controls group, click the Properties button.**

5. **Type a title.**

    The Title's text can help the user understand what needs to go into the content control.

6. **Place a check mark by the option Allow Carriage Returns (Multiple Paragraphs).**

7. **Click OK.**

With the multiple paragraph setting active, users can type as much text into the content control as they like. You cannot, however, apply formatting to any specific part of the text; it all carries a single text format.

To exit the control, click elsewhere in the document or press the → after typing the last item in the content control.

Inserting an image

The Picture content control expands the realm of content control possibilities. You use the control to preset, format, and position a picture location in a document or template. The user simply chooses a photo from the PC's library or the Internet.

To insert a Picture content control, follow these steps:

1. **Position the insertion pointer to the picture's eventual location.**

    If you're using advanced layout options, don't worry: You can apply them after inserting the content control.

2. **Click the Developer tab.**

3. **In the Controls group, click the Picture Content Control button.**

The Picture content control is dropped into the document. It appears similar to but as a content control it features a title and command buttons, as illustrated in the figure.

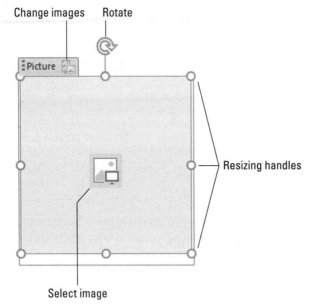

FIGURE 27-4:
The Picture
content control.

4. **Position and format the Picture content control's layout.**

Picture layout options are covered in Chapter 10. Also refer to Chapter 12 for additional picture formatting options.

To use the Picture content control, click on the button in the center. A dialog box appears, listing three sources for placing an image: from a file on your PC, from a Bing image search, or from your online OneDrive storage. Options for Facebook and Flickr might also be available.

TIP

>> The content control shows the text *Picture* in Figure 27-4. That's the content control title, which you can replace. Refer to the earlier section "Setting a content control's properties."

>> Just as you can type preset text into a text content control, you can preset a picture. If you do so, change the Picture content control title to read, "Click the icon to the right to set a new picture," or something similar.

- » The Change Images button (refer to Figure 27-4) lets the user replace the content control's original image with something else. This icon doesn't work if the option Contents Cannot Be Edited is set in the content control's Properties dialog box.

- » The default picture sources (Bing, OneDrive, and so on) cannot be changed. These are Microsoft's resources, which makes sense because Microsoft develops Word. You are free to choose any source for the image, such as Google Image Search. Just save the image to your PC's storage and choose that option when setting the content control's image.

Selecting the date

Perhaps the most unique content control is the Date Picker content control. It's a text content control, but it restricts input to a date format. It also provides a handy menu from which the user can choose a specific date.

Figure 27-5 illustrates the Date Picker content control. In the figure, the content control's menu is shown, where a date is selected.

FIGURE 27-5:
The Date Picker content control.

The date format is selected in the Date Picture Content Control's Properties dialog box. Even if the user types in another date format, the resulting date is displayed in the format chosen in the Properties dialog box.

 To insert the Date Picker content control, click its icon, shown in the margin. The content control is inserted at the insertion pointer's position.

Building a drop-down list

Two content controls let you create menus or lists in ... ~~~~ ~~~ ~~~~ ~~~~ ~~~~~ items, which then become the content control's text. The two content controls are the Combo Box and Drop-Down List.

Both content controls serve a similar function and look nearly identical. The main difference is that you can edit and format text in a Combo Box. The Drop-Down List content control shows text that cannot be changed.

To insert a Combo Box content control into your document, obey these directions:

1. **Position the insertion pointer where you want the combo box to appear.**

2. **Click the Developer tab.**

3. **In the Controls group, click the Combo Box content control.**

The combo box (or drop-down list) looks like any content control. Its text says *Choose an item.* When you click the menu button, shown in Figure 27-6, a list of choices appears.

The choices, shown in Figure 27-6, don't appear until you add them.

Menu button

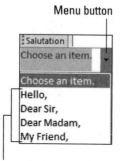

FIGURE 27-6:
A Combo Box
content control.

Items in the list

4. **In the Controls group, click the Properties button.**

The Combo Box Properties dialog box looks different from the standard Content Control Properties dialog box. In Figure 27-7, you see the portion of the dialog box that sets items in the drop-down list.

5. **Click the Add button to set a new item in the list.**

6. **In the Add Choice dialog box, type a Display Name.**

The Value field echoes the text typed in the Display Name field.

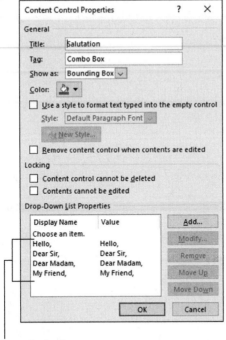

FIGURE 27-7:
Adding combo
box entries.

Items in the list

7. **Click OK to add the item.**

8. **Repeat Steps 5 through 7 to add more items.**

9. **Click the OK button to create the list.**

The user selects the combo box's menu to choose an item, one that you selected. That text is placed into the document. At that point, the content control can disappear, but only if you select the item Remove Content Control When Contents Are Edited in the Content Control Properties dialog box.

To create a Drop-Down List content control, choose that item's icon (shown in the margin) in Step 3. The Drop-Down List content control works just like the Combo Box content control, but the user cannot edit text inside the content control.

Chapter 28

Final Document Preparation and Protection

You may think that the final task for writing a document is to print. Or, better, to *save* and then print. That's fine, but it's not the bottom line when it comes to features Word offers for final document preparation. Along with checking for missing items or things you've overlooked, Word also offers forms of document protection. You can even encrypt a document and slap on a password. And if you lose your document, Word offers multiple painless options to help get it back.

Document Inspection

inspection regimen serves as a farewell of sorts to your document. Consider it a final blessing, confirming that a few technical tidbits have been addressed, such as items you might not want included in the final document, issues surrounding accessibility, and compatibility problems with older Word documents.

>> The tools mentioned in this section are the last ones you use before publishing the document, especially when publishing electronically.

>> Document inspecting isn't the same thing as proofing. It doesn't involve reading the text, looking for mistakes, or checking the layout.

Finding things you forget

To help ensure that your document enters publication without any regrets, Word offers a tool called the Document Inspector. It's designed to remove certain items from your document, such as comments, hidden text, revision marks, and other items that might be necessary for document production but unwanted for publication.

Follow these steps to give your document one last swipe before you commit it to paper or silicon:

1. **Save your document.**

   Always save before performing a document inspection. Some of the changed items cannot be reversed, in which case the saved copy serves as a backup.

2. **Click the File tab.**

   The Info screen appears. If not, click Info on the left side of the window.

3. **Click the Check for Issues button and choose Inspect Document.**

4. **If you haven't recently saved your document, you're prompted to do so; click Yes.**

   The Document Inspector dialog box appears, shown on the left in Figure 28-1. It lists items you might have overlooked or forgotten about. You can add or remove check marks to direct the inspector to find or ignore specific items.

Results

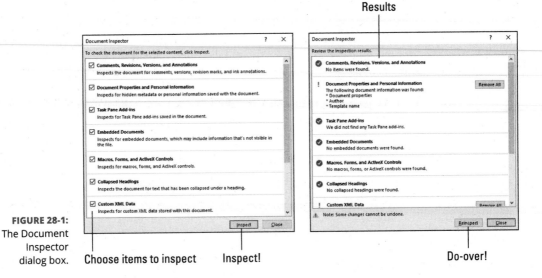

FIGURE 28-1:
The Document
Inspector
dialog box.

Choose items to inspect   Inspect!   Do-over!

5. **Click the Inspect button.**

   Word scours the document, checking for those items you selected in the
   Document Inspector dialog box. A summary appears, listing items of concern,
   as shown in the right in Figure 28-1.

6. **Click the Remove All button to purge your document of the unwanted
   items.**

   Repeat this step as necessary.

7. **Click the Close button.**

8. **Examine the document.**

   Look to ensure that none of the changes did something unintended.

In case something untoward happened and you can't undo the action, do not save
the document! Close it, and then open the copy you saved in Step 1. That's your
best avenue for recovery.

REMEMBER

The purpose of the Document Inspector is to ensure that unwanted items don't
remain in your document before you release it into the wild. This holds true especially for electronic documents.

Using the Accessibility Checker

You may think nothing of reviewing your document when your vision is good and
you can ably use a mouse or keyboard. Not everyone is so blessed. To ensure that

you don't unintentionally create a trap for someone who may not have your same abilities, you can run the Accessibility Checker. As with document inspection (see the preceding section), this activity takes place late in the writing and publishing schedule.

To check your document for accessibility issues, obey these directions:

1. **Save your document.**

   Seriously, this step should be the first step for all the listed procedures in this book.

2. **Click the File tab.**

   The Info screen appears.

3. **Click the Check for Issues button and choose Check Accessibility.**

   The Accessibility Checker pane, shown in Figure 28-2, appears on the right side of the document window. It lists any parts of the document that need addressing with regard to accessibility.

4. **Click to select an individual item.**

   Word highlights the item in your document and displays the reasons why they need addressing.

5. **Scroll the Additional Information item in the Accessibility Checker pane to review the fix.**

   In the case of the Picture issue selected in Figure 28-2, the item lacks alternative text. The solution is to add a text description to the image.

6. **Continue to review the document; repeat Steps 4 and 5.**

7. **Close the Accessibility Checker pane when you're done.**

   Click the X (Close) button.

Some of the items flagged for accessibility issues are relevant only for documents you plan to publish electronically, such as an eBook, a blog post, or a web page. For example, the alternative text suggestion shown in Figure 28-2 is irrelevant for a printed document.

Checking document compatibility

Not everyone is as up-to-speed with Word as you are. Some folks still use Word 2002, Word 98, and even Word 97. My point isn't to change anyone's mind about software upgrade choices, but rather to help you maintain compatibility with individuals or organizations that cling to those older versions of Word.

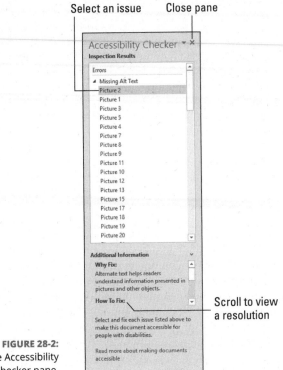

Select an issue   Close pane

Accessibility Checker ▾ ×
Inspection Results

Errors
▲ Missing Alt Text
   Picture 2
   Picture 1
   Picture 3
   Picture 5
   Picture 4
   Picture 7
   Picture 8
   Picture 9
   Picture 11
   Picture 10
   Picture 12
   Picture 13
   Picture 15
   Picture 17
   Picture 18
   Picture 19
   Picture 20

Additional Information ▾
Why Fix:
Alternate text helps readers
understand information presented in
pictures and other objects.

How To Fix:

Select and fix each issue listed above to
make this document accessible for
people with disabilities.

Read more about making documents
accessible

Scroll to view
a resolution

FIGURE 28-2:
The Accessibility
Checker pane.

To check your document's compatibility, you can run the compatibility checker. Heed these directions:

1. **Save your document.**

2. **Click the File tab.**

3. **On the Info screen, click the Check for Issues button and choose Check Compatibility.**

   The Microsoft Word Compatibility Checker dialog box appears, similar to what's shown in Figure 28-3. It lists any issues your document may have for users of an older version of Word. For example, features such as special text attributes, content controls, or document add-ins would be incompatible with those users' software.

4. **Choose which versions of Word to check.**

   Use the Select Versions to Show drop-down menu to select specific Word versions. For example, the content controls (refer to Figure 28-3) are unavailable to Word versions 97 through 2003. The text effects attribute is available in Word 2010 but not in Word 2007.

5. **Click the OK button when you're done checking the document.**

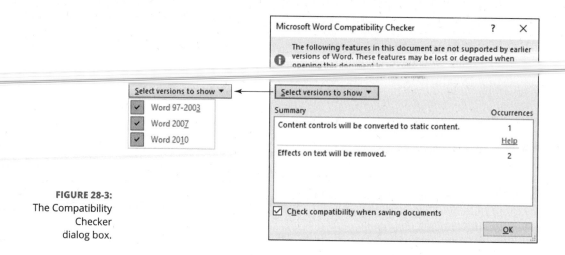

FIGURE 28-3:
The Compatibility
Checker
dialog box.

The compatibility checker doesn't show you specifically where the items are located in the document. That's really not an issue: The point is whether or not you save the document by using an older file format. When you do, the items listed in the dialog box are lost to that version, typically converted to plain text.

If you place a check mark by the item at the bottom of the dialog box, Word displays the Microsoft Word Compatibility Checker dialog box when you attempt to use an older Word file format to save the document. At that point, you can click the Cancel button to stop the save or click Continue to save the document with translated features.

Refer to Chapter 15 for details on using other file formats when saving documents.

Document Encryption and Password Protection

The most extreme form of document security is to encrypt the entire document and apply a password. This might be a bothersome choice for a document you frequently edit, but for finished documents or stuff you don't want anyone to see, it's the best security.

Encrypting your document

To lock up your document with encryption and a password, follow these steps:

1. **Save your document.**

2. **Click the File tab.**

   The Info screen appears. If not, choose Info from the list of items on the left side of the window.

3. **Click the Protect Document button and choose Encrypt with Password.**

   The Encrypt Document dialog box appears.

4. **Write down the password you plan to use.**

   I'm serious: Before you type the password, write it down somewhere obvious to you but not apparent to someone out to snoop for passwords. You need that backup password because — if you forget the document's password — it remains forever locked.

5. **Type a password into the Encrypt Document dialog box.**

   The password is case-sensitive.

6. **Click OK.**

7. **Retype the password to ensure that you know it.**

8. **Click OK.**

   The document will be encrypted when it's saved.

You can use an encrypted document just as you would any document in Word. Unless you've further applied editing restrictions (covered elsewhere in this chapter), you'll notice little difference between working on an encrypted document and working on a regular Word document.

When you open an encrypted document, a password prompt appears on the screen. Type the document's password and click the OK button. The document opens and you can do whatever with it.

>> A password-protected document can be copied, renamed, moved, or deleted. In File Explorer, however, you cannot use the Preview pane to peek at an encrypted document's contents.

WARNING

>> There is no ability to recover a lost password. I can't do it. Microsoft can't do it. Apparently, even the FBI can't do it. If you forget your password, you are totally screwed.

Removing encryption

To free your document from an encrypted and password-protected state, obey:

1. **Open the password-protected, encrypted document.**

2. **Type the password when prompted; click OK.**

   The document is open. The key is to save it in a nonprotected state.

3. **Click the File tab.**

4. **Choose Save As from the items on the left side of the window.**

5. **Click the Browse button to summon the traditional Save As dialog box.**

6. **Near the bottom right part of the dialog box, click the Tools menu.**

7. **Choose General Options.**

   The General Options dialog box appears, shown in Figure 28-4. It contains locations to set an encryption password and a modification password.

8. **Delete the password from the Password to Open text field.**

   You don't need to know the password. That's because Word assumes you knew the password when you opened the document. Still, I consider the lack of double verification to be a security risk.

Erase current password

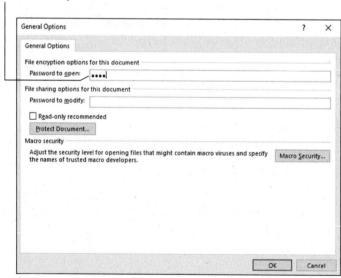

FIGURE 28-4.
The General
Options
dialog box.

9. **Click OK.**

   Document encryption is removed, as is the document's password.

10. **In the Save As dialog box, click the Save button to resave the document.**

11. **Click the Yes button to overwrite the encrypted document with the new, non-encrypted document.**

TIP

You can use the steps in this section to encrypt and password-protect the document: In Step 8, add the password. You can also simply add a password to modify the document by filling in the Password to Modify field (shown in Figure 28-4).

Restrict and Control Document Changes

Often times, you don't want to go full-on with document encryption and password protection. That step is a bit drastic. Instead, you may simply want to curtail access to specific parts of your document. Perhaps you want to restrict style and formatting choices. Or maybe you want to restrict editing in an entire document, save for one small part. These features are available, providing you know where to look for them.

Setting text-editing restrictions

Word's editing restrictions limit the user's ability to create new text in a document or edit existing text. You can apply the restrictions to the entire document, or you can allow editing within given blocks, or editing areas. The basic form of restriction, however, allows you to limit what can be done to the document. Follow these steps:

1. **Save your document.**

2. **Click the File tab.**

3. **On the Info screen, click the Protect Document button.**

4. **Choose Restrict Editing.**

   The Restrict Editing pane appears.

5. **Place a checkmark in the box below Editing Restrictions.**

   The Editing Restrictions area expands, as shown in Figure 28-5. Specifically, the list of exceptions appears, but your focus for now is on the menu, as illustrated in the figure.

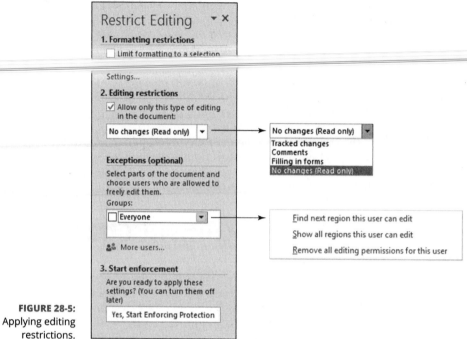

FIGURE 28-5:
Applying editing
restrictions.

6. **Choose a restriction level from the menu.**

   The options are

   No Changes (Read Only): The document cannot be edited or changed.

   Tracked Changes: Modifications can be made, but only with the Tracked Changes feature active.

   Comments: Other authors can insert only comments.

   Filling in Forms: Only content controls are available for typing text or adding information to the document.

   If you're collaborating and you want to ensure that your text is unmolested, choose Tracked Changes or Comments.

   TIP

   If you choose the restriction levels No Changes (Read Only) or Comments, you can set any exceptions and create editing areas. See the following section.

7. **Click the button Yes, Start Enforcing Protection.**

8. **Type a password into the dialog box: once to set the password and again to confirm.**

9. **Click OK to begin enforcing the editing restrictions.**

The restrictions remain applied to the document until you remove them. Refer to the earlier section "Removing restrictions" for further information.

Refer to Chapter 16 for information on Word's Track Changes feature as well as how to insert comments into a document.

Marking a document as "final"

When you're truly determined that your document is perfect and needs no more writing, editing, changing, modifying, or mutilating by anyone else, you mark it as *final*. Truly, this is the last thing you need to do to a document in Word.

Follow these steps to mark a document as final and apply read-only protection:

1. **Click the File tab.**

2. **On the Info screen, click the Protect Document button and choose the command Mark As Final.**

3. **Click OK to confirm.**

   If you haven't yet saved the document, you'll be prompted to do so now. And shame on you for not yet saving!

   Another dialog box appears with some complicated explanations about marking a document as final.

4. **Don't read the information in the dialog box and just click OK.**

What the dialog box says in Step 4 is that the document's status property is set to Final and that all editing and proofing and such is deactivated. The document's title (at the top of the window) is suffixed with the text [Read Only], which is a visual clue that no further changes can be made. Also, the Ribbon is hidden, and you might see a banner displayed, similar to what's shown in Figure 28-6.

FIGURE 28-6:
Perhaps "final" needs a new definition?

MARKED AS FINAL An author has marked this document as final to discourage editing. [Edit Anyway]   ✕

That's correct: To remove a document's Final status, you merely need to click the Edit Anyway button. But at least the steps outlined in this section might make you feel better about finally finishing something.

You can also remove final protection by repeating Steps 1 and 2 in this section.

Refer to the section "Setting text-editing restrictions" if you really don't want anyone messing with your document. Or see the following section if more protection.

Document Recovery

When disaster strikes, Word does its best to help you recover a lost document. Copies of your document are saved automatically. If anything sudden happens, and Word closes before you can save a document, chances are good that some of your unsaved work can be recovered. You can even peruse Word's deepest, darkest recesses to locate long-lost documents that Word has kept but that you don't know about.

Activating automatic backup

To ensure that Word frequently saves your document even when you forget — and you should be saving the document every few minutes — you can activate the AutoRecover feature. Even when you know that feature is active, it's good to confirm its settings. Heed these directions:

1. **Click the File tab.**

2. **Choose Options from the File screen.**

   The Word Options dialog box appears.

3. **On the left side of the dialog box, choose Save.**

4. **Ensure that a check mark appears by the first option, Save AutoRecover Information Every.**

5. **Ensure that the time setting shows 10 Minutes.**

   Or, if you find the that duration too great, set it to 5 Minutes.

6. **Click OK to close the Word Options dialog box.**

You appreciate the AutoRecover feature when you experience a computer crash, or perhaps when Word suddenly freezes. When that happens, you see a document recovery panel appear when you open Word. You're given the chance to restore an older version of a file or continue to work with the document as is. If you choose to recover a document, save it so that Word knows which version you're using.

>> When AutoRecover is set to a 10-minute interval, the largest chunk of information you can lose is whatever you typed during the last 9 minutes and 59 seconds of editing. For me, that text is fresh enough in my brain so that I can retype it. I'm not happy about the situation, but at least I don't have to redo the entire document.

>> See Chapter 32 for solutions to common Word problems.

Viewing an older version of your document

Have you saved your document recently? Every time you do, Word keeps track of the older versions. These versions are listed on the File tab's Info screen, as shown in Figure 28-7. The number of entries you see depends on how many times you've saved your document since it was last opened. (These items are not the same as AutoRecover backups, mentioned in the preceding section.)

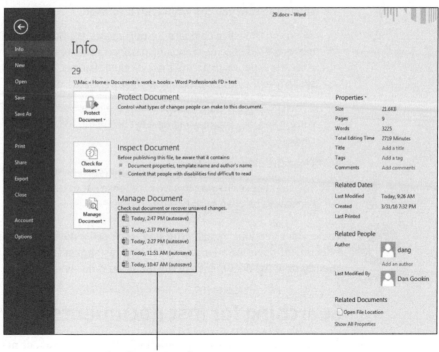

FIGURE 28-7:
Backup files for the current document.

AutoRecover versions of the current document

You can pluck any old copy of your document from the Manage Document list to compare it with the current document. To do so, follow these steps:

1. **Click the File tab.**

   The Info screen appears, looking similar to Figure 28-7. You may not see as many old versions listed. The number of items depends on how long you've been working on the document and how frequently you save. If you close the document, the list is wiped clean.

2. **Click to select one of the older versions of the current document.**

   The older version opens in a new window; it doesn't replace the current document.

   The document is shown in Read Mode view. The Ribbon is unavailable. The document title says [Read Only].

3. **Click the Compare button to compare items from the saved document to the current document, or click the Restore button to restore that older version so that you can work with it further.**

   When you choose to compare the documents, the Revisions tab appears and the recovered document and original document appear side by side. You can scroll the windows to peruse the individual changes. This feature works similarly to the document-compare feature, discussed in Chapter 16.

   If you choose to restore the document, the older version overwrites the current version. This may not be what you want, so use this option with caution.

4. **Close the older document.**

   You can choose whether to save it. I choose not to because the old document can always be opened and reviewed again.

REMEMBER

These older versions vanish after you've closed a document. Only when you leave a document open for a long time (all day, as shown in Figure 28-7) *and* you frequently save the document are the older versions available.

Searching for lost documents

Word keeps a crypt of sorts, populating it with lost, dead, or not-recovered documents. It's not a feature you'll use often, but if you're hunting for a document you've lost or misplaced, it's a place where you should look.

To peruse the purgatory of lost documents, obey these directions:

1. **Click the File tab.**

2. **On the Info tab, click the Manage Document button.**

3. **Choose the Recover Unsaved Documents item.**

   A traditional Open dialog box appears. It reveals the location where Word places its unsaved files — the Word crypt.

4. **Click to select a file to open.**

   The filenames listed in the Open dialog box are similar to the original Word document names. They contain a special suffix, which Word uses to track the document's origins.

5. **Click the Open button.**

   The file appears in a Word document window, but it's tagged as [Read Only]. A banner appears in the window. The banner features the Save As button.

6. **Peruse the document to determine whether it's worthy of recovery.**

   If you choose to recover the document, proceed with Step 7. If not, close the document and click the Don't Save button when prompted.

7. **Click the Save As button on the document's RECOVER UNSAVED FILE banner.**

8. **Work the Save As dialog box to find a location for the document and to give it a proper filename.**

9. **Click the Save button to save the file.**

If the Recover Unsaved Documents feature doesn't help you locate the document you're looking for, use other, traditional Word tools. For example, check the list of recently opened documents in Word, use the Search command in Windows, or look in the Recycle Bin for the file.

6

Beyond Word Processing

Discover how to use Word on a web page, explore cloud storage, and set up a Word online presentation.

Use Word to create web pages.

Tame Word's many options and settings, adding customizations of your own.

Fix Word when it's broken.

Chapter 29

Word and the Internet

Word has a friendly relationship with the Internet. This bond includes the ability to access files stored online, or "on the cloud," as well as access to Word on a web page. Combine these capabilities with the Office 365 program, and Word is pretty Internet savvy. As a bonus, many of these capabilities are offered free of charge. The only thing preventing people from using the online services is that, just like that free Slurpee at 7-11 on July 11, they just don't know about them.

The Backstage

Microsoft introduced the Backstage in Word 2013. It supplanted the traditional Save As and Open dialog boxes, replacing them with a full-window screen to augment their functions specific to cloud storage. The change also provided some consistency between the Save As and Open commands, as well as the Print and New commands.

>> The old Save As and Open dialog boxes are still available when you need them, so it's good that you have a choice.

>> *Cloud storage* is another term for *Internet,* or online, *storage.* It's integrated into your PC's local storage. See the later section "Cloud Storage Options."

>> Unlike with the Save As and Open dialog boxes, you cannot summon the old Print dialog box.

Using the Backstage

For both the Save As and Open commands, the Backstage provides quick access to recently opened files, folders, and storage locations. Figure 29-1 illustrates both screens.

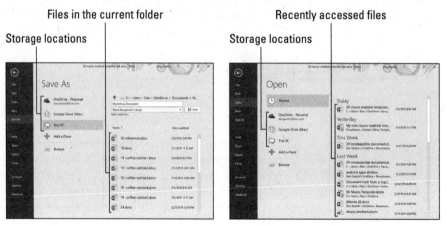

Files in the current folder

Recently accessed files

Storage locations

Storage locations

FIGURE 29-1:
The Backstage.

Save As Backstage

Open Backstage

A list of storage locations and options appears on the left side of the screen, illustrated in Figure 29-1. These locations include Microsoft's OneDrive cloud storage as well as This PC, which represents *local* files (stored on your computer). Additional storage locations may appear, such as Google Drive, shown in the figure, though I confess that this solution was a test and it wasn't successful.

The Browse button summons the old Save As and Open dialog boxes.

On the right side of the Backstage appears a list of files. The files listed in the Save As Backstage are located in the current folder on the selected storage location.

The files listed on the Open Backstage are recently accessed files. To quickly open a recent file, click it in the list.

The Save As screen features options for saving the current document. The relevant part of the screen is illustrated in Figure 29-2. The functions shown are identical to their counterparts in the traditional Save As dialog box.

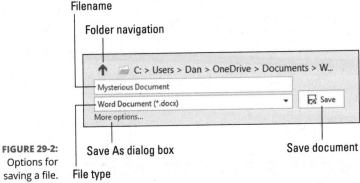

Filename

Folder navigation

FIGURE 29-2:
Options for
saving a file.

Save As dialog box

Save document

File type

For a quick save, you can type the filename, optionally set the document (file) type, and then click the Save button. The More Options link simply surrenders the Backstage to the more practical Save As dialog box. If you find yourself clicking that link frequently, see the later section "Disabling the Backstage."

>> The keyboard shortcut to access the Open screen is Ctrl+O.

>> To access the Save As screen, press Ctrl+S, though this shortcut key works only on unsaved document. When you need to save a document under another name, in a new location, or with a new file type, access the Save As screen from the File tab.

>> The Print-command keyboard shortcut is Ctrl+P, which summons the Print screen on the File tab.

>> The Ctrl+W keyboard shortcut closes a document window, which is the equivalent of the Close command on the File tab.

Removing a file from the Open Backstage

The Open screen lists recently accessed files. Some of the files listed might be invalid, removed from their storage locations, renamed, or what-have-you. When that happens, Word doesn't remove the filenames from the list. Further, you might simply want to evict a file that you don't want lurking in the list. To do so, follow these steps:

1. **Press Ctrl+O to access the Open screen.**

   You can also click the File tab and then choose Open from the left side of the screen.

2. **Right-click on the offending file.**

3. **Choose the Remove from List command.**

   And it's gone!

If you access the file again, it shows up in the list again. If so, repeat the steps in this section.

REMEMBER

Removing a document from the list of recent files doesn't delete the file.

Adding a storage place to the Backstage

Both the Save As and Open screens on the Backstage feature an enticing button labeled Add a Place. You would suppose that this button adds a new storage location, such as Dropbox or perhaps a favorite network drive. That's an inaccurate supposition, however; Word isn't as smart as you are.

The Add a Place button is limited to adding only two storage locations: Microsoft's OneDrive cloud storage and an Office 365 SharePoint folder. Curiously enough, both of those locations are controlled by Microsoft. Further, the two items relate to collaboration more than other opportunities to connect to online storage resources.

See the later section "Cloud Storage Options."

Summoning the traditional dialog boxes

When you dearly miss the old Save As and Open dialog boxes, you can quickly summon them from the Backstage. Figure 29-3 illustrates the locations where you can click in the Backstage to summon the traditional dialog boxes.

To access the Save As dialog box, click the Browse button, the More Options link, or the folder pathname above the filename text box, as illustrated on the left in Figure 29-3.

To access the Open dialog box, click the Browse button or the folder pathname, as illustrated on the right in Figure 29-3.

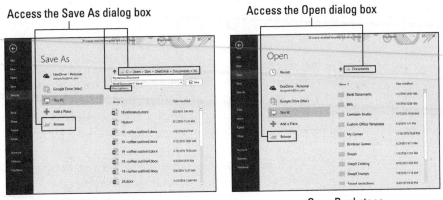

Access the Save As dialog box   Access the Open dialog box

Save As Backstage   Open Backstage

FIGURE 29-3:
Getting to the old
Save As and Open
dialog boxes.

The dialog boxes can also be accessed directly when you disable the Backstage, as described in the next section.

Disabling the Backstage

When you've had enough with the Backstage, or find yourself ending up in the old Save As or Open dialog boxes often enough anyway, follow these steps to skirt the Backstage:

1. **Click the File tab.**

2. **Choose Options.**

   The Word Options dialog box appears.

3. **From the list on the left side of the dialog box, choose Save.**

   Options for saving documents appear on the right side of the dialog box.

4. **Place a check mark by the option Don't Show the Backstage When Opening or Saving Files.**

   It's the third check box from the top.

5. **Click OK.**

These steps affect the Ctrl+S and Ctrl+O keyboard shortcuts. You can still access the Backstage from the File tab: Choose Save As or Open.

>> The Backstage still appears when you press Ctrl+P to print. Don't go looking for the old Print dialog box; it's been purged from Word.

>> The Save As dialog box also appears when you attempt to close a document that hasn't been saved and you click the Save button.

Cloud Storage Options

...e ...storage is that it provides a repository of files you can access from just about anywhere. As long as an Internet connection is available, the files you store "on the cloud" are within reach. These include your word processing documents as well as any other files you need to keep handy or maintain online for collaboration purposes or to foil your enemies.

» Cloud storage is accessed from a computer, laptop, tablet, or cell phone. All the device needs is Internet access to get to your cloud storage.

» One of the best ways to access cloud storage is to obtain a specific cloud storage program or app. Install that program on your computer or laptop, and the app on your phone or tablet. Even without a program or app, you can use the web to access cloud storage files.

» Cloud storage is touted for how well it lends itself to collaboration, but it also offers individuals a way to synchronize files. When a file stored on the cloud is updated on one device, it's updated on all other, connected devices. Cloud storage also provides a form of backup, though I wouldn't rely upon it exclusively.

Understanding OneDrive

OneDrive is Microsoft's online storage system, which is well-integrated into Word and all the Microsoft Office applications. It allows for cloud storage and access to your files from any Internet-connected device. It's also well-integrated into your PC's local file system: You'll find a OneDrive folder in your user profile, or home, folder in Windows, as illustrated in Figure 29-4.

The same folders and files

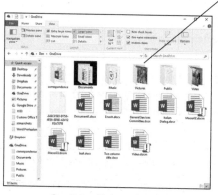

FIGURE 29-4: OneDrive on the local storage system.

OneDrive files on the PC

OneDrive files on the web

Whether you save a document in Word, copy a file on your PC, or upload an image from a computer you rent in a library, all OneDrive locations reflect the same contents. In Figure 29-4, you see the same folders shown in the File Explorer program as in a web browser window.

So which do you use?

It doesn't matter. OneDrive is easy to access from Word's Save As or Open screens: Click the big OneDrive button. Otherwise, you can click the This PC button (refer to Figure 29-1), and then navigate to the local OneDrive folder. Either way, the files end up in the same place and are available to any device connected to the Internet.

>> OneDrive features its own location on the Save As and Open screens, as described elsewhere in this chapter.

>> Any item you save to OneDrive is echoed on all other devices that can access your OneDrive storage.

>> OneDrive on the web is accessed from https://login.live.com.

>> For your mobile device, obtain the OneDrive app, either at the Apple App Store for the iPhone or iPad or the Google Play Store for your Android phone or tablet.

>> A free OneDrive account comes with 5GB of online storage. More storage is available for a subscription, or if you sign up for Office 365. See the later section "Word and Office 365."

TECHNICAL STUFF

>> OneDrive was originally called SkyDrive, which is a much cooler name, but was owned by another company, so Microsoft had to think of a new name. On some older PCs, you may still find a SkyDrive folder, which works the same as OneDrive.

Adding OneDrive to other devices

To help keep your files organized, consider adding OneDrive to all your devices. First, check to confirm whether OneDrive is available on your PC. Follow these steps:

1. **Press Win+E to summon a File Explorer window.**

2. **Click the chevron at the far left end of the Address bar.**

   Refer to Figure 29-5 for the chevron's location. Upon success, you see a menu drop down, as illustrated in the figure.

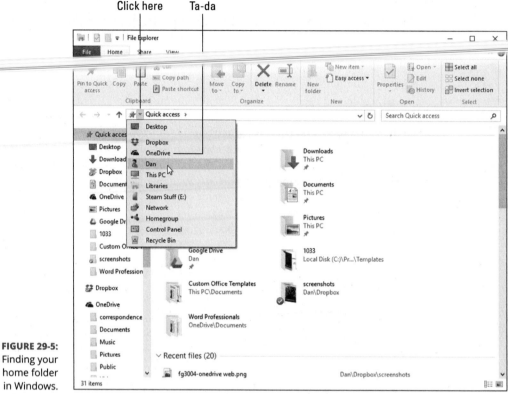

FIGURE 29-5:
Finding your
home folder
in Windows.

3. **Look on the menu for the OneDrive folder.**

    If you see the OneDrive folder, you're good to go. Otherwise, continue at Step 4:

4. **Visit onedrive.live.com on your computer or device.**

5. **Click or tap the Download item.**

6. **Choose your device's operating system from the list.**

    For example, tap Android for your Android phone.

7. **Continue obeying the directions on the screen to obtain the program or app.**

The web page displays the proper link where you can obtain the OneDrive app. Or if you're familiar with the Apple App Store or Google Play Store, search for *One-Drive* and download the app. Ensure that you choose the app provided by Microsoft.

With the OneDrive program or app installed, you can access your Word documents saved to OneDrive storage. The files are updated instantly, so if you're working away from home, when you get back you'll find the same, updated files.

Fixing OneDrive sync issues

It bothers me, but unlike other cloud storage solutions, OneDrive seems to have synchronization issues. I've never lost any files, but I do occasionally see errors about issues with documents and the PC somehow unable to access OneDrive.

In Figure 29-6, you see a OneDrive error notification in Windows 10. To resolve the issue, you can click the notification and see what's up or you can run the Microsoft Office Upload Center program for general OneDrive synchronization troubleshooting.

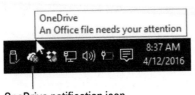

FIGURE 29-6: OneDrive has a boo-boo.

OneDrive notification icon

To troubleshoot in the Microsoft Office Upload Center program, heed these steps:

1. Tap the Windows key on your PC's keyboard.

The Start menu appears.

2. Choose All Apps or All Programs.

Windows 10 uses All Apps; Windows 7 uses All Programs.

3. Open the Microsoft Office 2016 Tools folder.

The name may be subtly different, to reflect the Office version.

4. Choose Office 2016 Upload Center.

The Upload Center program appears, looking similar to Figure 29-7. In the figure, you see the file that needs attention, which is why the notification icon (refer to Figure 29-6) sported a red X.

5. Click the Action button to the right of a problem file.

The button might also be labeled Resolve.

6. Choose the Upload command to see if that fixes the problem.

If so, the document is removed from the list and you're done; skip to Step 8.

7. If uploading doesn't work, open the file.

In Word, you might see more details that help you further address the issue.

8. Close the Upload Center window.

Problem file

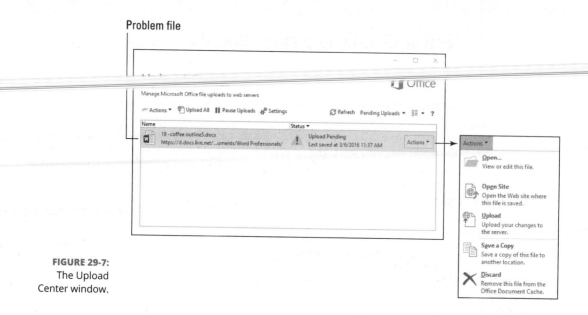

FIGURE 29-7:
The Upload
Center window.

On my PC, Word is claiming that the file shown in Figure 29-7 is in use by someone else. Most likely, I opened the document in another copy of Word or online. To address the issue, that other copy of Word needs to close the document. This is one of the foibles of using cloud storage, but keep in mind that Word is just being cautious so that you don't accidentally screw up a document.

Exploring other cloud storage solutions

OneDrive isn't the only cloud storage option available. I also use Dropbox as well as Google Drive. I find these services to be more reliable, though OneDrive has the advantage of being well-integrated with Word.

All cloud storage services are fairly similar when it comes to features and options: They synchronize files across devices, and they integrate with your PC's local storage system.

For accessing files on other cloud storage systems, you must use your own PC's storage, not the Word Backstage: Access the Open or Save As dialog box to navigate to the Dropbox folder and access any Word document you've stored there. For example, you would follow these steps to save a document on your Dropbox storage:

1. Click the File tab.

2. Choose Save As.

3. **Click the Browse button.**

You must summon the Save As dialog box, shown in Figure 29-8. If you can press Ctrl+S to get there, great; refer to the earlier section "Disabling the Backstage."

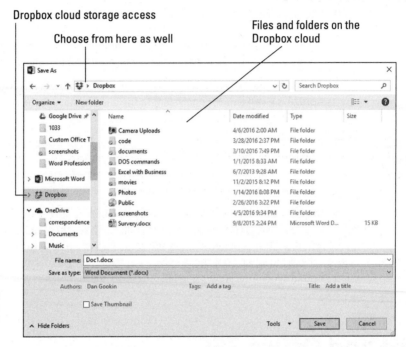

FIGURE 29-8:
Saving on
Dropbox cloud
storage.

4. **Choose Dropbox from the list of items on the left side of the dialog box.**

Use Figure 29-8 as your guide. And you could choose another cloud storage location if it appears in the list. They all work similarly.

5. **Browse to locate the folder into which you want to save your file.**

The file is saved locally in the Dropbox folder, but is also echoed on the cloud as well as on any other device that has access to your Dropbox account.

These steps apply to just about every online storage service, including Google Drive, Box, and others.

>> Visit dropbox.com to obtain the Dropbox software for your PC. Look for the download link. You can obtain the Dropbox app for your mobile device at the Apple App Store or Google Play Store.

>> Google Drive is available from drive.google.com. Look for a link or button to download the Google Drive software for your PC. Google Drive is included with all Android mobile devices.

>> Another popular cloud storage service is box.com. I could list even more choices, but the bribery checks haven't yet arrived.

>> Nearly all cloud services offer a given amount of storage at no cost, usually 5GB or so. You obtain more storage by buying a subscription to the service. Some services offer additional storage incentives, such as when you buy software, purchase an online movie, or lure a friend to sign up for the service.

>> In all cases, the cloud storage is echoed in your home folder in Windows. The storage is given a name equivalent to the service, such as the Dropbox folder or the Google Drive folder for Google Drive.

TECHNICAL STUFF

>> You might notice in Figures 29-1 and 29-3 that Google Drive appears as an option on the Backstage. That's a bug from software I experimented with on another computer. The experiment failed, but the Google Drive reference remains; it's a tombstone and doesn't work.

>> The issue I have with OneDrive is reliability. More than the other cloud services I use, OneDrive seems to lose files or have them needing extra attention. This problem has never cropped up when I use Dropbox or Google Drive. Even when I use those services to store Word documents, I don't get the kind of synchronization or "failed to upload" warnings I see with OneDrive.

Word and Office 365

You can purchase Word as a stand-alone software program, or you can pay for a subscription to the Office 365 service. Both methods allow you to access the same Word program described in this book. With Office 365, however, you get more: You get free updates to the latest version, up to five separate installations of Word (and the rest of the Office suite) on PCs, Macs, and mobile devices, and you get additional OneDrive storage.

>> Office 365 is a subscription service. It provides you access to the Microsoft suite of programs for an annual fee.

>> Not every Office 365 subscription offers the full Office suite, but they all include Microsoft Word.

>> The term *Office 365* is synonymous with the current release of Office. So the version of Word used with an Office 365 subscription is currently Word 2016. When a newer version of Word is released, Office 365 users update automatically.

Obtaining Office 365

I'm not here to sell Office 365, which is sad, considering the lucrative commissions I'd make. If you find that buying Word as an individual software package works for you, great! In a professional situation, or perhaps when you own a few gizmos and are tired of frequently buying each one a new copy of Word, then the Office 365 subscription is worthy.

If you're curious about Office 365, visit office.com. You can download a free trial, read about options for mobile devices and the web, and gauge whether it's a worthy offer.

>> As this book goes to press, the annual price for a single Office 365 subscription is $70 for an individual. This license includes access to Word on the web as well as the installation of Office 365 on a PC and mobile device.

>> Included with the basic ($70) Office 365 subscription is 1TB (terabyte) of OneDrive online storage.

>> Your organization or school may offer you a complementary Office 365 subscription. This access includes a copy of Word that you can download, access to Word on the web, as well as specific online storage and other goodies.

Checking your Office 365 subscription

To confirm that you have a current Office 365 subscription, follow these steps in Word:

1. **Click the File tab.**

2. **Choose Account from the items listed on the left side of the screen.**

If you have an Office 365 subscription, you see details similar to what's shown in Figure 29-9.

3. **If you don't see your user information on the left side of the window (refer to Figure 29-9), click the Sign In button to sign in to Office 365.**

Account information   Subscription details

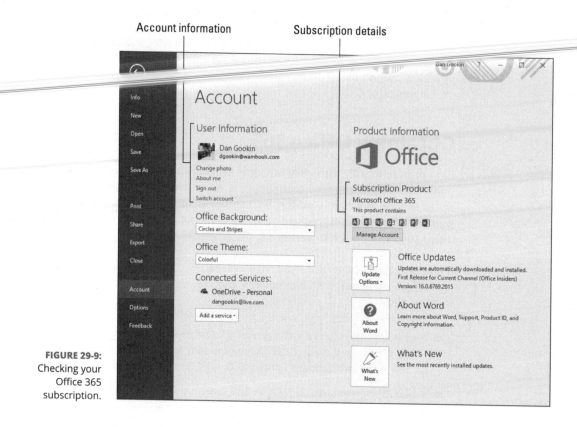

FIGURE 29-9:
Checking your
Office 365
subscription.

To check on your account's status, confirm your renewal date, check credit card information, or perform other subscription tasks, click the Manage Account button on the Account screen. (Refer to Figure 29-9.) You're taken to a web page where you can sign in to your Office account and review various settings.

One of the items you can perform on the Office website is to install Office 365 on another computer, such as your laptop or perhaps another system in a home office. You can also manage those installations, for example, removing an installation from your old laptop so that you can add it to your new laptop.

TIP

If you start Word and it informs you that your Office 365 installation has become invalidated, follow the steps in this section and sign in again to reactivate the account.

Word on the Web

Perhaps the most interesting thing you get with an Office 365 subscription is the capability to run Word from a web page. This option is also available to people without a subscription, though Word's features are limited to a subset of what you'll find online with an Office 365 subscription. And in both instances, the online version of Word isn't the same as the full version of the program.

To use the web-based Word, follow these steps:

1. **Steer your web browser software to** `office.com`.

2. **Click the Word app button.**

   Its appearance may change in the future, but the current icon is shown in the margin.

3. **Click to sign in with a Microsoft account.**

   If you don't have a Microsoft account, click the link to sign up for a new account.

   If you use a Microsoft account to sign into Windows 10, use that account.

   Eventually you see the New screen for Word online.

TIP

4. **Click New Blank Document to start up a new document.**

   You see Word as it appears in a web browser, similar to what's shown in Figure 29-10. The Ribbon appears, the document portion of the window is available, and you even see the status bar, as illustrated in the figure.

5. **When you're done editing the document, save just as you would when you use the Word program.**

   Click the File tab and choose the Save As command. The default location for files created or edited with Word online is on your OneDrive storage.

6. **To exit Word online, close the web page window.**

You'll notice subtle differences between Word on your PC and Word online; it's not the same program. Still, it's a handy way to edit your OneDrive files from any device that features a web browser.

TIP

» Word on the web is stripped down to just the basic commands. You won't find the Design or Reference tabs, fields, content controls, macros, or the ability to save in a format other than a standard Word document. Still, for quick edits, it's a handy tool that's available any time you can access the web.

» To open a document from Word on the web to Word on your PC, click the button OPEN IN WORD (refer to Figure 29-10). Click through a few confirmation dialog boxes (because a web page is starting a program on your computer), and soon the document is open in the full-blown version of Word, ready for editing.

Ribbon

Tabs   Status bar

Open another online app

Access file in
Word on your PC

Writing area

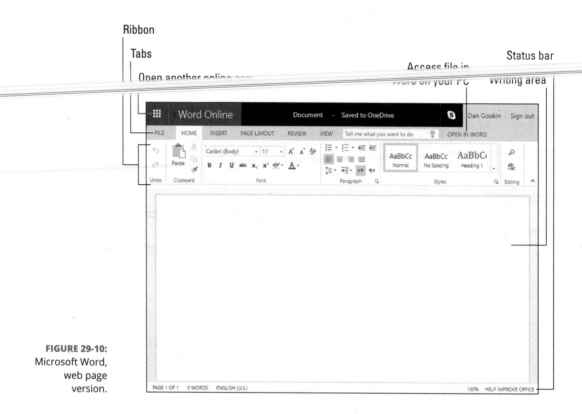

FIGURE 29-10:
Microsoft Word,
web page
version.

REMEMBER

>> Word on the web is tied directly into your OneDrive account. That's where files are saved and where Word looks to find files to open.

>> Sometimes a document opens in Word on the web for viewing only. If you need to edit the document, click the Edit Document button and choose the Edit in Word Online command. That command makes the document appear more familiar to you, as shown in Figure 29-10.

>> Documents created with Word on the web are saved to your OneDrive storage. Because OneDrive is coordinated with your PC's local files, the file is eventually available on your computer. Refer to the earlier section "Understanding OneDrive."

Chapter 30

Web Page Publishing

ay back in the 1990s, Microsoft added Internet features to *everything*. The overreaction was to compensate for being late to the Internet party. So Microsoft Office, which is a productivity platform, and Word in particular, which is designed to generate documents, suddenly became a web page creation tool. As someone who writes HTML code and designs web pages, I can promise you that it wasn't Word's proudest historical achievement.

The fallout of those hectic times is that Word still offers web page creation features. I know of no web page author, designer, or programmer who uses Word for that task, let alone who would even consider it. Still, the features are available and can be used to create web pages in a pinch.

Ode to Web Publishing

A web page is a text document. It's formatted by using HTML code, which handles the rudiments of designing the page layout, formatting the text, setting elements like pictures, and adding links. Current web technology uses variations of HTML, including DHTML, PHP, and others, but at the base all web pages are text documents that are interpreted by a web server and web browser to look like the web you see and enjoy all too often when you should be doing something else.

This section provides an insanely quick introduction to the web publishing process. If you plan on taking this task seriously, obtain a web page development program — one that's ~~specifically~~ ~~and publish web pages.~~

>> HTML stands for Hypertext Markup Language.

>> DHMTL is the Dynamic Hypertext Markup Language.

>> PHP stands for Personal Home Page. It's a programming language that helps automate web pages.

>> Web page documents use the html and htm filename extensions.

>> The best software to use for creating a web page is a specific web page editor. Many free programs are available. I use Dreamweaver, which is part of the Adobe Creative Cloud suite (and not cheap). If you know HTML codes, you can use any text editor to craft a web page lickety-split. This book doesn't go into further details.

>> A *web server* is software that runs on the Internet. It replies to HTTP requests. So when you visit a web page, your computer is requesting that information from a web server.

>> HTTP stands for Hypertext Transfer Protocol. Another web address prefix is HTTPS, which adds the word *Secure* to the acronym. HTTPS is used for secure websites, such as online shopping and access to cloud storage.

>> The *web browser* is software on your PC that fetches web pages from the Internet.

Obtaining a web host

To toss up a web page on the Internet in a professional manner, you need a domain and a web hosting service. Here's what those two terms mean:

Domain: This is a name, such as dummies.com or wambooli.com. It's not a web page, a location, or anything physical. It's just a name registered to you or your organization.

Web host: This is a service you subscribe to. The service provides web access associated with a domain. So when people visit dummies.com or wambooli.com on their web browsers, they find a web page.

You can register a domain and obtain a web host at the same place. For example, the online service GoDaddy offers domain names as well as web hosting. Other services are also available, and they all work similarly: You get a domain first and then a web hosting service attached to that domain.

>> It's possible to register domains and never assign a hosting service (or any Internet service) to those domains. For example, I own the domain blorfus. com, but it hosts no web pages.

>> Some people make a living buying various domains and then selling them later. This activity isn't as lucrative as it once was, because people and various organizations caught on.

>> Some people use Internet-based web page production services. These sites let you design a web page on the Internet and then have the same service host that page. These services do okay for promotions and small businesses, but the truly professional way to publish websites is to obtain a domain and a web host.

Understanding web page production

The web page production cycle works like this:

1. **Create a web page document.**

   The document is plain text, but saved with the html or htm filename extension.

2. **Upload the web page document to the web host.**

   The host has a specific address to which you upload the web page document. If the web page creation software doesn't handle this task, you can use an FTP utility. FTP stands for File Transfer Protocol, and it's usually the name of the program that transfers the files.

3. **Visit the web page on the Internet to see how it looks.**

   If you want to be diligent, you use a host of web browsers to view the web page to ensure that everything looks peachy.

4. **Repeat the process because it's often necessary to do things over.**

   Also, creating a web page can be fun.

Most web page development programs handle all these tasks. Word is good at doing Step 1. So if you use Word to develop web pages, you still need an FTP (File Transfer Protocol) program or its equivalent to get that page on your hosted domain.

>> The web page filename can be anything, though you must avoid spaces and certain special characters. My advice is to use only letters and numbers for the web page filename.

>> If you name the web page file index.html or index.htm, it becomes the main page that opens when the user visits ~~your site~~ ~~~~ ~~When~~ you visit ~~~~ `www.gookin.com`, you're actually loading the file `http://www.gookin.com/index.html`.

>> Just as you can create folders on your PC's storage system, you can build folders on a website. The folders help you organize the site. Either the web page development software lets you create these folders or you can use the FTP program. Within each folder, the index.html document is the one that opens when a web page document isn't specified.

TECHNICAL STUFF

>> Older versions of Windows created web page documents ending in *htm*. That's because ancient operating systems allowed only three characters in a filename extension. The html extension is more popular. It makes no difference to the web browser which extension you use. Word uses *htm* for documents you save as web pages.

Examining a web page document

You don't need to code HTML to create a web page; that's why you're using Word. It handles all the coding tasks for you, helping you to concentrate on the final result. Still, I would be shot with arrows by various members of the nerd public if I didn't at least show you a basic HTML document and all its pieces and parts.

Figure 30-1 shows a crude HTML document and the web page it creates. This is the simplest form of web page, far more primitive than what you can accomplish when you use Word as a web page editor.

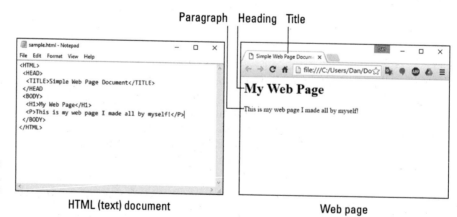

FIGURE 30-1:
An HTML document and web page.

HTML (text) document

Web page

On the left in Figure 30-1 is the Notepad text editor. It lists a basic HTML skeleton. On the right you see that document displayed in a web browser. It's a file on my computer, which I didn't upload to the Internet. Still, it appears the same as if the browser had fetched it from the web.

HTML code consists of tags. These tags define parts of the web page, formatting, and special features such as an image or a link. The tag is enclosed in angle brackets. Within the brackets you find the HTML code name, plus any options.

Most HTML tags come in pairs: a start tag and an end tag. For example, in Figure 30-1 you see the <HTML> tag in Notepad as the first line of text. That tag defines the start of the web page. The last line of text is the closing tab, </HTML>. That tag marks the end of the web page.

Here's the breakdown of the code shown in Figure 30-1:

```
<HTML>
```

The *HTML tag* identifies the start of the document. Within the document are two chunks: a head and a body. The head contains information about the page and other options. The body chunk contains items that appear on the web page itself.

The HEAD tag defines the header information for a web page. In this simple example, only one tag appears in the head: the TITLE. You can see the title text displayed on the web browser tab in Figure 30-1.

```
<HEAD>
  <TITLE>Simple Web Page Document</TITLE>
</HEAD>
```

Next comes the BODY, which is the part of the document that appears on the web page:

```
<BODY>
  <H1>My Web Page</H1>
  <P>This is my web page I made all by myself!</P>
</BODY>
```

The *H1 tag* is the top-level heading tag, Heading 1. It marks text that appears in a large, bold font, as shown on the right in Figure 30-1.

The *P tag* is the paragraph tag. It marks a section of text as a paragraph.

Both H1 and P feature closing or end tags so that their elements are contained.

Finally, the *ending* HTML tag marks the last line of the document:

```
</HTML>
```

REMEMBER

You don't need to know HTML to create web pages in Word. In fact, quite a few people create web pages without knowing a lick of HTML. I do recommend, however, that you be familiar with what it looks like so that you can impress your friends; point at an HTML document and proudly announce, "That's HTML!"

TECHNICAL STUFF

You can peek at any web page's HTML code just to see how complex it can be: Press Ctrl+U in any popular Windows web browser to view its source code. In Microsoft Edge and Internet Explorer, press the F12 key.

Web Page Creation in Word

Any Word document can be saved as a web page. Word does its best to retain those elements that are relevant to the web page and toss away anything that doesn't translate, such as macros or content controls. You can read more in the later section "Saving a web page document." But if you set out to use Word to create a web page, you had best follow the advice in this section.

>> Not every web page document ends up on the web: Many eBook publishers require document submission in the web page or HTML format. See Chapter 22 for information on eBook publishing.

>> To create a web page, Word converts the current document into the web page format. That's far different from software specifically designed to create web pages and build websites.

>> Refer to Chapter 12 for details on inserting images into a document, which translate into pictures and graphics on a web page.

Setting Web Layout view

The web doesn't have page margins. You can set a web page to be as narrow as a cell phone touchscreen or as wide as a PC sporting dual widescreen monitors. That's a heck of a range. To best understand that format, it helps to work on your web page document in Word's Web Layout view.

To switch to Web Layout view, obey these directions:

1. **Click the View tab.**

2. **In the Views group, click the Web Layout button.**

   The writing part of Word's document window changes. It looks blank, just like an empty web page.

From the and-now-he-tells-us department: The Web Layout shortcut button is found on the right end of the status bar and illustrated in the margin.

REMEMBER

>> When you close a document in Web Layout view, subsequent documents may open in Web Layout view. To fix this annoyance, set a document to Print Layout view, and then close that document.

>> To return to Word's preferred document view, repeat the steps in this section and choose Print Layout in Step 2. Or you can click the Print Layout button on the status bar, as illustrated in the margin.

Formatting a document for the web

The primary difference between a web document and one printed on paper is the page size; unlike a sheet of paper, a web page size is variable. To drive home this point, you can resize Word's document window to be wide or narrow and in Web Layout view watch the text wrap and reformat as you do so. For a traditional document, the window size is irrelevant.

The variable page size affects a document primarily with page-level formatting commands. Click the Layout tab and observe all commands in the Page Setup group, shown in Figure 30-2. Those commands highlighted in the figure have no effect on a web page.

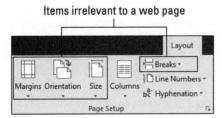

FIGURE 30-2:
Page formatting
commands.

Page Setup group commands that affect a web page include formatting columns and line numbers. But margins, orientation, paper size, and page breaks are irrelevant.

TIP

» My advice is to design the web page as a regular document. Save the regular document. Then switch to Web Layout view and make adjustments. Afterward, save the d~~ocument in~~ ~~~~~~~~~~~~~~~~~ ~~later section~~ "Saving a web page document."

» Though a document's page margins don't matter to a web page, a paragraph's left and right indentation still holds. The difference is that a page's margins measure the text area as offset from the edge of a page. A paragraph's indentation is measured from the page margin boundary. On a web page, a paragraph's indentation is measured from the edge of the web browser window.

» You can split your web page into columns, but keep in mind that a web page is infinitely tall. To split the column, you must insert a column break. Refer to Chapter 5.

» You can place text into boxes to obtain more formatting control. Text boxes are covered in Chapter 11, but be aware that the text boxes are converted to graphical images when the web page document is saved.

» Web pages don't use page numbers. If you need to reference something elsewhere on a page, set a bookmark and build a reference field or hyperlink. Refer to Chapter 21 for information on references.

» Don't bother setting headers and footers for a web page document.

» Macros may help you create the document, but they won't be saved with the web page. Ditto for content controls.

» Fields are converted to static text when you save the web page.

» Drawing objects are converted to images for the final web page.

Inserting a hyperlink

The web is called "the web" because of the hyperlinks that connect web pages, documents, images, and other fun stuff. Hyperlinks, or *links*, for short, can be inserted into any Word document, not just a web page document. You can link to document elements, such as bookmarks, chapter headings, and even other documents, and you can also add links to websites. For a web page, the links most frequently go to other pages or locations on the Internet.

To insert a common web page link into your document, obey these steps:

1. **Place the insertion pointer at the location where you want the link to appear.**

2. **Press Ctrl+K.**

The Insert Hyperlink dialog box appears, illustrated in Figure 30-3.

Link text (in the document)   Add pop-up bubble text

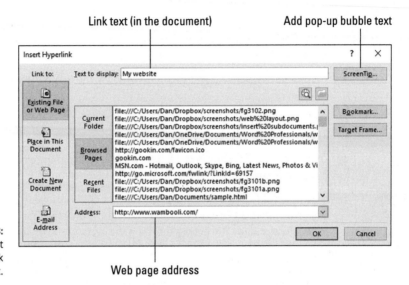

FIGURE 30-3:
The Insert
Hyperlink
dialog box.

Web page address

3. **From the list of Link To buttons on the left side of the dialog box, click Existing File or Web Page.**

If you're building a cross-reference link within the document, you choose Place in This Document. Refer to Chapter 21 for details.

4. **In the center of the dialog box, click the Browsed Pages button.**

This step may help you locate a page you've visited recently. If you see it in the list, click to select it. This step saves typing time; otherwise, you must type the address.

5. **Click the mouse in the Address text box and type the full web page address.**

The text you type is echoed in the Text to Display text box.

6. **Edit the text in the Text to Display dialog box to reflect the link text.**

You can use the full web page address or type other text to click. For example, "Here is the article" is more obvious than showing a complex web address to a news site.

7. **Click the OK button to build the link and insert the link's text.**

In the document window, the link appears in the traditional blue underlined text. Press the Ctrl key and click the link to launch your computer's web browser and visit the web page.

>> You can directly edit text in a link, but doing so is imprecise. Instead, right-click the link and choose Edit Hyperlink. You see the Edit Hyperlink dialog box, which looks the same as Figure 30-1 but with all the fields filled in.

>> To remove a hyperlink, right-click it and choose the Remove Hyperlink command.

>> Click the ScreenTip button (refer to Figure 30-3) to add text to a pop-up bubble that appears whenever the user hovers the mouse over the link.

>> The Hyperlink command is located on the Insert tab, in the Links group. The Ctrl+K shortcut is quicker, but not easy to remember.

TECHNICAL STUFF

>> A web page address is often called a *URL,* though this usage is inaccurate. URL stands for Uniform Resource Locator. It refers to only the first part of the web page address: http. The proper term is *web page address,* or just *address.*

Saving a web page document

Word offers three formats for a web page document. Well, it's actually four formats if you want to also save your work using Word's standard document format. The formats are chosen from the file type menu on the Save screen or in the traditional Save As dialog box. They are listed here:

Single File Web Page (*.mht, *.mhtml): This format includes all graphics and images saved in the document. It's not a traditional web page file format, but it includes everything in a single file.

Web Page (*.htm, *.html): In this format, more details are saved to keep the document compatible with many of Word's features.

Web Page, Filtered (*.htm, *.html): This format is more compatible with traditional web pages, because many of the extra features are omitted.

The Single File Web Page format isn't a traditional HTML document, though the file that's saved is a plain-text file. It folds pictures and other items into the file as text elements. Some web browsers can read this type of file, but I don't recommend it for uploading to the web or for sharing with people who may not use Microsoft Office.

The two Web Page file formats save the document as a plain text, HTML document. The Web Page format saves a lot of information in the document, stuff that most web designers consider obnoxious and superfluous, but data that makes opening the document in Word more compatible.

The Web Page, Filtered format is preferred for actual web page production. It's not as clean as a web page created specifically in HTML or written by a web page designer, but it's better than the unfiltered format.

For both file formats, supplemental information for the web page may be saved in a companion folder. The folder is given the same name as the document, and when the Web Page, Filtered file format is used, the folder contains the word *filtered* as part of its name.

To save a web page document, follow these steps:

1. **If you plan to keep a Word document copy of the file, perform one final save on it as a Word document.**

2. **Click the File tab.**

3. **Choose Save As.**

   The Save As screen appears on the Backstage.

4. **Type a name for the file.**

   Web page filenames do not contain spaces. Just stick with letters and numbers and, if you need a space, use the underscore character.

5. **Choose the web file type from the File Type menu.**

   The two types I recommend are Web Page and Web Page, Filtered, as described in this section. See Figure 30-4.

6. **Click the Save button to save.**

   You may see a warning appear, informing you that the document contains elements that don't translate into a web page. Those items will be missing from the final document.

REMEMBER

If any extra elements were involved with the web page, such as images or other media, or when you choose the Web Page format, extra files are held in a folder given the same name as the web page file. For example, if your web page file is named index.htm, then the folder index_files is also created. If you plan to upload the web page, you must send both the file and the folder. Place them in the same location so that the web page document can access its files.

>> If you use text boxes in your web page, don't use the Filtered option to save the document. That setting may not properly convert the text box into a graphical image.

>> Elements that don't save into a web page include fields, macros, content controls, and other fancy items. These pieces are stripped from the document as soon as it's saved in the web page format.

>> If file size is a consideration, be aware that the Web Page file size can be up to 15 times larger than the Web Page, Filtered file size. All that extra information occupies more space in the Web Page document.

>> For more information on HTML and web page publishing, I recommend the book *Web Design All-in-One For Dummies,* by Sue Jenkins (Wiley).

Web page file formats

Web page filename

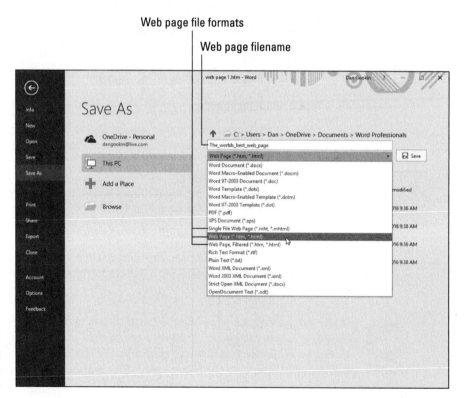

FIGURE 30-4:
Saving a document as a web page.

Chapter 31

Customize Word

Customization options can be a blessing or a curse. The blessing part deals with changing Word's behavior and appearance to match what you prefer. The curse comes from a departure from the traditional and well-documented ways that Word looks and acts. As long as you can keep in mind that your custom settings will make your copy of Word different, you're good to go.

TECHNICAL STUFF

Changes to Word's options and all customization settings are saved as part of the Normal template.

General Options and Settings

options and settings. The traditional way to open that dialog box is to obey these directions:

1. **Click the File tab.**

2. **Choose Options.**

   The Word Options dialog box appears, similar to what's shown in Figure 31-1.

Categories　　　　　　　Settings and options　　　　　　Areas

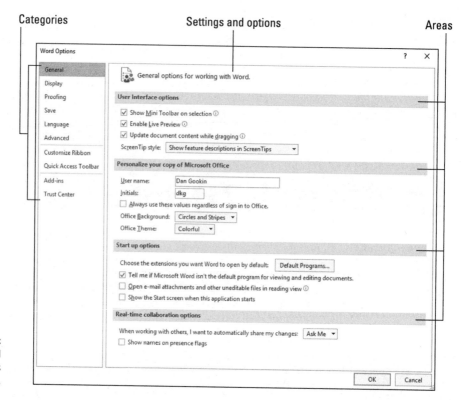

The dialog box lists categories on the left side. The right side lists controls and options for each category, organized into specific areas, such as User Interface Options, Personalize Your Copy of Microsoft Office, and the others shown in Figure 31-1.

The following sections reference items in the Word Options dialog box. These options control word's appearance and behavior.

Showing special characters

Word hides some items in the document that affect your text. You may not see these items, but you see their effects. For example, when you press the Enter key to start a new paragraph, you add a New Paragraph character to the text. It doesn't show up — unless you tell Word to show it.

¶ All the secret characters can be shown at one time when you use the Show/Hide command. If you find that the command junks up the document to the nth degree, you can select individual characters to show all the time, such as the New Paragraph character or perhaps the tab. Follow these steps:

1. **Click the File tab and choose Options.**

The Word Options dialog box appears.

2. **Choose the Display category.**

The list of special characters appears in the Always Show area, illustrated in Figure 31-2.

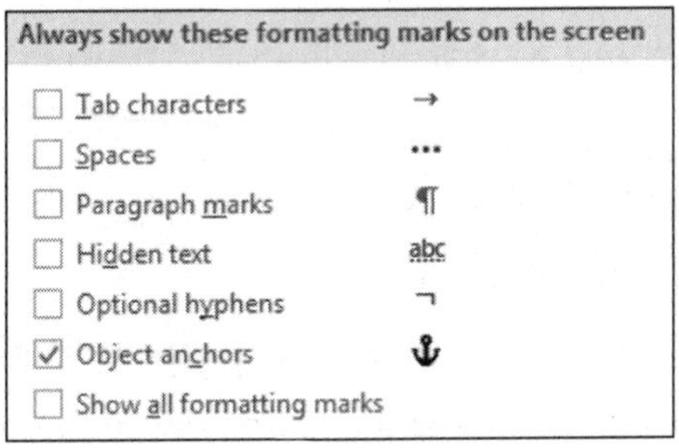

Always show these formatting marks on the screen

☐ Tab characters → →
☐ Spaces ···
☐ Paragraph marks ¶
☐ Hidden text abc
☐ Optional hyphens ¬
☑ Object anchors ⚓
☐ Show all formatting marks

FIGURE 31-2:
Special characters to show in a document.

3. **Place a check mark by the character you want to always see.**

For example, you may want to see the New Paragraph character or the tab. In Figure 31-2, you see that the Object Anchors character is selected. That character helps anchor (get it?) an image or another object to a paragraph of text. Refer to Chapter 10 for details on how it works.

4. **Click the OK button to lock in your choices and close the Word Options dialog box.**

The Show All Formatting Marks option (refer to Figure 31-2) activates all marks, similar to the Show/Hide command.

» When the paragraph mark is activated, heading styles in a document are prefixed with a square bullet.

>> The Spaces option directs Word to show space characters as small dots. One dot appears for every space character in the —

>> Hidden text is a text formatting attribute, like bold or italics, but hidden text doesn't show up in a document — unless you activate the Hidden Text option as described in this section. Even then, the hidden text won't print unless you set that option: Follow Steps 1 and 2 in this section, and in the Printing Options area, place a check mark by the Print Hidden Text setting. Of course, then what's the point of hiding the text in the first place?

>> Use the Font dialog box to apply the hidden-text format. It's listed as an "effect." See Chapter 1 for details.

Controlling text selection

Word believes that it's being helpful when it automatically selects text by the word as you drag the mouse. That setting allows for rapid text selection, but it might not be what you want. For example, I prefer to select text by the character, which can be tedious, but it's what I like.

To direct Word to select text by character instead of by word, obey these handy directions:

1. **Open the Word Options dialog box.**

   Click the File tab and choose Options.

2. **Select Advanced from the items listed on the left side of the dialog box.**

3. **Remove the check mark by the option When Selecting, Automatically Select Entire Word.**

4. **Click OK.**

One of my primary motivations in making this change is to better select text at the end of a paragraph. If you keep word selection active, selecting those words can be difficult. Also, I select text in the middle of a word to edit the word or change its meaning.

Setting text-pasting options

When you paste text into a document, you probably assume that the text carries its original format. That's a good assumption, but sometimes pasting in formatted text can be annoying. For example, you copy text from an email message and the dorky email message format is pasted into your Word document.

The immediate way to fix text-pasting options is to press and release the Ctrl key right after you paste the text. You see a pop-up menu with several paste options, as illustrated in Figure 31-3.

Press Ctrl to see the menu

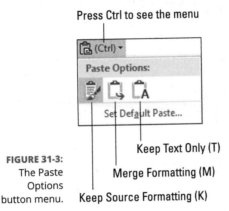

Keep Text Only (T)

FIGURE 31-3:
The Paste
Options
button menu.

Merge Formatting (M)

Keep Source Formatting (K)

Choose the options as shown in Figure 31-3 to control how the text is pasted. For example, if you choose the Keep Text Only option, the text formatting is removed and Word pastes the text as though you typed it.

The keyboard shortcuts for each text-pasting option are shown in Figure 31-3. To use the keyboard shortcuts, tap the Ctrl key after you paste the text. Then tap one of the keys T, M, or K for each of the options illustrated in the figure.

To override all settings, click on the Set Default Paste item. You're taken to the Word Options dialog box, Advanced category. In the Cut, Copy, and Paste area, you see all the settings for pasting text, as illustrated in Figure 31-4.

Show Paste Options button

Paste options menus

Cut, copy, and paste

Pasting within the same document: Keep Source Formatting (Default) ▾
Pasting between documents: Keep Source Formatting (Default) ▾
Pasting between documents when style definitions conflict: Use Destination Styles (Default) ▾
Pasting from other programs: Keep Source Formatting (Default) ▾
Insert/paste pictures as: In line with text ▾
☑ Keep bullets and numbers when pasting text with Keep Text Only option
☐ Use the Insert key for paste
☑ Show Paste Options button when content is pasted
☑ Use smart cut and paste ⓘ   [Settings...]

FIGURE 31-4:
Paste options and
other settings.

Menus to the right of the first four settings (refer to Figure 31-4) set the way Word pastes the text. The options are similar to those f̶̶̶̶̶̶̶̶̶̶̶̶̶̶̶̶̶̶ ̶̶̶̶̶̶Paste Options button:

Keep Source Formatting (Default): The text retains its format from elsewhere in the document, from the other document, or from its original source.

Merge Formatting: The text is reformatted to match the paragraphs before and after. If the text is a bulleted or numbered list, the bullets and numbering match the paragraphs before and after.

Keep Text Only: Only text is pasted, just the same as if you typed the text. Any existing text formats are applied.

Between Word documents, keeping the source formatting makes sense. The Pasting from Other Programs setting, however, is one you might want to reset to Keep Text Only.

If you don't desire to see the Paste Options button appear after you paste text (shown in the margin), remove the check mark by the option Show Past Options Button When Content Is Pasted.

TIP

If you want to choose the formatting options before you paste, use the Paste Special command. Follow these steps:

1. **Click the Home tab.**

2. **In the Clipboard group, click the Paste button.**

3. **Choose one of the paste options buttons shown in the menu.**

   Merrily, the buttons match what you see on the Paste Options button menu. (Refer to Figure 31-3.)

The text is pasted according to the format you chose, though it's probably easier to press Ctrl+V, Ctrl, and then the corresponding letter for the format you desire.

Disabling annoying features

Is it possible to count Word's annoying features? And what might be annoying to you might be a godsend to someone else. That's why Word has options and settings for turning off some of its "helpful" features. These include the items in the following five sections:

AutoCorrect and AutoFormat

Refer to Chapter 23 for details on disrupting the behavior of these Auto commands.

Click-and-Type

The Click-and-Type feature allows you to click anywhere on a blank page and start typing. Word formats the document instantly, providing whatever spacing commands are necessary to let you plop down text just anywhere.

Click-and-Type shows itself by changing the mouse pointer. The pointer's appearance reflects the Click-and-Type format applied to the text, as illustrated in Table 31-1.

TABLE 31-1

Click-and-Type Mouse Pointers

Pointer	Effect on Paragraph Formatting
	First line is indented.
	Paragraph is left-justified; no first-line indent.
	Paragraph is centered.
	Paragraph is right-justified.

You probably won't see Click-and-Type unless you use Print Layout view and you whip the mouse pointer around the blank page. If that mouse pointer change bugs you, disable Click-and-Type. Heed these directions:

1. Click the File tab and choose Options.

2. Choose the Advanced category.

3. In the Editing Options area, remove the check mark by Enable Click and Type.

4. Click OK.

The Backstage

The *Backstage* is the full-screen ~~~~~~~~~~~~~~~~~~~~~~~~~ Save As and Open commands, ~~~~~~~~ the traditional Save As and Open dialog boxes. Refer to Chapter 29 for details on disabling the Backstage.

The Mini Toolbar

The *Mini Toolbar* is that pop-up thing that appears whenever you select text or right-click on text. Its two flavors are illustrated in Figure 31-5.

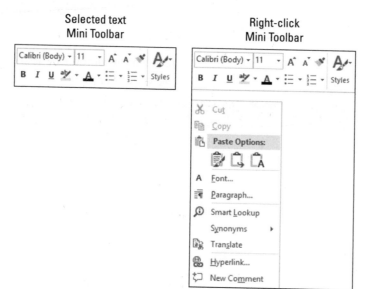

FIGURE 31-5:
The two types of
Mini Toolbar.

I like the Mini Toolbar. If you don't, disable it by heeding these steps:

1. Click the File tab and choose Options.

2. In the General category, under the User Interface Options area, remove the check mark by the option Show Mini Toolbar on Selection.

3. Click OK.

The Start screen

The *Start screen* is the first screen you see when you open the Word program, unless you double-click to open a document. In that instance, the Start screen doesn't horn in on your day and you can directly edit the document. If you'd rather never see the Start screen, and just start Word to behold a blank document, obey these steps:

1. **Click the File tab and choose Options.**

   The Word Options dialog box appears.

2. **In the General category, under the Start Up Options area, remove the check mark by Show the Start Screen When This Application Starts.**

3. **Click OK.**

If you miss the Start screen, repeat these steps, but in Step 2 add the check mark.

Specifying the default document folder

Word enjoys saving new documents in the Documents folder. That's the first place it looks, because the Default Local File Location option is set to your home folder, the Documents subfolder. If you prefer to use another folder, then — providing you know the folder's pathname — you can set that folder as the default local file location. Obey these directions:

1. **Click the File tab and Choose Options.**

2. **Click the Save category.**

3. **In the Save Documents area, click the Default Local File Location box and type a folder's pathname.**

   That's the folder in which Word saves documents by default.

If you save a document in any folder, Word uses that folder as the current folder. It's where documents are saved until you select another folder.

TECHNICAL STUFF

A *pathname* is a file's full, formal name. It starts with the storage device, and then all parent folders for the current folder, and, finally, the current folder. A filename can be appended to a pathname, which gives the file's precise location in the local storage system or on the network.

Word's Appearance

The Word window is your oyster. You can keep it as is, you can eat it whole, you can even pluck out the pearls. You just need to know what can be changed and how to change it.

Refer to Chapter 18 for information on using Word full-screen as well as how to show and hide the Ribbon.

Showing the ruler

I like the Ruler. It's ~~a great tool~~ to inspect a paragraph's margins and first-line indent, as well to position and work with tab stops. The Ruler doesn't, however, show up unless you bid it come.

To summon the Ruler, follow these steps:

1. **Click the View tab.**

2. **In the Show group, place a check mark by Ruler.**

To banish the Ruler, repeat these steps, but in Step 2 remove the check mark.

A Vertical Ruler is also available in Print Layout view. You can use it for anything, but it shows up and lets you gauge how the text lays out on the page.

To summon the Vertical Ruler, as well as determine whether the scrollbars appear in the document window, obey these steps:

1. **Click the File tab.**

2. **Choose Options.**

   The Word Options dialog box appears.

3. **Choose the Advanced category.**

4. **In the Display area, ensure that a check mark appears by the option Show Vertical Ruler in Print Layout View.**

5. **Click OK.**

REMEMBER

The Vertical Ruler appears only in Print Layout view.

Revealing the scrollbars

You may think nothing of having scrollbars in the document window, but you can control whether or not they show up. Two settings in the Word Options dialog box determine whether the horizontal or vertical scrollbar shows up.

To access the scrollbar settings, follow Steps 1 through 3 in the preceding section. In the Display area, you'll find two options for the scrollbars: Show Horizontal Scroll Bar and Show Vertical Scroll Bar. Add or remove the check marks to set either item.

I always write it as one word: scrollbar. What is Microsoft thinking?

Removing the Style Area view

In the Draft and Outline views, you might see a list of paragraph styles appear to the left of the document part of the window. This area is called the *Style Area pane*, and some people believe it should be titled *pain* and not *pane*.

To remove the area, follow these steps:

1. **Click the File tab and choose Options.**

2. **In the Word Options dialog box, click the Advanced category.**

3. **In the Display area, set the Style Area pane width to zero inches: Type** 0″ **into the box.**

   The command title is Style Area Pane Width in Draft and Outline views.

4. **Click OK.**

The Style Area pane isn't the same as the Style pane, which typically shows up on the right side of the window or appears as a floating palette. To banish the Style pane, click its X (Close) button.

Moving the Quick Access toolbar

The easiest thing to customize on the Ribbon is the Quick Access toolbar. You can add and remove icons, which is covered elsewhere in this chapter, but you can also set where the toolbar appears, either above or below the Ribbon. Figure 31-6 illustrates the differences.

To relocate the Quick Access toolbar, follow these directions:

1. **Click the Quick Access toolbar menu button.**

   Refer to Figure 31-6 for its location. It's always to the right of the last icon on the toolbar.

2. **Choose Show Below the Ribbon or Show Above the Ribbon to move the toolbar.**

   The command changes to reflect the toolbar's current position.

Menu

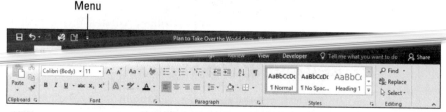

Quick Access toolbar above the Ribbon

FIGURE 31-6:
Quick Access
toolbar positions.

Quick Access toolbar below the Ribbon

At minimum, the Quick Access toolbar shows up as the Menu button only. You cannot completely remove the toolbar.

TIP

>> When you find the Quick Access toolbar populated with more than a handful of items, place it below the Ribbon.

>> If you really want a lot of icons on the Quick Access toolbar, consider creating a custom tab on the Ribbon instead. See the later section "Build a Custom Tab on the Ribbon."

Fun with the Quick Access Toolbar

I consider the Quick Access toolbar to be home for those commands I use frequently and those that I want to use but are absent from the Ribbon. In fact, if I don't use a command on the toolbar, I remove it. All these configuration options are available and easy to use, which is the essence of the Quick Access toolbar.

Configuring the toolbar

The Quick Access toolbar features some handy commands that you can access quickly. You can also add or remove commands at your whim. To do so, use the Quick Access toolbar menu, as illustrated in Figure 31-7.

The toolbar shown in Figure 31-7 lists the standard (or default) commands available on the toolbar. These are Save, Undo, and Redo.

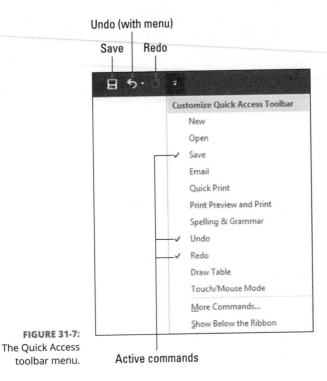

Save · Redo · Undo (with menu)

Customize Quick Access Toolbar

- New
- Open
- ✓ Save
- Email
- Quick Print
- Print Preview and Print
- Spelling & Grammar
- ✓ Undo
- ✓ Redo
- Draw Table
- Touch/Mouse Mode
- More Commands...
- Show Below the Ribbon

Active commands

FIGURE 31-7:
The Quick Access toolbar menu.

To add another command, such as Open, choose it from the list and follow these steps:

1. **Click the Quick Access toolbar menu button.**

2. **Choose the command from the list.**

The command is added.

To remove a command, select it from the list in Step 2. Visible commands feature a check mark, as shown in Figure 31-7. The command is removed.

> ➤ The Undo command on the Quick Access toolbar features a menu button. (Refer to Figure 31-7.) Click the triangle to peruse the last few tasks completed. Select an item from the list to undo all actions up to that point.

> ➤ The Redo command appears dimmed on the Quick Access toolbar until there is some action to redo.

> ➤ If your computer has a touchscreen or you use a tablet PC, the Touch/Mouse Mode command also appears on the Quick Access toolbar. Use that command to reposition items in the window so that they're more accessible when using a finger for input instead of a mouse.

Adding special commands to the toolbar

Not every command that appears on the Quick Access toolbar appears on its menu. To dig up additional commands, choose the More Commands item from the menu. Instantly, you behold the Word Options dialog box, with the Quick Access Toolbar item visible, as shown in Figure 31-8.

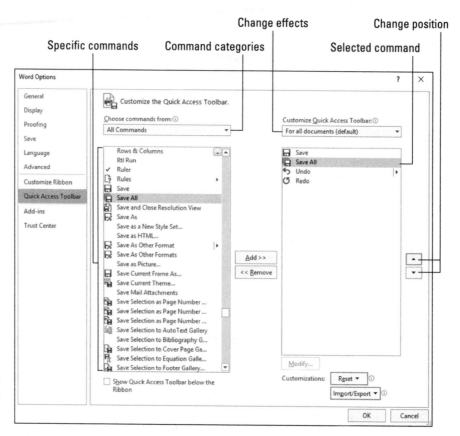

Unlike the paltry selection of commands available on the default toolbar, the items shown in the Word Options dialog box represent an exhaustive list of all of Word's commands. This list includes commands you can't access from the Ribbon as well as macros you created.

To add a command that's not listed on the Quick Access toolbar menu, follow these steps:

1. **Click the Quick Access toolbar menu.**

2. **Choose More Commands.**

   You see the Word Options dialog box appear, as shown in Figure 31-8.

3. **Choose a command category from the list.**

   For example, choose All Commands, as shown in Figure 31-8. This choice helps only when you know Word's specific name for the command. The names are, as you might guess, obnoxiously cryptic.

   If you've created macros you want to assign to the Quick Access toolbar, choose the Macros category.

4. **Select the command you want to add.**

   In Figure 31-8, the Save All command is selected. This command was available in earlier versions of Word, but doesn't appear on the Ribbon. What it does is save all open documents.

5. **Click the Add button.**

   The command is shoved over to the second column. See the next section for information on changing its position.

6. **Repeat Steps 3 through 5 to add more commands.**

7. **Click the OK button to lock in your changes and close the Word Options dialog box.**

The changes you make affect all documents in Word — unless you choose the current document from the Customize Quick Access Toolbar menu, as illustrated in Figure 31-8. Also, if you have an Office 356 subscription, the changes affect only the current installation of Word, not the copies of Word on other devices.

>> If you're specifically hunting for commands not found on the Ribbon, choose the category Commands Not on the Ribbon in Step 3.

>> Refer to Chapter 25 for information on macros.

Rearranging commands on the toolbar

A philosophy exists for where to place commands on a menu or, in the case of Word, on a toolbar. The prevailing wisdom is to keep the most-accessed commands at the top or left side of a list. You can choose whether to obey this line of thinking when you place commands on the Quick Access toolbar, but in the end you can move the commands to any location you like. After all, customization is about what you prefer and not what countless studies have shown.

To rearrange items on the Quick Access toolbar, follow these steps:

1. Click the Quick Access toolbar menu and choose More Commands.

2. **Select an item on the toolbar from the right column.**

   As an example, the Save All command is selected in Figure 31-8.

3. **Click the up or down arrows to shuffle the command up or down in the list.**

   Refer to Figure 31-8 for the arrows' location. Up or down in the list corresponds to left and right on the toolbar.

4. **Click the OK button to lock in your changes.**

Commands added to the Quick Access toolbar are placed below any selected item in the list in the Word Options dialog box. When no item is selected, the command is placed at the bottom of the list.

Separating command groups on the toolbar

To help you group commands on the toolbar, you can add a separator element. This item appears as a vertical bar on the toolbar, as illustrated in Figure 31-9. It's not a command, but rather a visual element.

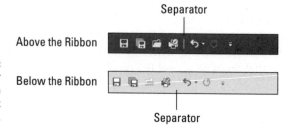

Separator

Above the Ribbon

Below the Ribbon

Separator

FIGURE 31-9:
The separator element on the Quick Access toolbar.

To add a separator, follow these steps:

1. **Click the Quick Access toolbar menu and choose More Commands.**

2. **From the list of commands in the left column, choose <Separator>.**

   The <Separator> command is the first item in the list, no matter which category you choose.

3. **Click the Add button.**

   The <Separator> is inserted into the Quick Access toolbar command list, on the right. It's placed below any selected command or at the bottom of the list.

4. Use the Up and Down buttons to position the separator element.

5. Click OK.

A limit isn't set on the number of separators you can have on the Quick Access toolbar. Heck, you could set a toolbar with all separator elements, if you thought such a thing to be useful.

>> Yes, the separator is more difficult to see when the Quick Access toolbar is below the Ribbon (refer to Figure 31-9). It does, however, add a smidge more space between the commands.

>> Those who know such things claim that it's best to group similar commands together. In Figure 31-9, you see the file-related commands — Save, Save All, Open, and Quick Print — grouped as a unit, and then the separator, and then Undo and Redo. Consider organizing your Quick Access toolbar in a similar manner. It would please the user interface design gods.

TIP

Removing commands

When you find yourself not using a Quick Access toolbar command, or when you just feel the urge to purge, pluck a command from the toolbar. Obey these directions:

1. Click the Quick Access toolbar menu.

2. Choose More Commands.

The Word Options dialog box appears (refer to Figure 31-8).

3. Select a command in the second (right) column.

Those commands currently appear on the toolbar.

4. Click the Remove button.

The command is gone.

5. Repeat Steps 3 and 4 to purge the list.

6. Click OK.

Behold the new Quick Access toolbar.

It doesn't matter which category is chosen in the Word Options dialog box. Clicking the Remove button doesn't affect items on the scrolling list of commands.

Yes, you can remove all the commands. All that remains is the Quick Access toolbar menu button. The button becomes very sad when you remove all the commands.

Resetting the toolbar

When you want a do-over, you can reset the Quick Access toolbar ~~installation, as it appeared~~ when Word first installed and before you began messing around. To do so, heed these steps:

1. **Click the Quick Access toolbar menu and choose More Commands.**

   The Word Options dialog box appears, with the Quick Access Toolbar category showing.

2. **Click the Reset button menu.**

   The button is found near the lower right corner of the dialog box.

3. **Chose the command Reset Only Quick Access Toolbar.**

4. **Click the Yes button to confirm.**

   The commands shown in the right list reflect only the original items that were preset for the toolbar.

5. **Click OK.**

   If you click Cancel instead of OK, the reset isn't effective. So click OK.

Resetting the Quick Access toolbar may not affect any documents where you've configured a custom Quick Access toolbar. And if you're using Office 365, the reset affects only the current installation of Word.

Build a Custom Tab on the Ribbon

When you fill up the Quick Access toolbar, or perhaps you just need more diversity than it offers, you can create your own custom tab on the Ribbon. The task isn't that difficult to do, but like most customizations you're locking yourself into a feature set that's available only on your copy of Word.

Creating a new tab

To build your own tab on the Ribbon, heed these directions:

1. **Right-click on the Ribbon.**

2. **Choose the Customize the Ribbon command.**

   The Word Options dialog box appears, shown in the Customize Ribbon area, as illustrated in Figure 31-10. You see a list of Word's commands in the left column and the Ribbon's current tabs on the right.

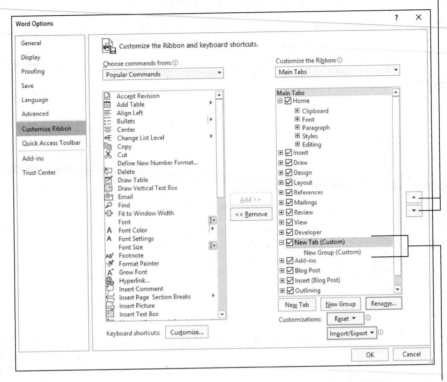

Set tab's position

FIGURE 31-10:
Customizing the
Ribbon in the
Word Options
dialog box.

New tab and new group

The list of tabs on the right side of the window (refer to Figure 31-10) shows all tabs available in Word. Don't be shocked if you see a tab in the list but haven't seen that tab on the Ribbon. Some tabs appear only in context to whatever you're currently doing in Word.

3. **Click the New Tab button.**

The new tab is inserted into the list, along with a new group; all tabs must have at least one group. The new items are given the names New Tab (Custom) and New Group (Custom), as illustrated in Figure 31-10.

4. **Select the New Tab (Custom).**

5. **Click the Rename button.**

6. **Type a new name for the tab.**

For example, type **My Commands**, or if the tab contains your macros, type **Macros**. Whatever you type into the Rename dialog box becomes the tab's name on the Ribbon. Shorter names work best.

7. **Click OK to lock in the new name.**

8. **Click OK to create the new tab.**

The Word Options dialog box ~~closes~~ .... ~~on the Ribbon~~.

The tab is empty until you add commands and groups. Continue reading in the next section.

> » The new tab appears on the far right end of any existing tabs. To change its location, select the tab and use the up and down arrows to set a new position. The tabs at the top of the list appear on the left side of the Ribbon.
>
> » The custom tab shows up as long as it features a check mark in its box.
>
> » Rather than remove a new tab, simply uncheck its box in the list. That way, the tab remains available, just hidden.
>
> » To delete a custom tab, click to select it and then click the Remove button in the center of the dialog box.
>
> » Don't mess with the check marks by other tabs listed in the Word Options dialog box.

WARNING

Adding commands to a new tab

The idea behind creating a custom tab on the Ribbon is to populate it with commands you desire or use frequently. These can be commands already available on the Ribbon, commands you need but aren't easily accessible from the Ribbon, and macros you've created.

To add commands to your custom tab, follow these steps:

1. **Right-click the Ribbon and choose the Customize the Ribbon command.**

2. **Select a group on your custom tab.**

   If you've just created a custom tab, the group is named New Group (Custom). See the next section for information on changing the name.

3. **Choose a category from the list of commands on the left side of the dialog box.**

   For example, Commands Not in the Ribbon or Macros. All of Word's commands are listed in the All Commands category.

4. **Select a command.**

5. **Click the Add button.**

   The command is placed into the group selected in the list on the right side of the dialog box.

6. Repeat Steps 3 and 4 to populate the group with a clutch of commands.

7. Click OK to close the dialog box and survey the group you've created on a custom tab.

In Figure 31-11 you see a custom tab and group, as shown in the Word Options dialog box, as well as how it appears on the Ribbon.

As edited in the Word Options dialog box

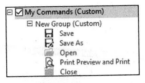

FIGURE 31-11: As shown on the Ribbon

A custom tab with a custom group of commands.

To change the command order, return to the dialog box and select a command from the list on the right side. Use the up and down arrows to reposition a command within a group. For example, in Figure 31-11, the Close command might be more useful if placed next to the Open command.

To remove a command, select it and click the Remove button. The command is pulled from the custom tab.

WARNING

You cannot add or remove any command from one of Word's standard tabs. You can try, but Word gets huffy and displays an angry warning, thwarting your efforts.

Changing command and group names

Commands placed into a group should be related — unless it's simply your intention to have an eclectic group of commands. Either way, give the group a name more interesting than New Group. Heed these directions:

1. Right-click the Ribbon and choose the Customize the Ribbon command.

   The Word Options dialog box appears, with the Customize Ribbon area open for action.

2. Select a group on your custom tab.

3. **Click the Rename button.**

The colorful R~~e~~ appears, as shown in Figure 31-12. It's more interesting than the Rename dialog box for setting the tab's name. That's because you can assign icons to a group in addition to slapping down a new name.

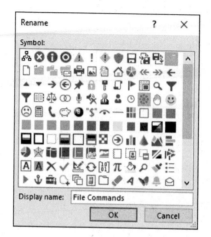

FIGURE 31-12:
Renaming a
group or
command.

4. **Type a new name for the group.**

The best name is descriptive of the group's contents. Even *My favorite commands* is better than *New group*.

You can choose an icon for the group, though Word doesn't show the icon anywhere.

5. **Click OK to set the group's name.**

The new name appears in the list.

6. **Click OK.**

The group name appears below the group on the Ribbon.

You can follow these same steps to rename a command in a group. I recommend that you do so for macros because their names tend to be long and meaningless. Also, you can assign another icon to a command name: After Step 4, select an icon from the list that appears in the Rename dialog box. The selection is rather limited, but the options are better than using some of the generic icons. Also, some of Word's more obscure commands lack icons altogether.

Building more groups

To help with organization, I recommend that you attempt to organize commands on your custom tab into groups of related commands. For example, you can have a group of favorite commands, commands you use but can't find on the Ribbon, macros, commands with funny names, or whatever groups you desire.

To add another group to a custom tab, follow these steps:

1. **Right-click the Ribbon.**

2. **Choose the Customize the Ribbon command.**

3. **In the list of tabs on the right side of the dialog box, select your custom tab.**

4. **Click the New Group button.**

   A new group is inserted into the tab.

5. **Use the up and down arrows to position the group.**

6. **Click the Rename button to assign the group a proper name.**

7. **Add commands to the group.**

   Refer to the earlier section "Adding commands to a new tab" for details.

8. **Click OK to create the new group.**

Peruse the new group as it sits on your custom tab on the Ribbon. If you need to make adjustments, change its name, reposition its commands, or make any other modifications, refer to the proper section elsewhere in this chapter.

When you tire of a group, you can either hide it or remove it. To hide the group, remove its check mark in the Word Options dialog box. The group is still available, merely hidden. To remove the group, select it and click the Remove command.

TIP

A limit exists for the number of groups on a tab. It's a practical limit, in that Word starts hiding commands when too many are available on the Ribbon and the window isn't wide enough to show them all. A logical limit also exists, which is that too many commands look junky and are difficult to access. A visual examination of your custom tab helps, as does practice; the more you use the custom tab, the more you'll recognize what works and what doesn't. Don't be too timid to change things.

Stealing another group from the Ribbon

A quick way to build up a custom tab is to lift an existing group from elsewhere on the Ribbon and stick it into your custom group. This type of theft is legal in 47 states. Here's how it works:

1. **Right-click the Ribbon and choose Customize the Ribbon from the menu.**

2. **From the list of command categories,** choose ~~~~

~~~~ndard and special tabs appear in the list on the left side of the dialog box.

3. **Open a tab to view its groups.**

4. **Click to select the group.**

5. **On the right side of the dialog box, click to select your custom tab.**

6. **Click the Add button.**

    The group is copied from the list of Word's tabs to your custom tab, complete with all its commands.

7. **Use the Up and Down buttons to rearrange the group.**

    The Up and Down buttons set the group's order, with top groups appearing on the left side of the tab.

8. **Click OK.**

    The group is added to your custom tab.

Because the group was born in one of Word's tabs, you cannot edit its contents or add or remove any commands. The group looks exactly as it does on the original tab.

Keyboard Customization

Of all the things you can customize in Word, I believe assigning keyboard shortcuts to be the scariest. Especially for Word's core commands — any of the Ctrl keyboard shortcuts — I strongly recommend that you don't remove the shortcut or allot it to another command. But don't worry: Plenty of other keyboard shortcut combinations are available to assign to any command you choose.

Assigning a keyboard shortcut to a command

The list of Word's keyboard shortcuts is pretty intensive. The variables involved include all the letter and number keys on the keyboard, a smattering of symbols, plus the Shift, Ctrl, and Alt keys in various mixtures and blends. Also included are the function keys. By my math, that's well over 60,000 different keyboard shortcuts available for assignment in Word.

The best way to create a custom keyboard shortcut is to first find a command you use frequently, one for which a keyboard shortcut isn't currently available. For example, I prefer having the Ruler visible when I edit, but the Ruler command lacks a keyboard shortcut. To assign a shortcut to the Ruler command, or any other command in Word, follow these steps:

1. Right-click the Ribbon.

2. Choose the command Customize the Ribbon.

A direct access to the Customize Keyboard dialog box isn't available, but a shortcut is found in the Word Options dialog box in the Customize Ribbon area.

3. Click the Customize button, found by the text Keyboard Shortcuts.

The Customize Keyboard dialog box appears, looking similar to the one shown in Figure 31-13.

Existing shortcut keys

Command categories   Individual commands

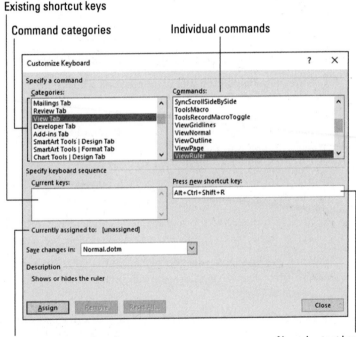

FIGURE 31-13: The Customize Keyboard dialog box.

Keys already assigned   New shortcut key

4. Choose a category to help you hone down the command you want to assign to a keyboard shortcut.

You can select a specific category from the Categories list or select All Commands to view all of Word's commands.

If you're assigning a keyboard shortcut to a macro, choose Macros from the Categories list.

5. Select the command from the Comma~~nd~~ ~~l~~

If th~~e~~ ~~already~~ features a keyboard shortcut, it appears in the Current Keys list. If so, you can assign a second keyboard shortcut, or just commit to memory the current shortcut.

6. Click to select the Press New Shortcut Key text box.

7. Type the shortcut key combination.

8. Check to confirm that the shortcut key combination isn't currently assigned.

Refer to the Currently Assigned To text in the dialog box to confirm, as illustrated in Figure 31-13. If the text [unassigned] appears, the shortcut isn't being used by any other command. That's what you want. If so, you're good to go; otherwise, repeat Steps 6 and 7.

9. Click the Assign button.

The shortcut isn't set until you click the Assign button.

10. Click the Close button to dismiss the Customize Keyboard dialog box.

11. Click OK to banish the Word Options dialog box.

The first thing you should do is test the new keyboard shortcut: Press the key combination to confirm that it works. It should work, unless you chose the improper command in Step 5.

>> I recommend either using the keyboard shortcut right away or writing it down until you can commit it to memory.

>> It's okay to reassign a shortcut key. For example, if you never use the Alt+Ctrl+O keyboard shortcut to enter Outline view, feel free to reassign it.

>> When you reassign an existing keyboard shortcut, even a trivial shortcut like Alt+Ctrl+O, you are deviating your copy of Word from its documentation and Help information.

>> I strongly recommend never reassigning any of the plain Ctrl keyboard shortcuts, such as Ctrl+S to Save, Ctrl+C to copy, and so on.

Setting a symbol's shortcut key

You need not be limited to assigning a keyboard shortcut to a command. Any of Word's special symbols can also sport shortcut keys. In fact, you may find short-cut keys available for symbols you use without knowing the shortcut.

To assign a symbol to a shortcut key, follow these directions:

1. **Click the Insert tab.**
2. **In the Symbols group, click the Symbol menu button.**
3. **Choose the More Symbols command.**

   The Symbol dialog box appears. It lists a host of symbols and squiggles you can stick into your document.

4. **Select a symbol to assign to a shortcut key.**

TIP

   Some symbols may already sport a shortcut key. If so, you see it listed next to the Shortcut Key button. Three types of shortcuts are available: a standard keyboard shortcut, an Alt+ keyboard shortcut, or the Alt+X shortcut.

   For example, the € symbol uses the Alt+Ctrl+E keyboard shortcut. Press Alt+Ctrl+E to see the € symbol.

   The × symbol has the keyboard shortcut Alt+0215. To generate that symbol, press and hold the Alt key and type **0215** on the numeric keypad (with Num Lock on).

   The Ω (omega) symbol uses the 03A9, Alt+X keyboard shortcut. Type **03A9** and then press Alt+X to generate that symbol. See the nearby sidebar "The Alt+X keyboard shortcuts" for details.

5. **Click the Shortcut Key button.**

   A special version of the Customize Keyboard dialog box appears. It looks similar to what's shown in Figure 31-13, but the "command" listed is the symbol you chose in Step 4.

6. **Click to select the Press New Shortcut Key box.**
7. **Press the shortcut key combination.**
8. **Confirm that the shortcut key isn't in use.**

   As long as the text [unassigned] appears by the Currently Assigned To prompt, you're good to go. Otherwise, choose another key combination; repeat Step 6.

9. **Click the Assign button.**

   The shortcut isn't set until you click the Assign button.

10. **Click the Close button to return to the Symbol dialog box.**

    Once in the Symbol dialog box, click the Insert button to insert the symbol, or close the dialog box and practice using your new keyboard shortcut.

If an Alt+ or Alt+X keyboard shortcut starts with a zero, you must ~~~~~~~
complete the code.

Unassigning a keyboard shortcut

To remove a keyboard shortcut, follow these steps:

1. **Summon the Customize Keyboard dialog box.**

    Follow the steps in the preceding sections to summon the Customize Keyboard
    dialog box for a specific command or symbol.

2. **For a command, select that command in the Customize Keyboard dialog
    box.**

3. **Confirm that the current keys for the command are those you assigned.**

4. **Select the current keys in the Current Keys box.**

5. **Click the Remove button.**

6. **Click the Close button to dismiss the Customize Keyboard dialog box.**

If you merely want to reassign the keyboard shortcut, after Step 5 select a new key
combination: Click the Press New Shortcut Key box, and then take a stab at choosing a new shortcut.

THE ALT+X KEYBOARD SHORTCUTS

Just about every symbol available in the known universe can be inserted into your document, provided that you know its Unicode value. The Unicode system is an international
standard for representing characters on computers. Thousands of symbols, from the
basic Latin alphabet to special characters and symbols used by aliens from other galax-
ies, are assigned code values. The list is comprehensive, and Word uses those Unicode
values as keyboard shortcuts.

As an example, the code for the 5/6 fraction character is listed as 215A, Alt+X. To insert
that character, you type — right in your document — the code **215A** and then press the
Alt+X keyboard shortcut. Word converts the 4-digit code into the symbol: ⅚.

Unicode values are hexadecimal, using the base 16 counting system. This system consists of numbers 0 through 9 and letters A through F. You can browse the full list of
Unicode characters online. The official site is unicode.org. A good online reference
can be found at unicode-table.com.

Chapter 32

Breaking Your Word

Word is a pretty solid program, which is amazing when you consider how much it does. When bad things happen, they can be blamed on Windows or faulty computer hardware, but Word can also raise its hand meekly and admit some of the guilt. In a program you rely upon, software issues can be a source of unwelcome woe.

The good news is that Word is packed with features to help mitigate any of its weaknesses. When problems arise, a solution is frequently at hand. You may not know the solution, because many of them aren't obvious and, naturally, Microsoft isn't going to crow about why it included recovery features in what is otherwise a solid program. So where do you look for help when Word breaks? Right in this chapter.

Quick Problems and Solutions

Some problems happen suddenly, raising the issues you'll find addressed in this section.

"What did I just do!"

REMEMBER

The ~~~~~~~~~~ in your Word arsenal is the Undo command. Before you freak out, press Ctrl+Z to see whether you can bring back whatever you lost.

» Word's Undo command remembers several layers of actions, so keep pressing Undo to reverse time and, hopefully, recover from the situation.

» Some commands cannot be undone, such as a search-and-replace operation in a long document. Warnings appear when you attempt such actions. If you were warned, Undo doesn't fix the problem.

» If you undo too much, use the Redo command to re-create your steps. The Redo command is Ctrl+Y.

"I just saved my document, and now I can't find it!"

The first place to look for the document is on the list of recently accessed files on the Open screen. Follow these steps:

1. Click the File tab.

2. Choose Open.

3. Locate your document on the list of recently accessed files.

If you point the mouse at the document name, you see a pop-up bubble that lists the document's full path, similar to what's illustrated in Figure 32-1.

In Figure 32-1, the document was saved on OneDrive, in the Documents folder, in the Word Professionals folder. Those folder names, which appear in the bubble, are part of the document's pathname, or its specific location on your computer's storage system.

If you have trouble reading a pathname, open the document and save it again. This time, ensure that you save it in a location you won't forget.

» Word prefers to use the Documents folder in your account's home folder in Windows. That would be the first place to look.

» Working with folders and finding documents is part of Windows, not Word. Windows is the computer's operating system, and I strongly recommend that you become familiar with how it works and why it's considered separate software from Word.

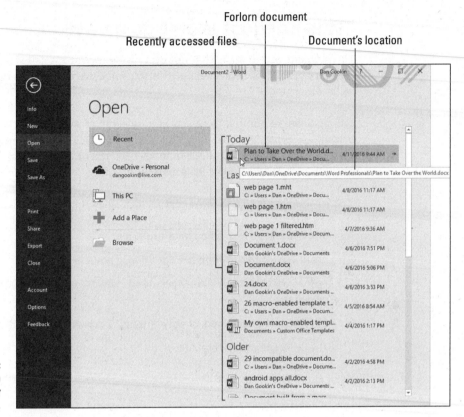

Forlorn document

Recently accessed files

Document's location

FIGURE 32-1:
Locating a
recently
saved file.

>> You can also use the Windows Search command to locate a missing document. In Windows 10, press the Win+S key combination and type the filename into the search text box.

>> When the Windows Search command cannot locate the file, consider looking in the Windows Recycle Bin. Again, this is a Windows function and has nothing to do with Word.

>> If you saved the file directly to removable storage, such as a thumb drive, look for the file there as well. By the way: I do not recommend that you save anything from Word directly to a thumb drive. Save to your PC's primary storage first, and then copy the file to a thumb drive.

>> If multiple people use the same computer, ensure that you're logged in under your own account. Windows keeps multiple account storage areas separate.

"This line just won't go away!"

The problem with this topic is that not everything in Word is called a *line*. Some lines are text borders, some are text attributes, some are revision marks, and some — believe it or not — are lines.

The first step in eliminating a line is to select it. If you can click on the line and it becomes selected, it's a drawing object. Press the Delete key to remove it. Be aware that drawing objects can appear in the document's header or footer. Refer to Chapter 7 for header/footer information.

The second step is to check the text format. Obey these directions:

1. **Select the text with a line in or around it.**

2. **Press Ctrl+D to summon the Font dialog box.**

3. **Ensure that the Underline Style menu shows "(none)" as the current selection.**

4. **If the text is underlined, choose "(none)" from the menu and click OK.**

   The underline style is removed.

Next, check the paragraph formatting to ensure that the line isn't a border style. Follow these steps:

1. **Select the text that features a line nearby.**

   The line can be above, below, to the right or left of, or even inside the text.

2. **Click the Home tab.**

3. **In the Paragraph group, ensure that the Borders button isn't highlighted.**

   The highlighted button is shown in Figure 32-2.

4. **If the paragraph has a Border style applied, click the Borders button and choose No Border from the menu.**

   The border should be gone. If a line remains, it wasn't a border.

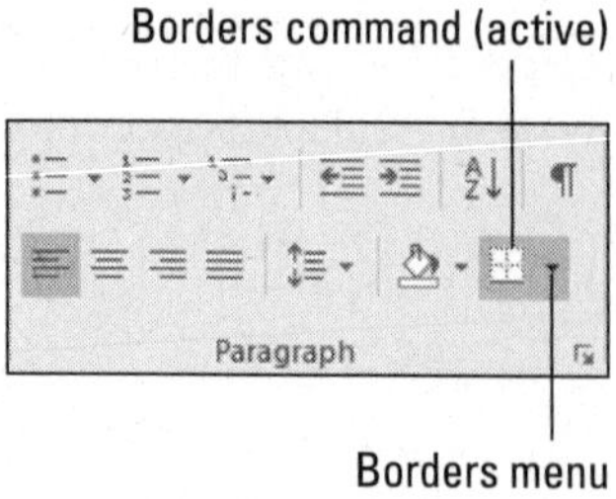

Borders command (active)

FIGURE 32-2:
The Paragraph group on the Home tab.

Borders menu

Another source of lines next to the text are revision marks. These lines may appear below the text or to the side of an edited paragraph. Refer to Chapter 16 for information on turning off revision marks, though they do serve a purpose and you should ask why the marks are present before you eliminate them.

Finally and literally, in Draft and Outline views, a squat horizontal line marks the end of the document. You cannot remove that line.

"How can I get this extra page not to print!"

The document's done printing — or is it? At the end of the text you find a single blank page. It doesn't look like a blank page is tailgating your document on the screen. What's up?

The process of typing words in a word processor causes excess spaces and paragraphs to accumulate like dirt in front of a plow. When spaces appear at the end of a paragraph, no one notices; the spaces don't print and no one is the wiser. When paragraphs (Enter key presses) accumulate at the end of a document, you get an extra, blank page.

To remove the extra blank page, follow these steps:

1. **Press Ctrl+End to move the insertion pointer to the end of your document.**

2. **Press the Backspace key.**

3. **Repeat Step 2 until you've backspaced over all the extra paragraphs and spaces at the end of your document.**

Eventually, you'll back up into the last bit of text on the true last page. That's when you stop pressing Backspace (obviously).

If you still find a blank page at the end of your document, you probably have an extra hard page break or section break. Switch to Draft view to confirm. If so, remove the page break. Refer to Chapter 6 for details on page breaks.

TIP

If you have trouble finding extra paragraphs at the end of a document, use the Show/Hide command to make them visible. See Chapter 17.

The Document Needs a-Fixin'

Malfunctioning documents don't happen as frequently as they once did in Word; document integrity is better today than in the old days, thanks to the docx file format. When you do encounter weirdness when opening a document, turn to this section for advice and fixes.

>> To determine whether the problem is with a specific document or all of Word, try to open other documents and see whether the behavior is repeated.

>> The document's weirdness may be related to its template. Try opening documents with another type of template to confirm whether or not the template is corrupted.

Opening a document in the proper format

The most common cause of a document looking weird is that you've chosen the wrong file type in the Open dialog box. So:

1. **Close the busted document; do not save it!**

2. **Use the Open dialog box to open the document again: Click the File tab and choose Open.**

3. **On the Open screen, click Browse.**

   The Open dialog box appears.

4. **From the file type menu, ensure that All Word Documents is chosen.**

5. **Use the tools in the dialog box to locate and select the document file.**

6. **Click the Open button.**

If the document fails to open properly, repeat these steps, but in Step 4 choose a specific Word document file type, such as Word Documents (*.docx).

TIP

>> To open an older-format Word document, choose Word 97-2003 Documents (*.doc).

>> Rather than use Word to open the document, locate the document's file icon and double-click. Word opens the document in its native format.

>> If these steps don't work, continue reading in the next section.

Opening a document for repair

If a document exhibits odd behavior and the format isn't the problem, you need to open it for repair. Follow these steps:

1. **Click the File tab and choose Open.**

2. **Click the Browse button to summon the traditional Open dialog box.**

3. **Select the file you need to open and repair.**

4. **Click the menu by the Open button and choose Open and Repair.**

See Figure 32-3 for the menu's location.

Selected document   Open button menu

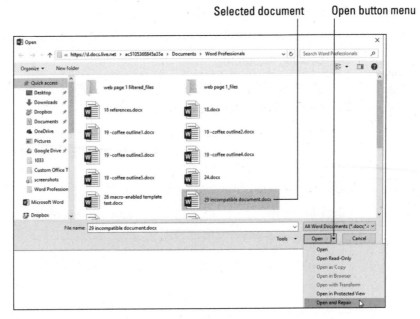

FIGURE 32-3:
Opening a
document for
repair.

The document is opened, and Word attempts to fix any obvious boo-boos. It's placed into a new document window, so the filename isn't retained. This change is made so that you can save the repaired document under a new name, if you like, and keep the original.

After making any further fixes, save the repaired document.

Reassigning the document's template

A reminder appears that your document is okay but its template may be fouled up. In that case, you can reattach the Normal template to the document and see if that fixes things. Obey these directions:

1. Save the document.

You want to ensure that you have a copy, just in case these steps don't work.

2. Click the File tab and choose Options.

The Word Options dialog box appears.

3. From the left side of the Word Options dialog box, choose Add Ins.

4. From the Manage menu, choose Templates.

The Manage menu is located near the bottom center of the dialog box.

5. Click the Go button.

The Templates and Add-Ins dialog box appears, shown in Figure 32-4.

6. Ensure that the Templates tab is selected.

If the Normal template shows up in the Document Template box, the problem most likely lies elsewhere. Otherwise, you can reattach the Normal template:

Ensure that template settings are updated

Current template   Set a new template

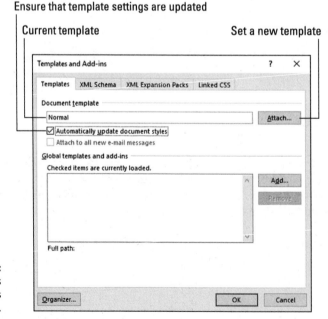

FIGURE 32-4:
The Templates and Add-Ins dialog box.

7. **Click the Attach button.**

The Attach Template dialog box appears. It works similarly to an Open dialog box. In the list of files, you see available templates.

8. **Select the Normal.dotm template.**

9. **Click the Open button.**

10. **Place a check mark in the box Automatically Update Document Styles.**

This step ensures that all styles and settings in the template are updated in the document, including any changes made to the Normal template.

11. **Click OK.**

Reattaching the Normal template may fix some template-based issues, specifically when the issue itself is with the Normal template. See the later section "Fixing the Normal template."

> » Some of the document's odd behavior may be due to macros in the template. Refer to Chapter 25.

> » Keyboard reassignments in the template may also cause things to behave oddly. Refer to Chapter 31.

> » If the document's old template was the issue, consider reediting the problem template, deleting it, or even re-creating it again.

Extracting a fouled document's text

One surefire cure is an almost last-ditch, desperate act: Select all the document's text, copy it, and then paste it into a new document. Delete the original document.

If that technique doesn't work, try again but select the entire document except for the last paragraph mark. Obey these steps:

1. **Press Ctrl+End to zoom to the end of a document.**

2. **Press ←.**

The insertion pointer is positioned just before the final paragraph mark.

3. **Press Shift+Ctrl+Home.**

The entire document is selected, save for the final paragraph mark.

4. **Press Ctrl+C.**

At this point you can paste the text into a new document. Hopefully whatever mess is causing trouble doesn't make the transfer.

If the copy-and-paste solution brings with it ~~~~~~~~~~~, consider saving the document in the Pl~~~~~~~~~~~. All the document's fancy formatting and ~~~~~ are extracted when you save it as plain text, but that may purge the issue. You'll need to reformat the document after you open it again, but you won't have to retype it.

Refer to Chapter 15 for information on saving documents in other formats.

Word Repair and Recovery

The most visible sign that Word is broken is that it just looks damn peculiar on the screen. Things may be missing. Things may be added. Other things may appear or disappear. This could be due to someone's attempt to customize Word, or as these things sometimes go, "stuff" just happens.

Running the Office Repair utility

Recognizing that "stuff" happens, Microsoft offers an Office Repair utility. Because Word is a part of the Office suite of programs, the Office Repair utility works to fix anything horrifically wrong with Word. Obey these steps:

1. **Close Word and any other Office programs.**

You should do so now; otherwise, you'll be asked to do so again later.

2. **Press the Win+X keyboard shortcut.**

In Windows 10, the Windows-and-X key combination brings up the super-secret shortcut menu in the lower left corner of the screen. If you're using Windows 7, just click on the Start button.

3. **Choose Control Panel.**

4. **Below the Programs heading, click the Uninstall a Program link.**

Don't freak out: You're not uninstalling Word. The link should read "Uninstall or Change a Program," which is the title of the Control Panel screen you see next.

5. **Select Microsoft Office from the list of programs.**

The name may be subtly different, such as Microsoft Office 2016 or Microsoft Office 365.

6. **Click the Change button.**

The Office Repair utility runs, showing a screen similar to Figure 32-5.

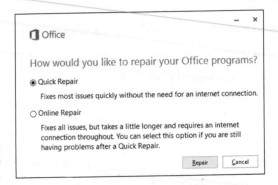

FIGURE 32-5:
The Office
Repair utility.

7. **Choose Quick Repair.**

If this choice doesn't work, go back and choose Online Repair when you try again.

8. **Click the Repair button.**

9. **Click the Repair button again to confirm.**

10. **Wait.**

The Office Repair utility attempts to figure out what's wrong. What happens next depends on whether anything is fixed. If something needs attention, obey the directions on the screen. If everything is fine, you see the Done Repairing message (even if nothing was actually wrong).

11. **Click the Close button.**

If the repair didn't work, try again but choose Online Repair in Step 8. If that doesn't work, consider reinstalling your Office installation.

Fixing the Normal template

Sometimes the evil lurks in what's supposed to be Word's main repository of sanity: the Normal template file. To fix the Normal template, you must delete it (or rename it) and then Word automatically builds a new, proper Normal template.

WARNING

If you rebuild the Normal template, you're removing any customizations you've added, macros you've created, or default settings you've modified. On the other hand, those changes may be causing your problem, so it's time for a fix.

To have Word re-create the Normal template, follow these initial steps to rename the original file:

1. **Quit Word.**

2. **Press Win+E to summon a File Explorer window.**

3. **Click the Address box to se~~~~~~~~ ~~~~ name appears there.**

4. ~~~~~~~~ **~~~~~~~ Delete key to clear the Address box.**

5. **Type** %USERPROFILE%\AppData\Roaming\Microsoft\Templates**.**

As you start typing **AppData**, you see hints appear below your typing. These hints help to direct you and confirm that you're on the right track. Eventually, you see the Templates folder, illustrated in Figure 32-6.

Word's templates pathname   The Normal template file

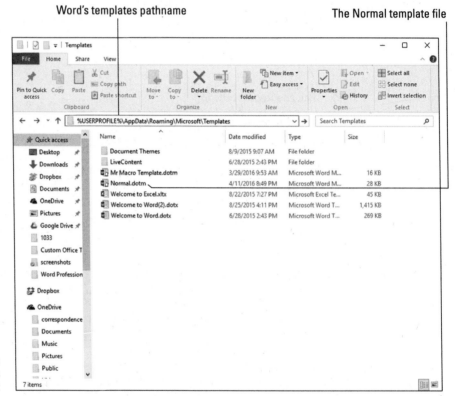

FIGURE 32-6:
Where Word's templates lurk.

6. **Right-click on the Normal.dotm file.**

The file might show only the first part of the name, Normal.

7. **Choose the Rename command from the shortcut menu.**

8. **Edit the name to** Normal-old.dotm **or** Normal-old**.**

If you can see the dotm part of the name, don't change it.

9. **Press Enter to lock in the new name.**

Keep the File Explorer window open.

10. **Restart Word.**

    You don't need to do anything in Word, though you may notice that any problems you have related to the old Normal template are gone.

11. **Quit Word.**

    In the File Explorer window, you see the rebuilt Normal.dotm file.

This trick may or may not work and, as I warned at the start of the section, it does remove any modifications that you've made to Word. To restore the original Normal.dotm file, quit Word and rename the file back to Normal.dotm or Normal.

> » Word stores its templates in the folder referenced by the pathname you type in Step 5. This location holds true for Word 16 and Office 365. Earlier versions of Word stored the template files in a different location.
>
> » Refer to Chapter 9 for more information on document templates.
>
> » The %USERPROFILE% thing is a Windows environment variable. It represents your account's home folder on the PC's primary storage device.

Entering Startup mode

Sometimes the problem you're experiencing with Word has to do with an add-on or extra feature. These features extend Word's capabilities, but they might also lead to problems. To ensure that the problem isn't with those extensions, you can run Word in Startup mode. I like to call it Naked mode, but Bill Gates frowned upon that suggestion.

To run Word in Startup mode, obey these directions:

1. **Ensure that Word is closed.**

    You can't enter Startup mode when Word is open.

2. **Press the Win+R keyboard shortcut.**

    The Run dialog box appears.

3. **Type** WINWORD /A **into the box.**

    WINWORD is Word's secret program name.

4. **Click OK.**

Word starts normally at this point, minus any add-ons. If they were the source of woe, the problem should be gone. If not, try running Word in Safe Mode; see the next section.

Running Word in Safe Mode

Safe Mode works similarly to Startup mode. The difference is that Word starts without add-ons, modifications, or custom settings. What you get is the "raw" version of Word with no frills.

Follow these steps to start Word in Safe Mode:

1. **Ensure that Word is closed.**
2. **Press the Win+R keyboard shortcut.**
3. **Type** WINWORD /SAFE **into the Run dialog box.**
4. **Click OK.**

   Word starts, perhaps even filling the entire screen. The window title reads "Microsoft Word (Safe Mode)." A dialog box appears, explaining what you might do next.

5. **Click the Accept button, if prompted.**
6. **Attempt to replicate the problem in Word.**

   Do whatever you did before to see whether the issue arises. If so, the problem is with either the Normal template or an add-on; solutions are offered elsewhere in this chapter, but also refer to the earlier section "Running the Office Repair utility."

WARNING

Do not attempt to create or edit any documents while running Word in Safe Mode. You can poke around, but keep in mind that Safe Mode is for trouble-shooting and not for creating or editing documents.

7. **Quit Word when you're done troubleshooting.**

If the problem isn't resolved in Safe Mode, something else is at fault. You may have a PC hardware issue, a problem with Windows, malware, or any of a number of meddlesome issues. Check elsewhere in this chapter for information on troubleshooting document problems as well as using the Office Repair utility.

TIP

You can also start Word in Safe Mode by pressing and holding the Ctrl key as Word starts.

7
The Part of Tens

Chapter 33

Ten Fun Macros

Can macros be fun? Sure! Especially when someone else writes them.

The Visual Basic for Applications (VBA) programming language is vast, complex, and intimidating. That means it has great potential, but isn't something that you'll sit and learn in a casual afternoon.

Chapters 25 and 26 touch on macros and VBA programming in this book. As promised, this chapter contains ten macros you can type in or record and then use in your documents.

>> I assume that you've read Chapters 25 and 26, that you know how to use the VBA Editor, and that the Developer tab shows up on the Ribbon in your copy of Word.

» Many of the macros shown in this chapter ~~...~~ but most of them require ~~...~~ programming code into the VBA Editor. Refer to Chapter 26 for assistance.

» To make the best use of macros, you can assign them to command buttons or keyboard shortcuts. Details are provided in Chapter 25.

Message Pop-Ups

The most basic type of programming is code that spits out a simple message on the screen. In fact, most beginner programming books start out with a sample program to display the text *Hello, World!* Word macros are no different.

The following macro, *message_popup1*, displays a dialog box with a single line of text and an OK button, as illustrated in Figure 33-1:

```
Sub message_popup1()
'
' message_popup Macro
' Display a pop-up message
'
    MsgBox "This Word macro requires your attention", vbOKOnly, "Hey there!"
End Sub
```

The first argument to the *MsgBox* command is the text to display in the dialog box. The second argument, *vbOKOnly*, directs Word to show only the OK button. The final argument — "Hey there!" — is the dialog box's title, as shown in Figure 33-1.

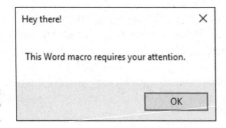

FIGURE 33-1:
A simple pop-up message macro.

Document Cleanup

Before that final save, or any time you're working on a large document, consider doing some document cleanup. It's a process that involves searching for rogue characters and other problematic text.

My document cleanup routine involves looking for trailing spaces at the end of paragraphs, double spaces, double tabs, and double Enter keys (empty paragraphs). These are all items to be avoided, but they end up in long documents anyway.

The process of eliminating these unwanted elements involves using the Find and Replace dialog box. You need to use the Special button to input special characters, such as Space, Tab, and Enter.

The macro I created to perform the document cleanup chore recorded the keystrokes I used to search and replace for the various characters. I then used the Visual Basic Editor to remove some of the redundant code. Here is the result:

```
Sub document_cleanup()
'
' document_cleanup Macro
' Remove trailing spaces and double spaces, tabs, and Enter keys
'
    Selection.HomeKey Unit:=wdStory
    Selection.Find.ClearFormatting
    Selection.Find.Replacement.ClearFormatting
' Remove trailing spaces from a paragraph
    With Selection.Find
        .Text = "^w^v"
        .Replacement.Text = "^v"
        .Forward = True
    End With
    Selection.Find.Execute Replace:=wdReplaceAll
' Remove double spaces
    With Selection.Find
        .Text = "  "
        .Replacement.Text = " "
    End With
    Selection.Find.Execute Replace:=wdReplaceAll
' Remove double tabs
    With Selection.Find
        .Text = "^t^t"
        .Replacement.Text = " ^t"
```

```
        End With
        Selection.Find E...
    .muve double Enter keys (blank paragraphs)
    With Selection.Find
        .Text = "^v^v"
        .Replacement.Text = "^v"
    End With
    Selection.Find.Execute Replace:=wdReplaceAll
End Sub
```

The first search-and-replace operation removes trailing spaces. The search text is ^w^v, which looks for any white space (^w) characters before the Enter key (^v). These whitespace characters — space, tab, and so on — are replaced with the Enter key, which removes the trailing spaces.

The second search-and-replace removes double spaces. I pressed the spacebar twice for the search text and pressed the spacebar a single time for the replacement text.

The third search-and-replace removes double tabs. The ^t represents tab characters in the Find and Replace dialog box.

The final search-and-replace removes empty paragraphs. The ^v characters represent the Enter key, so replacing ^v^v with ^v removes any empty paragraphs.

This macro works okay, but it could be better. For example, it doesn't handle triple spaces or triple tabs. You'd have to run the macro a second time for that. If you provide the programming talent, the macro's code can address those issues.

Double-Indent Paragraph

The double-indent paragraph macro modifies a paragraph's indentation, increasing both left and right attributes by half an inch. This effect could be applied by using a style, but a style sets the indentations to a specific value. When the macro is run, no matter what the current indentations are, the new values are a half-inch greater.

Here is the code for the *double_indent* macro:

```
Sub double_indent()
'
' double_indent Macro
' add half inch to both sides of the current paragraph
```

```
    pleft = Selection.ParagraphFormat.LeftIndent + InchesToPoints(0.5)
    pright = Selection.ParagraphFormat.RightIndent + InchesToPoints(0.5)
    With Selection.ParagraphFormat
        .LeftIndent = pleft
        .RightIndent = pright
    End With
End Sub
```

The macro takes the current paragraph indent values and adds a half-inch to each. These values are saved in the *pleft* and *pright* variables. The current paragraph's format is then modified, reset to those values.

>> This macro cannot be faked with recorded keystrokes. You must code it directly.

>> The Ctrl+M keyboard shortcut works similarly to the *double_indent* macro, but it affects only the paragraph's left indent value.

Word Swap

Here is a handy macro that I use all the time. The *word_swap* macro swaps two words. It cuts the first word and then pastes it after the second word:

```
Sub word_swap()
'
' word_swap Macro
' Swap two words, left-right
'
    Selection.MoveRight Unit:=wdWord, Count:=1, Extend:=wdExtend
    Selection.Cut
    Selection.MoveRight Unit:=wdWord, Count:=1
    Selection.Paste
End Sub
```

I recorded keystrokes to make this macro:

1. **Ctrl+Shift+→**

   The word to the right of the cursor is selected.

2. **Ctrl+X**

   The word is cut.

3. **Ctrl+→**

   moves after the second word.

4. **Ctrl+V**

   The original word is pasted.

REMEMBER

Word macros cannot record mouse clicks. When you need to select text, use the cursor keys plus the Shift key, or use the F8 (extended selection) key.

Also, for this macro to work, the insertion pointer must be positioned at the start of the first word.

And/Or Word Swap

Another word swap macro that I use frequently is what I call the *and_or_word_swap* macro. Unlike a regular word swap, the goal with this macro is to swap words on either side of a conjunction. For example, changing *this or that* to *that or this*.

As with the *word_swap* macro, covered in the preceding section, this macro was recorded from keystroke input:

```
Sub and_or_word_swap()
'
' and_or_word_swap Macro
' Swap two words in a conjunction
'
    Selection.MoveRight Unit:=wdWord, Count:=1, Extend:=wdExtend
    Selection.Cut
    Selection.MoveRight Unit:=wdWord, Count:=1
    Selection.Paste
    Selection.MoveRight Unit:=wdWord, Count:=1, Extend:=wdExtend
    Selection.Cut
    Selection.MoveLeft Unit:=wdWord, Count:=2
    Selection.Paste
End Sub
```

Here are the keystrokes I used to record this macro:

1. **Ctrl+Shift+→**

2. **Ctrl+X**

   The first word is cut.

3. **Ctrl+→**

The insertion pointer hops over the conjunction, *and* or *or*.

4. **Ctrl+V**

The word is pasted after the conjunction.

5. **Ctrl+Shift+→**

6. **Ctrl+X**

The word after the conjunction (now after the first word you pasted in Step 4) is selected and cut.

7. **Ctrl+←, Ctrl+←**

The cursor moves back to just before the conjunction.

8. **Ctrl+V**

The second word is pasted.

The net effect of these keyboard shortcuts is to cut a word on one side of an *and* or *or* and then paste the word on the other side. Then the second word is cut and pasted before the *and* or *or*.

TIP

For this macro to be effective, the insertion pointer must blink at the start of the first word.

Swap Sentences

Just as you can swap two words in a row, you can also swap two sentences. The *swap_sentences* macro does just that. And, as in other text manipulation macros, use the keyboard — not the mouse — to select text.

In the following code, the *Selection.Extend* command represents pressing the F8 key on the keyboard. When you press that key three times, a sentence is selected.

```
Sub swap_sentences()
'
' swap_sentences Macro
' Swap two sentences
'
    Selection.Extend
    Selection.Extend
    Selection.Extend
```

```
        Selection.Cut
        Sel
      Selection.Extend
      Selection.Extend
      Selection.EscapeKey
      Selection.MoveRight Unit:=wdCharacter, Count:=1
      Selection.Paste
   End Sub
```

Here are the keystrokes I recorded to create the *swap_sentences* macro:

1. **F8, F8, F8**

   The current sentence is selected.

2. **Ctrl+X**

3. **F8, F8, F8**

   The next sentence is selected.

4. **Esc, →**

   The selection is canceled, and the insertion pointer is placed at the start of the
   next sentence.

5. **Ctrl+V**

   The first sentence is pasted after the second sentence.

When you run this macro, ensure that the insertion pointer is set somewhere
within the first sentence.

Swap Header and Footer Text

The *swap_header_footer* macro swaps the document's header text and footer text.
You could complete this process manually, but the problem is that the macro
doesn't accurately record all the actions. So, although you can record the basic
keystrokes, you must return to the Visual Basic Editor to complete the macro:

```
Sub swap_header_footer()
'
' swap_header_footer Macro
' Exchange header/footer text
'
```

```
    If ActiveWindow.View.SplitSpecial <> wdPaneNone Then
        ActiveWindow.Panes(2).Close
    End If
    If ActiveWindow.ActivePane.View.Type = wdNormalView Or ActiveWindow. _
        ActivePane.View.Type = wdOutlineView Then
        ActiveWindow.ActivePane.View.Type = wdPrintView
    End If
    ActiveWindow.ActivePane.View.SeekView = wdSeekCurrentPageHeader
    Selection.WholeStory
    Selection.Cut
    ActiveWindow.ActivePane.View.SeekView = wdSeekCurrentPageFooter
    Selection.HomeKey Unit:=wdLine
    Selection.Paste
    Selection.EndKey Unit:=wdLine, Extend:=wdExtend
    Selection.Cut
    ActiveWindow.ActivePane.View.SeekView = wdSeekCurrentPageHeader
    Selection.Paste
    ActiveWindow.ActivePane.View.SeekView = wdSeekMainDocument
End Sub
```

The overall effect of this macro is to edit the document's header, select and cut all that text, and then switch to the footer. Once in the footer, the header's text is pasted, and then the footer's text is selected and cut. The macro switches back to the header and pastes the footer's text. Then the macro closes the header.

Update Document Fields

The *Update_all_fields* macro is discussed in Chapter 26. Its purpose is to refresh all fields in a document, which may or may not happen when the document is first opened:

```
Sub Update_all_fields()
'
' Update_all_fields Macro
' Refresh all of the document's fields
'
    Selection.WholeStory
    Selection.Fields.Update
    Selection.HomeKey
EndSub
```

The key to the macro is the Fi~~...~~ property. It's the command that affects fields i~~...~~. By setting it into a macro, you can place the command on a toolbar or assign it to a keyboard shortcut.

See Chapter 26 for more details.

Place Parenthetical Text into a Footnote

One of the sins you can commit in writing a term paper or thesis is placing too many parenthetical notes on a page. Many professors appreciate it when you instead use footnotes. You'll also appreciate the *parenthetical_to_footnote* macro, which automates the process.

I used keystrokes to record this macro, but the insertion pointer must be precisely positioned for it to work: Click the insertion pointer before the parenthetical sentence, just before the period where you want the footnote to appear. Figure 33-2 illustrates the positioning and the result after running the macro.

Before running the macro:

Insertion pointer position   Parenthetical text

Suspendisse dui purus, scelerisque at, vulputate vitae. Mauris eget neque at sem venenatis eleifend. Fusce aliquet pede non pede. (Suspendisse dapibus lorem pellentesque magna.) Integer nulla. Donec blandit feugiat ligula. Donec hendrerit, felis et imperdiet euismod, purus ipsum pretium metus, in lacinia nulla nisl eget sapien.

After running the macro:

Footnote

Suspendisse dui purus, scelerisque at, vulputate vitae. Mauris eget neque at sem venenatis eleifend. Fusce aliquet pede non pede.[1] Integer nulla. Donec blandit feugiat ligula. Donec hendrerit, felis et imperdiet euismod, purus ipsum pretium metus, in lacinia nulla nisl eget sapien.

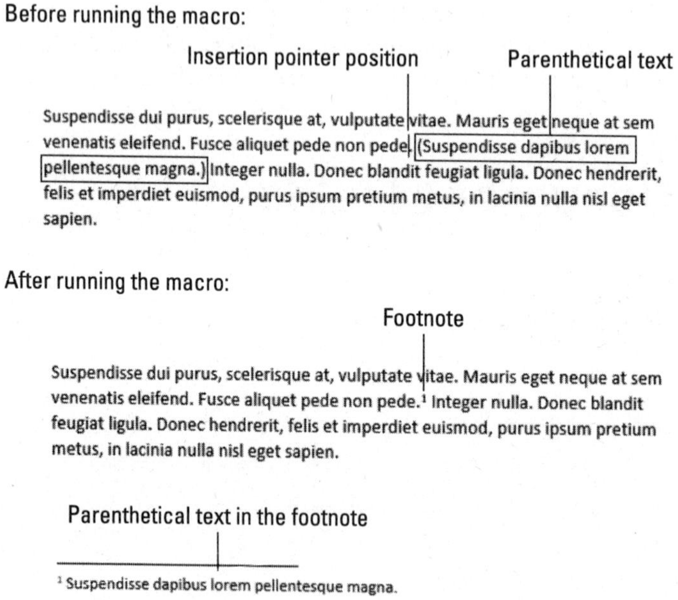

FIGURE 33-2:
Running the
parenthetical_to-footnote macro.

Parenthetical text in the footnote

_____

[1] Suspendisse dapibus lorem pellentesque magna.

```
Sub parenthetical_to_footnote()
'
' parenthetical_to_footnote Macro
' Convert parenthetical text following the cursor into a footnote
'
    Selection.Extend
    Selection.Extend Character:="("
    Selection.EscapeKey
    Selection.MoveRight Unit:=wdCharacter, Count:=1
    Selection.Extend
    Selection.Extend Character:=")"
    Selection.MoveLeft Unit:=wdCharacter, Count:=1, Extend:=wdExtend
    Selection.Cut
    Selection.MoveRight Unit:=wdCharacter, Count:=1
    Selection.TypeBackspace
    Selection.TypeBackspace
    Selection.TypeBackspace
    Selection.TypeBackspace
    Selection.TypeText Text:="."
    Selection.MoveLeft Unit:=wdCharacter, Count:=1
    With Selection
        With .FootnoteOptions
            .Location = wdBottomOfPage
            .NumberingRule = wdRestartContinuous
            .StartingNumber = 1
            .NumberStyle = wdNoteNumberStyleArabic
            .LayoutColumns = 0
        End With
        .Footnotes.Add Range:=Selection.Range, Reference:=""
    End With
    Selection.Paste
End Sub
```

I used keystrokes to create this macro. They're pretty complex:

1. **Press F8 and then the ((left parenthesis) character.**

The F8 command enters extended selection mode. When you press a key, such as the (key, text is selected up to and including that character.

2. **Esc, →**

Selection is canceled, and the → key moves the insertion pointer to the start of the parenthetical text.

3. **F8,)**

   Text is selected up to and including the) character.

4. **←**

   The) character is removed from the selection.

5. **Ctrl+X**

   The parenthetical text is cut. The next few keystrokes remove the parenthesis and position the insertion pointer for the footnote.

6. **Backspace, Backspace, Backspace, Backspace, . (period), ←**

7. **Click the References tab and, in the Footnotes group, click the Insert Footnote button.**

8. **Ctrl+V**

   The text is pasted into the footnote.

Refer to Chapter 21 for more information on footnotes.

Spike Text

A long time ago, I knew a friend who had a particular writing habit. Rather than delete large chunks of text, he would *spike* it. The text was selected, and he'd move it down to the end of the document. When he was done writing, he'd review his spike to see whether anything was worth saving.

I've never employed the spiked-text trick, but I did code a *spike_text* macro that automates the process:

```
Sub spike_text()
'
' spike_text Macro
' Move selected text to the end of the document
'
    If Selection.Type = wdSelectionNormal Then
        Selection.Cut
        Selection.EndKey Unit:=wdStory
        Selection.TypeParagraph
        Selection.Paste
        Application.GoBack
        Application.GoBack
```

```
        Else
            MsgBox "Nothing to spike"
        End If
End Sub
```

This macro contains an *if-else* structure. The *if* test determines whether text is selected. If so, the text is cut and pasted at the end of the document. When text isn't selected, the *else* part of the equation displays a message box with the text "Nothing to spike."

This macro was recorded initially. I used these keystrokes:

1. **Ctrl+X**
2. **Ctrl+End**
3. **Ctrl+V**
4. **Shift+F5, Shift+F5**

   The Shift+F5 keyboard shortcut returns you to the previous editing location in the document.

After recording the keystrokes, I added the *if-else* structure to ensure that the macro didn't display an ugly error message when text isn't selected. This process is part of defensive programming, where you anticipate that not every macro starts under ideal conditions. In this instance, a non-ideal condition is when text isn't selected.

Chapter 34

Ten Function Key Shortcuts

A long time ago, it was popular to use something called a keyboard template. You'd place this cardboard cutout over the top of the computer's keyboard. Its legend described commands associated with the function keys. Back in those days, the keyboard was the primary input device, and people preferred using function keys over using the mouse.

Thanks to the Ribbon interface, Word is now a lot easier to use than in the old keyboard days. Still, those keyboard shortcuts linger. Some of them are pretty handy, though not memorable. I've listed them all here in this chapter.

And yes, ~~I realize that~~ because 12 function keys adorn the top of your PC's keyboard, this chapter features 12 function key shortcuts, not the as advertised 10.

TECHNICAL STUFF

The function key commands here are listed as they are mapped within Word. Other programs installed on your computer may hijack certain key combinations. Also, some laptop computers may require you to press the Fn key in combination with the function keys to fully access their features.

F1

Unmodified	Display the online Help for Word 2016. You can search for help, browse categories, and be otherwise baffled by the information displayed.
Shift	Display (or hide) the Reveal Formatting pane.
Ctrl	Show or hide the Ribbon.
Alt	Go to the next field. See Chapter 24 for information on fields.
Shift+Ctrl	Maximize the document window to fill the screen and hide the Ribbon.
Shift+Alt	Go to the previous field in the document.
Ctrl+Alt	Display the System Information window.

F2

Unmodified	Move To command. Select text and press F2. Click to position the insertion pointer, and then press the Enter key to cut and paste the selected block.
Shift	Copy To command. Select text and press Shift+F2. Move the insertion pointer and press Enter to copy the selected text.
Ctrl	Summon the Print Preview screen; the same as pressing Ctrl+P.
Shift+Alt	Save command; same as Ctrl+S.
Ctrl+Alt	Summon the Open dialog box.

F3

Unmodified	Insert building block. Type the first part of the building block text, and then press F3. See Chapter 23.
Shift	Change Case command. Press Shift+F3 to cycle between lowercase, uppercase, and Sentence Case formats.
Ctrl	Cut selected text and store it in the Spike. The Spike can contain a collection of cut items, similar to the Clipboard; however, spiked items are not stored in the Clipboard.
Alt	Create a new Building Block entry. After you press Alt+F3, the Create New Building Block dialog box appears. See Chapter 23 for details.
Shift+Ctrl	Paste the contents of the spike. All spiked items (cut with Ctrl+F3) are inserted into the document. This is not the same command as Ctrl+V.

F4

Unmodified	Repeat command; the same as Ctrl+Y or Redo.
Shift	Repeat last browse object, such as Repeat Last Find or repeat the last Go To command, such as Go to Page.
Ctrl	Close the window; the same as the Ctrl+W command.
Alt	Quit the program. The Alt+F4 keyboard shortcut is the standard Windows command to close any window or program.
Shift+Alt	Close the window; the same as Ctrl+W and Ctrl+F4.

F5

Unmodified	Summon the Go To dialog box, or the Find and Replace dialog box with the Go To tab forward.
Shift	Move the insertion pointer to the last edit in the document. This command can be repeated four times to cycle through various locations.
Ctrl	Restore document window.
Alt	Restore program window.
Shift+Ctrl	Display the Bookmark dialog box. See Chapter 20.

F6

Unmodified	Cycle to the next open frame or pane.
Shift	Cycle to the previous open frame or pane.
Ctrl	Cycle to the next document window.
Alt	Cycle to the next document window; the same as Ctrl+F6.
Shift+Ctrl	Cycle to the previous document window.
Shift+Alt	Cycle to the previous document window; the same as Shift+Ctrl+F6.

F7

Unmodified	Proof the document.
Shift	Open the Thesaurus pane for the current word.
Alt	Move the insertion pointer to the next misspelled word.
Shift+Ctrl	Update Source command. This command applies to the IncludeText field and directs Word to update the contents based on the source document.
Shift+Alt	Open the Translation pane for the current word.
Ctrl+Alt	Summon the Korean-language spell checker. (I believe that this assignment is a bug.)

F8

Unmodified	Activate extended selection mode. Use the cursor keys to extend the selection; type a character to extend the selection; press F8 again to select a larger document chunk.
Shift	Shrink the extended selection. Press Shift+F8 to undo the last F8 key press.
Ctrl	Change the window's size (though it doesn't work in Word 2016).
Alt	Display the Macros dialog box.
Shift+Ctrl	Enter block selection mode. In this mode, you select a rectangular chunk of text. Use the cursor keys or mouse to highlight a rectangle of text in the document. You can work with the block selection just as you can with any chunk of selected text.

F9

Unmodified	Update the current field: Click in a field and press the F9 key. The Ctrl+Shift+U key does the same thing.
Ctrl	Insert an empty field, a pair of curly brackets with nothing between them.
Alt	Toggle field codes for all fields in the document.
Shift+Ctrl	Convert the current field into plain text.
Shift+Alt	Simulate a user clicking on a field for programming macros.

F10

Unmodified	Display Ribbon accelerator-key shortcuts.
Shift	Nonfunctioning shortcut menu command.
Ctrl	Maximize the document window.
Alt	Show or hide the Selection pane.
Shift+Ctrl	Assigned to the WW2_RulerMode command, which no one knows anything about.
Shift+Alt	Displays the smart tag menu.

Unmodified	Go to the next field in the document.
Shift	Go to the previous field in the document.
Ctrl	Lock the field.
Alt	Display the Visual Basic Editor.
Shift+Ctrl	Unlock the field.

F12

Unmodified	Summon the Save As dialog box. This command works whether or not the document has been saved.
Shift	Summon the Save As screen if the document hasn't already been saved.
Ctrl	Summon the Open dialog box.
Shift+Ctrl	Summon the Print screen; the same as Ctrl+P.
Shift+Alt	Activate the button on a selected content control.

Index

I

I-beam pointer, 2

explained, 4
Spelling and Grammar
Check, 345–346
ignore proofing command,
undoing, 347
ignoring foreign text,
350–352
illustrations. *See* images
images
about, 221–222
adding, 222–223
adding artistic effects, 231
adding borders, 233–234
adding from web, 224–225
adding to shapes, 218–219
adjusting, 225–232
adjusting color, 230–231
applying frame effects, 234
captioning, 234–236
copying and pasting, 223
cropping, 226–228
in eBooks, 406–407
frame formatting, 232–234
inserting, 485–487
inserting into documents,
186
Make Correction command,
229–230
removing, 225
removing backgrounds,
228–229
replacing, 225
restoring, 231–232
selecting Picture Styles,
232–233
setting position of, 193–194

increasing space before
paragraphs, 45
indentation, 37
indents, 42–43
index
about, 398
in eBooks, 409
inserting, 400–402
marking entries for,
398–400
updating, 402
Index dialog box, 401–402
Inline option, 190
inline-with-text layout
option, 407
Insert Chart dialog box, 249
Insert Hyperlink dialog box,
407–408, 533
Insert Picture dialog box,
222, 224
Insert Subdocument dialog
box, 378
Insert Table dialog box,
86–88
Insert Video dialog box, 242
inserting
blank pages, 128–129
citations, 392
column breaks, 115–116
columns in tables, 94–95
comments, 300–302
content controls, 478–479
Date Picker content control,
487
into documents, 186–187
drawing objects, 198–199
fields, 432–433
hyperlinks, 532–534
images, 485–487
index, 400–402

lists of captions, 395–396
page number fields,
437–439
rows in tables, 94–95
section breaks, 130–131
soft returns, 269
Table of Authorities,
320–322
Table of Contents, 383–385
tables, 88–89
text boxes, 215–216
text from documents, 240
unbreakable hyphens, 52
videos in documents, 242
word count into
documents, 340–341
insertion pointer, 2, 61
International Standard Book
Number (ISBN), 413
Internet
about, 509
Backstage, 509–513
cloud storage, 514–520
Office 365, 520–524
Word on the web, 522–524
Internet resources
Adobe, 292
Dummies, 5
Gookin, Dan (author), 528
Microsoft Developer
Network (MSDN), 473
Microsoft Office, 257
Office 365, 521
OneDrive, 515
introduction, 404
invitations, sending, 311–312
ISBN (International Standard
Book Number), 413
italic, 329

614   Word 2016 For Professionals For Dummies

About the Author

Dan Gookin has been writing about technology for over 25 years. He combines his love of writing with his gizmo fascination to create books that are informative, entertaining, and not boring. Having written over 150 titles, and with 12 million copies in print translated into over 30 languages, Dan can attest that his method of crafting computer tomes seems to work.

Perhaps his most famous title is the original *DOS For Dummies*, published in 1991. It became the world's fastest-selling computer book, at one time moving more copies per week than the *New York Times* number-one bestseller (though, as a reference, it could not be listed on the *Times'* Best Sellers list). That book spawned the entire line of *For Dummies* books, which remains a publishing phenomenon to this day.

Dan's most popular titles include *PCs For Dummies*, *Word For Dummies*, *Laptops For Dummies*, and *Android Phones For Dummies*. He also maintains the vast and helpful website www.wambooli.com.

Dan holds a degree in Communications/Visual Arts from the University of California, San Diego. He lives in the Pacific Northwest, where he enjoys spending time with his sons, playing video games indoors while they enjoy the gentle woods of Idaho.

Publisher's Acknowledgments

Senior Project Editor: Paul Levesque

Copy Editor: Becky Whitney

Technical Editor: Elaine Marmel

Editorial Assistant: Serena Novesel

Senior Editorial Assistant: Cherie Case

Production Editor: Siddique Shaik

Cover Image: IJzendoorn/Shutterstock